THE SOCIOLOGY OF MENTAL DISORDERS

Third Edition

WILLIAM W. EATON

PRAEGER

Westport, Connecticut
London

MT

Library of Congress Cataloging–in–Publication Data

Eaton, William W.
 The sociology of mental disorders / William W. Eaton.—3rd ed.
  p. cm.
 Includes bibliographical references (p.) and index.
 ISBN 0–275–96323–3 (alk. paper)—ISBN 0–275–96324–1 (pbk. : alk. paper)
  1. Social psychiatry. 2. Community psychiatry. 3. Psychiatric epidemiology. 4. Mental
illness—Etiology—Social aspects.
  [DNLM: 1. Community Psychiatry. 2. Mental Disorders—etiology. 3. Psychology,
Social. WM 30.6 E14s 2001]
 RC465.E22 2001
 362.2'042—dc21   99–055308

British Library Cataloguing in Publication Data is available.

Library of Congress Catalog Card Number: 99–055308
ISBN: 0–275–96323–3
   0–275–96324–1 (pbk.)

First published in 2001

Praeger Publishers, 88 Post Road West, Westport, CT 06881
An imprint of Greenwood Publishing Group, Inc.
www.praeger.com

Printed in the United States of America

The paper used in this book complies with the
Permanent Paper Standard issued by the National
Information Standards Organization (Z39.48–1984).

10 9 8 7 6 5 4 3 2 1

6\18\08

The Sociology of
Mental Disorders

This book is dedicated to the memory of Morton Kramer

Contents

Contents   xiii

Illustrations

TABLES

FIGURES

BOXES

Preface

I continue to hope this book will be handy to those attempting to learn how sociologists approach the topic of mental disorder. It is heavily revised over the prior edition, reflecting what I have learned in the 15 ensuing years. Substantial additions have been made to each chapter, and the entirety of each chapter has passed under my fingers in the word processor.

This revision was produced in two separate sabbaticals of three months duration, afforded by the School of Hygiene and Public Health of the Johns Hopkins University. The first sabbatical in the spring of 1997 was at the Oregon Social Learning Center in Eugene, Oregon. The environment provided by John Reid, Gerald Patterson, and their collaborators was conducive to productive work and considerable insight into the social causes of mental disorders. The second sabbatical was in the spring of 1998 at the Department of Psychological Medicine at the Institute of Psychiatry in London, England. The environment provided by Simon Wessely and Robin Murray was rich in opportunities for learning and study. I am grateful to both these institutions and to the individuals in both locales, who made a brief intellectual home for me during my stay.

I would be grateful for comments and criticisms. In prior editions, comments and criticisms helped form the motivation to write another edition. I would especially welcome suggestions about data that might illustrate the arguments better than the data I have been able to find. If a future edition takes advantage of these suggestions, I will acknowledge the contribution. These should be sent to me at weaton@jhsph.edu.

1

The Social Construction of Bizarre Behaviors

INTRODUCTION

Sociology is the study of human populations and groups. A *human population* is a number of individuals with some common characteristic such as age, religion, country of origin, place of residence, blood type, or disease. *Demography*, a subfield of sociology, is the study of the size of populations. Since populations can be defined by the occurrence of disease, epidemiology—the study of diseases in populations—may be thought of as a type of demography. A *human group* is a population that possesses one or both of the following characteristics: (1) the individuals interact or communicate with each other more often than with persons outside the group; (2) the individuals are aware of a common characteristic that defines their membership in the group. It is important to note that the group is conceptualized either by a behavioral definition (interaction/communication) or by a mental definition (awareness).

A book of this type should ordinarily begin with a definition of the second half of the subject of inquiry, namely, *mental disorder*. The purpose of this first chapter is to show that a consequence of the interest in groups produces complexities in the definition of mental disorder. The problematic nature of defining mental disorder is a central theme of the book, and the entire content of the book is relevant to the definition. Defining the term *mental disorder* delimits discourse, and it is too early to do that. Necessarily, we must define some terms to begin, and we will define many relevant concepts as the discussion proceeds. For now, we use the term *bizarre emotions or behavior. Emotions* are clusters of thoughts and feelings. *Behavior* is an activity an individual is engaged in. Webster's dictionary defines *bizarre* as (1) odd in manner, (2) marked by extreme incongruities and contrasts, and (3) unexpected and unbelievable. Briefly, bizarre emotions and behaviors are rare, culturally deviant, and inexplicable. These terms are purposefully defined with a broad scope to cast the net of associated meanings and connotations as widely as possible. Later on, more precisely defined concepts are introduced as necessary.

There is controversy over the specific labels that should be applied to the variety of bizarre behaviors. Where several definitions exist for the same bit of reality, the reality is negotiated. The process of negotiating reality is the subject of this chapter. Ultimately, bizarre emotions and behaviors are not the central subject of this book: rather, the subject is a subset of bizarre emotions and behaviors that for complex historical, political, and scientific reasons have been classified together as mental disorder. Various alternative categorizations and theories exist for defining and dealing with different concepts of mental disorder, but in order to be able to discuss them without bias, it is necessary to have a broader category, such as that of bizarre behavior, that includes all the alternative categorizations.

This chapter begins with a section introducing the reader to the sociology of knowledge, where it becomes apparent why the sociologist pays such close attention to problems of definition. A second section presents one framework for understanding bizarre emotions and behaviors—the so-called medical model. A third section presents an alternative framework for comprehending bizarre behaviors—the sociological theory of deviance. The fourth section presents a biosocial framework for understanding the etiology of mental disorders. The chapter concludes with a definition of mental disorder.

THE SOCIAL CONSTRUCTION OF REALITY

The Sociology of Knowledge

The sociology of knowledge is "concerned with the relationship between human thought and the social context in which it arises" (Berger and Luckmann 1967). A central insight came from Marx, who recognized that individuals' places in society—in particular, whether they were laborers or owners—determined their consciousness. The generalization of this idea—that the structure of society determines its culture and thereby the thought processes of individuals— has enormous implications. The major early contribution to this field is from Karl Mannheim, who wrote *Ideology and Utopia* (Mannheim 1936). He defines the two major terms as follows:

The concept *ideology* reflects the . . . discovery that ruling groups can in their thinking become so intensively interest-bound to a situation that they are simply no longer able to see certain facts which would undermine their sense of domination. There is implicit in the word "ideology" the insight that in certain situations the collective unconscious of certain groups obscures the real condition of society both to itself and to others, and thereby stabilizes it.

The concept of [*utopia* and] utopian thinking reflects the [idea] that certain oppressed groups are intellectually so strongly interested in the destruction and transformation of a given condition of society that they unwittingly see only those elements in the situation which tend to negate it. (40)

Mannheim contended that both groups of ideas tended to direct attention toward certain aspects of the situation and away from other aspects of the situation. Intellectuals and scientists are not immune to this tendency, and in the modern world ideologies compete with each other, supporting their own worldview and status quo and defining not only values but even concrete objects in different ways. Application of the framework of the sociology of knowledge, in its focus on the creation of categories of emotions and behaviors to which we might or might not direct our attention, has the potential to be helpful in epidemiology:

Thought, besides being a proper subject matter for logic and psychology, becomes fully comprehensible only if it is viewed sociologically. This involves tracing of the bases of social judgments to their specific interest-bound roots in society, through which the particularity, and hence the limitations, of each view will become apparent. (Berger and Luckmann 1967: xxvi of the Introduction by Louis Wirth)

This line of inquiry has led some to question the validity of any sort of objective or scientific thought, which aptly has been termed the *vertigo of relativity*. But Mannheim believed that the proper task of the sociology of knowledge was to examine the object of thought from as many different viewpoints as possible and that the object of thought became progressively clearer with this accumulation of different perspectives on it. In this book the concept or "object of thought" is the category of emotions and behaviors that earlier were termed bizarre and the subset of these termed mental disorders, as defined later. One major purpose of the book is to examine these from as many viewpoints as possible, with the hope that the concept of mental disorder becomes progressively clearer. Even the use of a given category implies the adoption of the given ideology, so that it is difficult even to begin the discussion. For the moment we use the terms *bizarre emotions and behaviors* loosely, noting that, of many concepts used, they are less firmly attached to powerful ideologies. Later, when we use other, more specific terms (e.g., *mental illness or residual deviance*), it will be clear that we are adopting temporarily the ideological framework implicit in the term.

The Reality of Everyday Life and the Bizarre

An important work in the sociology of knowledge is Berger and Luckmann's *The Social Construction of Reality* (1967). A main product of their book is to integrate U.S. social psychology (especially its symbolic interaction approach) with European sociology (e.g., Mannheim), which tends to approach the subject on the level of society as a whole—that is, Berger and Luckmann integrate U.S.

microsociology with European macrosociology. They extend basic concepts from the sociology of knowledge to apply to the everyday life of the "man in the street," a subject they term the "reality of everyday life."

The *reality of everyday life* is where things are presented to the mind of the individual. Concepts for things (e.g., "ball") are learned in early childhood, and when appearing in the here and now they have an immediate, objective quality and pragmatic implication (it is round, it rolls, and so on). These things appear in the consciousness of the individual already *objectified*—that is, the concept does not require agreement with others as to its qualities, and the thing appears to have coexisted with the concept before the appearance of the individual. The facile control of our body, the fact that objects fall, and our perception of distances and shapes are all examples of the reality of everyday life. It is the ongoing, coherent interpretation of an outside, objective, pragmatic, and unproblematic world.

One value in conceiving of the reality of everyday life is that it implies other realities that are different. Some concepts immediately imply a reality distinct from the everyday—the concept of "God," for example. Typically, other realities appear to exist in a narrowly delimited province of meaning, compared to the everyday. They do not appear as already objectified, and thus it is necessary to negotiate agreement with other persons as to concepts required to discuss and deal with the other reality. These other realities produce a shift in attention away from the everyday. Aesthetic and religious experiences almost always require this sort of transition. Any sort of problem in dealing with everyday life produces a transition outside its realm.

An important part of the reality of everyday life consists of the face-to-face situation. Routine, face-to-face interactions contain *typifications* of others that guide the interaction. Thus, the other may be typified as "a man," "jovial," "a European," "a salesman," and so on. In interaction with a single other in the here and now, each expression of the actors is produced by the one and accessible to the other, so that the typifications are constantly negotiated, enlarged, and changed as the interaction proceeds. Still, the fact remains that we deal with other persons as types, just as we deal with things as types. We also typify situations, and the stability of everyday life depends on the routine interactions of typified individuals in typified situations.

Language is the repository of all these types and the major vehicle by which they are recalled. Language groups experiences together into concepts and types, so that we can generate expectations about situations in the future from our experiences in the past. As such, language provides predictability and stability in our everyday life. In so doing, language objectifies experiences from the present, so that they can be useful later on.

Bizarre emotions and behaviors—either in ourselves or in others—present problems in everyday life and take us automatically into more remote provinces of meaning. Consider the first-person experience in the selection from *Autobi-*

ography of a Schizophrenic Girl in Box 1.1 or the narration by Mark Vonnegut in Box 1.2. Translating between this more remote sphere of knowledge and everyday life, in order to deal with the bizarre behavior, involves the creation of concepts and types that will objectify and also distort the face-to-face situation. But how can one describe these feelings and behaviors in language that objectifies and typifies, allowing prediction for the future? Leaving the reality of everyday life produces a shift of attention into a creative and problem-solving type of thought, both for the performer of the bizarre behaviors and for those observing or interacting with them. In the reality of everyday life, response choices are available for the performer, but one is highly favored; in problematic situations, where no obvious typification exists for guidance, the choice as to how to behave is less obvious (Figure 1.1). Where the choice of behavior is not obvious, the individual engages in problem solving, involving at least some degree of abstract thought, prioritizing desires, and redirection of attention and energy. This type of psychological activity is called executive function (Lyon and Krasnegor 1996). Sometimes achieving a resolution, allowing return to the reality of everyday life, requires intense negotiation between individuals; in other situations the negotiation is with different aspects of our own selves—for example, resolving conflicts between different aspects of the world we inhabit or between our past history and our future plans.

Institutionalization, Legitimation, and Universe Maintenance

Human activity takes place in an organized, stable fashion, but this stability is not the result of an innate human drive or capability. Animals are born with a repository of drives and knowledge that stabilizes their social behavior. For example, the Canada goose has virtually its entire repertoire of behaviors— knowing how to fly, to hunt for food, to seek and care for a mate, when and where to migrate, how to react to the approach of a fox—from birth. Drives in the human, however, are almost infinitely plastic. Study of cultures across the world shows that the range of food consumed by humans in different groups occupies the entire spectrum of edible things, even though there is enormous variety between groups and individuals. Likewise, "ethnological evidence shows that, in sexual matters, man is capable of almost anything" (Berger and Luckmann 1967). The point is that the stability of human life—the constraints on choices implicit in the left side of Figure 1.1—is an ongoing social product.

How does this stability arise, and what does it consist of? On the most fundamental level, the social order consists of *typifications*, that is, habituated actions by types of actors, each acting with, and taking account of, the other. In the language of social psychology, as presented in Chapter 3, these typifications are equivalent to *roles*. The sum total of complex combinations of roles is the *social structure*, or, equivalently, the institutional structure. Roles and institutions imply control of human conduct by setting up predefined patterns that narrow the range of choices for human action. Institutions imply objectivity,

Box 1.1
Narrative Account of Psychosis with Derealization

We were walking on a country road, chatting as two friends do. I was telling her what went on at school, my triumphs and failures; I spoke of my brothers and sisters, sometimes of my troubles, and beneath this mask of tranquility, of normality, I was living a veritable drama. Around us the fields spread away, cut up by hedges or clumps of trees, the white road ran ahead of us, the sun shone in the blue sky and warmed our backs. But I saw a boundless plain, noted, the horizon Infinite. The trees and hedges were of cardboard, placed here and there, like stage accessories, and the road, oh the endless road, white, glittering under the sun's rays, glistening like a needle, above us the remorseless sun weighing down trees and houses under its electric rays. Over and above the vastness reigned a terrifying quiet, broken by noises making the silence still more quiet and terrifying. And I was lost with my friend in the limitless space. But is it really she, this woman who is speaking, gesticulating? I see her shining white teeth, her brown eyes looking at me. And I perceive a statue by my side, a puppet, part of the pasteboard scenery. What fear, what anguish! I say to her, "Jean, is it really you?" And she answers, amazed, "who do you think it is; you know very well it is I, don't you?" "Oh, Yes, yes; I know perfectly well it is you." But to myself I say, "Yes, it is she, but disguised." I continue, "Why do you behave like an automaton?" "Oh," she replies, offended, "you think I walk awkwardly, but it's not my fault."

My friend has not understood the question. I keep quiet, more alone and isolated than ever. Then comes the time to go our separate ways. The anxiety exacerbates. At any price, by any means, I must conquer this unreality, for an instant feel someone alive near me, experience for a second the life-giving contact that makes up in a moment for the loneliness of a day. . . .

For me, madness was definitely not a condition of illness; I did not believe that I was ill. It was rather a country, opposed to Reality, where reigned an implacable light, blinding, leaving no place for shadow; an immense space without boundary, limitless, flat; a Mineral lunar country, cold as the wastes of the North Pole. In this stretching emptiness, all is unchangeable, immobile, congealed, crystallized. Objects are stage trappings, placed here and there, geometric cubes without meaning. People turn weirdly about, they make gestures, movements without sense; they are phantoms whirling on an infinite plain, crushed by the pitiless electric light. And I am lost in it, isolated, cold, stripped, purposeless under the light. A wall of brass separates me from everybody and everything. In the midst of desolation, in indescribable distress, in absolute solitude, I am terrifyingly alone; no one comes to help me. This was it; this was madness, the Enlightenment was the perception of Unreality. Madness was finding oneself permanently in an all-embracing Unreality.

Source: From Marguerite Sechehaye, *Autobiography of a Schizophrenic Girl* (1970). Reprinted by permission of Grune & Stratton, Orlando, FL.

Box 1.2
Narrative Account of Psychosis with Somatic Delusions

Most people assume it must be very painful for me to remember being crazy. It's not true. The fact is, my memories of being crazy give me an almost sensual glee. The crazier I was, the more fun remembering it is. I don't want to go nuts again. I'd do anything to avoid it. Part of the pleasure I derive from my memories comes from how much I appreciate being sane now, but most of what's so much fun with my memories is that when I was crazy . . . everything I did, felt, and said had an awesome grace, symmetry, and perfection to it. My appreciation of that grace, symmetry, and perfection hasn't vanished with the insanity itself. It's regrets that make painful memories. When I was crazy I did everything just right. There were "problems" but somehow they didn't seem like problems at the time. Tasks that required only minimal concentration—cutting wood, building fires, pruning trees, fetching water—became progressively more difficult and then impossible, but that seemed too silly to worry about. Even if I managed by herculean effort to think something was worth doing, I couldn't keep my mind on it. There was so much else going on. I felt no lack of energy, in fact I had a supersurplus; but my hands, arms and legs were getting all confused. I'd get all hung up in how perfectly beautiful one muscle was, exactly what it did, and get it to do it just right. But then all the others would go off on their own little trip. I nicked my ankle with the chain saw. I was losing my coordination as well as my concentration. Ambivalence and disability. It was like something in me knew I would become unable to function, and got me ready by telling me ahead of time that it didn't matter.

A *half dream. I* am in heaven, where the senselessness of pain is clear. The feeling is of peace and fullness. . . . Then a sharp pain in my foot, a small bump on the sole, between my toes, like a plantar's wart. Around it tender and sore but there is no sensation in the bump itself. Picking at it. Little by little I separate it from the surrounding skin. It's a plug about a quarter-inch across. I pull at it. Pain. It seems to have some sort of roots reaching up into my foot. I adjust to the pain and continue to pull at it. It starts to come. The pain is very intense but strangely almost pleasurable. Amazed by the size of the thing and how I hadn't noticed it earlier. I've pulled about six inches of foreign growth out of my foot, and there's no end in sight. A feeling of relief, making my foot all warm and tingly—the more I pull out, the higher the warmth and relief spreads. I pull another six inches and panic for a moment. What if this is all there is? What will be left once I get this thing out? But the gentle strong feeling of warmth and relief reassure me I am doing the right thing and I continue extricating this foreign growth from my system. After each six inches or so I rest, basking in the warmth and relief, letting each part of my body feel its new freedom, past my knee, up to my thigh. . . . Down my left leg, until my left toes turn warm and free, and up my torso, bringing peace and warmth to my belly and my lower back. At my solar plexus the resistance increases again. I feel the roots pulling on my heart and stop, but only for a moment. . . . I can feel the root tentacles being pulled through my whole body: out it comes, more and more. I am ecstatic as the peace passes up my throat, over my Mouth, and through my nose to the top of my head. Ecstasy. That's what all the rushes of fear and pain were. Just getting free of the Shit. Nothing but nothing is going to turn me around. Pain? Fear? . . . I've seen heaven and nothing's gonna turn me around. What is it that wants to turn me around and make me crawl back into believing all the sham about pain being unavoidable, utopia impossible? I'm a freight train, baby, don't give me no side track, no. I want your main line, baby. Climb aboard the Eden Express. This train, this train is comin' through. THIS TRAIN IS BOUND FOR GLORY.

Source: From THE EDEN EXPRESS by Mark Vonnegut. Copyright © 1975 by Praeger Publishers, Inc. Used by permission of Dell Books, a division of Bantan Doubleday Dell Publishing Group, Inc., and Knox Burger Associates.

---

because once crystallized, they exist prior to the individuals who temporarily embody them. Institutions are somewhat immune from subjective and creative impulses on the part of individuals. Thus, for example, language appears to the child, who cannot grasp the notion of its conventionality, as inherent in the nature of things. The general point is that humans produce a world that is then experienced as existing beyond them.

Legitimation is necessary to the maintenance of an institutional order. Institutions are created out of the necessity to typify social situations, and the original creators are aware of the conditions of the creation and the necessity for it; but their descendants are not, and legitimation is the process of explaining and justifying the institutions to new generations, so that they can accept them with conviction. Legitimation serves to make objectively available and subjectively plausible the current institutions, that is, it imposes a de facto logic on the institutional order.

Legitimation may involve explicit theories by which an institutional sector is associated with a complex, differentiated body of knowledge, and specialized personnel who transmit that knowledge through formalized initiation procedures, such as the field of medicine. Legitimation may involve further a *symbolic universe*, which, encompassing the totality of the institutional order, links together the many, variegated institutions. The symbolic universe of a culture is able to describe, integrate, and justify the totality of human activity and our place in the cosmos. It is a general theory of humanity, such as the theory of positivism and the ethic of humanism and science.

Symbolic universes require constant maintenance, and the "legitimation of the institutional order is faced with the ongoing necessity of keeping chaos at bay. . . . All societies are constructions in the face of chaos" (Berger and Luckmann 1967: 103). Without institutions, social interaction would be chaotic; the threat of chaos is present whenever the symbolic universe is challenged by another universe. "The appearance of an alternative symbolic universe poses a threat because its very existence demonstrates empirically that one's own universe is less than inevitable" (Berger and Luckmann 1967: 108), and, thus, maintenance and defense are required.

The study of bizarre emotions and behaviors necessitates discussion of this realm of the social construction of reality because, by their very nature, bizarre behaviors tend to resist objectifications. The resistance to objectification occurs on the level of the individual, who may fail ever to have the comfortable feeling

Figure 1.1
The Problem of Directing Behavior

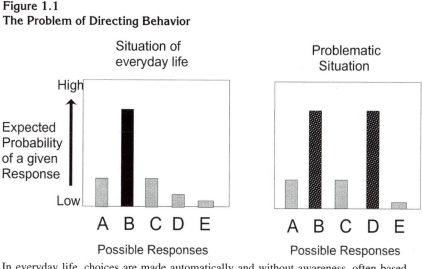

In everyday life, choices are made automatically and without awareness, often based on habit or instinct. In problematic situations, outcomes are less predictable, and seemingly trivial differences in social context can produce unexpected results.

of comprehension of his or her own bizarre behaviors; on the level of the small group, which may intensely negotiate meanings concerning the cause and intent of a group member's behavior; and on the level of society, where complex ideologies may compete with each other as to the definition of bizarre behaviors. Two ideologies that compete in the definition of bizarre behaviors are discussed next: the medical model, which comprehends bizarre emotions and behaviors as disease; and the sociological model, which comprehends bizarre emotions and behaviors within a general framework of deviance.

BIZARRE BEHAVIORS AS DISEASE

The Medical Model

The dominant interpretation for bizarre emotions and behaviors in modern, Western society is medical. The reality of everyday life for the average person contains medical concepts for explaining the occurrence of bizarre emotions and behaviors, acting upon the explanation, and referring this particular type of exception to everyday life to the medical institution. Bizarre behaviors are potential exceptions to the regularity of everyday life, presenting problems that are referred out of its realm to specialists. The medical framework is an ideology, because it directs our attention toward certain aspects of the situation and away from other aspects and because it supports the medical institution that is dominant in this area. It is, likewise, a legitimating theory, because it imposes de facto logic on the institutional order.

Models of disease and illness require adoption of certain terms and categories, including the following: symptom, sign, syndrome, pathology, disease, diagnosis, impairment, disability, and illness. A *complaint* is a statement about an unwanted or unpleasant feeling, and a *symptom* is a complaint reported by the individual that is assumed to be due to a disease—it is the medical model's more narrow version of a complaint about the way one feels. In the context of mental disorders, it concerns unwanted emotions. In its most common usage, symptom is the general medical term used to describe how we feel when we are sick. Unpleasant emotions like fear and sadness and pains and distress of whatever type are symptoms in the medical model. A *behavior* is any sort of activity of an individual, and a *sign* is an observable behavior that is assumed to be due to a disease—again, parallel to, but more narrowly defined than, behavior. In the medical model signs include laboratory tests, observations as from listening to the heart (auscultation), probing and palpation, and visual observation of such things as posture and facial expression. A *syndrome* is a group of complaints and behaviors or signs and symptoms that occur together more often than predicted by chance. Syndromes are usually defined by temporal co-occurrence (that is, cross-sectional clustering), but the notion also includes longitudinal clusters that occur predictably in individuals more often than would be expected by chance. The definition of syndrome is helpful because the concept can be applied within the medical model to signs and symptoms and also to the more general terms for complaints and behaviors.

Pathology is a biological process that occurs out of the normal context or out of the normal time frame that contributes to the death of the organism. *Disease* is said to be present when a pathological process is occurring, and the causal process leading up to the disease is referred to as its *etiology*. The early notions of pathology arose in the germ theory of medicine, in which an infectious agent instigated a process damaging or fatal to the individual. This might be termed a "single cause" model, because there was an agent that, by itself, could reliably produce the disease. Current notions of pathology are consistent with developments in genetics, in which a mutated gene is a sufficient cause of the pathology.

An important aspect of the medical model is the tendency to dichotomize. In common use, signs and symptoms are either present or absent, not present in degrees. The concept of syndrome can involve either dichotomous or continuous signs and symptoms. Where the syndrome is judged to be important, it is termed a *disorder*. Where an etiology is known for a disorder, a *disease* is named. *Diagnosis* is the process of determining the presence or absence of disease in an individual. *Impairment* is the damage to an organ that results from the disease, and *disability* is the reduction in functioning that such damage entails. *Illness* is the belief by the individual that complaints and behaviors might have a medical explanation.

Diagnosis is the basic medical methodology (Mechanic 1978). An accurate diagnosis explains how the individual became ill, the future of the illness, and treatment prescribed. Many diagnoses are made so often with such reliably beneficial effect that they are not questioned. For example, diagnosis of pernicious anemia is made when an individual complains of weakness and fatigue and shows signs of clumsiness. A blood count and bone marrow test yield highly reliable results. If the tests are positive, injections of vitamin B_{12} rapidly cure the disorder. Other diagnoses are made reliably but with less effect. The diagnosis of Beck's sarcoidosis is made when lymph nodes show up on a chest x-ray, and a biopsy and skin test exclude tuberculosis. But the cause of sarcoidosis is not well known, the course is not predictable, and there is little effective treatment. In some diseases the etiology is known, but no treatment exists (e.g., rabies); in others, effective treatment exists, but the etiology is unknown (e.g., hyperactive thyroid). Finally, there are many areas in medicine where diagnoses are not made with high reliability (e.g. in examination of X-rays or photographs of the retina). Thus, the reliability and validity of medical diagnoses in general have a wide range.

Feelings and behaviors that are painful or upsetting but not easily understood are distressing, and the distress can be relieved, in part, simply by the appearance of understanding that the process of diagnosis entails (Frank 1974). It seems likely that the relief is greater when there is a concrete quality to the diagnosis, as would exist when the agent of disease was, in principle, physically visible, such as might occur with a germ or a gene; but would be less likely to occur if the disease agent were some sort of process that was more difficult to conceptualize. This relief is generated in the modern medical system and in non-modern systems, even when the practical value of the diagnosis is trivial, as discussed earlier.

The medical model is an ideal-typical framework that doesn't apply very well in the specialty of psychiatry. A psychiatric category that falls usefully within the realm of the germ theory of disease is *general paresis*. The presenting symptoms of general paresis are very similar to those of schizophrenia, and in the nineteenth century there were thousands of general paretics in advanced stages of dementia in public mental hospitals. After years of speculation and generations of research, it was established that the syphilis bacterium was responsible and that paresis appeared in a certain proportion of persons who, years earlier, had contracted syphilis and not had it treated. Penicillin treatment for syphilis was introduced with widespread public health campaigns, and this disorder has all but disappeared. Further attempts to link other bacteria with psychiatric disorders have been less successful, and medical researchers began looking for other types of causes.

Another system of etiology that might link up to simple cause is the genetic theory of psychiatric disorder (Mendlewicz and Papadimitriou 1995; Papadimitriou and Mendlewicz 1996). Genes are units of heredity found in each living cell that influence the characteristics of an organism and that are transmitted as units, from generation to generation. All living matter passes its characteristics on to the next generation via genes, and, thus, experiments on fruit flies, pea plants, and monkeys are all relevant to humans. The theory of genetics ranges from the biochemical nature of the genetic material, to the molecular action by which genes relate to cell life, to the combined effects of genes on humans, to the variation and flow of genes in large populations of organisms. Recent research has shown that genetic material may be rearranged in living organisms, that is, even after conception. Genetic counseling may, further, forestall the birth of children with high likelihood of possessing unwanted traits. Thus, viable prevention and treatment of genetically caused disorders exist. There is one relatively rare psychiatric disorder in which a single gene has been established as a sufficient cause—*Huntington's chorea*. This disorder appears in late middle age, with symptoms resembling those of schizophrenia. There is currently no effective treatment. Thus, as with the germ theory, the search for a simple cause in genetic theory was logical and yielded some positive results.

Many emotions and behaviors and syndromes formed from clusters of them are produced by a subtle and complex combination of causes, with no single cause being either necessary or sufficient. Important conditions, such as many heart diseases and most psychiatric disorders, do not arise from simple etiologic processes. In the disease model the pathological process or its consequences are often observable with instruments like a microscope or modern radiologic imaging device. In the specialty of psychiatry many important brain and/or social processes are too subtle in their manifestations to be observed, at least with current technology. As a result, in psychiatry the pathologic process has had to be imagined from its distant consequences on the individual, more so than in other specialties of medicine. The additional complexity necessitates a wider range of perspectives than the simplistic disease model. Introductions to psychiatry for medical students often include a variety of frameworks, including the disease model but also dimensional models, such as might be used to describe continuous deviations in personality; behavioral and social frameworks; and psychodynamic or biographical "life story" approaches (McHugh and Slavney 1998; Tyrer and Steinberg 1993).

An important problem with the concept of disease in psychiatry is that many or most psychiatric disorders have a weak relationship to death, which makes the definition of pathology problematic. For example, it is true that individuals diagnosed with major depressive disorder have a much higher rate of suicide than the general population; but most people with this diagnosis do not commit suicide, and the rate of suicide also fluctuates markedly by other characteristics like age, sex, and cultural background. Other psychiatric disorders raise the individual's risk of death (Kouzis et al. 1995) but are not stronger risk factors for death than many other social and biological aspects of the individual.

Psychiatric Diagnosis

The dominant diagnostic system for research conducted in the United States after World War II was the American Psychiatric Association's *Diagnostic and Statistical Manual, Second Revision* (DSM-II, American Psychiatric Association

1968); the third revision of the DSM was published in 1980 (American Psychiatric Association 1980), and the fourth in 1994 (American Psychiatric Association 1994). Much of the research reviewed in the following was conducted using the DSM or its international equivalent, the World Health Organization's *International Classification of Diseases*, Chapter 5. This section presents discussion and complete diagnostic criteria for schizophrenia, major depressive disorder, and attention deficit disorder; in later sections abbreviated criteria are presented as required by the discussion.

In the DSM-II, the first step in classifying an individual is to decide whether he or she is psychotic or not. The definition of *psychosis* is gross inability to meet the ordinary demands of life, such as eating, dressing, responding to questions sensibly, and so forth—this is probably a diagnosis that would fit Mark Vonnegut (Box 1.2). In the late nineteenth century, the German clinician Emil Kraepelin grouped the signs and symptoms of the psychoses into two categories, based on what he saw as their different prognosis. The group with thought disorders and poor prognosis he called *dementia praecox* (adolescent dementia), which evolved into the diagnosis of *schizophrenia*; the group with signs and symptoms related mostly to mood and with relatively better prognosis he called *manic-depressive insanity*, which is now termed *bipolar disorder*. In the DSM-II, schizophrenia is characterized by a paragraph or two such as the following:

disturbances in thinking, mood, and behavior. Disturbances in thinking are marked by alterations of concept formation which may lead to misinterpretation of reality and sometimes to delusions and hallucinations. Corollary mood changes include ambivalent, constricted and inappropriate emotional responsiveness. Behavior may be withdrawn, regressive, and bizarre.

Schizophrenia is not difficult to diagnose where the individual is severely withdrawn (e.g., displaying distorted bodily movements or inability to converse), where the emotional behavior is highly inappropriate (e.g., inability to stop giggling or inappropriate smiles at odd moments), or where the thought disorder is dramatic (e.g., in producing a nongrammatic "word salad"). Diagnosis becomes difficult when the individual has only delusions or hallucinations. A *delusion* is a fixed, false belief (e.g., "the FBI is after me," which might be called a delusion of persecution; or "Adolf Hitler is still alive and inserting thoughts into my head," which might be termed a "bizarre" delusion, since it could not possibly be true). A *hallucination* is a perception when no stimulus has occurred, for example, when the individual sees or hears things that have no basis in reality (e.g., "voices from my dead mother"). Making the diagnosis of schizophrenia involves, first, defining what is real or true and, second, noting the deviation from reality of the individual's beliefs and perceptions. In field surveys, delusions and hallucinations are reported by as much as 5–10 percent of the population (Tien 1991), but only a small percentage of these persons would be diagnosed as schizophrenic. Since reality is socially defined, the psychiatrist risks defining as a schizophrenic an individual whose perceptions are simply out of line with the majority—a cultural or political deviant. Diagnosing across cultures becomes doubly difficult because cultures define reality differently. In our culture, conversing with God would probably not be classified in itself as a hallucination, but conversing with Woodrow Wilson would undoubtedly be classified as one. Seeing an unidentified flying object is about at the halfway point.

Affective psychosis is:

"a disorder characterized by a single disorder of mood, either extreme depression or elation, that dominates the mental life of the patient." The major subtypes of affective psychosis are the manic type, characterized by "elation, irritability, talkativeness, flight of ideas and accelerated speech and motor activity"; the depressed type, characterized by "severely depressed mood and by mental retardation progressing occasionally to stupor"; and the manic-depressive type, in which the depressive and manic phases alternate. (American Psychiatric Association 1968)

Hallucinations and delusions sometimes accompany affective psychosis, so that the distinction between it and schizophrenia may be difficult to make. In a study comparing the United States and England, it was found that the percentage of hospital admissions with schizophrenia was much higher in the United States and the percentage of hospital admissions with affective psychosis much higher in England (Kramer 1969b). Eventually, it was shown that the difference was an artifact of the different diagnostic criteria. In the United States hallucinations and delusions were counted as symptoms of schizophrenia whenever they were present; in England hallucinations and delusions were counted as symptoms of schizophrenia only when there was no depression. After correcting for diagnostic procedures in this single, simple way, many of the differences between the two countries vanished.

There are many changes in the diagnostic system from the second to the third and fourth editions of the DSM. For most disorders explicit *operational criteria* for the disorder have been written out—that is, the precise constellation of signs, symptoms, impairments, and duration necessary to meet the criteria for diagnosis. Many disorders have *criteria of exclusion*, such that the diagnosis is not made if another diagnosis is present—this is the situation for apparent symptoms of schizophrenia when there is a mood disorder also present. The new diagnostic system is *multiaxial*, with five axes: the first axis records the mental disorder diagnosis itself; axis 2 records personality traits that are regarded as relatively permanent but not severe enough to be called mental illness; axis 3 records any major physical illness diagnosis; axis 4 records the highest level of adaptive functioning the individual has reached, aids in prognosis, and gives a level to shoot for in the recovery process; and axis 5 records major stresses experienced in the period just prior to diagnosis to help assess the possible causes of the disorder and help predict recovery.

The operational criteria in the third and later editions of the DSM make it more difficult to meet the diagnostic threshold, so that the diagnostic is likely to be made less frequently. The operational criteria for DSM-IV schizophrenia are given in Box 1.3. The symptoms of thought disorder—such as the perceptual distortions, feelings of loss of will, grandiosity, and bizarre perceptions of the body and of social relationships experienced by the schizophrenic girl (Box 1.1) and by Vonnegut (Box 1.2)—are not enough to qualify for diagnosis: the symptoms must lead to some loss of functioning or disability for the individual, as they clearly did in Vonnegut's situation; they must endure for six months; and there must not have been a depressive episode that might have caused the symptoms. Transient experiences of these symptoms, if they are bizarre and disabling, are likely to be diagnosed as schizophreniform disorder, which is thought to be a distinct disease; if the symptoms are not so bizarre as to be disabling, but they endure over many years, the diagnosis of schizotypal personality disorder (on axis 2) may be made. This change in the way the diagnosis of schizophrenia is made brought U.S. diagnostic practice closer to European practice for this disorder. The narrative account by Mark Vonnegut can more easily fit into the DSM-II framework of the diagnosis of schizophrenia than it can into the DSM-IV framework.

In the DSM-II (American Psychiatric Association 1968) *neurosis* is described in the following way:

Anxiety is the chief characteristic of the neuroses. It may be felt and expressed directly, or it may be controlled unconsciously and automatically by conversion, displacement and various other psychological mechanisms. Generally, these mechanisms produce symptoms experienced as subjective distress from which the patient desires relief. The neuroses, as contrasted to the psychoses, manifest neither gross distortion or misinterpretation of external reality nor gross personality disorganization. . . . Neurotic patients, however severely handicapped by their symptoms, are not classified as psychotic because they are aware that their mental functioning is disturbed.

The problems of the neurotic tend to cause him or her anxiety and depression; the problems of the personality disorder tend to be directed outward, causing problems for others in the environment. Neurotics may be anxious to the point of panic, or they may direct their anxiety toward specific objects or places (as in a phobia); or they may displace or control the anxiety through compulsive activities or repeated unwanted thoughts.

A change in the diagnostic system from DSM-II to DSM-III is that the distinction between psychotic and nonpsychotic is no longer preeminent in the diagnostic process, being made after many other decisions. Another important change is that the diagnosis of neurosis was eliminated, noted with considerable chagrin by the *Washington Post* in its editorial "Goodbye, Neurosis!" (1978). Part of the resulting change was that the diagnosis of "affective psychosis" was

Box 1.3
Diagnostic Criteria for Schizophrenia

A. *Characteristic symptoms*: Two (or more) of the following, each present for a significant portion of time during a 1-month period (or less if successfully treated):

   (1) delusions

   (2) hallucinations

   (3) disorganized speech (e.g., frequent derailment or incoherence)

   (4) grossly disorganized or catatonic behavior

   (5) negative symptoms, i.e., affective flattening, alogia, avolition

B. *Social/occupational dysfunction*: For a significant portion of the time since the onset of the disturbance, one or more major areas of functioning such as work, interpersonal relations or self-care are markedly below the level achieved prior to the onset (or when the onset is in childhood or adolescence, failure to achieve expected level of interpersonal, academic, or occupational achievement).

C. *Duration*: Continuous signs of the disturbance persist for at least 6 months. This 6-month period must include at least 1 month of symptoms (or less if successfully treated) that meet Criterion A (i.e., active-phase symptoms) and may include periods of prodromal or residual symptoms. During these prodromal or residual periods, the signs of the disturbance may be manifested by only negative symptoms or two or more symptoms listed in Criterion A present in an attenuated form (e.g., odd beliefs, unusual perceptual experiences).

D. *Schizoaffective and Mood Disorder Exclusion*: Schizoaffective Disorder and Mood Disorder with Psychotic Features have been ruled out because either (1) no Major Depressive, Manic, or Mixed Episodes have occurred concurrently with the active-phase symptoms; or (2) if mood episodes have occurred during active-phase symptoms, their duration has been brief relative to the duration of the active and residual periods.

E. *Substance/general medical condition exclusion*: The disturbance is not due to the direct physiological effects of a substance (e.g., a drug of abuse, a medication) or a general medical condition.

F. *Relationship to a Pervasive Developmental Disorder*: If there is a history of Autistic Disorder or another Pervasive Developmental Disorder, the additional diagnosis of Schizophrenia is made only if prominent delusions or hallucinations are also present for at least a month (or less if successfully treated).

Source: American Psychiatric Association (1994: 285–86). Reprinted with permission from the *Diagnostic and Statistical Manual of Mental Disorders*, Fourth Edition. Copyright © 1994 American Psychiatric Association.

changed to "affective disorder" in DSM-III, and the symptoms no longer need be psychotic in severity to meet the criteria. The most important diagnosis in this group is *major depressive disorder*, for which the constellation and timing of the symptoms are explicitly laid out (Box 1.4): there must be a period of feeling sad and depressed ("dysphoria") or a loss of interest in things usually enjoyed ("anhedonia") that endures at least for two weeks and other symptoms leading to a total of at least five of the signs and symptoms from the symptom groups in the "A" criteria. These include somatic symptoms such as sleeplessness, the converse of too much sleep, loss or gain of appetite, loss or gain of weight, slowness in thinking, and preoccupation with death or suicide. The combination of depressed mood and somatic symptoms of a vegetative nature is sometimes referred to as "biological" depression by psychiatrists, and there are drug therapies that are thought to be specific to this disorder. Where episodes of depression occur interspersed with periods of normality and then episodes of manic excitement, the diagnosis of *bipolar disorder* may be made, and again, there is a specific chemotherapy for this specific type of disorder. Finally, another diagnosis within this group is called *dysthymia*, which is a mild, chronic, depressed mood.

The affective disorders in DSM-III cut away from neurosis the old neurotic depression, and most of the remainder of the neurosis category falls into the *anxiety disorders*. Anxiety is not a rare feeling, particularly in a situation as stressful as the experience of a mental disorder is likely to be—for example, in the narratives of the schizophrenic girl and of Vonnegut, there is intense anxiety. In DSM-III, one form this anxiety can take is a brief period of intense fear called a *panic attack* (Boxes 1.5 and 1.6). It is similar to depression in that there is an inexplicable mental symptom (the feeling of intense fear) accompanied by somatic symptoms, except that here the somatic symptoms have to do with the autonomic nervous system, such as trembling hands, sweaty palms, shortness of breath, and so forth. *Panic disorder* is a diagnosis given to individuals with several panic attacks within a short period.

Personality disorders are characterized by

deeply ingrained maladaptive patterns of behavior . . . including paranoid behaviors, alternating depression and elation, excessive shyness, daydreaming and avoidance of others, explosive personality, and hysterical and antisocial personality. (American Psychiatric Association 1968)

The antisocial personality is an important subtype. These are individuals who are

basically unsocialized and whose behavior pattern brings them repeatedly into conflict with society. They are incapable of significant loyalty to individuals, groups, or social values. They are grossly selfish, callous, irresponsible, impulsive, and unable to feel guilt or to learn from experience and punishment. (American Psychiatric Association 1968)

Box 1.4
Diagnostic Criteria for Major Depressive Episode

A. Five (or more) of the following symptoms have been present during the same 2-week period and represent a change from previous functioning; at least one of the symptoms is either (1) depressed mood or (2) loss of interest or pleasure.

(1) depressed mood most of the day, nearly every day, as indicated by either subjective report (e.g., feels sad or empty) or observation made by others (e.g., appears tearful)

(2) markedly diminished interest or pleasure in all, or almost all, activities most of the day, nearly every day (as indicated by subjective account or observation made by others)

(3) significant weight loss when not dieting or weight gain (e.g., a change of more than 5% of body weight in a month), or decrease or increase in appetite nearly every day)

(4) insomnia or hypersomnia nearly every day

(5) psychomotor agitation or retardation nearly every day (observable by others not merely subjective feelings of restlessness or being slowed down)

(6) fatigue or loss of energy nearly every day

(7) feelings of worthlessness or excessive or inappropriate guilt (which may be delusional) nearly every day (not merely self-reproach or guilt about being sick)

(8) diminished ability to think or concentrate, or indecisiveness, nearly every day (either by subjective account or as observed by others)

(9) recurrent thoughts of death (not just fear of dying), recurrent suicidal ideation without a specific plan, or a suicide attempt or a specific plan for committing suicide

B. The symptoms do not meet criteria for a Mixed Episode.

C. The symptoms cause clinically significant distress or impairment in social, occupational, or other important areas of functioning.

D. The symptoms are not due to the direct physiological effects of a substance (e.g., a drug of abuse, a medication) or a general medical condition (e.g., hypothyroidism).

E. The symptoms are not better accounted by Bereavement, i.e., after the loss of a loved one, the symptoms persist for longer than 2 months or are characterized by marked functional impairment, morbid preoccupation with worthlessness, suicidal ideation, psychotic symptoms, or psychomotor retardation.

Source: American Psychiatric Association (1994: 344–45). Reprinted with permission from the *Diagnostic and Statistical Manual of Mental Disorders*, Fourth Edition. Copyright © 1994 American Psychiatric Association.

Box 1.5
Abbreviated Diagnostic Criteria for Panic Disorder and Agoraphobia

Panic Attack

A discrete period of intense fear or discomfort, in which four or more of the following symptoms develop abruptly and reach a peak withing ten minutes:

1. Pounding or accelerating heart rate
2. Sweating
3. Trembling or shaking
4. Shortness of breath
5. Feelings of choking
6. Chest pain
7. Nausea
8. Dizziness
9. Feelings of unreality or being detached from oneself
10. Fear of losing control or going crazy
11. Fear of dying
12. Numbness or tingling sensations
13. Chills or hot flushes

Agoraphobia

A. Anxiety about being in places or situations from which escape might be difficult, or embarrassing, or in which help might not be available in the event of having a panic attack. Agoraphobic fears typically involve situations like being outside the home alone; being in a crowd or standing in a line; being on a bridge; or traveling on a bus, train, or car.

B. The situations are either avoided, endured with intense distress, or require the presence of a companion.

Panic Disorder

A. Both (1) and (2):

   (1) recurrent unexpected panic attacks

   (2) for one month or more:

      (a) persistent concern about having panic attacks

      (b) worry about the implications of panic attacks

      (c) a significant change in behavior related to the attacks

B. Agoraphobia present: *Panic disorder with agoraphobia*
   Agoraphobia absent: *Panic disorder without agoraphobia*

C. Not due to direct physiological effects of a substance, or a general medical condition

D. Not better accounted for by another mental disorder, such as social phobia, specific phobia, obsessive compulsive disorder, post-traumatic stress disorder, or separation anxiety disorder.

Source: American Psychiatric Association (1994: 395–96, 402–3). Reprinted with permission from the *Diagnostic and Statistical Manual of Mental Disorders*, Fourth Edition. Copyright © 1994 American Psychiatric Association.

This diagnosis again highlights the fact that diagnosticians must define their own reality (their own "society" and its "groups and social values") before they can decide that the individual is in conflict with them or lacks loyalty to them. For example, Charles Manson and his followers might be considered for the diagnosis of antisocial personality, but they had loyalty to their own small group and its social values.

A great number of individuals with bizarre and disabling emotions and behaviors do not fit precisely into any operational criteria. These include phenomena at the level of psychosis (Strauss et al. 1979); a wide range of complaints and behaviors resembling neurosis; feelings of distress or demoralization; and various complaints about the body that have no clear physical cause.

The Reliability and Validity of Psychiatric Diagnosis

Reliability is the consistency of measurement. It is considered the sine qua non of measurement, because it is quite possible to create and use a concept for which there is no referent in the empirical world. In the development of a new science, this process goes on all the time, and experience has taught us we need methods to evaluate our concepts. Compare, for example, the two concepts "ball" and "God." One can define a ball fairly easily by describing its shape and property of rolling, and good agreement could be reached among, say, 50 observers, as to whether a ball was present in the room or not. On the other hand, the 50 observers might have quite a low rate of agreement on whether "God" was present in the room. Even if a good deal of time were spent training the observers as to what was meant by God and precisely how to determine the presence of God, there might still be a lack of consistency between observers. In these two cases the observers would constitute the measures of the two concepts, and the reliability of the concept is the consistency with which its presence can be ascertained. "Ball" is probably a much more reliably measured concept than "God." In a similar manner, one can quantify the reliability of any other concept in social science, such as "depression," "schizophrenia," "bizarre behavior," and "residual deviance" (as discussed in Chapter 3). There are many varieties of reliability determined by the precise manner in which it is evaluated, but they all derive from this simple definition—the consistency of measurement.

There have been continuing efforts to assess the reliability of psychiatric diagnosis over the last few decades. The first edition of this book (Eaton 1980)

Box 1.6
Medical Case History of Panic Disorder

A 30 year old accountant was referred by his internist to a psychiatric consultant because of a 6-month history of recurrent bouts of extreme fear of sudden onset, accompanied by sweating, shortness of breath, palpitations, chest pain, dizziness, numbness in his fingers and toes, and the thought that he was going to die. His internist had given him a complete physical, an EKG, and glucose tolerance and other blood tests, and had found no abnormalities.

The patient has been married for five years; he has no children. He went to night school, while working, to get a master's degree in business administration and was quite successful and well liked at his firm. He and his wife, a teacher, generally get along well and have several couples with whom they enjoy going out.

Because of the attacks, which occurred unexpectedly and in a variety of situations several times each week, the patient started to avoid driving his car and going into department stores, lest he have an attack in these situations. He began to coax his wife to accompany him on errands, and, during the last month, he had felt comfortable only at home with his wife. Finally, he could not face the prospect of leaving home to go to work and took a medical leave of absence. When at home, he experienced only "twinges" of chest pain and slight numbness in his fingers, but no full-blown attacks.

When asked about circumstances surrounding the onset of his attacks, the patient said that he and his wife had been discussing buying a house and moving from their apartment. He admitted that the responsibilities of home ownership intimidated him and related the significance of the move to similar concerns his mother had that prevented his parents from ever buying a house.

Source: Spitzer et al. (1989: 213–14). Reprinted with permission from the American Psychiatric Association.

was produced just as the third edition of the DSM (American Psychiatric Association 1980) was published. The review of diagnostic reliability at that time revealed such poor reliability as to severely threaten the credibility of clinical practice and research based on the diagnoses. The review presented *kappa* statistics, which run below zero if agreement is less than would occur by chance, to zero at chance agreement, to 1 at perfect agreement. A kappa value of 0.50 is considered the minimum acceptable for good research, and still higher reliability is required for making decisions about individuals, such as treatment decisions. In reviews of diagnostic reliability from 1950 up to the DSM-III (Helzer, Clayton, et al. 1977; Helzer, Robins, et al. 1977), only one diagnosis (sociopathic) was above the 0.50 level in all the studies in which it was estimated (only two). Not a single study was able to attain values above 0.50 for all the diagnoses. The most reliable diagnosis was organic brain syndrome, which was low only in the latest study; the other reliable diagnosis was schizophrenia, which was above 0.50 in five out of seven studies. Psychotic depression (a subtype of affective psychosis) had low reliability, probably because of the difficulty in distinguishing it from milder depression. The two mild disorders, personality disorder and neurosis, had unacceptably low reliability. Since these reliability studies were conducted, for the most part, in research centers, the reliability of diagnoses in hospitals, clinics, and other treatment centers where little or no research was conducted was bound to be substantially lower. During the research leading up to the DSM-III, criteria necessary and sufficient for each diagnosis were written out in great detail. Standardized clinical interview questionnaires were designed that directed the clinician on the determination of each and every symptom. Training procedures were developed with videotapes that allowed psychiatrists to practice making diagnoses with the standardized interview questionnaires, ask questions, be corrected, and improve their rate of agreement with other psychiatrists so trained. Finally, measures of reliability were developed that took into account chance agreement such as the so-called kappa statistic.

The changes in the diagnostic system had the desired effect in improving reliability of disorders. Table 1.1 shows recent kappa estimates for diagnostic reliability for the recent American (DSM-III-R, Williams et al. 1992) and international (ICD-10, Sartorius 1988) systems. Only two anxiety disorders (agoraphobic disorder and social phobic disorder) fall below the threshold of 0.50 in the American study, and all values are acceptable, good, or even excellent in the ICD-10 system.

Validity is the degree to which the instrument measures the concept it purports to measure. It is not difficult to have a reliable measure with no validity. If observers were informed that God would be present whenever there was a plastic figurine of Buddha in the room, there would probably be a high degree of agreement as to its presence, but many would claim that the measure was invalid because the image of Buddha is not equivalent to God. For the purposes of this discussion two types of validity are of interest. The first is *criterion validity*, in which some independent measure of the concept is stated as the criterion; then the extent to which the instrument agrees with the criterion is quantified. A second type of validity is *construct validity*; here one builds a theory relating the concept to several others in a variety of ways. Then the theory is tested with empirical measurement; if it comes out as predicted, there is indirect evidence that the concept is being measured accurately. To the extent that the theory is broad and differentiated, the construct validity is believable. Often in social science there is no adequate criterion (e.g., on the presence of God), so that one must rely on construct validity. There is no external criterion by which to judge the validity of the psychiatrist's diagnosis. This fact arises out of the definition of *functional disorders*, which describes those disorders that have no known structural or organic basis. The result is that, in psychiatry, the most important way of judging the system of psychiatric diagnosis is by its construct validity. The construct validity consists of all the qualities and theories that connect to the various diagnoses. The germ theory of disease and the genetic theory of psychiatric disorder are relevant, as well as the relationships of disorders to

Table 1.1
Reliability and Validity of Psychiatric Diagnoses

Diagnosis	Reliability DSM-III-R	Reliability ICD-10	Chemical Treatment	Psycho-social Treatment	Recurrence Risk in MZ Twins
Disorders of children					
Autism	NA	.90	✕	✕	2,555.0
Attention Deficit	0.61	0.83	✚	✚	3.3
Disorders of adolescents					
Conduct Disorder	0.57	.90	✕	✚	NA
Eating Disorders	NA	.95	?	✚	8.0
Non-psychotic Disorders of Adults					
Agoraphobic Disorder	0.43	0.80	✚	✚	NA
Panic Disorder	0.58	0.64	✚	✚	4.0
Social Phobic Disorder	0.47	0.79	✚	✚	NA
Alcohol Disorder	0.75	0.93	✕	✚	NA
Antisocial Personality	0.63	NA	✕	✕	NA
Major Depressive Disorder	0.64	0.73	✚	✚	1.7
Psychotic Disorders of Adults					
Schizophrenia	0.65	0.88	✚	✚	48
Bipolar Disorder	0.84	0.82	✚	✕	60
Disorders of the elderly					
Dementia	0.83	NA	?	✕	NA

Notes: Reliability in the American diagnostic system: Williams et al. (1992). Reliability data for specific disorders not included in the Williams reference are: ADHD (DSM–IV)—Lahey et al. (1994), conduct disorder (DSM–IV)—Lahey et al. (1994); antisocial personality disorder (DSM–III)—Robins et al. (1981). NA: data are not available.

Reliability in the international diagnostic system (ICD–10): Sartorius (1988). NA: data not available.

Chemical treatment: ✚ indicates where data reveal statistically significant and non-trivial differences between a treated group and randomly assigned controls; ✕ indicates where there are no data, or the results show no difference; and ? indicates where the data are ambiguous. Taken from Nathan and Gorman (1998) with disorder-specific additions as below: ADHD—Wilens and Biederman (1992); anxiety disorders—Lydiard et al. (1996); depressive disorders—Thase and Kupfer (1996); schizophrenia—Prince (1985); bipolar disorder—Rickwood and Braithwaite (1994); eating disorders (question mark denotes proven chemotherapy for bulimia only)—Wilson and Fairburn (1998); dementia (question mark denotes proven chemotherapy of extremely limited use due to side effects,—Tune (1998).

Psychosocial treatment: ✚ indicates where data reveal statistically significant and non-trivial differences between a treated group and randomly assigned controls; ✕ indicates where there are no data, or the results show no difference; and ? indicates where the data are ambiguous. Taken from Nathan and Gorman (1998) with disorder-specific additions as below: conduct disorder—Dishion and Andrews (1995); eating disorders—Dare, Eisler et al. (1995); anxiety disorders—Barlow and Lehman (1996), Chambless and Gillis (1993); alcohol disorder—McCrady and Langenbucher (1996); major depressive disorder—Clarkin et al. (1996); schizophrenia—Lam (1991), Falloon et al. (1996), and Leff et al. (1990).

Genetics: Shows the relative risk for developing the disorder for a monozygotic twin whose cotwin has the disorder, compared to the risk in the general population. Taken from NIMH Genetics Workgroup (1997). NA: adequate estimates not available.

various medical and psychosocial treatments—all as contributions to the construct validity of the diagnostic system. Of course, many social conditions are also related to the various diagnoses, and these form part of the construct validity of the diagnostic system, even if they do not inhere strictly to the medical model itself. Thus, for example, if we find that urbanization is related strongly to schizophrenia and not to affective psychosis (as in Chapter 8), that is evidence for the construct validity of the diagnostic category of schizophrenia, even if no medical etiology or treatment is implied.

The *germ theory of disease* provided a theory for the origin of disease, a biological organism that could be used to establish the diagnosis, an effective treatment for individual cases (e.g., antibacterial medicines), and effective public health treatments for populations. Since the late nineteenth century, when this theory first appeared, diseases such as smallpox, diphtheria, and polio have been literally wiped out. Few would argue that these efforts were not fruitful or that the theory was a "myth." One reason for trying to extend this model into psychiatry is its notable success in the area of infectious diseases.

Characteristics in humans vary as to the extent they are influenced by genes. One good way of measuring the extent of genetic influence is with a *twin study*. Twins are of two types: one-egg twins, who are formed from the splitting of a single fertilized egg; and two-egg twins, who are formed from two separate fertilized eggs. One-egg twins share 100 percent of their genes, whereas two-egg twins share 50 percent of their genes. A twin study compares the percentage of twins in which both have the disease, comparing one-egg and two-egg twins. Where the concordance is much higher in one-egg twins than two-egg twins, there is evidence for strong genetic involvement in the characteristic. A statistic that helps assess the strength of genetic influence in a twin study is the *recurrence risk ratio for monozygotic twins*. This is the risk of having the disorder if one is a monozygotic twin of someone with the disorder, compared to the risk in the general population. The advantage of the recurrence risk ratio is that its value can be easily compared with other risk factors for the same disorder. For example, the relative risk for having an episode of major depression is about 2.0 for women compared to men; the relative risk for having an onset of schizophrenia is about 4.0 for persons born in urban areas versus those born in rural areas.

Most psychiatric disorders are influenced by inheritance, as shown in Table 1.1. There are no disorders in which there are not also strong influences by the environment (which includes the physical environment as well as the social environment), because all studies of monozygotic twins, who have identical genetic structures, show less than 100 percent concordance. But three disorders stand out as having strong genetic influences: *autism*, in which the risk is increased by a factor of 2,500; *schizophrenia*, in which risk is raised by a factor of nearly 50; and *bipolar disorder*, in which the risk is raised by a factor of 60. Aside from these three, the recurrence risks for those with monozygotic twins are not greatly different from the relative risks for social and other environmental characteristics, as presented later in this volume. There is considerable variation in the estimates given in the different studies, especially for the eating disorders, which range to well above 50 in some studies.

Geneticists are currently searching the entire set of genes in humans to locate those that might cause mental disorders, but it appears unlikely that any major mental disorders—even one of the three with the strongest evidence (autism, bipolar disorder, and schizophrenia)—will have a simple pattern of inheritance, devoid of environmental influence. The current genetic evidence seems to suggest that specific disorders are not inherited—rather, vulnerabilities to a broad range of disorders are inherited and then molded by environmental influences to specific patterns. For example, Kendler et al. (1987) found that genetic influences produced vulnerability for both anxiety and depression, and other studies have shown that depressive and anxiety disorders run in families (Weissman et al. 1984). Linkage studies of schizophrenia show that the highest genetic loading is produced by a broad concept of schizophrenia, rather than a narrow one (Kendler 1988). Thus, the genetic theory of psychiatric disorder adds to the construct validity of the diagnostic system, but only as regards broad categories of disorder.

Research on the treatment of psychiatric disorders also provides evidence of their validity. There are specific treatments for certain disorders that have been proved to be beneficial in randomized, double-blind studies, where the effectiveness of the treatment was matched against the effect of a placebo, and neither the patient nor the clinician knew whether the medication or the placebo was in use on a given patient. In a placebo study, it often occurs that about one-third of the patients report improvement—thus, the medication results summarized in Table 1.1 by a "✚" sign generally indicate improvement in a substantially higher proportion of patients than that. The nature of research tends to overemphasize the fit of specific medications with specific diagnoses. Research on drug treatments is funded, for the most part, by pharmaceutical companies that must prepare for approval by regulatory agencies such as the Food and Drug Administration (FDA) and is geared toward a single disorder category, especially for the first trial. For example, for attention deficit disorder with hyperactivity, there is ritalin; for schizophrenia, there is phenothiazine and other neuroleptics developed and used from the 1950s onward and later generations of neuroleptics such as clozapine and olanzapine; for bipolar disorder, lithium, electric shock, and various antidepressant medications; for the anxiety disorders, there is a variety of mild tranquilizers; and for depression, a range of antidepressants, including new medications that target a specific type of surface on brain cells (so-called selective serotonin reuptake inhibitors [SSRIs] like Prozac). As with the genetic research, the medications are specific to disorder categories only in the most crude sense. For example, tricyclic antidepressant medications are useful in the treatment of panic disorder and eating disorders; mild tranquilizers are used across the range of disorders. For some disorders, such as autism, conduct disorder, eating disorders, alcohol disorders, antisocial personality disorder, and dementia, there are no medications proven to be effective (indicated by an "☒" in Table 1.1).

Various nonchemical treatment modalities have been shown to be effective for mental disorders. The studies on psychosocial treatments are based on randomized, controlled trials with a placebo or other comparison, but since the therapy involves psychological or social counseling, they are less likely to be blinded as to condition. Cognitive behavioral therapy (CBT) involves teaching the individual new habits of thinking and behaving that lower the risk of onset of disorder, speed remission, and prevent relapse. One form or another of CBT or other psychosocial therapy has been found effective for all the nonpsychotic disorders of adulthood listed in Table 1.1, except for antisocial personality disorder.

BIZARRE BEHAVIORS AS DEVIANCE

In this section we consider the general framework within which the sociologist interprets bizarre behaviors: the theory of deviance. Second, we apply concepts from the sociology of knowledge to the social and cultural history of bizarre behaviors in modern Western society. One of the implications of this analysis is that the disease interpretation of bizarre behaviors may be unique to modern Western society. Therefore, we next examine contemporary, non-Western societies and our own society before it took on its present form.

The Sociology of Deviance

An assumption of the sociological framework is that no act is universally regarded as deviant (Erickson 1966). Deviance is defined as the breaking of a cultural norm—that is, a shared set of expectations about behavior. Deviance thus departs from the typifications of normal life, as discussed earlier. Norms vary so much between cultures that the definition of deviance always depends on the culture, and nothing is disapproved of universally. Incest and murder, for example, are not proscribed in many cultures, nor even in some subcultures in our own society. Norms change, too; for example, homosexuality is no longer proscribed in many parts of our society, and use of marijuana was not illegal before the Marijuana Tax Act of 1937 (Conrad and Schneider 1980: 22). The conclusion to be drawn is the central concept in the sociology of deviance: *acts are not deviant until they are so defined*. Individuals do not create deviance; rather, audiences create deviance. As Friedson puts it, the task is not so much the "explanation of the cause of behavior as it [is] the cause of the meaning attached to the behavior" (Freidson: 213, cited in Conrad and Schneider 1992: 19). According to Spector and Kitsuse (1977), "the theoretical problem is to account for how categories of social problems and deviance are produced."

Another aspect of the sociological framework is that deviance has functions at the level of society. The idea is that individual acts of deviance may serve some purpose not related to the individual. This part of the sociological theory of deviance ties into the more general theory of *functionalism* in sociology, which recurs in later chapters. A brief digression on this theory is necessary (Merton 1956). *Functions* are "those observed consequences [of an institution or cultural item] which make for the adaptation of a given [social] system." *Manifest functions* are functions that are "intended and recognized as such by the participants in the system"; *latent functions* are those that are neither intended nor recognized. An aim of functional sociological analysis is to identify latent functions in a social system.

One issue in the theory of functionalism is whether there exist functional requirements in a social system—that is, functions that are necessary for the survival of the system. The clearest example is reproduction, which is necessary for the survival of a society. Connected to this issue is the idea of functional alternative. If there are functional requirements, it may be that they can be satisfied by a range of different social institutions (e.g., different mating and kinship patterns).

Institutions for identifying, processing, and resocializing deviants have as their manifest function the correction of the deviant behavior of the individual. But sociologists have proposed two major latent functions of these ceremonies and institutions. The first is that the ceremonies surrounding the recognition, labeling, and public sanctioning of deviant individuals serve to define and publicize the norms of the community. In effect, deviants serve the community by promulgating the norms. A second major latent function of the labeling and sanctioning process is that it creates moral solidarity among nondeviants. Thus, deviance redefines the social boundaries of the community by ostracizing the deviant and reinforces the sense of group belonging among the majority.

One must separate prudently the idea of function from that of cause and necessity. Because deviance has manifest and latent functions does not mean that it is necessary, and the functions themselves are not necessarily inevitable. Likewise, functions are not causes; the need for moral solidarity does not necessarily cause deviance, for example. The question is, Is the processing of deviants a functional requirement for the continuance of the society? If so, the function may, in fact, cause deviance, but the causal network has to be traced out, from the societal level of function to the individual act of deviance. The cause does not follow directly and simply from the identification of function.

The question as to how a particular act comes to be defined as deviant is a part of the sociology of deviance that links directly with the sociology of knowledge. The general answer is that social order and stability derive from a constant process of legitimation and universe maintenance, and acts that threaten the process are deviant. There is a limitless range of human behavior; and complex and bizarre behaviors requiring considerable energy occur continually. But only some of these are singled out as deviant in a given culture. One aspect of legitimating theories is that they connect to one another, enhancing their logic and together building an abstract and powerful symbolic universe, which links all the theories together in a cosmic theory of humanity, explaining existence and providing a stable framework by which to view the world. Acts that challenge the logic of these theories will be defined as deviant, and the closer they come to challenging the symbolic universe on a very abstract level, and the more legitimating theories they link up to, the more societal effort will be spent in dealing with the deviant.

Medicalization

The social constructionist and functionalist approaches suggest that the diagnostic system in psychiatry is actually part of an ideology—that is, a system of ideas that supports the status quo. In fact, there is evidence that the diagnostic system has been expanding to define a wider and wider range of behaviors as medical illness, instead of simply disapproved. This movement from badness to sickness is termed *medicalization* (Conrad and Schneider 1980: 29):

the defining and labeling of deviant behavior as a medical problem, usually an illness, and mandating the medical profession to provide some type of treatment for it. Concomitant with such medicalization is the growing use of medicine as an agent of social control, typically as medical intervention. Medical intervention as social control seeks to limit, modify, regulate, isolate, or eliminate deviant behavior with medical means and in the name of health.

The notion is that this is part of a general expansion of medicine into everyday life. This might be termed the hypothesis of medicalization. As Friedson puts it:

Medicalization is thought to serve the interests of the medical profession. Medicine is . . . active in seeking out illness. The profession does treat the illnesses laymen take to it, but it also seeks to discover illness of which laymen may not even be aware. One of the greatest ambitions of the physician is to discover and describe a "new" disease or syndrome and to be immortalized by having his name used to identify the disease. Medicine, then, is oriented to seeking out and finding illness, which is to say that it seeks to create social meanings of illness where the meaning or interpretation was lacking before. (Friedson 1970: 252, cited in Conrad and Scheider 1992)

There is clear evidence of medicalization. The 1840 census of the United States included just one category for mental disorders, but this was expanded to seven categories in the 1880 census. In 1917 the American Psychiatric Association Committee on Statistics proposed 59 disorders (Pincus et al. 1992). In the first edition of the DSM, in 1952, there were 128 categories; the 1968 second edition had 159; the 1980 DSM-III had 227; the 1987 DSM-III-R had 253; the DSM-IV has 357 categories; and projections are that the future versions will contain yet more (Blashfield and Fuller 1996). Examples of behaviors and conditions that have been the subject of sociological analyses with regard to the hypothesis of medicalization are alcoholism, homosexuality, child abuse, criminal behavior, drug addiction, senility, and hyperkinesis.

The production of the third edition of the *Diagnostic and Statistical Manual* provides several specific examples of issues surrounding medicalization. In the 1960s many leaders felt that the profession of psychiatry would benefit by tightening their relationship to medicine in general. This has sometimes been called the *neo-Kraepelinian credo*, with some of the following tenets:

1. Psychiatry is a branch of medicine.
2. Psychiatry should base its practice on scientific knowledge.
3. Psychiatry treats people who are sick.
4. There is a boundary between the normal and the sick.
5. There is not one but many discrete mental illnesses. They are not myths.
6. Psychiatrists should focus on the biological basis of mental illness.
7. There should be explicit concern with diagnosis and classification.
8. Diagnostic criteria should be codified.
9. In research on diagnosis, appropriate statistical techniques should be used. (Kirk and Kutchins 1992; Klerman 1978)

The American Psychological Association (APA) objected on several occasions to the wording in the then-upcoming third edition of the *Diagnostic and Statistical Manual*, especially statements that mental disorders are medical in nature. The chairman of the group of psychiatrists that was composing the manual was eager to make the debate between the two professional groups public, because "it would make it clear that DSM-III helps psychiatry move closer to the rest of medicine" (letter from Robert Spitzer to APA medical director Melvin Sabshin, October 26, 1977)—(Kirk and Kutchins 1992). A letter from the president of the American Psychiatric Association to the president of the American Psychological Association asked:

Where do we go from here? You can continue to try to convince us that most mental disorders in the DSM-III classification are not medical disorders. You will not only fail to convince us, but we believe that it is inappropriate for you to attempt to tell us how we should conceptualize our area of professional responsibility. You can try to convince us that even if we believe that mental disorders are medical disorders, we should not explicitly say so in DSM-III. You will not convince us of this either. We believe that it is essential that we clarify to anyone who may be in doubt, that we regard psychiatry as a specialty of medicine. (Kirk and Kutchins 1992: 114)

The president of the American Psychological Association responded that the DSM-III "is more of a political position paper for the American Psychiatric Association than a scientifically-based classification system" (Kirk and Kutchins 1992: 115). In the end, however, the psychologists did not have the resources to come up with an alternative classification theory based on principles of psychology, such as learning theory, and the use of the DSM is now widespread even among psychologists.

There is a financial imperative to producing the *Diagnostic and Statistical Manuals*. They are heavily used in teaching and research and sell well, making a profit for the publisher, the American Psychiatric Association. The profit from the third edition, including its revision, was about $25 million, and the predicted profit from the fourth edition is about $40 million (Blashfield and Fuller 1996).

Expansion of the medical model is particularly evident in the area of childhood problems. The classic example is overactive behavior in children, to which the diagnosis of *attention deficit/hyperactivity disorder* (ADHD), in the third and fourth editions of the DSM, is sometimes applied. The criteria for the disorder in the DSM-IV are given in Box 1.7. Note that *all* of the criteria are behavioral, and *all* criteria describe behaviors that *all* children engage in at one time or another. For example, who has *not* known a child who "often has difficulty organizing tasks and activities . . . dislikes . . . to engage in tasks . . . such as school work or homework . . . loses things . . . fidgets . . . or squirms in seat . . . blurts out answers before questions have been completed . . . or . . . has difficulty awaiting [his or her] turn"? The crucial distinction is made by the diagnostician, who must decide where to place the threshold that determines when the behavior occurs "often." As well as occurring "often," there must be a wide range of types of behaviors, including attentional problems, overactivity, and impulsivity. The prevalence of the disorder will depend highly on the thresholds chosen. Another aspect of this disorder is that there is no room for complaints by the individual—that is, the disorder is based on signs alone, judged by an observer. A disorder based on behaviors whose presence is totally judged by others is, in some sense, totally dependent on the social ecology for its construction.

Conrad has developed the thesis of medicalization for this disorder most fully (Conrad and Schneider 1980). As early as 1937 it was discovered that amphetamine drugs had very strong effects on children who had problems learning in school or behaving well. The effect was termed paradoxical, because the drug was known to be a stimulant, but the effect on the children was to calm them down. Although the report was published in the prestigious *American Journal of Psychiatry*, there was not much attention paid to it for more than 20 years. About 10 years after the discovery of the effects of amphetamine, studies of children who had had inflammation of the brain were shown to have a range of behaviors including overactivity, and the term "minimal brain dysfunction" was used to describe the syndrome. Various terms were used over the ensuing 10 years, including the term "hyperkinetic impulse disorder," which described a problem similar to some problems with clearly organic causes but for which there was no evidence of organic involvement. In 1961 the drug Ritalin was approved for use with children by the Food and Drug Administration, and this drug became the treatment of choice for ADHD, remaining so until today. In

Box 1.7
Diagnostic Criteria for Attention Deficit/Hyperactivity Disorder

A. Either (1) or (2):

(1) six (or more) of the following symptoms of inattention have persisted for at least 6 months to a degree that is maladaptive and inconsistent with developmental level:

Inattention

(A) often fails to give close attention to details or makes careless mistakes in schoolwork, work, or other activities

(B) often has difficulty sustaining attention in tasks or play activities

(C) often does not seem to listen when spoken to directly

(D) often does not follow through on instructions and fails to finish schoolwork, chores, or duties in the workplace (not due to oppositional behavior or failure to understand instructions)

(E) often has difficulty organizing tasks and activities

(F) often avoids, dislikes, or is reluctant to engage in tasks that require sustained mental effort (such as school work or homework)

(G) often loses things necessary for tasks or activities (e.g., toys, school assignments, pencils, books, or tools)

(H) is often easily distracted by extraneous stimuli

(I) is often forgetful in daily activities

(2) six (or more) of the following symptoms of hyperactivity-impulsivity have persisted for at least 6 months to a degree that is maladaptive and inconsistent with developmental level:

Hyperactivity

(A) often fidgets with hands or feet or squirms in seat

(B) often leaves seat in classroom or in other situations in which remaining seated is expected

(C) often runs about or climbs excessively in situations in which it is inappropriate (in adolescents or adults, may be limited to subjective feelings of restlessness)

(D) often has difficulty playing or engaging in leisure activities quietly

(E) is often "on the go" or often acts as if "driven by a motor"

(F) often talks excessively

Impulsivity

(G) often blurts out answers before questions have been completed

(H) often has difficulty awaiting turn

(I) often interrupts or intrudes on others (e.g., butts into conversations or games)

B. Some hyperactive-impulsive or inattentive symptoms that caused impairment were present before age 7 years.

C. Some impairment from the symptoms is present in two or more settings (e.g., at school [or work] and at home).

D. There must be clear evidence of clinically significant impairment in social, academic, or occupational functioning.

E. The symptoms do not occur exclusively during the course of a Pervasive Developmental Disorder, Schizophrenia, or other Psychotic Disorder and are not better accounted for by another mental disorder (e.g., Mood Disorder, Anxiety Disorder, Dissociative Disorder, or a Personality Disorder).

Source: American Psychiatric Association (1994: 83–85). Reprinted with permission from the *Diagnostic and Statistical Manual of Mental Disorders*, Fourth Edition. Copyright © 1994 American Psychiatric Association.

1966 the U.S. Public Health Service sponsored a task force that chose the term "minimal brain dysfunction" from about three dozen competing terms. In the DSM-III the diagnosis became ADHD.

The sociological analysis focuses on the social construction of the diagnosis of ADHD. One question that arises is why it took 20 years for ADHD to take off as a scientific and public issue. Prior to 1966 there were few scientific articles and no published articles in the popular or educational media on this topic; but in about a decade the literature mushroomed (Conrad and Schneider 1980: 157). It could be that attaching the word "brain" to the disorder, which was suggested in 1947 and then confirmed in the government panel in 1966, had an important effect. It seems probable that the pharmaceutical industry's marketing efforts had an effect, also. Ritalin has been shown to be effective in randomized, double-blind trials in improving the behavior of children with hyperactivity (Table 1.1). Ritalin supplied an estimated 15 percent of the total gross profits to its company in 1971 (Conrad and Schneider 1980: 160). Attention deficit disorder may have satisfied the needs of pediatricians, who were possibly bored with treatment of minor respiratory illnesses in children. There may also have been some responsiveness among working mothers, who needed help managing a child with a great deal of energy and were forming an increasing proportion of mothers. The medical diagnosis of ADHD laid the blame for the problem squarely within the child, perhaps relieving feelings of guilt associated with parenting practices. Finally, the Association for Children with Learning Disabilities, an interest and lobbying group formed from groups of parents and professionals, played a role in making the public aware of the disorder and in accepting the idea of medication. There is interest in the occurrence of ADHD in adults (Wender and Garfinkel 1989), which might be taken as further evidence of medicalization.

New technologies strongly influence the spread of a diagnosis. Following the introduction of phenothiazines, there was an abrupt increase in the frequency of diagnosis of schizophrenia; following the introduction of lithium, there was an abrupt increase in the number of affective disorders diagnosed; and following the introduction of behavior therapy, there was an increase in the frequency of diagnosed phobias (Baldesserini 1970; Blum 1978, Hare 1974). Apparently, when there is doubt as to a diagnosis, the clinician is more likely to choose the diagnosis for which a good therapy exists or at least a diagnosis with therapy that has not yet been proved ineffective. When a specific drug is thought to be applicable to a new diagnosis, drug companies intensively promote the new diagnosis with research support, colorful advertisements in psychiatric journals, and symposia. The more prevalent the disease or diagnosis in the population, the more lucrative the drug and the more intensive the promotion campaign.

The existence of a proven medical treatment for ADHD is not a conclusive counterargument to the hypothesis of medicalization. The social research shows that availability of medical therapy is only one of the forces producing interest in the diagnosis and its use. Even though a medication is proven to change behavior, the etiology of the behavior is not understood, and it is not clear that a medical explanation is more beneficial to the public's health than an alternative psychological or social explanation or diagnosis might be. In our culture, chemicals are ingested, and medications prescribed, in many situations with no diagnosis available. An upward trend in the use of medications and chemicals for increasingly minor complaints and behaviors, personality traits, and social situations will continue. The point is to study the various forces that go into creating, using, and popularizing the diagnosis and to make a rational decision about whether the diagnostic category is a useful and good thing.

Another diagnosis relevant to the idea of medicalization is *masked depression*: "the term given to a depressive condition which manifests itself chiefly at the somatic level" (Dols 1987). In making the diagnosis, the psychiatrist is supposed to rule out possible physical etiologies and search for clinical signs of depression, such as sadness, guilt, sluggishness, and so forth. However, they may not always be present, in which case the clinician searches for diurnal or phasic variations in the somatic symptoms, which are thought to be characteristic of depression. Other questions cover the family and personal history of the individual, including questions about depression in relatives. However, "response to antidepressant therapy . . . is generally considered to be of decisive importance, but its value is not absolute." At this writing there appears to be no study of the reliability of the diagnosis of masked depression.

Drug companies have intensively promoted this diagnosis. A symposium on masked depression, later published, was organized by CibaGeigy and took place in 1973 in the most lavish resort in the world, St. Moritz, Switzerland. A second volume, *Somatic Manifestations of Depressive Disorders* (Leff et al. 1976), was "presented as a service to the medical profession by Pfizer Laboratories." There is an enormous potential since depression (masked or unmasked) is widespread. Also, doctors are accustomed to patients who have somatic complaints that are difficult or impossible to diagnose (sometimes referred to pejoratively by the doctors as "crocks"). In *Masked Depression* (Kielholz 1973) there are chapters on masked depression in children and adolescents, old age, general practice, and many other areas. One chapter recommends use of antidepressant medication for the treatment of "isolated aches and pains."

The hypothesis of medicalization is disconfirmed in several instances. In its 1974 annual meeting, the American Psychiatric Association (APA) held a vote to determine whether homosexuality, a prime example of medicalization, according to Conrad and Schneider (1992), should be considered a disease. The vote was slightly in favor of *not* designating it as a disease (Spector 1977), and it was removed from the psychiatric diagnostic manual in the third edition in 1980. The conscious and deliberate consideration by the APA is not in accord with the hegemonistic striving implied by the medicalization hypothesis. Many doctors resist medicalization by refusing to assign diagnostic categories in their everyday treatment of patients (Strong 1979). There is not complete acceptance of the diagnosis of ADHD, for example (Prior and Sanson 1986). Public and highly politicized discussions of which categories to include now take place before each revision of the manual, and disorders that should be considered in the manual in its next edition are now listed in the appendix to promote public discussion. The growth in number of categories and increasing rapidity of revision of the DSM are not popular with some leaders in the psychiatric community, who see the changes as impeding acquisition of knowledge about the categories (Cooper 1995; Guze 1995). The diagnostic corpus contained in the DSM is presumably weakened by inclusion of unpopular diagnoses, as well as those for which there is little demonstrable reliability or validity.

Mental Disorders in Recent History

The textbook application of the functional theory of deviance is manifested in the medieval *Inquisition* (Goode 1992). In the fifteenth century, European society was in considerable flux because ideas that challenged the dominant position of the church and religion had spread widely. There was an influx of scholars from Constantinople, which had fallen to Turks in 1453, a revival of traditions from classical Greece, and a new interest in humanism, reading, literature, art, and science.

Part of the response to this challenge to the ethic of the church and the idea of life based on faith was the publication in 1487 of *Malleus Maleficarum* (Witches' Hammer) by two Dominican monks. The gist of *Malleus Maleficarum* was that demons representing the devil could invade the souls of individuals and result in various deviant acts. Many behaviors now labeled as psychiatric disorders were included in the list of those thought to be caused by Satan. The title implied that women were more likely to fall prey to Satan than men. The publication of *Malleus Maleficarum* led to the creation of enormous and powerful inquisitions, whose functions were to search for, discover, label, and sanction deviant individuals. The book was the major diagnostic manual in the Inquisition and underwent 29 editions in the next two centuries. Many individ-

Figure 1.2
Saint Catherine Exorcising a Possessed Woman, **by Benvenuto (early
sixteenth century)**

Social control of bizarre deviance in medieval times was done by the church.

uals were persecuted and burned at the stake on the grounds they were Satan's
representatives. In other cases church figures such as Saint Catherine exorcised
the demons (Figure 1.2).

There is an interesting difference between the Spanish and Italian Inquisitions
(Szasz 1970). In Italy the focus was on various sexual acts regarded as deviant.
In Spain, however, there were different historical circumstances. In 1492 all
Jews had been required by royal edict to convert to Christianity or leave Spain.
Many Jews outwardly converted but continued to practice some tenets of Ju-
daism in private. The Spanish Inquisition focused not on sexual deviations or
bizarre psychiatric-like symptoms but on the location and punishment of these
crypto-Jews. Thus, for instance, aversion to pork was a "symptom" in the Spanish Inquisition. The implication is that both societies were threatened by the
development of the Renaissance and needed the Inquisition to build moral solidarity and reinforce the symbolic universe; but each somehow chose a different
cultural norm to emphasize and sanction. The Spanish and Italian Inquisitions
were functionally equivalent.

It seems amazing, with the aid of hindsight, that so much effort could be
spent in this process of cultural definition. But we find examples of processes
like these much closer to our own time and situation: the lynching of blacks

who appeared to threaten or blur the racial divisions of society in the 1940s, for example; or the threat of communism in the 1950s; or the persecution of Lenny Bruce or Timothy Leary in the 1960s; or the search for kidnappers of young children in the 1980s. The extension of this idea to psychiatry is obvious: is it the functional equivalent of the medieval Inquisition?

The Inquisition (similar to the DSM-III) is an example of universe maintenance that combines three major operations of creation of cultural systems (religion), therapy (exorcism), and annihilation (redefining the individual as nonhuman). Likewise, the institutional apparatus concerned with mental disorder in our society also combines these systems: we have an elaborate group of scientific theories for understanding mental disorder, a complex of therapeutic institutions, and a way of redefining the individual as nonhuman—as a "case" or "disease." The questions that now become paramount are: How is it that our culture came to regard these particular types of behaviors as deviant? How did mental illness enter our spectrum of deviance? In the words of Foucault in his *Madness and Civilization* (Foucault 1979: ix–x):

We must try to return, in history, to that zero point in the course of madness at which madness is an undifferentiated experience. [We must] determine the realm in which the man of madness and the man of reason, moving apart, are not yet disjunct [and] begin the dialogue of their breach. . . . Here madness and non-madness, reason and non-reason are inextricably involved; inseparable at the moment when they do not yet exist.

There appears to have been a period in our civilization sometime before the end of the fifteenth century when madness was an "undifferentiated experience." If it existed, it was not remarkable or was much less remarkable than currently and did not require departure from everyday life. It is difficult to find references to persons who engaged in bizarre behaviors, and when we do find them, the references are allegorical or only by implication. But between the 1487 publication of *Malleus Maleficarum* and the presentation of Shakespeare's plays a century later, madness had leaped to prominence as a cultural symbol. During that time there occurred the publication of Brant's allegorical *Narrenschiff* (Ship of Fools) and the satirical painting by Bosch with the same title; Erasmus' *In Praise of Folly*; the publication of *Don Quixote*, the first full-fledged novel in the Western world in which the central character is described repeatedly as crazy; the many plays by Shakespeare with themes of madness and mad individuals such as King Lear, Macbeth, and Hamlet. In *Hamlet* (act 4, scene 5) is found a gentleman's description of Ophelia's behavior that displays Shakespeare's gift for concise descriptions of difficult and complex ideas and emotions:

She speaks much of her father; says she hears there's tricks in the world, and hems, and beats her heart, spurns enviously at straws, speaks things in doubt that carry but half sense. Her speech is nothing, yet the unshaped use of it doth move the hearers to col-

Figure 1.3
Dulle Griet (Mad Meg), **by Breughel (late sixteenth century)**

This painting depicts bizarre deviance, at the time of the reformation, at large in society—that is, not socially controlled. One theory for this painting is that Breughel was representing a schizophrenic woman that he had actually observed.

lection. They aim at it and botch the words up fit to their own thoughts; which, as her winks and nods and gestures yield them, indeed would make one think there would be thought, though nothing sure, yet much unhappily.

In reading this, it is hard to imagine that Shakespeare had not come into contact with a schizophrenic with florid thought disorder.

Another cultural artifact of this age is Breughel's painting *Mad Meg* (Figure 1.3). It portrays the cultural transition of this period most clearly. Breughel was an artistic descendant of the Spaniard Hieronymus Bosch. Bosch had dealt with two themes relevant to the bizarre: human folly, as in his *The Cure of Folly* and his *Ship of Fools*; and chaos at the level of society, as in his *Temptation of St. Anthony, Garden of Earthly Delights*, and other paintings with legions of otherworldly monsters and grotesque, half-human forms. These paintings present as well as any representation to date the unleashing of chaos and the failure of order. A generation later in *Mad Meg*, Breughel personified chaos in the form of an individual crazy woman. There appear in *Mad Meg* the armies of monsters, the conflagrations, and the battles inspired by the chaos of Bosch; the same ship from Bosch's *Ship of Fools* is in the distance, as well as an upturned funnel, which appeared in *The Cure of Folly*. She marches along with a sword in one hand and a bag of inexplicable tools and implements in the other. On first examination she appears to be walking toward a large, open-mouthed head of Satan, representing the Gates of Hell; but on closer look, it is clear she will step right into a large tree. The painting is full of deliberate odd placements and proportions; for example, one of Meg's legs in noticeably longer than the other.

Mad Meg stands out from Breughel's other work because he tended to paint quite realistically; he is famous for his *Peasant Wedding* and *Returning Hunters*, for example. He painted deviants such as blind persons and cripples in realistic fashion. *Mad Meg* was not an afterthought or carelessly done: he apparently began the same painting over again after being displeased with the first try, because there are two complete versions extant, both by him. One conclusion is that *Mad Meg* is Breughel's attempt to represent as accurately and realistically as possible a woman who today would be called schizophrenic, including her hallucinatory world, the postulated causes of her affliction, her distorted social relationships, her supposed moral transgressions, and the force of her physical presence (Panse and Schmidt 1967). If this interpretation is correct, then the remarkable thing is not that he was able to paint her with such power but that he decided to paint her at all. He was representing the ever-threatening chaos of the world in one crazy woman. Madness had become an individualized phenomenon.

Foucault presents two compelling arguments for the rise to preeminence of madness as a cultural symbol during these centuries (Panse and Schmidt 1967). The first argument concerned the growing desire to organize society in a rational way, instead of basing organization on faith and the church. In this Age of Reason, the lack of reason that madness represented threatened the new and growing symbolic universe much more than it had heretofore, hence, the heightened concern over chaos in general and individual madness in particular. The second reason was an economic one: madness was perceived, as was poverty, as incapacity to work and inability to integrate with the group. The culmination of this new ethic was the *Great Confinement* in 1656. During this year the *Hospital General* was formed in Paris out of several existing structures; and beggars, lunatics, vagrants, and demented persons were rounded up and institutionalized. As many as 1 percent of the population of Paris was confined as a result of this one great effort. These arguments are consistent with the functionalist theory of deviance.

A wonderful exercise illustrating the change in conceptual approach to bizarre behavior is to compare the paintings of *Saint Catherine* and *Mad Meg* and a painting of the great Parisian clinician Charcot called *A Clinical Lecture at the Salpêtriére*, by Brouillet in the late nineteenth century (Figure 1.4). In all three paintings, the madness is personified in a woman. In *Malleus Maleficarum* and the picture of *Saint Catherine*, the chaos was to be controlled by the church. In *Mad Meg* it is unleashed onto the world. In the painting by Brouillet it is under the control of science. The woman, with breasts slightly bared, is fainting as a result of hysteria, almost at the snap of Charcot's fingers. There is the atmo-

Figure 1.4
A Clinical Lecture at the Salpêtriére, by Brouillet (nineteenth century)

Social control of bizarre deviance in modern times is done by the medical profession. Charcot's protégé Babinski is catching the woman, and Freud is seated at the front of the onlookers, wearing an apron. A painting at the far left shows a woman fainting.

sphere of scientific calm and rationality, and the fainting woman is being caught gently by Charcot's assistants. Only in *Mad Meg* is the crazy person the central subject of the painting.

The implications of the theory of deviance and this brief review of the cultural history of bizarre behaviors are insidious. If the cultural system has dictates of its own, then, as the culture evolves, categories may be created or emphasized in order to support or connect to others or to form a logical, cultural whole, with no necessary empirical underpinning. Thus, for example, we have today a category *unidentified flying objects* (UFOs), which fits into our culture well but has dubious empirical basis. We think these categories ought to exist, yet we cannot locate an empirical referent for them or show that they are reliable. If the discovery, labeling, and sanctioning of deviant individuals are functional for the society as a whole, then it may be that individuals are sacrificed for the higher goal of cultural stability and moral solidarity. In the special case of mental disorder, the starting point could be that period in the sixteenth and seventeenth centuries when insanity first came to be recognized. The conclusion is that the process is not inevitable and that mental illness need not exist as such. According to this logic, we ought to be able to find a functional alternative to mental disorder for our culture so that mental illness and psychiatrists have no part in it.

A deduction from this line of reasoning is that mental disorders are unique to Western society, because they developed as cultural concomitants of the Age of Reason and the capitalist economic order. Non-Western societies or our own society in the premodern era should display less or no evidence of the existence of mental disorders.

Mental Disorder in Non-Western Culture

It seems likely that all cultures have words for bizarre behaviors that translate roughly as "crazy." Native speakers from many cultures (e.g., Chinese, Arabic, American Indian, Yoruba Nigerian) can readily supply translations for words like "crazy," "mad," and so forth. In most cases the words do not have European origins but indigenous ones. The existence of a word for craziness is not proof that the behavior exists—it indicates only a need to express the concept.

Transcultural psychiatrists have studied the immense variation in types of mental disorders in different cultures (Kiev 1972; Marsella 1993; Simons and Hughes 1985). Some mental disorders are thought to be unique to particular cultures, and these are termed the *culture-bound syndromes*. An example is the so-called *koro* found infrequently in Chinese men (Cheng 1996; Chowdhury 1996). *Koro* is an intense fear that the penis is shrinking into the abdomen and will disappear. The word for *koro* is apparently of Malaysian origin, possibly a rough translation of "turtle's head." It is believed that if the penis shrinks all the way into the abdomen, death will result. The sufferer may tie a string to it or clamp a box around it. The fear, if it is strong, can severely disable the individual because he may be unwilling to let go of his penis and so may have difficulty in eating or working and may injure the penis in attempts to prevent its shrinkage. *Koro* is thought to be due to an imbalance of yin and yang forces, caused by sexual excesses, prostitution, or masturbation. *Koro* is found mostly among young men. *Koro* occurs sometimes in epidemic form (Cheng 1996).

Amok is a type of culture-bound syndrome found in Malaysia. It is characterized by outbursts of rage and violence, followed by amnesia. It is sometimes connected to violence directed at animals or persons, and it is the origin of our own phrase "running amok." As with *koro*, there are epidemic qualities to *amok*, such as diffusion of a particular form involving grenades (Westermeyer 1973).

Latah is a culture-bound syndrome found in Southeast Asia (Simons 1996). It is a group of behaviors usually occurring in women and is precipitated by startling them in some way. The startling is followed by a brief period of hypersuggestibility and automatic obedience. Sometimes there is automatic repetition of the words and gestures of others. On other occasions there is intense swearing and sometimes severe disorganization of thought. The startling is often a deliberate form of teasing of those known to be *latahs*. *Latah* has been discussed in the psychiatric literature for about a century (Yap 1951).

A variety of cultures include behaviors such as these that have been termed the *startle-matching syndrome* (Simons 1996). For example, something similar to *latah*, dubbed *jumpers*, was observed in loggers in isolated areas of the north-

Box 1.8
Observations of the Startle-Matching Syndrome

Latah in Malaysia:

"It happened to my sister at a wedding. People kept startling her with pokes in the ribs, over and over. After she became latah, they ordered her to eat and she ate; they ordered her to dance and she danced. They ordered her to do all sorts of things and she did whatever they ordered. Finally, someone ordered her to take her clothes off, and she did that too. She didn't know what was happening so she just stripped off.

When she took her clothes off, the people around her were embarrassed, and her children were embarrassed too. One of her children got angry. He gave her a stick and told her to hit the person teasing her. But instead of hitting him she smashed all the dishes and plates. Her children were furious, and they took her home.

When she came to her senses she was ashamed. It wasn't right or fair to do what they did to her, order her to strip! Startling her should have been enough. When she's that flustered she doesn't know what she's doing. Whatever they ordered she did, like a person without shame."

Mali-mali in the Philippines:

Aling Chayong, a widow in her sixties, lived in a small hut with her unmarried son. Her married daughter lived a few meters away with her own family. For many years, Aling Chayong had earned her living as an unlicensed midwife; she told us that she had assisted in the delivery of generations of babies in her own village and surrounding areas. She is well known locally both as a midwife and as a *mali-mali*. After having been startled, she says words such as "Ay uten!" [prick] or "Ay puki!" [cunt]. When alone, episodes are brief; in the presence of a crowd, episodes may last longer and include matching and obedience. When she assists in the delivery of a baby, others refrain from startling her intentionally.

Aling Chayong told us that she became a *mali-mali* during a wake. She was deep in thought about the dead child when a cat suddenly jumped from a window to her side. The sound and the unexpected appearance of the cat startled her violently. What happened next must have been a remarkable scene. Without conscious thought she picked up the dead child by the neck and ran with it as fast as she could, pursued by the mourners, led by the child's father. Ever since this wake she has been regarded by all as a mali-mali, and she now is frequently startled intentionally by the villagers to see what she will do.

Source: From BOO! CULTURE, EXPERIENCE, AND THE STARTLE REFLEX by Ronald C. Simons. Copyright© 1996 by Oxford University Press, Inc. Used by permission of Oxford University Press, Inc.

eastern United States in the nineteenth century. Box 1.8 provides examples from Simons' observations in Malaysia and the Philippines (where the behaviors are called *mali-mali* in the Tagalog language). Further examples given include Siberia (*miryachit*), Sweden (*Lapp Panic*), Thailand (*bah-tsche*), Yemen (*nekzah*), and Hokkaido (*imu*). Examples from modern Western cultures are more difficult to find, and the response is much less dramatic for these few cases. Simons feels a universal, biologically programmed startle response, which is characteristic of all human beings, provides the physiologic basis for this particular cultural expression. The startle response evolved to protect human beings in situations where immediate response, such as to avoid stepping on a snake, is beneficial to survival. The startle response is unusually swift, sometimes as fast as 10–20 microseconds, which precludes complex central cortical processing. The startle follows a wide variety of stimuli, such as loud or sudden noises, surprising images, or unsuspected touching or tickling. What follows seems to be an unusual state of focused attention, with behaviors that vary widely from culture to culture. The initiation of the startle and the responses that follow are patterned within each culture, and there are social psychological influences during the response itself: that is, *latah* is more than an individual phenomenon—in effect, it is a form of group behavior (a *role*, as described in Chapter 3).

Is *latah* a culture-bound syndrome or a universal aspect of human behavior? The similarities and differences across cultures are summarized by Simons (1996) as follows (beginning with the similarities and proceeding to differences):

1. The condition is not found prior to adolescence;

2. Once acquired, the hyperstartling response does not disappear over the lifetime;

3. For any subject, the range of effects produced is similar from episode to episode;

4. Lower status persons are more likely to receive startle-teasing than upper-status persons;

5. Although individuals differ in their degree of acceptance of the role, there is a frequent pattern of differential acceptance, by which startle-teasing is accepted if done in a friendly way, or in certain social situations such as a party, and distressing in other circumstances;

6. Hyperstartlers respond readily and more dramatically to stimuli that others in their own culture find innocuous, *but* there is a huge difference in the prevalence of hyperstartling from culture to culture;

7. Across cultures, the stimuli producing the response are broadly similar, as described above; *but* there are local stimuli which do not exist in other cultures.

8. The responses consist of those described above: exaggerated movements and vocalizations, naughty talk, throwing or dropping objects, and, in more extreme instances, imitative or disorganized behavior, and obedience to commands; *but* not all elements of the startle-matching syndrome occur in all cultures;

9. The first startle episode occurs in time of stress, *but* the nature of the stress is highly dependent on the culture;

10. Once a subject fills the culturally defined role (latah, mali-mali, etc.), the surrounding social group defines the individual according to the role, and expects future performances; *but* the relationship of the latah or startle-matching role to other roles differs considerably from culture to culture.

Some observers feel that the physiology of the startle response is irrelevant to *latah*, in that it is entirely culturally determined (Kenny 1978, 1983, 1990). Others feel it is conscious deception of the naive Western observer (Bartholomew 1994, 1995). The debate about conscious deception depends on the orientation of the observer to the concept of "conscious" behavior—focus on conscious and willful mechanisms may lead one astray in understanding the behavior, as shown in Chapter 3. The debate as to whether it is biological or cultural is a false dichotomy, since *all* behaviors have biological *and* cultural elements, as discussed in the section on the biosocial framework for the etiology of mental disorders.

The existence of culture-bound syndromes led many transcultural psychiatrists to give up hope that diagnoses could be made that were equivalent across cultures. The idea was not just that the culture influences the diagnostic process but rather that the etiology of the various disorders differed in the different cultures; therefore, any attempt at a pan-cultural scientific psychiatry was doomed. Other psychiatrists argued that the various culture-bound syndromes could be linked to Western diagnoses: for example, *koro* and other similar, culture-bound syndromes would be termed a phobia or panic reaction; *latah* and others, a transient psychosis linked to the physiology of the startle response; *amok* and others, a violent dissociative state; and so forth.

In studying disorders in different cultures, Devereux (1980) defined what he termed an *ethnic disorder* as follows:

1. The disorder is frequent relative to other psychiatric disorders;
2. The disorder is expressed continuously in a spectrum of intensity;
3. The disorder expresses core conflicts that are pervasive in the culture;
4. The disorder is a final common pathway for wide variety of idiosyncratic personal problems;
5. Symptoms of the disorder are direct extensions and exaggerations of normal behaviors and attitudes in the culture, often including behaviors that are widely valued;
6. The disorder is a highly patterned and imitated model for the expression of distress, a "pattern of misconduct" providing individuals with an acceptable means of being irrational, deviant, or crazy;
7. The disorder elicits highly ambivalent responses from others; awe and respect, as well as punitive and controlling reactions to deviance. The disorder gains notoriety for the individual in the culture.

In the following we will use the term *cultural disorder* for disorders fitting Devereux's criteria, with a change in criterion 1 to: The disorder is much more frequent in the individual's culture than in other cultures. The difference in frequency is so great that, for cultural disorders, names do not exist for them in many or most cultures. The point is that the disorder would not have a name— that is, it would not be socially constructed into a noticeable language entity—if the cultural causes were absent. As for many disorders found in non-Western cultures, *latah* does not really have a name in our culture. A cultural disorder, similar to the rather more loosely defined "genetic disorder" or "developmental disorder," is one in which cultural factors are necessary and sufficient causes (as defined later) in all, or nearly all, cases. The logic of the phrase "all, or nearly all" is to allow that idiosyncratic cases of the disorder may exist infrequently. With the revision, *latah* fulfills the criteria for cultural disorder.

A cultural disorder may be contrasted with a *universal disorder*, that is, a disorder believed to exist in all cultures. Many major mental disorders are found in most or all populations in which they have been studied. In a follow-up to the U.S.-U.K. study described earlier (Kramer 1969b), the World Health Organization coordinated diagnoses at 11 different centers around the world in its International Pilot Study of Schizophrenia, or IPSS (Lee 1996). At each center, psychiatrists were trained in the use of a standardized instrument called the Present State Exam, which had established reliability and validity (Wing et al. 1967). Symptom profiles for those diagnosed as schizophrenic were very similar at all the sites. For example, Figure 1.5 shows symptom profiles for patients in five of the 11 sites: Denmark, Moscow, Washington, D.C., Cali, Colombia, and Agra, India. The signs and symptoms of the disorder were present in all 11 cultures in which there was a search for them. Similar profiles at 11 sites is not very strong proof of universality, since there are thousands of distinct language/cultural groups in the world. Furthermore, the fact that these signs and symptoms had parallel profiles and clustered into diagnoses at each of the 11 sites of research is not conclusive proof of the universality of the diagnosis, because there is little evidence that the clustering is not due to chance or artifactually produced by the algorithm of diagnosis. Later studies under the leadership of the World Health Organization (WHO) showed that the frequency of schizophrenia in cultures around the world was similar (Sartorius et al. 1986). In most of these countries, similar chemical therapies have been found effective for those meeting the common diagnostic criteria, suggesting some degree of construct validity for the diagnosis. Thus, while *latah* is a candidate for a cultural disorder, schizophrenia is a candidate for a universal disorder.

BIOSOCIAL FRAMEWORK FOR THE ETIOLOGY OF MENTAL DISORDERS

The sociological framework of deviance does not provide enough focus on the etiology of mental disorders. The medical model does not provide enough focus on social causes of disorders. This section introduces a biosocial framework that addresses these gaps and helps organize the remainder of the book.

Etiology is the study of causes, and causes are important because they generate an understanding that eventually permits preventing the disorder. A *cause* of a disease is "an event, condition, or characteristic that plays an essential role in producing an occurrence of the disease" (Rothman 1986). A variety of criteria

Figure 1.5
International Pilot Study of Schizophrenia: Profiles of Selected Syndromes for Schizophrenics in Four Countries and for Psychotic Depressives in Nine Countries

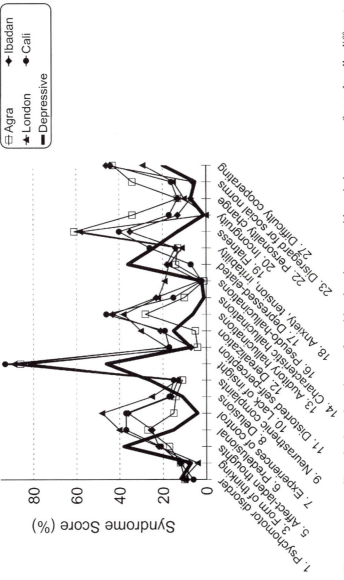

The symptom profiles of selected syndromes for schizophrenia, even with variations across five culturally different sites, looks similar, and different from the profile for psychotic depression.

Source: World Health Organization (1975: Tables 9 and 23).

have been used to judge whether a cause exists (Hennekens and Buring 1987), such as:

1. a statistical association greater than would be expected by chance;
2. a plausible mechanism which explains how the cause has the effect it does (termed *biologic plausibility* by epidemiologists working in the medical model);
3. consistency of the association across a range of studies;
4. clear evidence that the cause occurs before the disease has started;
5. a dose-response relationship, such that more of the cause is associated with quicker or more serious occurrence of the disease; and
6. specificity, such that the cause effects a single disease and not an entire range.

Although it is simplest to think of a one-to-one relationship between cause and effect, as sometimes seems to happen in infectious diseases, most causes consist of a complex set of components that act together in a very particular manner. A *sufficient cause* is "a set of minimal conditions and events that inevitably produce disease" (Rothman 1986); a *necessary cause* is one that is required to be present for the disease to occur. There are few psychiatric disorders where the causal status is known with the detail implied by the preceding list of criteria.

Causes have been studied at different levels of organization. The *ecologic* or area-based study of causes is common, for example, but there is also study of causes at the level of the *individual* and at a level smaller than the individual, such as the *microbiological* level (Stallones 1980). In the epoch of sanitary engineering in the early nineteenth century, the focus was on improving public health through collective efforts at the ecologic level, such as drainage, sewerage, and sanitation. In the latter part of the nineteenth century the focus was on infectious diseases, with laboratory identification of microbial agents, at a level below that of the individual, whose transmission from person to person might be interrupted through vaccination, isolation, and antibiotics. In the current era the focus is on the individual who engages in risky behavior, such as smoking and drinking, or protective behavior, such as eating well, getting enough sleep, and so forth (Susser and Susser 1996). As the discipline of epidemiology developed, especially as it began to study a range of diseases beyond those caused by infections, it became increasingly clear that most diseases had complex chains of causation—dubbed the *web of causation* in one text (Krieger 1994; Mac-Mahon et al. 1960). In some infectious disease epidemics, there is a relatively strong relationship between exposure to an infectious agent and acquiring the disease. Even for infectious diseases, however, the exposure is rarely a sufficient cause, in that characteristics of the host will affect whether the disease occurs after exposure. For noninfectious diseases, however, there is almost always a complex chain of causes, not one of which is sufficient to produce the disease—rather, there is a complex interaction between the individual ("host" in epidemiology), various external causal forces such as germs ("agent"), and the environment, occurring over an extended period of time. Many of the causes in such complex chains are necessary for the chain to continue and, thus, there are multiple opportunities for prevention.

Consider the following situation, which might appear as a case study (Muntaner, 1988). A truck driver commits suicide by shooting himself. What is the cause of the suicide? Is it because, as a male instead of a female, he had greater familiarity with firearms, typically a more "successful" method of suicide than ingestion of drugs? Is it because his levels of serotonin were severely depleted, inducing a depressed mood? Were the levels of serotonin depleted as the result of taking illegal stimulants? Did he take the stimulants because he was genetically vulnerable to addiction or, rather, because he needed to stay awake on a 16-hour run? Would the run have been 16 hours long if he had been a union trucker? Would he have been a union trucker if the political system were more supportive of unions? Would he have been making the 16-hour run if his income were sufficient to support his family? Would his income have been sufficient if the economy had been strong? Considering this complex web of causation, how do we choose target interventions to improve the public's health?

The study of social causes of mental disorder will benefit by considering causes at, below, and above the level of the individual, operating together in additive and synergistic fashion. This means deliberately incorporating factors in causal models that might not have, by themselves, a distinctly social characteristic. The point is that social life influences the individual's exposure to risk and protective factors that may not be distinctly social. In studying chains of causation, it is not wise to eliminate any particular chain because it includes so-called nonsociological elements. This narrowing of focus emasculates the influence of social variables and undermines strong potentials for prevention.

Figure 1.6 sketches a framework for understanding the interplay of disciplines and levels of analysis in the etiology of mental disorders. There are four basic levels at which causal processes occur: large group or macrolevel; small group or microlevel; individual level; and subindividual level. The texts represent processes involved in the generation of risk. Stratification, integration, and culture are processes that are expressed and measurable both at the societal level of large groups and also at the level of the small group. Learning, stress, and health care occur at the level of the individual and his or her immediate social environment. Individual mentation involving deliberate decisions and feeling states occurs at the level of the individual. Exposure to physical dangers converts to risk when physical or organic agents enter the body or strike it. In an attempt to reach and present the borders of a comprehensive framework, the figure sacrifices precision to some degree, omitting detailed description of the many possible levels of analysis, fine aspects of the causal processes, and complex interactions between the many possible causes.

Stratification is the process by which rewards in the society are distributed unequally, and it affects the degree to which individuals can control their environment. Stratification includes macrolevel processes occurring between social

Figure 1.6
Biosocial Framework for the Etiology of Mental Disorders

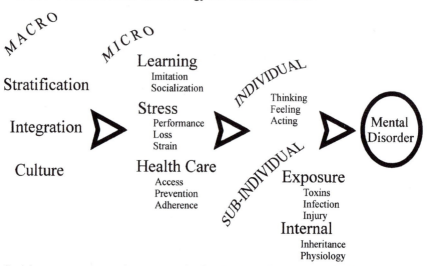

Social causes operate at the macro and micro levels, influencing psychological factors at the level of the individual and factors connected to exposures and bodily states below the level of the individual. Causes of mental disorders virtually always involve multiple levels.

groups such as political economics and class exploitation. Animals also appraise the power structure of their community, and changes in the stratification structure produce a range of hormonal and physiological effects in individuals (Jones et al. 1995; Yeh et al. 1996). These effects often involve awareness by the individual, but such awareness is not necessary for there to be strong influences. The effects of stratification on health have historically been very strong and continue to exert powerful influences on the range of medical conditions and mental disorders, as shown in Chapter 5.

Integration is the process of interaction and coordination within social groups by which they are generated, recognized, and reinforced. It affects the individual's degree of attachment to others, and its effect on mental disorder has been studied at least since Durkheim (1966). As with stratification, animals are aware of the level of social integration, and the degree of integration is related to a range of physiological activities (Uchino et al. 1996). Integration occurs in the context of large and small family and friendship groups. Integration is taken up in Chapter 4.

Culture is the beliefs, norms, and values of social groups that affect the individual's ability to attribute meaning and coherence to his or her existence, to understand his or her history, and to plan for his or her future—in short, to give the individual a *sense of biography* (also discussed below in Chapter 3). The effects of culture and meaning on physical and mental health have also been studied in epidemiologic research (Antonovsky 1979, 1993a, 1993b; Burton, 1998) and are considered throughout this volume. Culture is a uniquely human phenomenon.

Stratification and integration, sometimes termed status and solidarity, have been termed two basic dimensions of human interaction (Brown 1965). Studies of group processes repeatedly reveal these two basic dimensions (Borgatta 1964). Darwinian psychiatrists see these two dimensions in operation in virtually all primate groups and surmise they have arisen through millions of years of evolution in which aggression, submission and cooperation helped to preserve individual genes and the survival of the species (Gilbert 1992; Stevens and Price 1996). The three processes of stratification, integration, and culture are all distinctly social in nature—that is, as Durkheim would have said, they are *social facts* that constrain the behavior of the individual (Durkheim 1966; Eaton 1994a). Examples of the macrosocial theaters in which they operate and where they can be measured are the family, neighborhood, job, and larger institutions such as bureaucracies and societies. These three processes also operate at the level of the small group, and they are affected by the decisions and behaviors of individuals, as well as by the decisions and behaviors of small groups.

The social psychological processes affecting the health of the individual can be roughly divided into those involving learning of some type or those involving stress. *Learning*, the acquisition of new responses, is roughly divided into *imitation*, which occurs relatively quickly, and *socialization*, which takes much longer. The discussion of imitation is presented in Chapter 6 under the rubric of collective behavior. The discussion of socialization is presented in Chapter 5, because a long-term emotional relationship is the most common vehicle for socialization, which usually occurs in the family or other stable social environments.

Stress is the situation of environmental demands exceeding the response capacity of the organism. At the social psychological level, there are at least three separate processes (Lazarus 1993) called "stress": *performance demand*—the situation of performing a response or behavior that is highly acquired, such as in an athletic event; *loss*—the situation of an unexpected disruption in social life, such as the death of a spouse, which demands a response that is not in the current repertoire of the organism; and *strain*—the situation of repetitive, non-catastrophic overload, sometimes called "role strain" or "hassles." These concepts are taken up in Chapter 3 on social psychology.

In the modern world *access* (the ability to obtain health care), *prevention* (engaging in health-promoting behaviors), and *adherence* (complying with medical regimens) are strongly connected to health and survival. These health care processes are strongly affected by the other social processes, such as the individual's location in the power structure, his or her friendship networks, and his or her cultural background. These processes are considered in Chapter 7.

Processes related to the *individual* are difficult to separate from the social psychological level of analysis, since thought and emotion are inevitably social.

Processes related to *exposure* to toxins, infections, and injuries are not, by definition at least, always strictly social in nature, but social processes, including stratification, integration, culture, learning, imitation, and health care, inevitably impinge on them in important ways. These exposure variables are included in the relevant chapters, where there is evidence that they are part of a causal chain that involves social variables. They are inherently more proximal to the individual, since their effects actually can be seen on the body, as in an injury, or extracted from the body, as in a toxin or infection.

Some social scientists have proposed that certain social factors, such as social inequality, be considered as *fundamental causes*, because they continue to exert influences on health even after mediating causes are eliminated or evolve into different forms (Link and Phelan 1996). It may be useful to think of "proximal" and "distal" causes; "powerful" and "weak" causes; or "malleable" and "difficult-to-change" causes: all concepts subject to more or less straightforward empirical scrutiny. But the idea of the fundamental cause seems useful mostly as a disciplinary polemic. Focusing on social processes that are strictly social, or assuming that social factors have some sort of causal priority, may blind us to important social processes that are mediated by nonsocial variables. Thus, in our consideration of the social causes of mental disorders, we include any causal chain that includes, somewhere in its length, a social factor, as shown in Figure 1.6.

A Definition of Mental Disorder

Having traced some of "the bases of social judgments to their interest-bound roots in society" and having examined the object of thought from "many different viewpoints," we may be in a position to define the term *mental disorder*. The psychiatric definition is:

a clinically significant behavioral or psychological syndrome or pattern that occurs in an individual and that is associated with present distress (e.g., a painful symptom) or disability (i.e., impairment in one or more important areas of functioning) or with a significantly increased risk of suffering death, pain, disability, or an important loss of freedom. (American Psychiatric Association 1994)

The most informed attempt to give a social definition to the concept of mental disorder is by Morris Rosenberg, whose entire career was spent in this subfield of sociology. In *The Unread Mind* (Rosenberg 1992), which he finished shortly before his death, he reviewed various approaches to the definition of mental disorder. He noted that the public view of mental disorder involves the twin notions of *unpredictability* and *dangerousness*. But unpredictability is not a sufficient criterion because certain unpredictable acts (such as suddenly standing up and shouting in a room full of people) are not regarded as mentally disordered if the behavior is understandable (e.g., if there is a fire). Dangerousness is insufficient because so often dangerous acts are understandable (e.g., the perpe-trators of the St. Valentine's Day massacre in Chicago, who were involved in mob warfare). Social scientists often rely on the concept of statistical rarity, but this, too, is insufficient, and Rosenberg gives examples of rare behaviors (such as grimacing and waving one's hands excitedly in front of several others, with-out talking) that are not judged as mentally disordered once they are understood (playing charades). Normative abnormality, as opposed to statistical, has been proposed, but counterexamples show it is insufficient (e.g., not responding when spoken to is not normative, but if the person is deaf, it is understandable and not judged to be due to mental disorder).

Researchers in the area of autism propose that the central difficulty concerns what they term the *theory of mind*. A theory of mind is the capacity to under-stand that other human beings have a mind, which has certain complementary aspects to one's own mind (Gardner 1983). For example, in talking, the human being must be able to "index" the first-and second-person pronouns, so that when the other person says "you," the meaning is transferred to "me" in the receiving persons' mind. This is certainly a social capacity, but it is also built deeply within the human brain structure, presumably since the dawn of language and the human species (Crow 1991). Autistic children lack this capacity, ac-cording to this notion, and that is why they cannot form social relationships. Autistic children cannot take the role of the other (in the terms to be discussed in more detail in Chapter 3).

Rosenberg proposes that mental disorder is defined by *the failure of others to take the role of the individual*. In his conception, mental disorder is thus defined dyadically, by an individual and by others in his or her social environ-ment. Only when others cannot devise the motivation for the behavior is the judgment made that the individual is mentally disordered. This notion is the converse of the theory of mind in autistic children; for them, in effect, every other human being fits Rosenberg's definition of mental disorder, since they cannot understand even a single other person's behavior as being motivated rationally.

There is much wisdom in Rosenberg's notions, but role-taking failure alone is not a sufficient definition. For example, there are instances of role-taking failure that occur when another person is suffering enormous pain, humiliation, or grief—a common reaction is, "I can't imagine how that must feel"—and there are instances of widespread behaviors that are not comprehensible, even to the individuals involved—an example is warfare, as described so eloquently in *Catch-22* (Heller 1961). So the definition must involve both cultural and statistical abnormality, as well as the failure in role taking.

It is necessary to include in the definition of mental disorder a criterion of severity so that common occurrences of trivial or unimportant emotions and behaviors are not included. Earlier it was noted that the concept of pathology is less clear for mental disorders than for many physical illnesses because mental disorders do not have a strong connection to mortality. Instead, the psychiatrist establishes the *clinical importance* of disorders by their effects on distress and disability. But the notion of "clinical" importance is vague and implies that the clinician must be involved in the definition. Necessitating a clinician implies the necessity of a discipline of clinicians and, in effect, the entire apparatus of Western medicine that generates clinicians. Therefore, the definition of mental disorder used in the DSM, given earlier, is historically and culturally limiting.

It is also possible to use social criteria to evaluate the importance of disorders. How much does the disorder disrupt social life? By what dimensions shall we measure such disruption? The framework given earlier and outlined in Figure 1.6 suggests that the dimensions that should be considered are the three basic social processes of stratification, integration, and culture. The criteria for severity of mental disorder then become the degree to which it leads to loss of control over the social environment (stratification); the degree to which it leads to detachment from social networks (integration); or the degree to which it interferes with the individual's sense of biography (culture).

Thus, the *sociological definition of mental disorder* is:

A. a collection of emotions or behaviors that meet *all three* conditions:

  1. rare;

  2. culturally deviant;

  3. inexplicable;

and

B. that leads to *one or more* consequences below:

  1. loss of control over the environment;

  2. detachment from social networks;

  3. interference with the individual's sense of biography.

The short definition is "bizarre and disabling emotions or behaviors."

Discussion

It is probable that behaviors recognized as bizarre occur in all cultures and historical periods, but few patterns of behaviors have been established as historically stable and pancultural. Perhaps it is not too much to say that many diagnoses are close to unidentified flying objects, and it is not preposterous to call them "myths" or "ideologies." Myths and ideologies can be useful, but the reality of their content depends on their utilities for human beings, not on some objective relationship to the nonhuman world. There is a variety of ways in which human societies create and deal with bizarre behaviors. This variety occurs despite certain regularities in the patterns of behavior and the characteristics of societies. The basic conclusion is that many of the details of our own system for dealing with bizarre behaviors have no inevitable logic. In studying diagnosis, rather than discovering naturally occurring categories of health and illness, we are negotiating the creation of categories with more or less utility to various social groups.

The field of mental illness is a linguistic zone of linked categories and meanings, and the general conclusion is that concepts within these zones differ considerably in quality but are evaluated, to varying degrees, by the quality of the entire zone and the logical linkage of the singular concepts. Thus, the medical model of mental disorder tends to be evaluated as a whole, and stronger and more useful concepts such as general paresis, Huntington's chorea, and schizophrenia can carry more than their own weight and take "unidentified flying objects" such as neurosis, personality disorder, or dysthymia with them. Thus, concepts and categories tend to gain durability and believability from their neighboring concepts.

Many of these ideas on the competition of cultural subsystems are exemplified by the situation of Copernicus and his follower Galileo. They espoused a conceptual framework for astronomy that involved the revolution of the earth and planets around the sun, instead of the Ptolemaic theory held by the church that the earth was the center of the universe, and other heavenly bodies moved in relation to it. The Copernican theory struck deeply into the symbolic universe of that time because of the belief in the divine origin of human beings and their deliberate placement on what was believed to be the central heavenly body. The reliability of measurement was an important issue: one proof of Copernicus' theory was the revolution of newly discovered moons around Jupiter. When the church fathers looked through Galileo's telescope at these moons, they saw nothing or, at least, claimed to have seen nothing. The church fathers forced Galileo to recant his theory, and the Ptolemaic theory held the day. Many people do not realize that Copernicus' theory was no better in predicting the movement of heavenly bodies than were existing calculations of the Ptolemaic theory— that is, the utility of the theories at that time was roughly equivalent. We could, in fact, still use the Ptolemaic framework today if we chose to. But it is a less elegant theory than the Copernican, and the elegance has to do with its ability to explain many occurrences with few principles and with its linkage to other bodies of thought. For example, the Copernican theory eventually linked up with Keplerian formulas for the revolution of the planets and with Newtonian physics, so that an enormous mass of information could be generated by a few simple principles. Thus, neither the power structure of the time, nor the immediate utility of the theories, predicted the outcome of this particular cultural competition. Rather, the overall elegance of the system and the developing linkages to other growing systems of thought determined the outcome.

2

The Social Epidemiology of Mental Disorders

INTRODUCTION

Epidemiology is the study of diseases in populations. A *population* is a number of individuals having some characteristic in common, such as age, gender, occupation, nationality, a disease, and so forth. Population, a broader term than *group*, has awareness of itself, or structured interactions. Populations are typically studied by demographers, whereas groups are typically studied by sociologists. Thus, sociology, demography, and epidemiology are closely allied disciplines.

The *general population* is not limited to any particular class or characteristic but includes all persons without regard to special features. In the context of epidemiologic research studies, the general population usually refers to the individuals who normally reside in the locality of the study. Many epidemiologic studies involve large populations, such as a nation, state, or a county of several hundred thousand inhabitants. In such large studies, the general population includes individuals with a wide range of social and biologic characteristics, and this variation is helpful in generalizing the results. In the broadest sense, the general population refers to the human species. The fundamental parameters used in epidemiology are often conceptualized in terms of the population; for example, prevalence is sometimes used to estimate the population's need for health care; incidence estimates the force of morbidity in the population. Diseases generally have the characteristic of rarity in the population. As discussed later, rates of disease are often reported per 1,000, 10,000, or 100,000 population.

Various definitions of epidemiology reflect the notion of pathology in populations. Mausner and Kramer (1985) define epidemiology as "the study of the

distribution and determinants of diseases and injuries in human populations."
Lilienfeld and Stolley (1994) use a very similar definition but include the notion
that "epidemiologists are primarily interested in the occurrence of disease as
categorized by time, place, and persons." A less succinct, but nevertheless classic, statement is by Morris (1975), who listed seven "uses" of epidemiology:

1. To study the history of health of populations, thus facilitating projections into the
   future;

2. To diagnose the health of the community, which facilitates prioritizing various health
   problems and identifying groups in special need;

3. To study the working of health services, with a view to their improvement;

4. To estimate individual risks, and chances of avoiding them, which can be
   communicated to individual patients;

5. To identify syndromes, by describing the association of clinical phenomena in the
   population;

6. To complete the clinical picture of chronic diseases, especially in terms of natural
   history;

7. To search for causes of health and disease.

The seventh use is regarded by Morris as the most important, but, in reviewing
the literature on psychiatric disorders for the third (1975) edition of his text, he
was surprised at

the sad dearth of hard fact on the causes of major as well as minor mental disorders,
and so on how to prevent them . . . [and] the dearth of epidemiological work in search
of causes. . . . Lack of ideas? Methods? Money? It wants airing. Of course, the popular
trend open-endedly to hand over to psychiatry (and to social work), in hope or resig-
nation, the whole of the human condition is no help. (220)

Epidemiology's base in medicine has led it to focus on the dichotomy of the
presence or absence of disease. There is the old adage in epidemiology: "The
world is divided into two types of persons: those who think in terms of dichotomies, and those who do not." The result for statistical analysis is recurring
focus on forms involving dichotomies: rates and proportions (Fleiss 1981), the
two-by-two table (Bishop et al. 1975), the life table (Lawless 1982), and logistic
regression (Kleinbaum et al. 1982). Much of the logic that distinguishes the
methods of epidemiology from those of sociology and psychology involves the
epidemiologic focus on rare dichotomies. The case-control method maximizes
efficiency in the face of this rarity by searching for, and selecting, cases of
disease very intensively—for example, as in a hospital or a catchment area
record system—and selecting controls at a fraction of their representation in the
general population. Exposures can also be rare, and this possibility is involved
in the logic of many cohort studies that search for, and select, exposed individ-

uals very intensively—for example, as in an occupational setting with toxins present—and select nonexposed controls at a fraction of their representation in the general population. In both strategies the cases, exposed groups, and controls are selected with equal care; and in both strategies they are drawn, if possible, to represent the population at risk of disease onset: the efficiency comes in the comparison to a relatively manageable sample of controls.

THE METHODS OF EPIDEMIOLOGY

Ecologic Method

The ecologic approach compares populations in geographic areas as to their rates of disease and has been a part of epidemiology since its beginnings. A classic ecologic study in epidemiology is Goldberger's work on pellagra psychosis (Cooper and Morgan 1973). The pellagra research also illustrates the concept of the causal chain and its implications for prevention. In the early part of this century, pellagra was most prevalent in the lower classes in rural villages in the southeastern United States. As the situation may be today for many mental disorders, discussed in Chapter 6, the relationship of pellagra prevalence to low social class was a consistent finding: a leading etiologic clue among many others which had less consistent evidence. Many scientists felt that pellagra psychosis was infectious and that lower-class living situations promoted breeding of the infectious agent. But Goldberger noticed that there were striking failures of infection—for example, aides in large mental hospitals, where pellagra psychosis was prevalent, seemed immune. He observed certain exceptions to the tendency of pellagra to congregate in the lower class: upper-class individuals with unusual eating habits. Goldberger became convinced that the cause was a nutritional deficiency connected to low social class. His most powerful evidence was an ecologic comparison of high- and low-rate areas: two villages that differed as to the availability of agricultural produce. The comparison made a strong case for the nutritional theory using the ecological approach, even though he could not identify the nutrient. He went so far as to ingest bodily fluids of persons with pellagra to demonstrate that it was not infectious. Eventually, a deficiency in vitamin B was identified as a necessary causal agent. Pellagra psychosis is now extremely rare in this country, in part, because of standard supplementation of bread products with vitamin B.

Goldberger understood that low social class position increased risk for pellagra, and he also believed that nutritional deficiencies that resulted from lower class position were a necessary component in pellagra. With the advantage of hindsight, nutritional deficiency appears to have a stronger causal status, because there were many lower-class persons who did not have pellagra but few persons with pellagra who were not nutritionally deprived: vitamin B deprivation is a *necessary* cause, but lower social class position is a *contributing* cause. The concept of the causal chain points to both causes and facilitates other judgments

Table 2.1
Rates and Proportions in Epidemiology

Rate	Minimum Design	Numerator	Denominator
Lifetime Prevalence	Cross section	Ever ill	Alive
Point prevalence	Cross section	Currently ill	Alive
Period prevalence (1)	Cross section	Ill during period	Alive at survey
Period Prevalence (2)	Two waves	Ill during period	Alive during period
First Incidence	Two waves	Newly ill	Never been ill
Attack Rate	Two waves	Newly ill	Not ill at baseline
Proportion of Cohort Affected	Birth to present	Ever ill	Born and still alive
Lifetime Risk	Birth to death	Ever ill	Born

about the importance of the cause. Funneling resources to the medical profession to cure pellagra would have been one approach to the problem consistent with the power arrangement in the social structure; another approach would have been redistributing income so that nutritional deficiency is less common. As it happens, neither approach would have been effective. The consensus to redistribute income—in effect, to diminish social class differences—is not easy to achieve in a democracy, since the majority of persons are not affected by the disease. Bread supplementation for the entire population was a relatively cost-effective public health solution. The more general point is that Goldberger's work encompassed the complexity of the causal process.

Epidemiology accepts the medical framework as defining its dependent variable, but it is neutral as to discipline of etiology. Goldberger did not eliminate one or the other potential cause due to an orientation toward social versus biological disciplines of study. He did not favor one or the other potential cause because it focused on the individual versus the collective level of analysis. This eclecticism is an important strength in epidemiology. The public health approach is to search for the most important causes and to concentrate on those that are malleable, since they offer possibilities for prevention.

Rates

An early and well-known epidemiologist, Alexander Langmuir, used to say that "stripped to its basics, epidemiology is simply a process of obtaining the appropriate numerator and denominator, determining the rate, and interpreting that rate" (cited in Foege 1996: S11). In the sense in which Langmuir was speaking, the term *rates* includes proportions such as the prevalence "rate," as well as the incidence rate, as explained later. Table 2.1 shows the minimum design requirements and the definitions of numerators and denominators for various types of rates and proportions (Eaton et al. 1985). The table is ordered from top to bottom by increasing difficulty of longitudinal follow-up.

Prevalence is the proportion of individuals ill in a population. Temporal criteria allow for several types of prevalence: point, lifetime, and period. *Point prevalence* is the proportion of individuals in a population at a given point in time. The most direct use of point prevalence is as an estimate of need for care or potential treatment load, and it is favored by health services researchers. It is also useful because it identifies groups at high risk for having a disorder, greater chronicity of the disorder, or both. Finally, the point prevalence can be used to measure the impact of prevention programs in reducing the burden of disease on the community.

Lifetime prevalence is the proportion of individuals who have ever been ill and who are alive on a given day in the population. As those who die are not included in the numerator or denominator of the proportion, the lifetime prevalence is sometimes called the *proportion of survivors affected* (PSA). It differs from the lifetime risk because the latter attempts to include the entire lifetime of a birth cohort—both past and future—and includes those deceased at the time of the survey. Lifetime risk is the quantity of most interest to geneticists. Lifetime prevalence also differs from the *proportion of cohort affected* (PCA), which includes members of a given cohort who have ever been ill by the study date, regardless of whether they are still alive at that time.

Lifetime prevalence has the advantage over lifetime risk and PCA in that it does not require ascertaining who is deceased, whether those deceased had the disorder of interest, or how likely those now alive without the disorder are to develop it before some given age. Thus, lifetime prevalence can be estimated from a cross-sectional survey. The other measures require either following a cohort over time or asking relatives to identify deceased family members and report symptoms suffered by them. Often, these reports must be supplemented with medical records. The need for these other sources adds possible errors: relatives may forget to report persons who died many years before or may be uninformed about their psychiatric status; medical records may be impossible to locate or inaccurate; and the prediction of onset in young persons not yet affected requires assuming that they will fall ill at the same rate as did the older members of the sample and will die at the same ages if they do not fall ill. If risks of disorder or age-specific death rates change, these predictions will fail.

Lifetime prevalence requires that the diagnostic status of each respondent be assessed over his or her lifetime. Thus, accuracy of recall of symptoms after a possibly long symptom-free period is a serious issue; symptoms and disorders that are long past, mild, short-lived, and less stigmatizing are particularly likely to be forgotten. For example, data from several cross-sectional studies of depression seem to indicate a rise in the rate of depression in persons born after World War II (Cross-National Collaborative Group 1992, Klerman and Weissman 1989). These persons are older, however, and it may be that they have forgotten episodes of depression that occurred many years prior to the interview

(Simon and VonKorff 1995). Data showing that lifetime prevalence of depressive disorder actually declines with age (Parker 1987, Robins et al. 1984) are consistent with the recall explanation.

Period prevalence is the proportion of the population ill during a specified period of time. The numerator customarily is estimated by adding the prevalent cases at the beginning of the defined period to the incident (first and recurrent) cases that develop between the beginning and the end of the period. This form is shown as period prevalence (2) in Table 2.1. In research based on records, one customarily counts all cases of a disorder found over a one-year period. The denominator is the average population size during the interval. Thus, the customary definition of period prevalence requires at least two waves of data collection. There are certain advantages of period prevalence for the study of psychiatric disorders (Kleinbaum et al. 1982; Mausner and Kramer 1985), where onset and termination of episodes are difficult to ascertain exactly (e.g., the failure to distinguish new from recurrent episodes is unimportant in the estimation of period prevalence). Furthermore, the number of episodes occurring during the follow-up is unimportant; it is important only to record whether there was one or more versus none. The disadvantage of period prevalence is that it is not as useful in estimating need as point prevalence or as advantageous in studying etiology as incidence.

Another type of period prevalence, sometimes labeled by a prefix denoting the period, such as *one-year prevalence*, is a hybrid type of rate, conceptually mixing aspects of point and period prevalence, which has been found useful in the Epidemiologic Catchment Area (ECA) Program (Eaton et al. 1985). This type of period prevalence is labeled period prevalence (1) in Table 2.1. It includes in the numerator all those surveyed individuals who have met the criteria for disorder in the past year and in the denominator, all those interviewed. It is not a point prevalence rate because it covers a longer period of time, which can be defined as six months, two years, and so forth, as well as one year. But one-year prevalence is not a period prevalence rate because some individuals in the population who are ill at the beginning of the period are not successfully interviewed, because they either die or emigrate. As the time period covered in this rate becomes shorter, it approximates the point prevalence; as the time period becomes longer, the rate approaches the period prevalence. If there is large mortality, the one-year prevalence rate will diverge markedly from period prevalence.

Incidence is the rate at which new cases develop in a population. It is a dynamic or time-dependent quantity and can be expressed as an instantaneous rate, although, usually, it is expressed with a unit of time attached, in the manner of an annual incidence rate. In order to avoid confusion, it is essential to distinguish *first incidence* from *total incidence*. The distinction itself is commonly assumed by epidemiologists, but there does not appear to be consensus on the terminology. Most definitions of the incidence numerator include a concept such as "new cases" (Lilienfeld and Stolley 1994: 109) or persons who "develop a disease" (Mausner and Kramer 1985: 44). Morris (1975) defines incidence as equivalent to our "first incidence" and "attack rate" as equivalent to our "total incidence." First incidence corresponds to the most common use of the term "incidence," but since the usage is by no means universal, we prefer to keep the prefix.

The numerator of *first incidence* for a specified time period is composed of those individuals who have had an occurrence of the disorder for the first time in their lives, and the denominator includes only persons who start the period with no prior history of the disorder. The numerator for *attack rate* (or *total incidence*) includes all individuals who have had an occurrence of the disorder during the time period under investigation, whether or not it is the initial episode of their lives or a recurrent episode. The denominator for total incidence includes all population members except those cases of the disorder that are active at the beginning of the follow-up period.

A baseline and follow-up are generally needed to estimate incidence. *Cumulative incidence* (not shown in Table 2.1) is the proportion of the sample or population that becomes a case for the first time between initial and follow-up interviews (Kleinbaum et al. 1982). But incidence is generally measured per unit of time, as a rate. When the follow-up period extends over many years, the exposure period of the entire population at risk is estimated by including all years prior to onset for a given individual in the denominator and removing years from the denominator when an individual has onset or dies. In this manner, the incidence is expressed per unit time per population, for example, "three new cases per 1,000 person years of exposure." This method of calculating facilitates comparison between studies with different lengths of follow-up and different mortality.

First incidence can be estimated by retrospection if the date of onset is obtained for each symptom or episode, so that the proportion of persons who first qualified in the year prior to the interview can be estimated. For this type of estimate (not shown in Table 2.1), only one wave of data collection is needed. This estimate of first incidence is subject to the effects of mortality, however, because those who have died will not be available for the interview.

The preference for first or total incidence in etiologic studies depends on hypotheses and assumptions about the way causes and outcomes important to the disease ebb and flow. If the disease is recurrent, and the causal factors vary in strength over time, then it might be important to study risk factors not only for first but for subsequent episodes (total incidence). For example, one might consider the effects of changing levels of stress on the occurrence of episodes of neurosis (Tyrer 1985) or of schizophrenia (Brown et al. 1972). For a disease with a presumed fixed progression from some starting point, such as dementia, the first occurrence might be the most important episode to focus on, and first incidence is the appropriate rate. In the field of psychiatric epidemiology, there is a range of disorders with both types of causal structures operating, which has led us to focus on this distinction in types of incidence.

The two types of incidence are functionally related to different measures of prevalence. Kramer et al. (1980) have shown that *lifetime prevalence* (i.e., the proportion of persons in a defined population who have ever had an attack of a disorder) is a function of *first incidence* and mortality in affected and unaffected populations. *Point prevalence* (i.e., the proportion of persons in a defined population on a given day who manifest the disorder) is linked to *total incidence* by the queuing formula $P = f (I \times D)$ (Kleinbaum et al. 1982; Kramer 1957); that is, point prevalence is a function of the total number of cases occurring and their duration. In the search for risk factors that have etiologic significance for the disorder, comparisons based on point prevalence rates suffer the disadvantage that differences between groups as to the *chronicity* of the disorder—the duration of episodes, the probability that episodes will recur, or the mortality associated with episodes—affect the comparisons (Kramer 1957). For example, it appears that blacks may have episodes of depression of longer duration than whites have (Eaton and Kessler 1981). If so, the point prevalence of depression would be biased toward a higher rate for blacks, based solely on their greater chronicity.

Incidence and Onset

Dating the onset of episodes is problematic for most mental disorders for many reasons. One is that the diagnostic criteria for the disorders themselves are not well agreed upon, and continual changes are being made in the definition of a case of disorder, such as the recent fourth revision of the *Diagnostic and Statistical Manual* (DSM-IV) (American Psychiatric Association 1994). The DSM-IV has the advantage that criteria for mental disorders are more or less explicitly defined, but it is, nevertheless, true that specific mental disorders are often very difficult to distinguish from nonmorbid psychological states. Most disorders include symptoms that, taken by themselves, are part of everyone's normal experience; for example, feeling fearful, being short of breath or dizzy, and having sweaty palms are not uncommon experiences, but they are also symptoms of panic disorder. The clustering of symptoms, often with the requirement that they be brought together in one period of time or "spell," generally forms the requirement for diagnosis. Although the clustering criteria are fairly explicit in the DSM, it is not well established that they correspond to the characteristics generally associated with a disease, such as a predictable course, a response to treatment, an association with a biological aberration in the individual, or an associated disability. Thus, the lack of established validity of the criteria-based classification system exacerbates problems of dating the onset of disorder.

The absence of firm data on the validity of the classification system enjoins us to be very careful about conceptualizing the process of disease onset. One criterion of onset used in the epidemiology of some diseases is entry into treatment, but this is unacceptable in psychiatry since people with mental disorders so often do not seek treatment for them. Another criterion of onset sometimes used is detectability—that is, when the symptoms first appear—but this also is unacceptable because experiences analogous to the symptoms of most psychiatric disorders are so widespread. It is preferable to conceptualize onset as a continuous line of development toward manifestation of a disease. There is a threshold at which the development becomes irreversible, so that at some minimal level of symptomatology it is certain that the full characteristics of the disease, however defined, will become apparent. This concept of onset as irreversibility is consistent with some epidemiological uses (Kleinbaum et al. 1982). Prior to this point, the symptoms are thought of as "subcriterial." At the current state of knowledge in psychiatry, longitudinal studies in the general population, such as the ECA Program and others discussed later, are needed to determine those levels of symptomatology at which irreversibility is achieved.

There are at least two ways of thinking about development toward disease. The first way is the increase in severity or intensity of symptoms. An individual could have all the symptoms required for diagnosis but none of them sufficiently intense or impairing. The underlying logic of such an assumption may well be the relatively high frequency of occurrence of the symptoms in milder form, making it difficult to distinguish normal and subcriterial complaints from manifestations of disease. For many chronic diseases, it may be inappropriate to regard the symptom as ever having been "absent," for example, personality traits giving rise to deviant behavior, categorized as personality disorders on axis 2 of the *Diagnostic and Statistical Manual*. This type of development we can refer to as *symptom intensification*, indicating that the symptoms are already present and have become more intense during a period of observation. This concept leads the researcher to consider whether there is a crucial level of intensity of a given symptom or symptoms in which the rate of development toward a full-blown disease state is accelerated or becomes irreversible.

A second way of thinking about progress toward disease is the occurrence of new symptoms that did not exist before. This involves the gradual *acquisition* of symptoms so that clusters are formed that increasingly approach the constellation required to meet specified definitions for diagnosis. A cluster of symptoms that occur more often together than would be expected by their individual prevalence in the population—that is, more often than expected by chance—is a *syndrome*. "Present" can be defined as occurrence either at a nonsevere or at a severe level; thus, decisions made about the symptom intensification process complicate the idea of acquisition. This idea leads the researcher to consider the order in which symptoms occur over the natural history of disease and, in particular, whether one symptom is more important than others in accelerating the process.

Figure 2.1 is an adaptation of a diagram used by Lilienfeld and Lilienfeld (Zola 1975: Figure 6.3) to visualize the concept of incidence as a time-oriented rate that expresses the force of morbidity in the population. In their original figure (2.1a) the horizontal axis represents time, and the presence of a line

Figure 2.1
Incidence, Intensification, and the Force of Morbidity

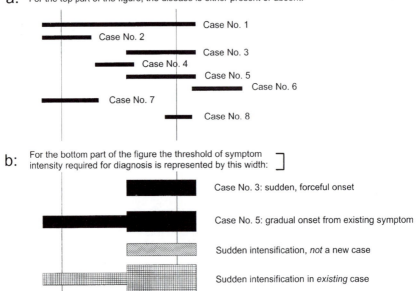

a: For the top part of the figure, the disease is either present or absent.

Case No. 1
Case No. 2
Case No. 3
Case No. 4
Case No. 5
Case No. 6
Case No. 7
Case No. 8

b: For the bottom part of the figure the threshold of symptom intensity required for diagnosis is represented by this width: ⌐

Case No. 3: sudden, forceful onset

Case No. 5: gradual onset from existing symptom

Sudden intensification, *not* a new case

Sudden intensification in *existing* case

Incidence is the force of morbidity in the population. Figure 2.1a shows a diagram from a classic text in epidemiology in which the disease is judged to be either present or absent (redrawn from Lilienfeld and Stolley 1994: Figure 6.2). Figure 2.1b adapts these concepts to continuous variations in intensity of a single symptom of disease.

indicates disease. Our adaptations in Figure 2.1b give examples of the several distinct forms that onset can take when the disorder is defined by constellations of symptoms varying in intensity as is the case with mental disorders. In Figure 2.1b, the topmost subject (1) is what we might consider the null hypothesis, and it corresponds to simple onset as portrayed in the original. Figure 2.1b shows how intensity, represented by the vertical width of the bars, might vary. The threshold of disease is set at four units of width, and in the null hypothesis subject 1 progresses from zero intensity to four units, becoming a case during the observation period. Subject 2 changes from nearly meeting the criteria (width of three units) to meeting it (four units) during the year. Both subjects 1 and 2 are new cases, even though the onset was more sudden in subject 1 than in subject 2—that is, the force of morbidity is stronger in subject 1 than subject 2. Subjects 3 and 4 are *not* new cases, even though their symptoms intensify during the year as much or more than do those of subject 2.

Figure 2.2 adapts the diagram to conceptualize acquisition of symptoms and the development of syndromes. At one point in time there is no correlation

Figure 2.2
Incidence, Acquisition, and the Emergence of Depressive Syndromes

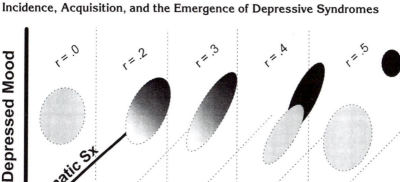

Concepts shown in Figure 2.1 have been adapted to variations in number of different symptoms required for the presence of disease.

between symptoms, but the correlation gradually develops until there is a clear separation of the population into one group with no association of symptoms and another group where the two symptoms co-occur. This example could be expanded to syndromes involving more than two symptoms.

Acquisition and intensification are indicators of the force of morbidity in the population, as are more traditional forms of incidence rate. But they are not tied to any one definition of caseness. Rather, these concepts allow study of progression of disease independently of case definition. Risk factors at different stages of the disease may be differentially related to disease progression only above or below the threshold set by the diagnosis. In this situation, we might reconsider the diagnostic threshold.

Morbidity Surveys

Morbidity surveys are cross-sectional surveys of the general population. They are used to estimate prevalence of disease in the population as well as to estimate need for care. Morbidity surveys address Morris' (1975) second "use" of epidemiology—"diagnosing the health of the community, prioritizing health problems and identifying groups in need"; as well as the third use—"studying the working of health services"; and the fifth use—"identifying syndromes." Morbidity surveys are sometimes called the *descriptive* aspect of epidemiology, but

Figure 2.3
Prevalence of Mental Disorder in the Past Six Months (ECA Program—
Percentage of the Population)

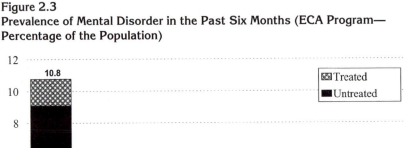

The ECA program provided prevalence for a range of specific disorders, for the first time in the United States. The large proportion of cases that were not under treatment was surprising and used to justify outreach programs for disorders such as depression, for which effective treatments exist.

Source: Eaton (1994b).

they can also be used to generate hypotheses about associations in the population and to generate control samples for cohort and case-control studies.

An example of a morbidity survey is the Epidemiologic Catchment Area (ECA) Program, sponsored by the U.S. National Institute of Mental Health from 1978 through 1985. The broad aims of the ECA Program were "to estimate the incidence and prevalence of mental disorders, to search for etiological clues, and to aid in the planning of health care facilities (Eaton et al. 1981). The program involved sample surveys of populations living in the catchment areas of already designated community mental health centers. The methods of the ECA Program are described in Eaton and Kessler (1985), and the cross-sectional results are described in Robins and Regier (1991).

A principal advantage of the morbidity survey is that it includes several or many disorders, which helps in assessing their relative importance from the public health point of view. Another advantage is that estimates of prevalence and association are measured without regard to the treatment status of the sample (Shapiro et al. 1984). Figure 2.3 displays results from the ECA study, showing the relatively high prevalence of phobia and relatively low prevalence of schizophrenia. The figure also shows the proportion meeting criteria for a given dis-

Figure 2.4
Sampling Strata for Residents in the ECA Study Design

In contrast to many earlier surveys, the definition of "normal residents"—that is, the target population—included persons in long-term institutions and temporary group quarters as well as those residing in households.

order within the last six months who had seen either a physician or mental health specialist during that period. These proportions are well under 50 percent, with the exception of schizophrenia and panic disorder. For depression, which is disabling and highly treatable, less than a third of those with the disorder have received treatment.

Defining the target population for the morbidity survey is the first step. The best way to define the target population is not always clear, and different definitions have implications for the ultimate value of the results as well as the feasibility of the study. A good definition of a target population is an entire nation, such as in the National Comorbidity Survey (Kessler 1995), or, better yet, a birth cohort of an entire nation, such as the British Perinatal Study, which included all births in Britain during a single week in March 1958 (Butler and Alberman 1969). Other studies usually involve compromises of one form or another. The goal of the sampling procedure is that each respondent is selected into the sample with a known, nonzero probability. Strict probabilistic sampling characterizes high-quality epidemiologic surveys and is a requirement for generalization to the target population.

Most surveys are of the household-residing, noninstitutionalized population, where the survey technology for sampling and interviewing individuals is strongest (Sudman 1976). The ECA design defined the target population as "normal" residents of previously established catchment areas. Sampling was conducted in two strata, as shown in Figure 2.4. The household residing population was sampled via area probability methods or household listings provided by utility companies (Sudman 1976). This stratum included short-stay group quarters such as jails, hospitals, and dormitories. After making a list of the residents in each household, the interviewer asked the person answering the door as to whether there were any other individuals who "normally" resided there but were temporarily absent. "Normally" was defined as the presence of a bed reserved for the individual at the time of the interview. Temporarily absent residents were added to the household roster before the single respondent was chosen randomly. If an individual was selected who was temporarily absent, the interviewer made an appointment for a time after his or her return or conducted the interview at the person's temporary group quarters residence (i.e., in the hospital, jail, dormitory, or other place). The ECA sampled the institutional populations separately by listing all the institutions in the catchment area as well as all those nearby institutions that admitted residents of the catchment area. Then the inhabitants of each institution were rostered and selected probabilistically. Sampling the institutional population required many more resources, per sampled individual, than the household sample, because each institution had to be approached individually. Inclusion of temporary and long-stay group quarters is important for health services research because many of the group quarters are involved in provision of health services and because residents of group quarters may be high utilizers. The ultimate result of these procedures in the ECA was that each normal resident of the catchment area was sampled with a known probability.

It is not enough to crisply define a geographic area, because different areas involve different limitations on generalizability of results. A nationally representative sample, such as the National Comorbidity Survey (Kessler 1995), may seem to be the best. But how does one apply the results of the national sample to a given local area, where decisions about services are made? In the ECA the decision was made to select five separate sites of research in order to provide the possibility of replication of results across sites and to better understand the effects of local variation (Eaton et al. 1981). Thus, the ECA target population consisted not of the nation but rather of an awkward aggregation of catchment areas. Nevertheless, the ECA data were considered benchmarks for a generation of research (Eaton 1994b) because there was sufficient variation in important sociodemographic variables to allow generalization to other large populations, that is, sufficiently large subgroups of young and old, men and women, married and unmarried, rich and poor, and so forth. Generalization to other target populations, such as Asian Americans or Native Americans, or to rural areas was not logical from the ECA. But note that generalization from a national random sample to all rural areas or to small ethnic groups would likewise not always be possible. The point is that the target population should be chosen with a view toward later generalization.

General population surveys are not efficient designs for rare disorders or unusual patterns of service use. Even for research on outcomes that are not rare, sample sizes are often larger than 1,000. A common statistic to be estimated is the prevalence, which is a proportion. For a proportion, the precision is affected by the square root of the sample size (Blalock 1979). If the distribution of the proportion is favorable—say, 30–70 percent—then a sample size of 1,000 produces precision that may be good enough for common sample surveys such as for voter preference. For example, a proportion of .50 has a 95 percent confidence interval from 0.47 to 0.53 with a sample of 1,000. For rarer disorders, the confidence interval grows relative to the size of the proportion (i.e., 0.82–0.118 for a proportion of .10; from 0.004 to 0.160 for a proportion of .01). Often there is interest in patterns broken down by subpopulations, thus challenging the utility of samples with as few as 1,000 individuals. Many community surveys, such as the ECA, have baseline samples in excess of 3,000.

Assessment in epidemiology should ideally be undertaken with standardized measurement instruments that have known and acceptable reliability and validity. In community surveys and automated record systems, reliable and valid measurement must take place efficiently and in "field conditions." The amount of training for interviewers in household studies depends on the nature of the study. Interviewers in the Longitudinal Study on Aging (LSOA) (Kovar et al. 1992), a well-known cohort study in the United States, received about 1½ days of training (Fitti and Kovar 1987), while ECA interviewers received slightly more than a week (Munson et al. 1985). Telephone interviews, such as in the LSOA, can be systematically monitored by recording or listening in on a random basis (as long as the subject is made aware of this possibility), but it is difficult to monitor household interviews, since it cannot be predicted exactly when and where the interview will take place.

The ECA Program involved a somewhat innovative interview called the Diagnostic Interview Schedule, or DIS (Robins et al. 1981). The DIS was designed to resemble a typical psychiatric interview, in which questions asked are highly dependent on answers already given. For example, if an individual responds positively to a question about the occurrence of panic attacks, a series of questions about that particular response is asked; if the response to the question on panic is negative, the interviewer skips to the next section. In effect, the interview adapts to the responses of the subject, so that more questions are asked where more information is needed. The high degree of structure in the DIS required more than one week of training, as well as attention to the visual properties of the interview booklet. The result was that the interviewer could follow instructions regarding the flow of the interview and the recording of data smoothly, so as not to offend or alienate the respondent. Household survey questionnaires are becoming increasingly adaptive and response-dependent, because more information can be provided in a shorter amount of time with adaptive interviews. Inexpensive laptop computers will facilitate such adaptive interviewing. Self-administered, computerized admission procedures are becoming more widely disseminated in the health care system, expanding the database, and facilitating the retrieval and linkage of records.

The reliability and validity of measurement are usually assessed prior to beginning a field study. Often the assessment involves pilot tests on samples of convenience to determine the optimal order of the questions, the time required

Table 2.2
Case Control and Cohort Studies

		Case-Control Study		
		Cases	Controls	
Cohort	Exposed	a	b	a + b
Study	Not Exposed	c	d	c + d

$$\text{Relative Risk} \quad == \quad \frac{a/(a+b)}{c/(c+d)}$$

$$\text{Relative Odds} \quad == \quad \frac{a/b}{c/d} \quad == \quad \frac{ad}{bc}$$

for each section, and whether any questions are unclear or offensive. Debriefing subjects in these pilot tests is often helpful. The next step is a test of reliability and validity. Many pretests select samples from populations according to their health or services use characteristics, in order to generate enough variation on responses to adequately estimate reliability and validity. In order to economize, such pretests are often conducted in clinical settings. But such pretests do not predict reliability and validity under the "field" conditions of household interviews. The ECA Program design involved reliability and validity assessment in a hospital setting (Robins et al. 1981) and later under field conditions (Anthony et al. 1985). The reliability and validity of the DIS were lower in the household setting.

Studying Exposure and Disease

Two basic research designs in epidemiology are the *cohort* and the *case-control* design. These designs are used mostly in addressing Morris' seventh "use" of epidemiology—the search for causes (Morris 1975). This is sometimes called the *analytic* aspect of epidemiology. These designs differ in their temporal orientation to collection of data (prospective versus retrospective) and in the criteria by which they sample (by exposure or by caseness), as shown in Table 2.2.

In a *cohort design*, incidence of disorder is compared in two or more groups that differ in some exposure thought to be related to the disorder (Table 2.2). The cohort design differs from the morbidity survey in that it is prospective, involving longitudinal follow-up of an identified cohort of individuals. As well as the search for causes, the cohort design addresses Morris' (1975) fourth "use" of epidemiology—"estimating individual risks"—and the sixth "use"—"completing the clinical picture, especially the natural history." The entire cohort can be sampled, but when a specific exposure is hypothesized, the design can

Table 2.3
Mental Disorder and Low Birth Weight (British Perinatal Study)

	Prevalence per 1,000		Odds Ratio
	Low Birth Weight n = 727	Normal Birth Weight n = 16,812	
Narrow Schizophrenia (n=35)	7.03	1.86	3.8
Broad Schizophrenia (n=57)	9.82	3.09	3.2
Affective Psychosis (n=32)	8.43	1.61	5.3
Neurosis (n=76)	4.23	4.51	0.9

Source: Adapted from Sacker et al. (1995: Table 1).

be made more efficient by sampling for intensive measurement on the basis of the putative exposure, for example, children who live in an area of toxic exposures or with parents who have been convicted of abuse or who have had problems during delivery; and a control group from the general population. Follow-up allows comparison of incidence rates in both groups.

An example of a cohort design in psychiatric epidemiology is the British Perinatal Study, a cohort study of 98 percent of all births in Great Britain during a single week in March 1958 (Butler and Alberman 1969; Done et al. 1991; Sacker et al. 1995). The cohort had assessments at the ages of 7 and 11 years, and, later, mental hospital records were linked for those entering psychiatric hospitals between 1974 and 1986, by which time the cohort was 30 years old. Diagnoses were made from hospital case notes using a standard system. There was some incompleteness in the data, but not too large; for example, 12 of the 49 individuals diagnosed as "narrow" schizophrenia were excluded because they were immigrants or multiple births or because they lacked data. It is difficult to say how many individuals in the cohort had episodes of disorder that did not result in hospitalization, but that does not necessarily threaten the results, if the attrition occurred equally for different categories of exposure. Table 2.3 shows results for one of 37 different variables related to birth—that is, "exposures"— that were available in the midwives' report: birth weight under 2,500 grams. With the "n" given at the head of the columns in Table 2.3, the reader can fill in the four cells of a two-by-two table, as in Table 2.2, for each of the four disorders. For example, the cells, labeled as in Table 2.2, for narrow schizophrenia, are: a—5; b—706; c—30; d—16,160. The number with the disorder is divided by the number of births to generate the risk of developing the disorder by the time of the follow-up—the cumulative incidence. The risks can be compared across those with and without the exposure: in Table 2.2, the incidence of those with the exposure is $a/(a+b)$, and the incidence of those without the exposure is $c/(c+d)$. The *relative risk* is a comparison of the two risks: $[a/(a+b)]/[c/(c+d)]$. For narrow schizophrenia the relative risk is ($RR=[5/711]/[30/16,136]$), or 3.78.

The relative risk is closely related to causality since it quantifies the association in the context of a prospective study, so the temporal ordering is clear. The relative risk is closely approximated by the *relative odds* or *odds ratio*, which does not include the cases in the denominator (i.e., OR=[5/706]/[30/ 16, 106] = 3.80, not 3.78). The odds ratio has many statistical advantages for epidemiology. It is easy to calculate in the two-by-two table by the cross-products ratio (i.e., ad/bc). The odds ratio quantifies the association without being affected by the prevalence of the disorder or the exposure, which is important for the logic of cohort and case control studies, where these prevalences may change from study to study, depending on the research design. This lack of dependence on the marginal distribution is *not* characteristic of many measures of association typically used in sociology and psychology, such as the correlation coefficient, the difference in proportions, or the kappa coefficient (Bishop et al. 1975). The odds ratio is a standard result of logistic regression and can be adjusted by other factors such as gender, age, and so forth. The odds ratio for low birth weight and narrow schizophrenia in the British Perinatal Study, as it happens, was 3.9, after adjustment for social class and other demographic variables.

The logic of the cohort study includes assessing the *natural history* of the disorder, that is, the study of onset and chronicity in a population context without specific intervention by the researcher. Study of natural history requires repeated follow-up observations. In the British Perinatal Study, there were assessments of the cohort at ages 7 and 11. Once the case groups had been defined, it was possible to study their reading and mathematics performance well before hospitalization. Those destined to become schizophrenic had lower reading and mathematics scores at both 7 and 11 years of age (Crow et al. 1996). Males who would eventually be diagnosed schizophrenic had problems relating to conduct during childhood, while females were anxious, as compared to children who did not end up being hospitalized with a diagnosis of schizophrenia later. Later follow-ups in this study may economize by studying only those who have had onset, and a small random subsample of others, to estimate such factors as the length of episodes, the probability of recurrences, prognostic predictors, and long-term functioning.

In the *case control study*, the disease or disorder drives the logic of the design, and many factors can be studied efficiently as possible causes of the single disorder (Schlesselman 1982). The case control study may be the most important contribution of epidemiology to the advancement of public health, because it is so efficient in searching for causes when there is little knowledge. For example, adenocarcinoma of the vagina occurs so rarely that, prior to 1966, not a single case under the age of 50 had been recorded at the Vincent Memorial Hospital in Boston. A time-space clustering of eight cases, all among young women born within the period 1946–1951, was studied (Herbst et al. 1971). There was almost no knowledge of etiology. A case control study was conducted, matching four controls to each case. The study reported a highly significant (p < 0.00001)

Table 2.4
Depression and Life Events and Difficulties in London

	Cases		Cases		Controls	
	(Patients)		(Survey)		(Survey)	
One or more severe event	70	61%	52	68%	76	20%
No severe events	44	39%	24	32%	306	80%
	114	100%	76	100%	382	100%

Source: Brown and Harris (1978: 57–58, 103).

association between treatment of the mothers with diethylstilbestrol during pregnancy and the subsequent development of the adenocarcinoma of the vagina in the daughters. The results led to the recommendation to avoid administering stilbestrol during pregnancy. *Logistic regression*, developed by epidemiologists and used in case control studies, has distinct advantages over analysis of variance, ordinary least squares regression, discriminant function analysis, and probit regression, used by sociologists and psychologists, especially when the dichotomous dependent variable has a very skewed distribution, that is, is very rare.

The most convincing demonstration of social factors in the etiology of any mental disorder is *The Social Origins of Depression*, by George Brown and Tirril Harris (1978). That study used the case control method to demonstrate the importance of life event stresses and chronic difficulties as causal agents provoking onset of depression. The method involved in-depth diagnostic and etiologic interviews with a sample of 114 patients and a sample of 458 household residents. The target population is that residing in the Camberwell area in south London.

The analysis presented by Brown and Harris is logical but does not always follow the standard epidemiologic style. Table 2.4 presents the crucial findings in the typical epidemiologic manner (following Table 2.2). Two case groups are defined: the 114 women presenting at clinics and hospitals serving the Camberwell area, diagnosed by psychiatrists using a standardized clinical assessment tool called the Present State Examination; and 76 women in the community survey (17 percent) who were depressed at the time of the survey, as judged by a highly trained, nonmedical interviewer using a shortened version of the same instrument. Sixty-one percent of the patient cases (70/114) and 68 percent of the survey cases (52/76) experienced the "provoking agent" of a severe life event during the year prior to the onset of depression. Twenty percent (76/382) of the healthy controls experienced such an event in the year prior to the interview. Patient cases had 6.4 times the odds of having experienced a severe life event than the controls (i.e., [70/44]/[76/306]).

The case control study is very efficient, especially when the disease is rare, because it approximates the statistical power of a huge cohort study with a relatively limited number of controls. For a disease like schizophrenia, which occurs in less than 1 percent of the population, 100 cases from hospitals or a psychiatric case register can be matched to 300 controls from the catchment area of the hospital. A cohort study with this number of cases would involve measurements on 10,000 persons instead of 400! Since the disease is rare, it may be unnecessary to conduct diagnostic examinations on the group of controls, which would have only a small number of cases. Furthermore, a few cases distributed among the controls would weaken the comparison of cases to controls, generating a conservative bias. The statistical power of the case control study is very close to that of the analogous cohort study, and, as shown earlier, the odds ratio is a close estimate of the relative risk. The case control study can be used to test hypotheses about exposures, but it has the very great ability to make comparisons across a wide range of possible risk factors and can be useful even when there are very few hypotheses available.

Using Available Records

Many sources of data for psychiatric epidemiologic research are available to the public from *government surveys* of various types. These include statistics from treatment facilities and from large sample surveys of the populations conducted by large organizations such as national governments. Often the measures of interest to sociologists are only a small part of the survey, but the availability of a range of measures drawn from other disciplines can be a strong advantage. In the United States an important source of data is the National Center for Health Statistics (NCHS). For example, the Health and Nutrition Examination Survey (HANES) is a national sample survey conducted by the NCHS involving physical examinations of a sample of the U.S. population. Its first phase included the Center for Epidemiologic Studies Depression Scale as part of its battery of measures, which included anthropometric measures, nutritional assessments, blood chemistry, medical history, and medical examinations (Eaton and McLeod 1984). Later phases of the HANES included portions of the DIS. The Health Interview Survey conducts health interviews of the general population of the United States and includes reports by the respondent of named psychiatric disorders such as schizophrenia, depressive disorder, and so forth. The National Medical Care Utilization and Expenditure Survey (MCUES) is conducted by the NCHS to help understand the health service system and its financing. The MCUES samples records of practitioners from across the nation, and there are several questions on treatment for psychological problems.

Some governments also sponsor national surveys that focus on psychological disorders. The ECA is one such example, although it was not, strictly speaking, a sample of the nation. The later National Comorbidity Survey includes 8,058 respondents from a probability sample of the United States, with its major measurement instrument being a version of the Composite International Diagnostic Interview (CIDI), a descendant of the DIS used in the ECA surveys (Weissman et al. 1989). The British government conducted a large survey of psychological disorders in a national sample, using a similar instrument to the DIS and CIDI (Meltzer et al. 1995). Anonymous, individual-level data from the ECA, the British survey, and the NCS are available at nominal cost. Governments also generally assimilate data on *vital statistics*—that is, births, deaths, and marriages— from states, provinces, or localities, ensuring some minimal degree of uniformity of reporting and creating data files for public use. The mortality files usually list the cause of death, including suicide. These data files are often available from the government at nominal cost.

Statistics originating from treatment facilities can also be put to good use in psychiatric epidemiology. Many early epidemiologic studies used hospital statistics as the numerators in estimating rates and census statistics in the denominators (Kramer 1969a). The utility of rates estimated in this manner is dependent on the degree to which the clinical disorder is associated with treatment—a stronger association for severe schizophrenia than for mild phobia, presumably. The value of these rates also depends on the relative scarcity or abundance of treatment facilities. In the United States, Medicaid and Medicare files, which include such data as diagnosis and treatment, are available for research use. Many health maintenance organizations maintain data files that could be used in psychological epidemiological research.

Statistics from treatment facilities are considerably enhanced by linkage with other facilities in the same geographic area, serving the same population (Mortensen 1995). Although the number has declined, there still exist several psychiatric case registers that attempt to record and link together all psychiatric treatment episodes for a given population (ten Horn et al. 1986). Linkage across facilities allows multiple treatment episodes for the same individual (even the same episode of illness) to be combined into one record (so-called unduplicating). Linkage across time allows longitudinal study of the course of treatment. Linkage with general health facilities and with birth and mortality records provides special opportunities. The best-known example of a comprehensive health registry is the Oxford Record Linkage Study (ORLS) (Baldwin and Evans 1971), which links together all hospital treatment episodes in its catchment area. The database of the ORLS consists of births, deaths, and hospital admissions, which is a strong limitation. However, due to the catchmenting aspect of the British National Health Service, the data are not limited to household-residing population, as is the National Comorbidity Survey, for example, or the LSOA. In automated data collection systems such as the ORLS, the recordation is often done under the auspices of the medical record systems, with data recorded by the physician, such as the diagnosis. It cannot be presumed that physician's diagnosis is "standardized" and therefore more reliable than other interview or record data. In fact, there is significant variation in diagnosis among physicians. Research using measurements and diagnoses recorded by the physician—as in record linkage systems such as the ORLS—should ideally include studies of reliability and validity (Loffler et al. 1994).

An example of the benefits of record linkage in psychiatric research is the adoption study of schizophrenia in Denmark (Kety et al. 1975, 1994). Familial and twin studies of schizophrenia suggested strongly that schizophrenia was inherited, but these studies were open to the interpretation that the inheritance was cultural, not genetic, because family members are raised together, and identical twins may be raised in social environments that are more similar than the environments of fraternal twins. The Danish adoption study ingeniously combined the strategy of file linkage with interviews of cases, controls, and their relatives. In Denmark each individual receives a number at birth, which is included in most registration systems. The registration systems are potentially linkable, after appropriate safeguards and clearances. In the adoption study, three registers were used. First, all 5,483 individuals in the county and city of Copenhagen who had been adopted by persons or families other than their biological relatives, from 1924 through 1947, were identified from a register of adoptions (Figure 2.5). These were linked to the psychiatric case register, wherein it was determined that 507 adoptees had ever been admitted to a psychiatric hospital. From case notes in the hospitals, 34 adoptees who met criteria for schizophrenia (about one-half of 1 percent of the total number of adoptees) were selected and matched on the basis of age, sex, socioeconomic status of the adopting family, and time with biologic family or in institution prior to adoption. The relatives of these 68 cases and controls were identified by linkage with yet another register in Denmark that permits locating families, parents, and children. After allowing for mortality, refusal, and a total of 3 who were impossible to trace, a psychiatric interview was conducted on 341 individuals. Eleven of the 118 biologic relatives of the index adoptees were schizophrenic (9 percent), versus one in the 35 relatives of adoptive families of the index adoptees (3 percent) and three of the 140 biologic relatives of the control adoptees (2 percent). The findings for schizophrenia spectrum disorders (including uncertain schizophrenia and schizoid personality) also show a pattern consistent only with genetic inheritance (26/118 in the biologic relatives of index cases, or 22 percent versus 16/140 biologic relatives of control adoptees, or 14 percent).

The Logic of Prevention

Some of the earliest epidemiologists used interventions in the community to stop an epidemic or to gather information about the causes of diseases in the population. This is sometimes called the *experimental* aspect of epidemiology. The best-known experiment is that conducted by John Snow in the cholera epidemic in London. Snow's work exemplifies epidemiologic principles in several ways (Cooper and Morgan 1973). It was widely believed that cholera was spread through the air, in a miasma, leading many to seek safety by retreating to rural areas. Snow showed with ecologic data in London that areas serviced by a water company taking water from upstream in the Thames had lower rates of cholera than areas serviced by a company taking water from downstream. This ecologic comparison suggested cholera was borne by water. In the context

Figure 2.5
Danish Adoption Study of Schizophrenia

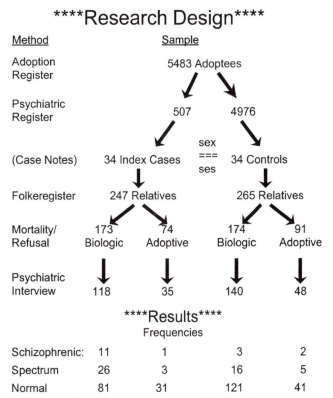

****Research Design****

Method	Sample
Adoption Register	5483 Adoptees
Psychiatric Register	507 4976
(Case Notes)	34 Index Cases sex===ses 34 Controls
Folkeregister	247 Relatives 265 Relatives
Mortality/ Refusal	173 74 174 91 Biologic Adoptive Biologic Adoptive
Psychiatric Interview	118 35 140 48

****Results****
Frequencies

Schizophrenic:	11	1	3	2
Spectrum	26	3	16	5
Normal	81	31	121	41

The Danish adoption study took advantage of multiple, linkable registers and clinched the evidence on the heritability of schizophrenia.

Source: Kety et al. (1973).

of a single cholera epidemic, Snow identified individual cases of cholera, showing that they tended to cluster around a single water pump at Broad Street. He further showed that many exceptional cases—that is, cases of cholera residing distant from the pump—had actually drawn or drunk water from that pump (e.g., on their way home from work). His action to remove the handle of the pump, which roughly coincided with the termination of the epidemic, is regarded as an early instance of experimental epidemiology.

In epidemiology, as with medicine generally, intervention is valued if it is effective, regardless of whether the causation of the disease is understood or not. Table 2.5 shows examples of preventive measures that were implemented well prior to knowledge of the cause, discovered much later in many cases. This logic leads to experimentation even in the absence of causal information.

Various conceptual frameworks have been used to organize the area of pre-

Table 2.5
Knowledge of Prevention and Etiology

Disease	Prevention		Etiology		
	Discoverer	Year	Agent	Discoverer	Year
Scurvy	Lind	1753	Ascorbic Acid	Szent-Gyorgi	1928
Pellagra	Casal	1755	Niacin	Goldberger	1924
Scrotal Cancer	Pott	1775	Benzopyrene	Cook	1933
Smallpox	Jenner	1798	Orthopoxvirus	Fenner	1958
Puerperal Fever	Semmelweis	1847	Streptococcus	Pasteur	1879
Cholera	Snow	1849	Vibrio cholerae	Koch	1893
Bladder Cancer	Rehn	1895	2-Napththlamine	Hueper	1938
Yellow Fever	Reed	1901	Flavirus	Stokes	1928
Oral Cancer	Abbe	1915	N-nitrosonornicotine	Hoffman	1974

Source: Wynder (1994).

vention research. The Commission on Chronic Illness (1957) divided prevention into three types, dependent on the stage of the disease the intervention was designed to prevent or treat. Prior to onset of the disease, the prevention was *primary*, and its goal was to reduce incidence; after disease onset, the intervention was directed at promoting recovery, and its goal was to reduce prevalence— so-called *secondary* prevention. *Tertiary* prevention was designed to prevent impairment and handicap that might result from the disease. The Institute of Medicine (Mrazek and Haggerty 1994) integrated this framework into that of Robert Gordon (1983), who directed attention at the population to which the preventive intervention was directed: *universal* preventions at the entire general population; *targeted* interventions at subgroups at high risk for development of disorder; and *indicated* interventions, directed at individuals who have already manifested signs and symptoms of the disease. Curative medicine is generally operating in the area of secondary prevention, with indicated interventions. Rehabilitative medicine is in the area of tertiary prevention. Primary universal and targeted interventions are the province of experimental epidemiology. Prominent examples of universal interventions in the area of epidemiology are various smoking cessation campaigns and such studies as the Stanford Five-City Project, which was designed to reduce risk for heart disease by lowering levels of several associated risk factors (Farquhar et al. 1990).

From among many possibilities, how should interventions be selected? Epidemiology provides a helpful tool in the form of the *population attributable risk*, sometimes called the *attributable fraction* or the *etiologic fraction* (Lilienfeld and Stolley 1994; 202). The attributable risk is the maximum estimate of the proportion of the incidence of disease that would be prevented if a given risk factor were eliminated. For a given disease, the attributable risk combines information from the relative risk for a given exposure with the prevalence of the exposure in the population. The formula for attributable risk is:

$$\text{Attributable risk} = \frac{P\ (RR\ -\ 1)}{P\ (RR\ -\ 1)\ +\ 1}$$

where:

P = Prevalence of exposure; and

RR = Relative risk of exposure to disease.

The relative risk can be estimated from a cohort study, as described earlier; and the prevalence of the exposure can be estimated from a separate survey. A simple case control study also provides the information for attributable risk under certain conditions. The relative risk is approximated by the relative odds, as discussed earlier. If the controls are selected from the general population, the level of exposure can be estimated from them. For example, case control studies of smoking and lung cancer in the early 1950s showed that the odds of dying from lung cancer were about 15 times higher for smokers as for nonsmokers. About one-half the population smoked, leading to the attributable risk estimate of about 80 percent. In the United States, this meant that about 350,000 of the 400,000 annual deaths due to lung cancer would not occur if smoking were totally eliminated. In the situation of many possible risk factors, the attributable risk is a tool that helps prioritize them.

Epidemiologic cohort studies can provide information that may help to stage the intervention at the most appropriate time. The intervention should occur before most onsets in the population have taken place, but not so far before onset that the effects of the intervention wash out before the process of disease development has begun. The appropriate stage for prevention in many situations would appear to be that of precursors, in which there are subgroups that can be identified as at high risk, but before the disease prodrome has started (Eaton et al. 1995).

Bias

Epidemiologic research entails bias, and it is beneficial to anticipate bias in designing research studies. Common biases in epidemiology take a slightly different form than in typical social science research (e.g., as enumerated in Campbell and Stanley 1971), but the principle of developing a language to conceptualize bias and to attempt to anticipate, eliminate, or measure bias is common to both disciplines. In this section five basic types of bias are considered: sampling bias, divided into three subtypes of treatment bias, prevalence bias, and response bias; and measurement bias, divided into subtypes of diag-nostic bias and exposure bias.

Sampling bias arises when the sample studied does not represent the popu-lation to which generalization is to be made, and an important type of sampling bias is *treatment bias*. The case control design often takes advantage of treatment facilities for finding cases of disorder to compare with controls. With severe diseases that invariably lead to treatment there is less bias than for disorders that are less noticeable, distressing, or impairing to the individual. As shown in Figure 2.3, data from the ECA Program indicate that, among the mental disor-ders, only for schizophrenia and panic disorder are as many as half the current cases under treatment. In 1946 Berkson showed that, where the probability of treatment for a given disorder is less than 1.0, cases in treatment overrepresented individuals with more than one disorder—*comorbid cases*. In studying risk fac-tors for disorder with the case control design, where cases are found through clinics, the association revealed in the data may be an artifact of the comorbidity; that is, exposure x may appear to be associated with disease y, the focus disorder of the study, but actually related to disease z (perhaps not measured in the study). This type of bias is so important in epidemiologic research—especially case control studies—it is termed *Berkson's bias*, or sometimes "treatment bias." The existence of this bias is possibly one factor connected to the rare use of the case control design in studies of psychiatric disorders.

Another type of sampling bias very common in case control studies arises from another type of efficiency in finding cases of disorder—the use of prevalent cases. This is sometimes termed *prevalence bias*, or the "clinician's illusion" (Cohen and Cohen 1984). The ideal is to compare relative risks among exposed and nonexposed populations, which entails comparison of incidence rates, as discussed earlier. But the rate of incidence is often too low to generate sufficient cases for analysis and necessitates extending the data collection over a period of months or years during which new cases are collected. Prevalent cases are easier to locate, either through a cross-sectional survey or, easier yet, through records of individuals currently under treatment. The problem with study of current cases is that the prevalence is a function of the incidence and chronicity of the disorder, as discussed earlier. Association of an exposure with the pres-ence or absence of disease mixes up influences on incidence with influences on chronicity. Influences on chronicity can include treatment. For example, com-paring the brain structure of prevalent cases of schizophrenia to that of controls showed differences in the size of the ventricles—possibly an exciting clue to the etiology of schizophrenia. But a possible bias is that phenothiazine or other medication, used to treat schizophrenia, produced the changes in brain structure. Later studies of brain structure had to focus on schizophrenics who had not been treated in order to eliminate this possibility. The study of depression among women in London is possibly subject to prevalence bias since cases were se-lected on the basis of presentation to treatment, and controls were selected via a cross-sectional (prevalence) survey. Thus, it may be that provoking agents such as life events contribute only to the recurrence of episodes of depression, not necessarily to their initial onset.

Attrition bias is a third general threat to the validity of findings from epidemiologic research. The epidemiologic design includes explicit statement of the population to which generalization is sought, as discussed earlier. The sampling procedure includes ways to designate individuals thought to be representative of that population. After designation as respondents, before measurements can be taken, some respondents become unavailable to the research, usually through one of three mechanisms: death, refusal, or change of residence. If these designated-but-not-included respondents are not a random sample, there will be bias in the results. The bias can result from differences in the distribution of cases versus noncases as to response rate or to differences in distribution of exposures or both. In cross-sectional field surveys (Von Korff et al. 1985) and in follow-up surveys (Eaton et al. 1992), the attrition bias connected to psychopathology has not been extremely strong. Persons with psychiatric diagnoses are not more likely to refuse to participate, for example. Persons with cognitive impairment are more likely to die during a follow-up interval; and persons with antisocial personality disorder or abuse of illegal drugs are more likely to change address and be difficult to locate. Differential attrition is particularly threatening to studies with long follow-up periods, such as the British Perinatal Study and the Danish Adoption Study, since there was sizable attrition in both studies.

Bias in measurement is called *invalidity* in the social sciences, and this term is also used in epidemiology. But the study of validity in epidemiology has been more narrowly focused than in social sciences. The concentration in epidemiology has been on dichotomous measures, as noted earlier. The medical ideology has ignored the notion that concepts for disease and pathology might actually be conventions of thought, as discussed in Chapter 1. Where the psychometrician takes as a basic assumption that the true state of nature is not observable, the epidemiologist tends to think of disease as a state whose presence is essentially knowable. As a result, discussion of construct validity is rare in epidemiologic research. Instead, the focus has been on sensitivity and specificity, which are two aspects of *criterion validity* (also a term not used much in epidemiologic research).

Sensitivity is the proportion of true cases that are identified as cases by the measure (Table 2.6). *Specificity* is the proportion of true noncases that are identified as noncases by the measure. In social research criterion validity is often estimated with a correlation coefficient, but this statistic is inappropriate because the construct of disease is dichotomous, and differences in rarity of the disorder will constrain the value of the correlation coefficient. Furthermore, use of sensitivity and specificity has the advantage over correlation in that it forces quantification of both types of error, that is, false positive and false negative error. These errors and the calibration of the measurement to adapt to them depend heavily on the prevalence of the disorder.

Bias also exists in the measurement of exposure. The epidemiologist's ten-

Table 2.6
Sensitivity and Specificity

		True Disease Status		
		Present	Absent	
Test Results	Present	a (True Positives)	b (False Positives)	a + b
	Absent	c (False Negatives)	d (True Negatives)	c + d
		a + c	b + d	

Sensitivity $= a / (a + c)$

Specificity $= d / (b + d)$

dency to categorical measurement leads to the term *misclassification* for this type of bias. A well-known example is the study of Lilienfeld and Graham (1958, cited in Schlesselman 1982: 137–38), which compared male patients' declarations as to whether they were circumcised to the results of a doctor's examination. Of the 84 men judged to be circumcised by the doctor (the "gold standard" in this situation), only 37 reported being circumcised (44 percent sensitivity). Eighty-nine of the 108 men who were not circumcised in the view of the doctor reported not being circumcised (82 percent specificity). In social research, the exposures are often subjective happenings, such as emotions, or objective events recalled by the subject, such as life events, instead of, for example, residence near a toxic waste dump, as might be the putative exposure in a study of cancer. The importance of subjective reporting of exposures threatens the validity of the case control design in psychiatric epidemiology and may be one reason it has been used so little. The cases in a case control study by definition have a disease or problem that the controls do not. In any kind of case control study where the measure of exposure is based on recall by the subjects, the cases may be more likely than controls to recall exposures, because they wish to explain the occurrence of the disease. In the study of depression in London, depressed women may be more likely to recall a difficult life event that happened earlier in their lives because of their current mood, than women who are not depressed; or depressed women may magnify the importance of a given event that actually did occur. These problems of recall raise the importance of strictly prospective designs in psychiatric epidemiological research.

BASIC DATA IN PSYCHIATRIC EPIDEMIOLOGY

Development of the Field of Psychiatric Epidemiology

Epidemiologic studies in the field of psychiatry have been undertaken for about as long as the fields of psychiatry and epidemiology have been in existence as we know them. As with other fields of medicine and academic study, research has burgeoned in this century. Dohrenwend and Dohrenwend (1982) have described three generations of research in psychiatric epidemiology that are useful in summarizing briefly the history of the field. The first generation of research in psychiatric epidemiology was distinguished by studies of hospital statistics. Many hospitals produced voluminous statistics on the characteristics of their patients, often on a yearly basis. These statistics formed the basis for numerators of rates of prevalence and incidence of disorder, as discussed earlier, as long as a suitable denominator could be found from the census or other estimate of the population. In 1939 a study of the rate of first admission to hospital for the entire Chicago area was published (Faris and Dunham 1939), which showed a relationship of the rate with the area of the city (reviewed further in Chapter 8), stimulating widespread debate about the effects of city life. These studies in the first generation relied completely on the diagnosis as obtained from the medical records. Another classic study in this generation was conducted in New Haven, Connecticut, using the 1950 census as the basis for the denominators and admission to psychiatric treatment facilities as the numerators (Hollingshead and Redlich 1958). It showed a strong relationship of social class to rate of mental disorder (reviewed further in Chapter 5). In the 1950s the federal government shifted the responsibility for statistics about mental disorders to the newly formed National Institute of Mental Health, under the leadership of the Office of Biometry, led by Morton Kramer. Kramer organized the reporting systems of the individual states into a national system of data collection, based on the records of the state mental hospitals in the early 1950s and eventually including private mental hospitals, psychiatric wards of general hospitals, and community mental health centers. The culmination of this effort was reflected in Kramer's *Applications of Mental Health Statistics*, written in 1969 for the World Health Organization (Kramer 1969a).

After World War II, there was intensified interest in mental disorders less serious than to cause hospitalization and a concomitant realization that many serious disorders did not come into treatment. The problem of untreated cases was recognized by sociologists Kitsuse and Cicourel (1963), as well as by epidemiologists such as Kramer (1969a, Appendix). There was also increasing interest in stress as a possibly unifying cause of mental disorders (partly out of the realization that a large number of potential recruits to the armed services had been rejected due to psychiatric reasons, as reviewed in Chapter 3) and associated decline in interest in the specific mental diagnoses found in medical records. Finally, there developed during the period shortly after the war the technology of area probability sampling and social survey interviewing, which made possible, in theory at least, efforts to determine the total prevalence of mental disorders in the population. The psychiatric epidemiologic surveys of this era, such as the Midtown Manhattan Study (Langner and Michael 1963; Srole and Fischer 1989) and its analogue for rural areas, the Stirling County Study in Nova Scotia (Leighton et al. 1963), used relatively uncomplicated scales of about 20–30 items, which yielded the probability that an individual was a "case" of mental disorder. The methods of these second-generation studies thus ignored cases of mental disorder in hospitals and focused on only one form of mental disorder.

In undertaking reviews of the scientific literature in the area of psychiatric epidemiology during the decade of the 1960s, Bruce and Barbara Dohrenwend revealed two basic aspects (1969, 1974b). One conclusion they drew was that the dominant factor related to mental disorders was lower social class status. A second aspect of the literature that their work illuminated was that the epidemiologic research on specific mental disorders, which had continued throughout the century in Europe, revealed that specific disorders had specific patterns of relationships to such basic risk factors as age, sex, social class status, and rural or urban residence—these patterns might be called the "sociodemographic fingerprint" of the disorder. Their work thus renewed interest in the specific diagnoses at the same time as the field of psychiatry was moving away from the unitary concept of "caseness" into the so-called neo-Kraepelinian revolution, of interest in specific diagnoses. The revolution in psychiatry led to ultimate rejection of the psychoanalytic theory, the gradual ascendance of biological theories as to the cause of mental disorder, and the design and implementation of the third revision of the *Diagnostic and Statistical Manual* (American Psychiatric Association 1980).

The third generation of psychiatric epidemiology reflected these trends by incorporating highly sophisticated diagnostic interviewing techniques into social surveys. The Diagnostic Interview Schedule (DIS) was designed by Lee Robins (a sociologist, as it happens, married to Eli Robins, a psychiatrist and leader of the neo-Kraepelinian revolution) and others to achieve this goal (Robins et al. 1981). The DIS was implemented in the National Institute of Mental Health Epidemiologic Catchment Area Program, as discussed earlier.

The description of the three generations of research is useful as a summary and raises the question as to where psychiatric epidemiology will turn now, as it enters a potential "fourth" generation (Anthony et al. 1995; Eaton and Merikangas, 2000). Before the third revision of the DSM, there was only one textbook in the area of psychiatric epidemiology (Cooper and Morgan 1973); at the time of the fourth edition there are several texts (Tsuang, et al. 1995) and edited collections (Anthony et al. 1995; Williams et al. 1989) as well as recent texts in social psychiatry (Bebbington 1991; Bennet and Freeman 1991; Bhugra and Leff 1993). One development is the current strong interest in *comorbidity*, in which a specific mental disorder is highly associated with another (Kessler 1995). Comorbidity possibly reflects the trend to split mental disorders into too many subdiagnoses, which occurred as the second generation (the "caseness" concept of one disorder) evolved into the third generation (DSM and its hundreds of categories). As noted earlier, evidence regarding the discriminant validity of the disorders—that is, the proof through construct validation that each is unique—is questionable. It may be that the time is ripe for psychiatric epidemiology to change from the descriptive to the analytic mode of research. This will involve explicit hypothesis testing, using the full range of epidemiologic methods, instead of the purely head-counting approach that has dominated the first three generations. This stage will benefit from progress in biologic assays and explicit, rejectable, social and biologic theories of the causation of mental disorder.

The Extent of Mental Disorders in the Population

This section presents basic data for 14 disorders reviewed in the first chapter in the section on the medical model. Table 2.7 presents results on crude prevalence and incidence. The table is divided into sections on children (0–10 years), adolescents (10–20 years), adults (15–65 years), and the elderly (65 + years). The age ranges are necessarily arbitrary, allowing reporting of (albeit rough) age-specific rates. The prevalence rates reported are lifetime prevalences, specific to the age range. For most disorders there are dozens or scores of field studies reporting lifetime prevalence, so the figures reported are the interquartile range and exemplar study. The *exemplar* study is a high-quality study at or very near the median (i.e., the study reporting a rate below which half the literature falls). The interquartile range is the minimum and maximum rate in the central 50 percent of the studies (i.e., eliminating the bottom and top 25 percent of studies). The interquartile ranges are not interpolated, so that the figures in the table represent prevalences actually reported in the relevant studies. The number of studies gives the reader a feeling for the size of the literature. For incidence there are many fewer studies, and the figures reported in the table are from studies selected by this author and reported in the notes to the table. The reader should note that the prevalence data are reported in percentages, while the incidence data are presented as rates per 1,000 population per year.

Symptoms of mental disorder do not cluster in children in the same way as they do in adults, and, thus, the diagnoses that we apply to adults are not useful for children. The table includes the diagnostic categories of autism as an example of a pervasive and severe disorder and attention deficit disorder with hyperactivity as an example of a learning disorder. In adolescence adult disorders such as panic (Hayward et al. 1989) and depression arise (Lewinsohn et al. 1994), in much the same form as exist for adults. Prior to adolescence, the symptoms may occur, even in a form permitting of diagnosis (Kovacs et al. 1984), but they do not always cluster in the same manner as in adults; they do not have the same standard epidemiologic correlates, such as gender; and the standard treatments for them are not effective or much less so. While there are continuities between childhood and adulthood in general and broad behavioral and emotional tendencies, specific syndromes resembling adult disorders that occur in childhood do not predict strongly their occurrence in adulthood (Moffity 1993; Robins 1966; Robins et al. 1971).

There are twenty-three studies of the epidemiology of autism, with a large range of prevalences. The range of the middle three quartiles is 0.04 to 0.10 per

Table 2.7
Summary of Descriptive Epidemiology of 14 Psychiatric Disorders

Diagnosis	Review	Exemplar Lifetime Prevalence (%)	Inter-quartile Range (%)	Number of studies	Annual Incidence per/1000
Disorders of children 0 - 10					
Autism	Fombonne 1999	0.049	0.041-0.104	23	NA
Attention Deficit	Anderson and Werry 1994	6.2	2.2-6.7	6	NA
Disorders of adolescents 10 - 20					
Conduct Disorder	Offord et al 1987	5.4	NA	1	NA
Eating Disorders	Hsu 1996	1.2	1.0 - 2.8	7	0.18
Non-psychotic Disorders of Adults 15 - 65					
Agoraphobic Disorder	Eaton 1995	5.3	3.6 - 5.7	7	22.0
Panic Disorder	Eaton 1995	1.6	1.1 - 2.2	11	1.4
Social Phobic Disorder	Eaton 1995	1.7	1.7 - 2.7	6	4.0
Alcohol Disorder	Helzer and Canino 1992	13.0	10.7-15.9	15	17.9
Antisocial Personality	de Girolamo 1993	1.4	0.4 - 2.6	13	NA
Major Depressive Disorder	Kaelber et al 1995	9.0	8.4-16.0	15	3.0
Suicide	this volume	NA	0.08-0.19	57	0.14
Psychotic Disorders of Adults 15 - 65					
Schizophrenia	Eaton 1985	0.3	0.16 - 0.56	25	0.2
Bipolar Disorder	Bebbington and Ramana 1995	0.6	0.4 - 0.8	9	0.3
Disorders of the elderly 65 +					
Dementia	Henderson 1994	4.9	3.6 - 7.2	23	6.0

Sources:

Reviews column: autism Fombonne (1999); attention deficit disorder—Anderson and Werry (1994); conduct disorder—Offord et al. (1987); eating disorder—Hsu (1996); agoraphobic disorder, panic disorder, and social phobic disorder—Eaton (1995); alcohol disorder—Helzer and Canino (1992), excluding studies of American Indians and French Canadians because they were not population-based, and Mexican Americans because the data were redundant with the Los Angeles ECA site; antisocial personality disorder—de Girolamo and Reich (1993); major depressive disorder—Kaelber et al. (1995), with four studies added from Angst (1990); suicide—data from Figure 4.1 in this volume; schizophrenia—Eaton (1985); bipolar disorder—Bebbington and Ramana (1995); dementia—Henderson (1994:23 studies of populations aged 65 or years older, designated as moderate or severe impairment).

Table 2.7 (continued)

Exemplar studies column: Autism—Steffenburg and Gillberg (1986); attention deficit disorder—
Offord et al. (1987); conduct disorder—Offord et al. (1987); eating disorders—Szmukler
(1985); agoraphobic disorder—Magee et al. (1996); panic disorder—Eaton et al. (1994); social
phobic disorder—Bland et al. (1988); alcohol abuse or dependence—Wittchen and Bronisch
(1992); antisocial personality disorder—Kinzie et al. (1992); major depressive disorder—
Wittchen et al. (1992); schizophrenia—Nielsen and Neilsen (1977); bipolar disorder—Bland
et al. (1988); dementia—Gurland et al. (1983, New York site).
Incidence studies column: eating disorders—average of 1982 rates in Lucas et al. (1991) and Eagles
et al. (1995); agoraphobic disorder—Eaton and Keyl (1990); panic disorder—Eaton et al.
(1998); social phobic disorder—Neufeld et al. (1999); alcohol abuse or dependence disorder—
Eaton et al. (1989); major depressive disorder—Eaton et al. (1997); suicide—Figure 4.1 in this
volume (Norway); schizophrenia—average of 27 studies in Eaton (1999); bipolar disorder—
Leff et al. (1976); dementia—Schoenberg et al. (1987).

1,000, and the exemplar study is that of Steffenberg and Gillberg (Williams and
Calnan 1996) with prevalence of 0.45 per 1,000.

The nonpsychotic disorders reviewed in the table usually involve marked
disability, but the individuals often or even usually do not come in for treatment.
Therefore, these two sections of the table review only studies in which surveys
were conducted, and cases are identified without regard for their treatment samples. There are six studies of ADHD reviewed by Anderson (Anderson and
Werry 1994), with a median prevalence of 6.2 and interquartile range of 2.2–
6.7. There is sufficient controversy about the value of this disorder, and there
are unsolved problems of epidemiologic method, so no credible incidence studies exist. Similarly for conduct disorder, there appear to be no strong reviews
of this disorder using common criteria for diagnosis, so that median, interquartile
range, and incidence cannot be estimated. The prevalence figure for conduct
disorder (5.4 percent) is from a single strong study in Ontario and is based on
occurrence within the six months prior to the interview (Offord et al. 1987).

The eating disorders consist of anorexia nervosa and bulimia (more details
on these diagnoses are given in Chapter 6). These disorders usually do not
overlap at any given time, but they do tend to overlap in the lifetime of the
individual, with many girls beginning with anorexia and then going on to bulimia. The review by Hsu (1996) presents 7 studies that include data on both
disorders, with sufficient data to focus on the age range 15–25. The median
lifetime prevalence rate for both disorders combined is about 1 percent. A review
of 25 studies of point prevalence of anorexia alone, by Fombonne (1995), reports
a lower median of 0.12 percent. Fombonne's review includes a separate table
of studies of bulimia, and it is clear that even if one added together the rates
for the two disorders, the median would be lower than 1 percent, which suggests
either that the disorder is quite transient or that the prevalence is very sensitive
to the threshold chosen for diagnosis and the methodology of the study used to
estimate prevalence. Also, the prevalence and incidence of the disorder have
been changing, with the term "bulimia" being used only after its introduction

in 1979. Both reviews include only studies that relied on the survey method, since it is believed that many cases do not receive treatment. The exemplar study is that of Szmukler (1985), who reports a prevalence of 1.2 percent. The incidence rate presented is the average of the reports from Minnesota (Lucas et al. 1991) and Scotland (Eagles et al. 1995).

The specific diagnoses in the area of anxiety changed markedly with the introduction of DSM-III in 1980, so that the epidemiology of the anxiety disorders is sharply demarcated by that point, and the number of studies is limited. The reviews for agoraphobia, panic, and social phobia are based on a 1995 compilation of survey studies by Eaton in 1995. There were 7 studies of agoraphobia, with an interquartile range of lifetime prevalence from 3–6 percent of the adult population. The median, exemplar study is the national comorbidity survey (Magee et al. 1996), which reported a prevalence of about 5 percent. The incidence estimate is from the one-year follow-up of the ECA sample (Eaton and Keyl 1990). There are 11 studies of panic disorder, with a median lifetime prevalence of 1.6, as reported in the ECA program (Eaton et al. 1991). Panic disorder is often not treated and often treated outside the psychiatric treatment sector, so it is important that the review is of survey studies only. The interquartile range is about 1–2 percent of the population. The incidence estimate for panic disorder is 1.4/1,000/year, from the 13-year follow-up of the Baltimore ECA sample (Eaton et al. 1998). There are 6 studies of social phobia, with a median of 1.7 percent and an interquartile range from about 1.5 percent to about 3 percent. The exemplar study is the Edmonton survey of Bland, which used the DIS (Bland et al. 1998). The incidence data come from the follow-up of the Baltimore ECA sample (Neufeld et al. 1999).

There are more than a dozen field studies in which the diagnosis of major depression is made, as reviewed in Kaelber et al. (1995), and also including four further studies reported in the review of Angst (1990). About 9 percent of the population report an episode of major depressive disorder over the course of their adult lives, with an interquartile range of about 8–16 percent. The exemplar study is a field study in Munich (Wittchen et al. 1992). The incidence estimate of 3.0/1,000/year is from the 13-year follow-up of the Baltimore ECA site (Eaton et al. 1997).

Table 2.7 includes the two major psychotic disorders of adults—schizophrenia and bipolar disorder (formerly called manic-depressive disorder). These disorders produce such a disruption in social life that, in Western societies, the individuals end up seeing a psychiatrist at some time or other in their lives. Since both disorders involve loss of contact with reality and lack of insight into the disorder itself, the individual is not a good reporter for his or her own symptoms, and a credible diagnosis must necessarily involve a trained clinician such as a psychologist or psychiatrist. Since the symptoms can be produced by causes associated with physical illnesses and the ingestion of substances, the study benefits if the clinician has medical training. Therefore, the two reviews include only studies where the diagnosis is made by a psychiatrist. The reviews also include many studies based on data from treatment facilities, as long as there was some attempt to be comprehensive by including all the relevant facilities for a given population, such as occurs with a psychiatric case register. There are more than 30 such studies for the diagnosis of schizophrenia (Eaton 1985), with a median lifetime prevalence of about one-third of 1 percent (as reported in the exemplar study of Nielsen and Nielsen [1977]) and an interquartile range of about 0.2–0.5 percent. The incidence of schizophrenia is about 0.2/1,000/ year, as reported in the WHO study of schizophrenia (Sartorius et al. 1986). Bebbington and Ramana (1995) review nine studies of bipolar disorder, showing a median of 0.6 in the study of Bland et al. (1988) in Canada and an interquartile range of about 0.4–0.8 percent. The incidence is 0.3/1,000/year (Leff et al. 1976).

Since the prevalence of dementia is exquisitely sensitive to the age range, the 23 studies reported in Table 2.7 include a selection of those from 52 reported in Henderson (1994) in which the age range is exactly 65 or greater, and the diagnostic criteria used are in the "moderate" or "severe" range of impairment. About 5 percent of this age population have dementia, with an interquartile range from 3.6 to 7.2. The incidence is over one-half of 1 percent per year (Schoenberg et al. 1987).

Variation over the Course of Life

The crude rates reported in Table 2.7 obscure variation in incidence of disorders over the life span, especially in the adult disorders, where the age range is as long as 50 years. For some disorders there does not appear to exist remarkable variation over the life course, with new cases occurring from late adolescence through at least to the beginning of old age, such as agoraphobia (Eaton and Keyl 1990), social phobia (Wells et al. 1994), and antisocial personality disorder, which is defined as beginning before age 18 and continuing throughout life as a stable personality disorder. Figure 2.6 shows the force of morbidity over the life course for each gender for four disorders: autism, alcohol disorder, major depressive disorder, and dementia. These disorders are so dependent on the threshold of diagnosis and other methodologic factors that presenting data points is more precise than the data merit. Therefore, the y-axis in Figure 2.6 is not calibrated; however, the shape of the curves is estimated roughly from incidence data cited in Table 2.7. The incidence of alcohol disorder rises sharply in the teen years and then declines rapidly with age, reflecting heavy usage during the years just past adolescence (Figure 2.6). Males have nearly five times the rate of disorder as females. At around the age of retirement, there is an upturn in the rate of incidence, for males only. This upturn is generated by only a handful of cases in the numerator of the ECA Program data but also is present in the only comparable population-based study, in Lundby,

Figure 2.6
Force of Morbidity over the Course of Life for Four Mental Disorders

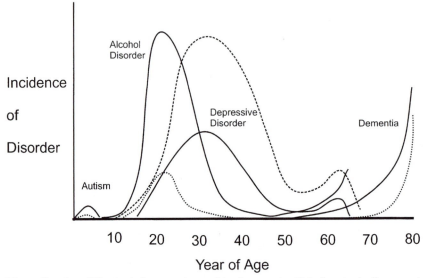

These disorders differ in their sex ratios and in the age at which they typically present. Autism is more frequent in males and occurs early in life. Alcohol disorders are more frequent in males and occur during young adulthood. Depressive disorders are more frequent in females and occur during the years of early and middle adulthood. Dementia is equally common in males and females in old age, but males have earlier onset.

Note: Males—solid lines; females—broken lines.

Sweden (Ojesjo et al. 1982, not shown in the figure). The upturn might well be accounted for by the physical decline of aging, in which a lifetime of heavy drinking finally takes its toll. It could also be that, among men, retirement provides new opportunities for drinking during the day. It could also be that stresses of retirement or of widowhood are risk factors for onset of alcohol disorder.

Major depressive disorder has onset in adolescence and young adulthood, with a peak onset at the age of about 30 for males and a few years later for females (Figure 2.6). The incidence is about twice as high for females as males. For both genders, the rate appears to be bimodal, with a second mode sometime after the age of 55. The second mode consists of only a few cases in the numerator, but the rise after the age of 50 is replicated, in retrospective data, in the National Comorbidity Survey data (Kessler et al. 1994). The effects of menopause might explain the rise after 50 in women, but not in men. It could be that the stresses of divorces and widowhood during this period of life contribute to the upturn.

The beginning and end of the life course are marked with the severe disorders

Figure 2.7

Incidence of Schizophrenia by Age and Sex, Rochester, New York, and Denmark

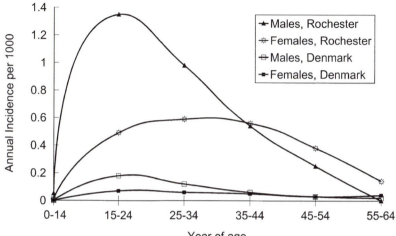

Schizophrenia occurs in young adulthood, somewhat earlier in males than females. This pattern is evident whether one uses the broad criteria of diagnosis, as in Rochester, or the narrow criteria, as in Denmark. An outlier point in the Rochester males, 45–54, was edited from 0.49 to 0.25.

Source: Rochester data from Babigian (1985) and Denmark data from Munk-Jorgensen (1986).

of autism and dementia, respectively. Autism is very rare, and the peak incidence is in the age range of two to five years, with no new cases occurring after the age of about eight. There are about five times as many males as females with autism. Dementia rises in old age, somewhat earlier in males than in females.

The age of high risk for schizophrenia is in young adulthood, but the risk period extends throughout the adult years (Figure 2.7). The data presented are from psychiatric case registers in Monroe County, New York, with principal city of Rochester (Babigian 1985), and the nation of Denmark (Munk-Jorgensen 1986). The two sets of data are presented together to show how the threshold for diagnosis can contribute to large variations in the incidence rate. Diagnoses in the Rochester data are based on the DSM-II, prior to implementation of the results of the U.S.-U.K. study; whereas diagnoses in Denmark, with rates about one-fifth as large, are based on the ICD and traditionally conservative practice in Denmark. It is also important, in evaluating these two sets of data, to realize that the Monroe County register was extremely comprehensive in its case-finding net, including even private practice psychiatrists who may have treated an individual having a first episode of schizophrenia. In Denmark the register is limited to hospital admissions, but the nature of psychosis is such as to facilitate hospitalization for nearly all cases, especially where there is no financial barrier

to treatment, as in Denmark. In both locales, there are almost no onsets prior
to age 15 or after the age of 65. Even with the enormous difference in overall
rates, the much replicated differential shape of the age of onset curves for males
and females is evident in both sets of data. The peak is at about 25 years for
males and 30 years for females, and toward the end of the period of risk, at
about age 50, the rate for females is substantially higher than for males. The
differential shape of the incidence curve for males and females has been replicated many times, and the best evidence is that it is not due to differential delay
in hospitalization.

Prevalence of Complaints and Behaviors Not Meeting Criteria for Disorder

Estimation of rates requires use of diagnostic categories, obscuring variation
in the symptom picture below and above the diagnostic threshold. As discussed
in Chapter 1, there is evidence that diagnoses can be made reliably under research conditions, at least, and some evidence for the construct validity of broad
categories of disorder, such as anxiety, depression, and severe thought disorder.
The evidence for discriminant validity and the general utility of more narrowly
defined categories, as presented in Table 2.7, is much weaker. This section
presents data showing how the symptoms in the population aggregate to produce
prevalence of panic disorder and depressive disorder. It further shows prevalence
of selected complaints of distress and somatic symptoms for which no physical
illness is believed to be the cause.

Episodes of sadness that last for two weeks or more are common in the
population, with about 28 percent reporting such an episode over their lifetimes
(Table 2.8). The other symptoms of depressive disorder frequently occur outside
the context of obvious sadness, and the occurrence of these symptoms is common. The table shows lifetime prevalence of the occurrence of the symptoms
in the relevant symptom groups, as defined in the diagnostic manual (American
Psychiatric Association 1994) (Box 1.4), which occurred every day, or nearly
every day, for periods of two weeks or longer, so that the total lifetime occurrence of any of the symptoms reported is likely to be much greater than shown
in the table. Even so, the prevalence of two-week periods with the symptoms
is fairly high. For example, more than one-fifth of the population reports a period
of two weeks or longer when they had problems sleeping, problems with appetite, or thoughts of death; nearly one-fifth report episodes of fatigue. Many of
these occurrences are explained by an illness, injury, or medication or as an
effect of taking drugs or alcohol; but there exist sizable numbers of individuals
who report the symptoms and have no explanation for them (second column,
Table 2.8): for example, 10 percent have episodes of fatigue or problems in
concentration, with no explanation. A smaller number report the symptoms in
the context of an episode of sadness, thus meeting the criteria for depressive
syndrome. For example, only about 8 percent report sleep problems during such

Table 2.8
Symptom Groups Related to Depressive Disorder (Baltimore Epidemiologic Catchment Area Follow-up)

DSM-IV Symptom Groups	Lifetime Prevalence N = 1920		
	Any occurrence	Unexplained occurrence	
	Ever	Ever	During worst episode of depression
Dysphoric episode	27.9	--	--
Anhedonia	9.3	8.4	5.6
Appetite	20.7	20.7	7.0
Sleep	22.1	18.9	8.4
Slow or restless	9.8	6.0	3.7
Fatigue	17.1	10.2	5.0
Guilt	6.3	6.3	4.2
Concentration	11.7	10.0	6.9
Thoughts of death	21.0	21.0	7.1
Episode of depressive syndrome:			
symptoms in 1 + groups			12.0
symptoms in 2 + groups			11.8
symptoms in 3 + groups			10.6
symptoms in 4 + groups			9.6
symptoms in 5 + groups			7.6

Source: Estimated by the author.

an episode, and 7 percent, appetite problems. Episodes of depression appear to vary considerably in the breadth of accompanying symptoms, as shown in the bottom right section of Table 2.8. Twelve percent report an episode of the depressive syndrome, but only 7.6 percent have such an episode with symptoms in five or more groups, which is required to be eligible for the diagnosis of major depressive disorder. After incorporating other aspects of the episode, the diagnosis is reached by 6.6 percent of the sample. Nothing in these data or elsewhere in the scientific literature suggests that the threshold of symptoms in five or more symptom groups is better than any other threshold.

Anxiety is the dominant psychiatric complaint in the general population and can be manifested in physiological reactions, in the emotion of fear, and in behaviors such as avoidance (Marks 1987). In the ECA Program surveys, nearly one-quarter of the sample responded positively to the question, "Would you say you are a nervous person?" (Eaton et al. 1991). More than 50 percent of the samples responded positively either to this question or to at least one question about the occurrence over the lifetime of unreasonable fears (Eaton et al. 1991). This level of prevalence is such as to suggest anxiety is normal, not abnormal, in much the same way that acute respiratory illnesses happen to virtually everyone—phobia is sometimes called the "common cold" of psychiatry. The tendency to respond to stress with anxiety is the central aspect of the personality trait of *neuroticism*, which is distributed roughly normally in the population. The interest in anxiety in psychiatry tends to concentrate on episodes of relatively more intense anxiety, in which there does not seem to be a reasonable cause. These episodes can occur in the situation of a specific stimulus, such as a ride in an elevator or across a bridge, in which case they fit into one or another category of *specific phobia*. Table 2.7 shows estimates of prevalence and incidence for two important types of phobias: *social phobia*—about 2 percent lifetime prevalence—wherein an individual is unreasonably afraid of speaking or eating in front of other people and avoids that situation to a degree that is impairing; and *agoraphobia*—about 5 percent lifetime prevalence—in which the individual is unreasonably afraid to go outside or enter into any unpredictable situation where there might be sudden incapacitation and help needed. Agoraphobics sometimes curtail their life quite sharply to very predictable activities around or inside the house, going out only rarely and then with the accompaniment of someone they know and trust. Thus, phobias can be disabling if they lead to avoidance of the situation that provokes them, especially if that situation is common in the environment of the individual or if entrance into that situation is important to the individual's successful functioning in society. When intense anxiety arises quite suddenly, more or less without provocation or with a provocation that is difficult to discern, the diagnosis of *panic disorder*—about 1.5 percent lifetime prevalence—may be relevant. Panic disorder and agoraphobia are closely related, and the fourth edition of the DSM places them together in one category.

Complaints about the body that are rather nonspecific are quite common in the general population (Table 2.9). In the table, the complaint is registered as "unexplained" only if the respondent has stated that there was no apparent cause due to medication, drugs, alcohol, physical illness, or injury. Complaints like these are plausible psychiatric symptoms if there is no medical explanation. These complaints are not only prevalent but not trivial; for example, in Table 2.9 the complaint is recorded as positive only if the respondent stated that he or she talked to a doctor or other professional about it or took medication for it more than once or that it "interfered with your life or activities a lot." The complaints are listed in their order of descending lifetime prevalence. Complaints and behaviors attributed by psychiatrists to depression (Table 2.8), anxiety, or somatoform disorder (Table 2.9) are common in the population of the practice of general medicine, as well as psychiatry (Goldberg 1995; Goldberg and Huxley 1980).

Table 2.9
Prevalence of Unexplained Somatoform Complaints (Epidemiologic Catchment Area Program—Sites 2–5)

Complaint or Behavior	Point Prevalence	Lifetime Prevalence
Joint pain	8.1	14.4
Headache	4.5	12.3
Back pain	4.1	11.5
Chest pain	2.6	10.3
Belly pain	2.0	9.6
Dizziness	2.3	9.6
Gas	3.9	8.7
Pain in arm or leg	4.0	8.6
Heart beating hard	1.9	8.4
Shortness of breath	2.4	6.2
Nausea	1.6	5.7
Diarrhea	1.2	4.8
Weakness	1.8	4.3
Food allergy	1.4	3.0

$N = 13,537$.

Source: Estimated by the author.

The most common complaint in the general population is that of generalized distress or demoralization. *Distress* is the term used for the reaction to a stressful situation, as described in the next chapter. *Demoralization* is the term used by Jerome Frank (1974) to describe the way people feel when they seek psychiatric treatment of any sort. In an insightful review, Link and Dohrenwend (1980) showed that virtually all measures of psychiatric "caseness" in the second generation of psychiatric epidemiology were measuring this one construct of feeling unable to cope with the current situation. Therefore, the terms "distress" and "demoralization" are used equivalently. The most useful measure of this concept is the General Health Questionnaire (GHQ) designed by David Goldberg (Goldberg 1972, 1978). It measures adjustment to the current circumstances, relative to the "normal" way of functioning, in the time frame of the "last few weeks." Several of the items are:

Have you been taking things hard?

Have you been able to face up to your problems?

Have you found everything getting too much for you?

Have you been feeling unhappy and depressed?

Have you been losing confidence in yourself?

Figure 2.8
Distribution of Distress/Demoralization (Baltimore ECA Cohort—1981)

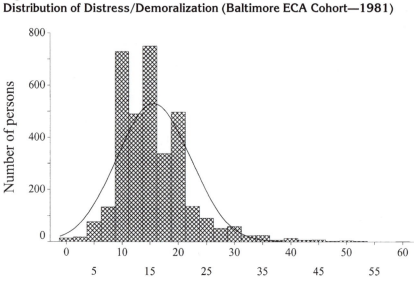

GHQ20 Score

Distress/demoralization is measured well by the General Health Questionnaire. It is distributed with wide variation in the population.

The response choices for each question are:

0   More than usual
1   Same as usual
2   Less than usual
3   Much less than usual

The original version of the GHQ included 60 items that formed a single homogeneous scale, but the scale could be reduced to 20 items without compromising its reliability. The GHQ has been validated in many ways and is widely used around the world. It is strongly related to the diagnosis of psychiatric disorder in samples from primary health care settings.

The distribution of scores for the 20-item GHQ is shown in Figure 2.8. An important quality of the GHQ score for the purpose of this discussion is its near normal distribution, which contrasts markedly with other measures in the field of psychiatric epidemiology. The mean score in this sample of Baltimore is 15. Although the force of morbidity for many disorders changes markedly over the life course, the mean value of the GHQ is virtually unchanged over the entire span of adult life. At first glance this lack of change is puzzling because so many physical illnesses appear later in life that require adaptations of various sorts—that is, the GHQ score should be higher in older people. The logic would appear to be in the nature of the wording of the response choices "more than usual, . . . less than usual," and "over the last few weeks." The GHQ is strongly associated with mental disorders because these disorders are usually episodic, being caused by environmental circumstances of a relatively short duration (as considered in the next chapter) or requiring adaptation of a temporary sort in many cases. It is invariant over the life span because human beings tend to adapt to their circumstances over a period of time greater than "over the last few weeks." The GHQ is not strongly related to schizophrenia or antisocial personality disorder, for example, because these conditions tend to be chronic, and individuals adapt to them. The notions of homeostasis and adaptation are crucial to the concept of stress, considered in the next chapter.

3

Role, Identity, Suggestibility, and Stress

INTRODUCTION

This chapter presents a social psychological framework for understanding the relationship of the individual to the surrounding group. It might be termed "microsociology" or social psychology, but the focus is more limited than the focus of those terms. The first section of the chapter concerns two related theories in the area of social psychology: role theory and identity theory. A second section considers the notion of suggestibility in the context of these theories, and a third section deals with stress.

ROLE AND IDENTITY

Befitting its place at the juncture of the individual and society, role theory has been developed by both psychologists and sociologists. The best source on the subject by psychologists is work by T. R. Sarbin and colleagues, such as his and Allen's chapter on "Role Theory" in the *Handbook of Social Psychology* (Sarbin and Allen 1968): work by sociologists has been within the so-called symbolic interactionist school of sociology, beginning with George Herbert Mead (1934) and continuing with Sheldon Stryker (1968), among others (Gross et al. 1957; Hewitt 1991; Linton 1956). Suggestibility and stress are two very general, social psychological conditions that can lead to mental disorders. Suggestibility reflects on the subjects of role modeling, hypnosis, hysteria, and labeling and recurs later in this volume at least once as a possible etiologic mediator in chapters on social integration, mass movements, organization, stratification, and modern urban society. The section on stress includes discussions of animal and experimental models of stress as well as naturally occurring stress situations that can produce mental disorders in humans. Stress is a mediator for macrosocial conditions, and the notion also recurs in all of the following chapters.

Roles and the Individual

Role theory deals with the problem of the guidance of behavior by the individual. How does one know what to do in any given situation (Figure 1.1)? Human beings retain clusters or patterns of behavior in their memory that provide guidance. One problem is to judge when to apply which pattern, and the notion of the role helps in that problem-solving process. A *role* is a cluster of behaviors associated with a position in the social structure. The behaviors are expected or normative in the culture. For example, the role of "mother" involves expectations about caring for a baby; the role of "left fielder" entails expectations about fielding fly balls; and so on. Every role has an *audience*, which is a person or group before whom the role is acted out. The audience is the complement to the role and is itself an integral part of the role: it is difficult or impossible to conceive of a given role without simultaneously conceiving of the audience—for example, the mother role entails the idea of the child, and the left fielder role entails the conception of other members of the baseball team. The idea that roles are expectations that are common to the culture links the individual to the larger group via his or her mental apparatus; the concept of role audience links the individual to the group via the more interactional social network.

Role performance (or role enactment) is the set of behaviors that the individual actually engages in while operating in the role, in the context of the role audience, and that others are likely to perceive as originating in the role. As the individual engages in behavior, she or he continuously monitors performance, comparing it to the standard stored in memory. This continuing conceptual activity is termed the *identity process* or *conceiving the self* (Burke 1991; Rosenberg 1986). Role performances vary in the degree to which they match the standard, and a valuation is attached to each role performance. In assessing performance, the individual uses information from other individuals in the social field, and in many cases these individuals are role audiences or are otherwise positioned in the social structure so that they may be thought of as "natural raters" for performance—for example, a job supervisor is a natural rater for the occupational role, and a wife is the natural rater for the husband role (Kellam, 1970). Consistent with the general approach to social life described in Chapters 1 and 2, it is useful to consider these valuations as falling on two dimensions related to stratification and integration. Each role performance, then, generates valuation or satisfaction with respect to power over others and with respect to affection received from them. Some roles generate high valuations on the power dimension, such as the role of executive; but these same roles may be very weak on the affiliation dimension. Other roles, such as that of "aunt," may be stronger on the affiliation dimension and not generate much power.

Roles differ in the energy required to enact them, and *role involvement* is the energy and intensity of the role performance. High involvement brings the entire attention and capacity of the individual to the role, as in an athletic contest, for example. High involvement is usually temporary because it is fatiguing. Role performances of high involvement have the capacity to interfere with other roles, and typically there is disengagement from other roles when involvement is high.

Roles differ in the degree to which they are *chosen versus assigned*. Some roles, such as gender and ethnic group, are assigned at birth and difficult to change. Other roles involve a single threshold of performance, decision, or activity to be entered, such as the role of "mother." Yet other roles involve a constant level of performance, such as the role of "ethical human being."

Some roles are conspicuous, well understood, and agreed upon, so that an individual and his or her audience have little doubt about the origin of the behavior—for example, they understand that the individual is catching the fly ball because he or she is a left fielder on a baseball team. But some roles that guide behavior are not accessible to the individual performing the role enactment, and the behaviors seem unmotivated, bizarre, and alien to the individual. The parallel in Freudian theory is the unconscious, which motivates bizarre behavior according to tenets of psychoanalysis. In the area of information-processing psychology, the notion of *parallel processing* allows for behaviors to occur that are not always understood or where the motivation for the behavior is not verbalizable by the individual (Power and Brewin 1992).

Roles can differ in the specificity of the context that calls them into play and the behaviors that they prescribe. In many situations the role has a convenient label and obvious role audience and examples that are relatively easy to define; but roles exist that are much more difficult to identify and characterize. For example, the roles "friend" and "ethical human being" have a wide variety of expectations associated with them that are idiosyncratic to the individual and the situation. The "mother" role is quite general, too; but the "left fielder" role is more specific. Some roles are so ubiquitous in human culture that they could possibly link to inherited predispositions to learn and retain a given pattern of behavior—that is, an *archetype* (Gilbert 1992). George Herbert Mead, even before the notion of role was well known, described three different types of learning that fit into the concept of role and display the possibilities for different levels of abstractness (Mead 1934). The first type involved simple *imitation* of behaviors by others, which even very small children do. Even the simplest imitation of a gesture, with almost no pattern of related meanings or evaluations and no association with a given social context, is the basic building block for a role. The second stage is what Mead would call *play*—learning to engage in a patterned series of behaviors, often with a position label and a social context (e.g., "doctor," "nurse," "mother," and so on; i.e., a role). Play usually involves an uncomplicated role with a simple role audience, that is, a dyad. The third stage involves the integration of several roles so that a *game* is formed, for example, fitting together the roles of mother, father, and child into a family or fitting together the various roles on a baseball team. In this situation the individual views himself or herself in relation to all the other roles and role actors, and Mead calls this conglomerate of persons *the generalized other*. In fitting the roles together, abstract and general roles like "friend" must be integrated and coordinated with more specific roles like "left fielder;" or consider the simultaneous engagement in the two roles of "ethical human being" and "lawyer." This discussion leads to the important conclusion that, at any given time, an individual is engaging in several roles simultaneously. Furthermore, roles are retained in memory that are not currently being enacted.

The Three-Dimensional Model of Social Identity

Each individual engages in many roles, and concepts are needed to describe this multiplicity. If we ask someone to answer the question, Who am I?, he or she will generate a list of roles such as "spouse," "secretary," "mother," and so forth. The *social identity* of the individual is the total of all the roles in which she or he engages. The social identity is the major link between the psychological, social psychological, and sociological study of the individual and society. The social identity of an individual identifies a social network for that person, that is, "the interpersonal linkages among a set of individuals" (Mueller 1980). The social identity of different individuals varies considerably in its size—most individuals in the general population have a network of about 25 to 40 people, among whom about 6 to 10 are known intimately (Hammer 1963). Networks in different cultures and subcultures differ in size and shape, and networks of certain types of individuals (e.g., psychotics versus executives) are very different also. The social identity consists of thousands or even millions of roles—in effect, the entire memory store of the individual as regards behaving in social situations is the social identity. The social identity includes the history of the individual's role performances and the expectation of future role performances.

It is helpful to think of the social identity as occupying a space, as shown in Figure 3.1 (adapted from Scheibe 1995: Figure 4.3). The dimensions of the social identity are the assignment/choice dimension (from front left to back right), the role valuation dimension (from top to bottom), and the role involvement dimension (from back left to front right).

Roles differ as to their importance to the individual. Rosenberg (1986) used the concept of *psychological centrality* to describe this quality, and this concept fits roughly with the evaluation attached to the role performance over an extended period of time. Figure 3.2 shows hypothetical ordinal rankings of psychological centrality of seven roles for three different types of social identities among women, as described later. Rankings such as those shown in Figure 3.2 can be determined empirically, from a survey, for example (Thoits 1992). Intimate and face-to-face relations are generally considered more central, whereas roles involving only acquaintances through work or professional associations tend to be less central; but these valuations depend on which of the two basic

Figure 3.1
Three-Dimensional Model of Social Identity

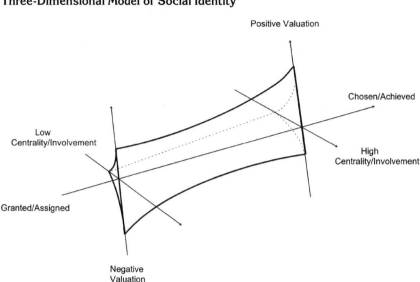

Positive Valuation

Chosen/Achieved

Low
Centrality/Involvement

High
Centrality/Involvement

Granted/Assigned

Negative
Valuation

The potential for valuation and involvement differs for roles at the achieved versus ascribed end. Each individual will have a different shape, but each identity can be usefully characterized by three dimensions.

Source: Redrawn from Scheibe (1995: Figure 4.3).

social dimensions of power or affiliation (Figure 1.6) is more heavily involved. In order to facilitate understanding of the social identity, comparisons of social identities between individuals, and changes in the social identity in a single individual, Figure 3.2 considers only seven roles that might often be central for a variety of individuals: roles in sports, hobbies, occupational role, parental role, and roles as spouse, sib, and daughter. The strength of the affiliation/solidarity valuation is cross-hatched in the figure and at the lower part of the role; the strength of the power/status valuation is clear and on the top part of the role. The overall size of the identity based on these seven roles can vary, so that the total area enclosed by the multiplex identity, for example, is larger than either the homemaker or careerist identity. The proportion of valuations from the affection/solidarity dimension is distinctly different for the homemaker, heavily involved with family roles, versus the careerist, intensely involved with occupational roles and also involved in athletics. Neither of these three identities is morally better than any of the other, but the shape of the social identity will have emotional consequences for the individual and presumably affect the intersection of her life with the social structure.

Stryker (1968) preferred the term *salience* instead of centrality, which he defined as the probability that the individual will actually engage in a particular

Figure 3.2
Positive Valuation for Three Ideal-Typical Social Identities

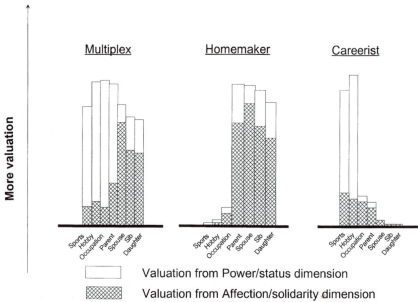

The total size of the positive valuations will vary between individuals, as will the absolute and proportional amounts of valuations from the power and affection dimensions. These variations will interact with the ongoing social context to produce emotional fluctuations.

role at any given time. These terms are not contradictory (Stryker and Serpe 1994) but actually different perspectives on the same process, with the difference being the temporal orientation. Psychological centrality incorporates the sense of biography into the identity process, that is, selecting, weighing, and prioritizing all the roles the individual has engaged in and anticipates engaging in for the future. This involves higher cortical processes involving the frontal lobe of the brain—so-called *executive function* (Lyon and Krasnegor 1996). Consideration of whether to take a new job, to marry a certain person, to join a club, and career planning in general involves this process, as do many of the conscious, judicious decisions individuals make in planning their lives. Psychological centrality is highly related to time spent in the role over an extended period of time. It is close to George Herbert Mead's (1934) notion of the *me*—that is, the conscious, reflecting self as object. Salience has to do with the choice of a role in the immediate present, which is closer to Mead's notion of the *I*—that is, the immediate self as actor. A careful comparison of the long-term valuations associated with various roles may take place when psychological centrality is being assessed, as might happen in responding to questions in a survey about the "importance" of roles (Thoits 1986). Salience is more likely to be affected by short-term factors in the current social context, which may temporarily emphasize or distract from certain roles, while directing focus to others. Salience is highly affected by processes of sustained attention and suggestibility, and the choice of the role may emerge from temporary dominance of lower cortical or noncortical processes that are not verbalizable and that seem bizarre, as discussed later.

The fact that each individual engages in a complex set of roles brings the problem of *role conflict*. *Inter-role conflict* involves two or more roles that have contradictory expectations associated with them, such as the role of "homemaker" and "career woman." Each of these roles demands large blocks of time and considerable personal involvement. *Intrarole* conflict occurs when the role audience is not homogeneous in its expectations, such as might occur in the role of "mother" to two children, who have different expectations about the role. Role conflict is associated with a drop in self-esteem, because at least one of the role enactments is likely to suffer. There are varying solutions to this problem: people can isolate the two roles (or role audiences), for example, so that there is no overlap between role enactments; they can withdraw from one or more of the roles that are in conflict; or they can change the audience's definition of the role so that their own enactment will be satisfactory.

Social identities can be quite varied in their shape. There are individuals with narrowly circumscribed identities of only a few roles, with self-esteem coming from only a few sources. Some individuals have identities with large, positive evaluations on the power dimension, whereas others have large foundations of self-esteem on the affiliation dimension. In Figure 3.2, the identity on the right is one whose valuations are almost entirely limited to occupational activities and dominated by the power dimension. The center individual is a homemaker whose social identity is largely determined by her family network, and the valuations are largely from affiliative aspects. Individuals with many roles and large social networks have been described as *multiplex identities* (Thoits 1983), in which the sources of self-esteem are spread throughout a large number of roles (identity on the left in Figure 3.2). The social identities of these different individuals are differentially subject to changes in the social structure.

How is it that individuals behave consistently over time? Why do they tend to have the same types of responses to varied situations? An intuitive answer is that individuals have personalities that define them as individuals and that their behavior expresses basic personality traits. A *personality trait* is a disposition to behave in a given fashion that is persistent over time and consistent across situations. The study of personality traits has traditionally formed an important part of the discipline of psychology (Gleitman 1981: Chapter 16). The stability and consistency of personality traits suggest that they are inherited or formed through early socialization experiences. A large body of research suggests that five basic traits explain much of the individual differences in personality in cultures using the English language (Norman 1963). The so-called *big five* are neuroticism, extraversion, openness to experience, agreeableness, and conscientiousness (Costa and McCrae 1992). The field of personality was criticized because the logic seemed circular, the traits as measured had low stability over time, and situational determinants seemed to be more important predictors of behavior than the traits (Mischel 1968). Later research has shown well-measured traits to have strong temporal consistency (Costa and McCrae 1988). The problem of predicting behavior in different situations has not been solved through personality measurement: in many situations, simply knowing the role the individual is enacting is far superior in predicting behavior than is understanding her or his personality.

The social identity provides an explanation for the relative stability and predictability of individuals' behavior throughout life, because it has a temporal dimension to it. Involvement in ongoing experience, which necessitates linking the past to the present and future, in the manner of a story, forms the basis for extracting meaning from the flow of events, and the meanings provide the basis for the feeling of the continuity of identity across time, that is, the *me*. Thus, the individual evaluates role enactments of the past and anticipates the evaluation of role enactments in the future in forming the sum total of evaluations about the social identity. Identity is thus linked to history of experience and the potential for action (Baumeister 1986). Solomon Asch (1952) has expressed the temporal aspects of self-consciousness as follows:

In the most highly developed anthropoids action and feeling are dictated almost exclusively by the immediate situation, with only the dimmest and most momentary premonition of a past and a future. . . . How utterly different is the situation with man! Living in a field that is not dominated by the immediate moment, his experiences acquire a new texture and enter into new organizations. He is able to encompass events and relationships that are inaccessible to other living creatures. . . . Because [humans] can look forward and backward and perceive causal relations, because they can anticipate the consequences of their actions in the future and view their relation to the past, their immediate needs exist in a field of other needs, present and future. Because they consciously relate the past with the future they are capable of representing their goals to themselves, to aspire to fulfill them, to test them in imagination, and to plan their steps with a purpose. (121)

This notion of identity is what is implied in the term *sense of biography*—that is, the comprehension of one's continuing existence in the social world.

There is a controversy in the field of social psychology as to whether individuals perform role-prescribed behaviors because they have selected roles agreeable to their basic personalities or because they have learned the role extremely well. Are insurance salespersons inherently aggressive people who have chosen a profession in line with their innate tendencies, or do they learn to be aggressive because they have ended up as insurance salespersons? Data support both alternatives (Borgatta 1961). Individuals choose roles that fit well with their social identities and personalities, but the same individuals will behave quite differently in different roles. The role theoretical explanation for stability of behavior through time is that the social identity guides experience through repeated selection from a repertoire of roles that have a historical constancy to them, that is, a sense of biography.

The Transformation of Social Identity

In the study of bizarre behaviors, changes in social identity as time passes are important. People gain and lose roles throughout their lives as they take new positions in the social structure and give up old ones. An early general term for this process was *status passage*, but later role theorists have used *transformation of social identity* to describe it (Sarbin 1968). In all cultures, important status passages are surrounded with ceremony and social gatherings of various sorts; for example, the passage from status of child to that of adult is recognized ritually in many so-called primitive cultures, and in our own culture, school graduations and marriage ceremonies are examples of ceremonies of status passage. As discussed later, unritualized or uncontrolled situations of status passage are much more likely than everyday life to involve bizarre behaviors. It seems fair to assume that the ceremonies of status passage are an implicit recognition of, and attempt to control, potential social instabilities that might arise—to guide the individual into the proper role, to introduce him or her to the appropriate role audience, to solidify their mutual bonds, and to remove permanently the former role or roles from the social identity.

Lower self-esteem or demoralization can result from failure in everyday roles or unexpected entry into demanding or unlearned roles. An individual will select roles that can be performed adequately and back out of roles in which there is failure in order to maintain an acceptable level of self-esteem. Each role is part of the social identity and participates in the process by which self-esteem is evaluated on a relatively continuous basis, even though only one or a few roles are enacted at any given time. Evaluation of a given performance is balanced against past and anticipated performances in that role and in other roles, so that the level of self-esteem is temporally fairly stable. Where self-esteem is low, there may be attempts to change the social identity (Kiecolt 1994).

An important aspect of the transformation of social identity is *role gain*, the process by which new roles are added to the social identity. Role gain involves selection of new roles by the individual before entry into the role or involuntary or inadvertent entry in the role, as well as maintaining the role after entry. Role gain necessitates learning about the role, which is not always a simple process. The basis for the learning of roles is the innate ability of humans to imitate others, and it is evident even in tiny infants, who imitate gestures of their parents before learning to talk. Role learning is a more complex cognitive task than bald imitation, however, because one has to learn not only the behavior itself, such as a given gesture, but also the situation to which the behavior belongs and the fit of the individual in that situation (Mead 1934). A child often learns a pattern of behaviors for a given role before he learns where the role belongs and whether he belongs in it. A two-year-old boy may learn mothering behaviors such as bathing or rocking a doll before he learns to whom they should be applied (his own baby brother or sister). But his parents may consider them slightly inappropriate for a male, and he may not learn that for several years.

A concrete example of role learning is Howard Becker's research on becoming a marijuana smoker (Becker 1967). The learning process even for this very specific role is complex and involves all three levels of imitation, play, and the game. Simple imitation is involved in learning the technique of smoking: the proper way to handle the marijuana, the proper way to inhale it, and so forth. The role also involves perceiving the effects of marijuana, learning to enjoy them, and understanding the borders of the role, that is, learning the entire pattern of behaviors and feelings associated with the role and where it stops and other roles begin (the play stage). Finally, learning the role of the marijuana smoker involves strategies of *role linkage*, that is, combining the role with other roles and hiding and isolating the role when necessary (the game stage). Roles tend to have emotional components associated with them; that is, they are valued, feared, disliked, enjoyed, and so forth.

Some roles are more difficult and complex to learn than others. A given role on an assembly line in a factory may be easily and quickly learned. On the other hand, learning sex roles is a complex and enduring task lasting many years. It appears that roles are learned more quickly and become more enduring parts of the social identity when the individual strongly identifies with a *role model* (Bandura 1977). A role model is someone enacting a role appropriate for the individual, who can observe the model easily. For simple roles direct imitation is all that is needed to engage in the role. An advantage of learning via a model is that the model can be observed selecting the role, that is, guiding the individual as to when it is appropriate.

Several characteristics of the relationship of the individual with the role model affect his or her willingness to enter into the role and involvement in it. The most important factor is his identification with the role model or, to put it another way, the strength of the affective bond with the role model. An intense positive bond, such as that between parents and children, is accompanied invariably by some effects of role modeling that can endure a lifetime. Another important characteristic is the similarity of the individual to the role model. Over the long run, a boy is more likely to emulate his father than his mother because he understands that many of the role behaviors are more appropriate for his own sex. Any similarity to other observable characteristics (e.g., age, race, religion, level of education, overall belief structure, and so forth) generates more role modeling, other things being equal. Finally, the prestige of the role model increases the probability that the role is entered into and that the behavior is imitated. These factors of identification, similarity, and prestige are among many that have been verified in the study of persuasive communications, a subfield in social psychology from which one can draw many relevant observations, even if this field did not use role theory as a framework for analysis.

Another important aspect of status passage is *role loss*, where roles are stripped from the social identity. Role loss is often a painful experience, especially if it is unexpected. The death of a close relative or friend or the loss of a friend through a fight, disinterest, or disfavor are examples of role loss that can be painful. A good study of the social psychology of role loss is Erving Goffman's (1962) study of confidence men. In this essay Goffman describes the process by which confidence men identify an individual they wish to defraud in some way (the "mark"). They then involve the mark in a seemingly reasonable role that leads, at some point, to the transfer of money. *Cooling the mark out* is the process by which the role is terminated in the most believable and least painful way, so that the mark is least likely to cause trouble.

Changes in the social identity over time are difficult to study because the salience and centrality of roles are difficult to assess, but centrality in particular is very important in predicting consequences of the change. Roles are linked together in clusters that are idiosyncratic. For example, an individual's network of close friends may be entirely outside the circle of acquaintances at work, so that the work role is not as central as it would be if the friendship and work networks were nested together. This might be the situation of the multiplex identity in Figure 3.2. Getting laid off has different implications for the two situations. Similarly, the spouse role can be highly involved with a friendship network, as in an extended family, or the friendship network can be entirely independent of the family; implications of separation, divorce, or widowhood are different for the homemaker versus multiplex identities. Compare also the effect of loss of a job on the two identities of homemaker versus career woman. The proportional effect is bound to be larger for the career woman.

In summary of this section, the social identity is best understood as a process of conceptualizing one's expected behavior in relation to other people. The process is a mental one, in the mind of the individual, but it involves concepts— histories, plans, anticipations—of social interaction.

SUGGESTIBILITY AND MENTAL DISORDERS
Acquisition of Bizarre Roles

A certain social psychological situation collects together many of the behaviors we tend to label as bizarre. The situation occurs where a single salient or central role conflicts with the remainder of the social identity (Sarbin and Allen 1968). It is especially dramatic when the role is subtle, unstated, or difficult to verbalize. This type of role conflict forms much of our social drama; a good example is the abdication of Edward VIII of England, who decided he preferred a single central role of high affiliative evaluation (lover–husband) to the remainder of his social identity, involving many roles of enormous power and rank, as king of England. Edward VIII made a conscious and careful decision and could verbalize the logic of his choice, which involved the psychological centrality of the lover-husband role. This situation comes to be defined as bizarre when the role performance is highly involved, and the role is not accessible to the individual, so that an explanation cannot be provided. In the following paragraphs this situation is described explicitly, several examples are given, and then conditions that may facilitate entry into such a situation are described. The examples given are the roles of urban guerilla, experimental subject, hypnotic subject, and voodoo death.

In the early 1970s Patty Hearst, the teenage daughter of a wealthy publishing magnate, was kidnapped by a small, urban, guerrilla group known as the Symbionese Liberation Army (SLA). In an almost unbelievable chain of events, she was held captive for more than one year, during which time the SLA engaged in several armed robberies (Hearst 1982). In the beginning of her captivity she was isolated and tightly guarded, but she increasingly became involved in SLA activities, seemingly of her own free will—making tape recordings denouncing her father, participating in armed holdups, and not trying to escape. Eventually, she was captured and convicted of her participation in robberies, even though she renounced the SLA. There was considerable public disagreement over her motives and, therefore, her culpability. The point of interest here is the time of her capture, when she was filling out police department forms and was asked to supply her occupation. She responded by writing in "urban guerrilla." This *role of urban guerrilla* is a central role with a high degree of choice and high involvement but questionable or even negative valuation. It conflicted with her social identity because it contributed to her image as a willing participant in illegal activities and destroyed her chances for defense on the basis that she had been forced to participate. One can only guess that she has even now only a vague notion of why she wrote "urban guerrilla" in the police registry.

A second example is the *role of the experimental subject*. For this role two bizarre behaviors that have been associated with the role in certain circumstances are examined: attempted murder as observed in the work of Stanley Milgram (Milgram 1965) and attempted suicide as described by Martin Orne (Orne 1959). Milgram was interested in discovering the highest degree of obedience he could extract from an experimental subject, so he invented an onerous, but believable, task: administering electric shock to a second learning subject in a learning experiment to "negatively reinforce" him or her upon failing to supply the correct answer. The "teacher" subject was instructed to increase the shock after each failure, well past a point where the dial reached a red zone marked "danger!" and up to a maximum of 450 volts. In some conditions the learning subject, who was strapped to a chair and unable to move, complained of the pain loudly, eventually responding to the shocks with only grunts and groans and for the final few shocks with silence. There was even one condition where the learning subject was introduced along with the information that he had a weak heart. In this final condition, at the least, the situation can only be interpreted by the teaching subject administering the shock as being extremely harmful to the learner, if not fatal; thus, this behavior has been labeled, perhaps too dramatically, as "attempted murder." Whether the label fits or not, the reader will agree that the behavior is certainly *bizarre*. Many of the subjects showed signs of extreme nervousness and resisted completing the experiment, but they were told by a scientist in a white coat, "The experiment must go on"; in most conditions, a majority of subjects pushed a lever administering the maximum 450-volt shock to an apparently unconscious man. Once the experiment was completed, the subject was introduced to the learner, who had, in reality, been a confederate and had not been receiving shocks.

Another example of bizarre behavior resulting from the role of experimental subject is by Martin Orne (1959), which was designed to compare the role of the experimental subject with that of the hypnotic subject. He was unable to show any behavioral difference between two roles, but, in the present schema, the role of hypnotic subject (discussed later) is at a lower level of accessibility. The subjects began, as in the Milgram research, simply by volunteering to participate in a psychology experiment. There is a series of experiments involving subjects who were hypnotized, those who were instructed to pretend they were hypnotized, and some who were just given a series of directions. In the most dramatic experiment, Orne gave a similar set of directions to hypnotized and nonhypnotized subjects. The directions were to perform behaviors that were technically easy to execute, but increasingly unpleasant and dangerous. In the last set of behaviors subjects were instructed to reach into a wooden box to pick up objects and animals. The second-to-last instruction was to reach into the box to pick up a live (harmless) lizard. After the lizard was removed, a live rattlesnake was introduced into the box, and an invisible glass partition was slid into place. The subjects were asked to pick up the snake, and 50 percent of each group rapped their knuckles on the glass partition while attempting to pick up the rattlesnake!

These two situations—the kidnapping of Patty Hearst and the role of the experimental subject—have been classified as roles of high salience. The word *salience* is used instead of *centrality* because the individual's choice of the given role performance had a temporary quality to it, generated by the immediate social context and recent experience in the role. The decision to sign the police register as "urban guerrilla," to administer the shock, or to pick up the snake might not have been taken if there had been thoughtful consideration of the history of the individual's social identity and the potential for future actions. The immediate situation distracted the individual from other roles. In each of these bizarre cases, however, performance of the role threatened or destroyed important other aspects of the social identity. In each case the individual could only partially verbalize a logical explanation for the bizarre behavior (e.g., "I was kidnapped and afraid," "I was a subject in an experiment and the guy told me to do it"). In the situations discussed later, hypnosis and voodoo death, the subject is generally unable to verbalize a reason, cause, or motivation for his or her behavior. In addition, there is high involvement in the role performance, which adds to the appearance of bizarreness.

The modern study of *hypnosis* is about 200 years old, beginning with Mesmer's work in France and many others throughout Europe (Ellenberger 1970). They discovered that a certain social psychological situation could be created that could have bizarre effects on some people. First, a volunteer subject agreed to place himself or herself under the mesmerist's influence. Second, the mesmerist would gradually shift the subject's attention away from normal roles and everyday matters and concentrate his or her attention solely on the passive role relationship with himself. Finally, the mesmerist would ask the subject to perform certain behaviors to demonstrate the power of the trance. Toward the end of a given session, these behaviors might be bizarre and specific: crowing like a rooster, imitating a dog walking on all fours, withstanding extreme pain, demonstrating feats of strength or agility seemingly impossible in everyday life, instantly falling asleep or waking up, and so forth. These behaviors were so dramatic that the original mesmerists thought that they were due to the influence of an invisible electromagnetic fluid surrounding the body that came under the control of the mesmerist during the trance.

In the nineteenth century the study of hypnosis was linked to the beginning of the study of abnormal psychology. At that time the disorder called hysteria was thought to be more prevalent than today, and investigators were interested in the connection with hysteria and hypnosis. The name *hysteria* was applied to a disorder that was thought to originate in the uterus and, therefore, common only in females. The symptoms were thought to be of two types; *dissociative* hysteria included various types of trance and fugue states, such as amnesia, sleepwalking, and multiple personality, and an exhibitionist or overly dramatic personality; in *conversion* hysteria the symptoms were physical in nature, ranging from autonomic nervous system paralysis to uncontrollable fainting, vomiting, coughing, and headaches. Today the conversion symptoms of hysteria are grouped in the area of somatoform disorder, and the symptoms of dissociative hysteria are grouped in the "dramatic" cluster of personality disorders (American Psychiatric Association 1994).

Hysteria in the nineteenth century bore a strong relationship to hypnosis (Ellenberger 1970). In the famous case of Sally Beauchamp, the condition of multiple personality began during a hypnotic trance, and there are other examples of the close relationship of dissociative hysteria with hypnosis. In the case of conversion hysteria, Charcot demonstrated that symptoms could be precipitated in the hypnotic trance, and Charcot and Bernheim demonstrated that hysteria could often be cured through hypnosis. For the moment, further discussion of hysteria is postponed to Chapter 6 on collective behavior. Here we stress the importance of the connection between hysteria, hypnosis, and role playing.

In the last half of the twentieth century there have been dramatic advances in understanding hypnosis (Hilgard 1977; Sarbin and Coe 1972). A standardized method for inducing the hypnotic state has been developed, and it has excellent test-retest reliability. The trait of hypnotic susceptibility has stability (correlation of 0.60) over more than 10 years, as high as the most stable personality traits (Morgan et al. 1974), and there is evidence it is moderately heritable (Morgan 1973). There is still disagreement as to whether hypnosis is a special state of consciousness (Hilgard 1977). There are slight differences between hypnosis and other rule-following or role-playing situations; for example, rule-following subjects and hypnotic subjects tolerate severe pain equally well (much better than persons in everyday situations), but the physiological response of the hypnotic subject is much less dramatic. Another distinction is that posthypnotic suggestion and amnesia seem to be possible only in the hypnotic situation.

How does hypnosis work? It appears to be a combination of concentration of attention with two very strong human impulses: to imitate and to plan. Imitation is a facility even very young infants possess, and the internal symbolic representation of another's gesture is enough to stimulate the imitative impulse. The classic, commonplace example of the imitative impulse at work is the after-dinner yawn. William James described a similar idea in his discussion of the ideomotor control of action: "Every representation of a movement awakens in some degree the actual movement which is its object; and awakens it in a maximum degree whenever it is not kept from so doing by an antagonistic representation present simultaneously to the mind" (1890, II: 526, from Hilgard 1977). Imitation is not always conscious, as occurs in "body English" among those watching an athletic contest. In hypnosis the planning function is taken over by the role induced by the hypnotist (Miller et al. 1960; Sarbin and Allen 1968). In hypnosis, the attention is concentrated, and the brain's executive function, which might allow diversion of attention to other roles, is lost.

Hypnosis is almost indistinguishable from other role-playing situations, such as the role of experimental subject (Orne 1959). It is impossible for trained observers to differentiate between hypnotized subjects and those who are told to act "as if they were hypnotized" (to play the role of hypnotic subject). Orne found that naive subjects will listen for subtle cues as to how a hypnotic subject acts and then act those cues later during their hypnosis (enacting a behavior that had never been recorded as occurring during hypnosis, such as paralysis of the left arm, after hearing it read as part of a list of other "typical" symptoms prior to hypnotic induction); and that other rule-following situations not involving hypnosis produce equally bizarre behaviors, such as picking up poisonous snakes, withstanding severe pain, and so forth.

The final example of a bizarre, high involvement role is that of the *voodoo victim*. This role is discussed despite the fact that it is not as well documented as the previous ones, because it literally destroys the entire social identity by ending in death. It is extremely rare, but there are documented cases of individuals who have entered into a relationship with a voodoo god who condemns them to die for certain willful transgressions. In some cases death has occurred on schedule, with no known medical explanation (Cannon 1942).

The purpose of presenting these four examples of high role involvement (urban guerrilla, experimental subject, hypnotic subject, and voodoo victim) is twofold. First, it is to remind the reader that behaviors we cannot help but label "bizarre" occur in a wide variety of contexts not necessarily related to mental disorder, so that mental disorders themselves are not viewed inevitably as unique exceptions to everyday life. In this connection it should also be noted that, although these behaviors might casually be thought of as crazy, one does not customarily apply a medical interpretation to them; therefore, there is somewhat more flexibility in choosing an interpretive framework for bizarre behaviors allegedly caused by mental disease. The second purpose of presenting these examples is to draw out similarities in the various situations examined.

These situations of high role involvement possess four common characteristics. First, the role is isolated from the social identity, so as to minimize conflict with the other roles: Patty Hearst was held captive in a closet with only very rare and highly controlled opportunities to communicate with former friends (role audiences) or to perform formerly held roles; the roles of experimental and hypnotic subjects are always in highly controlled environments; for the voodoo victim there is not enough data to let us conclude that the subject is isolated from other roles, and one can only speculate that the situation is similar to the other three situations in this respect. Thus, these behaviors occur in the context of an *impoverished social identity*. In the three-dimensional model of social identity, impoverishment is literally an identity with small volume. The impoverishment of the social identity can be temporary but can also occur in less transient situations, such as occurs through widowhood, job loss, catastrophe to the family, the prisoner of war experience, and so forth. In the situation of impoverishment, the individual may seek the appearance of stability and predictability that a new role offers, even if it is an unusual one. In effect, the individual must know how to act and will seek some degree of predictability about the future—where only a limited role provides that predictability, it will be chosen.

Second, there is the *perception of voluntary* entry into the role. It is difficult to know, but at some point Patty Hearst presumably decided she belonged with her captors of her own free will; this moment may have been when she fell in love with one of her captors, called Cujo. Experimental and hypnotic subjects always agree to their role entry more or less formally. In the case of voodoo death, the subject perceives him- or herself as guilty of a transgression that brings forth voodoo sanctions.

Third, the *role audience is prestigious or powerful*. Hearst's captors were in absolute control of her life, and she clearly feared that they would kill her. In the case of the experimental and hypnotic subjects, the role audience has the power and prestige of the scientist. For the victim of voodoo, the priest is regarded as powerful. Thus, the role audience has characteristics known to be associated with role learning and successful persuasion.

Finally, when observed over time, the *role expectations are shaped* from vague, easy-to-perform, and normative tasks, to specific, deviant, and more difficult ones. The clearest example of this role shaping is in hypnosis. The subject is first asked whether she or he is willing to be hypnotized and then asked to relax and close the eyes, with the instructions gently repeated so that there is a period of some minutes before the next instruction is given; then the subject is instructed to fall asleep while listening to the hypnotist's voice; then told to raise the arm; then told that the arm will feel heavy, then light; then the subject is told to try to catch an imaginary fly, act like a dog, and so forth; until, at the end, the subject may be asked to withstand the pain of electric shock or very cold water or to pick up a poisonous snake.

All of these conditions have been studied, in one form or another, in the literature on persuasive communication or marketing. But they seem to result in bizarre behaviors only when applied simultaneously, and even then only infrequently. The question that is taken up in the next section concerns whether the bizarre behaviors called mental disorders tend to occur in these types of situations also. Considerable work has been done on this problem under the rubric of labeling theory.

Labeling Theory

The labeling approach in sociology began with the work of Edwin Lemert (1951) in his *Social Pathology*. He studied deviants of all types, such as criminals, alcoholics, blind persons, the mentally ill, and so on. The central contribution of that work is the distinction between primary and secondary deviation. *Primary deviation* is instigated by the individual, but *secondary deviation* is deviant behavior that is a defense against, or adaptation to, society's reaction to initial primary deviation. Thus, the same act of deviant behavior (say, an angry outburst by a blind person) is interpretable analytically in these two distinct ways. Since in this framework the deviant label is the clearest expression of society's reaction, this school of thought is variously called the "labeling" or the "societal reaction" school.

In the early 1960s labeling theory was applied systematically to the special case of mental disorders by Thomas Scheff (1963) in a classic article entitled "The Role of the Mentally III and the Dynamics of Mental Disorder." The gist of this work is that most of the behaviors we regard as mental disorders are examples of secondary deviation caused by labeling and societal reaction. His framework provides an alternative etiologic theory to the medical model of mental disorders. He presents nine postulates:

1. Residual deviance originates from fundamentally diverse sources.
2. Relative to the rate of treated mental illness, the rate of unrecorded residual deviance is extremely high.

3. Most residual deviance is denied and is transitory.

4. Stereotyped imagery of mental disorder is learned in early childhood.

5. The stereotypes of insanity are continually reaffirmed, inadvertently, in ordinary social interaction.

6. Labeled deviants may be rewarded for playing the stereotyped deviant roles.

7. Labeled deviants are punished when they attempt to return to conventional roles.

8. In the crisis occurring when a primary deviant is publicly labeled, the deviant is highly suggestible and may accept the proffered role of the insane as the only alternative.

9. Among residual deviants, labeling is the single most important cause of careers of residual deviance.

The most important new concept Scheff introduced was *residual deviance*, defined as deviance for which society provides no explicit label. The idea is that cultures have many unspoken norms for which there is no handy noun to label those who break them. Many of these norms concern minor vagaries of personal hygiene, such as not picking or scratching oneself on the nose or crotch during a face-to-face conversation. Another such norm is that extremely emotional behavior should be accompanied by a motivation that can be explained to others; yet another is that if an individual is interacting on a face-to-face level with others, he or she should maintain a minimum level of involvement, not drift off into daydreams, not carry on long monologues, and not fail occasionally to meet the other's gaze. There are countless other such norms. The word "residual" means that the range of behaviors included in residual deviance is extremely broad because it includes the breaking of all nonexplicit rules. The range of human behavior is of unbounded diversity, defying categorization except by such a residual category. The causes of residual deviance could run the gamut of biological and social events, including genes and physiological actions, stress, volitional acts of defiance, and temporary situations of high role involvement.

Scheff's second postulate is based on the idea that the rate of treated mental illness is very low compared to the rate of residual deviance. Population-based estimates of the rate of mental disorder in any given year are about 10–20 percent (Kessler et al. 1994; Myers et al. 1984), but only about 3 percent of the population visit some kind of psychiatric service, and another 5 percent see a primary care physician for emotional problems (Shapiro et al. 1984). Thus, more than half of those with diagnosable mental disorders do not get treatment for them, and since residual deviance is a much broader category than diagnosable mental disorders, the second postulate is taken as correct.

The idea that residual deviance is denied and transitory (third postulate) is well supported. Children are almost immune to imputations of mental illness when compared with adults; observers barely raise an eyebrow, for instance, if a child has an uncontrollable temper tantrum or an imaginary playmate, whereas these would probably be considered "symptoms" in an adult. Many transitory occurrences of bizarre deviance occur in adulthood, too, and are denied, forgotten, or ignored. Most people spend a good deal of effort to structure their perceptual field so that certain bizarre behaviors in themselves or in others are seen as normal. They invent preposterous explanations for the bizarre behaviors, arrange their schedules so they do not come into contact with the offending individual, deny that the behaviors have occurred, or just avoid attempting to explain them (Sampson et al. 1962).

One important question is the timing of the decision to discontinue the process of denial and begin to label the individual as crazy. The denial process will continue indefinitely in many cases as long as the bizarre behavior is not violent and is predictable enough to allow stable patterns of social interaction. In some cases people outside the individual's usual social group (e.g. neighbors or representatives of social agencies) notice the behavior and begin the labeling process. In other cases the behavior changes enough to disrupt the evolved stable pattern of interaction, precipitating a change in the reaction to it. In still other cases outside events occur that disrupt the social equilibrium and stimulate the labeling process; for example, a caring member of the individual's family may die or move away, or someone may retire or lose his or her job so as to be close to the individual for long periods of time (Sampson et al. 1962).

Denial and *labeling* are examples of the perceptual principle of assimilation and contrast. Denial of the bizarre behavior effectively assimilates the individual being perceived into the category of normal. When labeling finally does occur, the behavior is suddenly contrasted sharply to the normal and assimilated to the bizarre. In both cases the process of stereotyping is at work: in denial, bizarre behaviors are underestimated or ignored; in labeling, they are exaggerated. The value of the stereotyping process is a certain perceptual efficiency to avoid dealing with the uncertainty of individuals in marginal categories. One might speculate that this principle is stronger for bizarre behaviors than for the range of normal behaviors, because bizarre behaviors already entail a degree of uncertainty. Thus, it may be that stereotypes of the "normal" and the "insane" tend to be even less accurate than other types of stereotypes.

The fourth and fifth postulates concern the *role of the mentally ill*. The implication is that a relatively well defined role in our culture exists that most individuals are aware of. The mass media continuously contain references to behaviors expected of insane individuals. About 10 percent of modern films and the same percentage of modern television programs in the United States involve portrayals of mental illness (Ezzy 1993). There are humor magazines wholly devoted to themes of insanity, with explicit role models, such as Alfred E. Newman. Cartoons and comics use insanity as a basis for humor, too. News reports repeatedly explain bizarre, violent behaviors in broad terms, such as "insanity" or "crazy." Even positive references reveal the stereotype, such as the following: "Mrs. Jones, a former mental patient, was elected secretary-treasurer of the Abbot Garden Club." The implication is that it is unusual for former mental patients to be able to hold minor public offices.

The sixth and seventh postulates in Scheff's framework concern the shaping of role demands. Most of the evidence for these postulates is from psychiatric treatment institutions, especially mental hospitals. Patients in psychotherapy (especially analytic therapy) are sometimes rewarded for "displaying insight": discovering or admitting to an unconscious desire, need, or hostility, having a vivid dream, or remembering an incident of abuse. Displaying strong emotion is regarded sometimes as cathartic for a mental patient, whereas it might be considered bizarre for a person in the same circumstances without that label. Also, patients can get attention or manipulate others by bizarre behaviors that would not be acceptable in "normal" individuals. There is evidence that mental patients more or less consciously change their symptomatology when they know it will help them achieve some desired goal, such as gaining admission to, or discharge from, the hospital or transfer to a more desirable ward (Braginsky et al. 1966). Another common situation is the acceptance by individuals of their illness. In commitment hearings the judge sometimes tries to persuade the patient to enter the hospital voluntarily; even where commitment takes place, the judge may try to get the patient to admit to illness and the need for help, in the hope the patient will be less rebellious to the staff later on. Hospital staff find it easier to deal with patients who admit to being sick and reward those who have this "insight" into their "illness."

The shaping of the role of the mentally ill by this type of reward and punishment would be called *operant conditioning* in the psychology of learning theory. Punishment for returning to conventional roles is the other side of the shaping behavior. Rosenhan and his colleagues documented the experiences of normal persons who claimed to have heard voices in order to be admitted to mental hospitals (Rosenhan 1973). They found it impossible to interact with the hospital staff in a normal way—they would be ignored as if they did not exist, for example; or the staff would carry on a conversation without maintaining eye contact. In this instance, talking to staff as a normal, equal person was punished; approaching the staff as a mental patient was rewarded by more attention, concern, and success.

The eight postulate implies that the primary deviant is more suggestible because there is a crisis and because she or he has no alternative. A transformation has begun to impoverish the social identity. In the "crisis occurring when a primary deviant is publicly labeled," the conditions for role enactment of bizarre behavior, discussed earlier, are all met. Salience of other roles is quite low for a variety of reasons. Some friendships are likely to have been broken off before the public labeling ceremony, such as the commitment hearing or the entry into psychiatric treatment. Some researchers have called this process a *betrayal funnel*, whereby friends and relatives gradually switch over from the point of view of the primary deviant to the point of view of the institution (Goffman 1961). Others have called it *status degradation*, in which certain statuses are removed from the social identity (Garfinkel 1956). In any sort of process involving psychiatric diagnosis and treatment, major roles are threatened, if not eliminated:

the ability to hold a job is challenged, and the spouse may sue for divorce when the individual enters a mental hospital. Visibility of other roles may be low to the extent that the labeling process takes place away from the individual's normal surroundings. The role of audience in the labeling situation is prestigious and powerful. A psychiatrist is a physician—one of the most prestigious of all occupations. In a commitment hearing there are one or two psychiatrists as well as a judge and sometimes police and former friends, forming a powerful combination. Finally, there is the attempt to get the individual voluntarily to enter the role, and the role is shaped over time, as noted earlier.

In the ninth postulate labeling theory is contrasted deliberately with medical theories as to its explanatory power. Only one theory can provide the *most* important cause. This concise and articulate piece of work from the sociological perspective had broad implications for the understanding of mental disorders. Much resulting debate has pivoted around this article and, in particular, the final postulate.

The labeling approach stimulated many research studies in different areas and organized prior research in innovative ways. The effect was to shift the focus of research away from medical (and even social) etiologies toward the study of the treatment system itself as a possible cause of disorder. The admission process was scrutinized, and it was shown that commitment procedures were inadequate and cursory and that the committing psychiatrists often presumed illness without good evidence. Focusing on psychiatrists as agents of social control led to research on the civil liberties of mental patients and, ultimately, to important changes in the law. In all of these ways it was beneficial to approach the study of bizarre behaviors from a labeling viewpoint.

The most important research hypothesis suggested by labeling theory and confirmed by research evidence is that nonmedical contingencies have powerful effects on the treatment process. One or more studies have demonstrated, for example, that characteristics of the individual such as age, sex, ethnicity, social class, access to resources, and so forth affect the treatment process in important ways (Scheff 1964). Other factors, such as the characteristics of relatives, the type of neighborhood in which the bizarre behavior occurs, the characteristics of the treatment institutions, and many others, all sometimes affect the treatment process.

The basic tenets of labeling theory were challenged by Walter Gove (1970a), who cited studies that fail to show an effect of social factors on the treatment process and contrasted them to studies showing beneficial effects of treatment. The most important failure of the labeling theory was the inability to explain the origin of severe primary deviance, such as psychotic behavior. The theory rests too heavily on a dramatic single instance of labeling, where temporary primary deviance suddenly shifts to chronic secondary deviance. Scheff's two postulates concerning role shaping use evidence based on the treatment system, and the effects of labeling are supposed to take hold right at the moment of institutionalization. The problem is that bizarre behaviors often occur over protracted periods of time prior to the beginning of psychiatric treatment and the moment of labeling. For severe mental disorders, such as the psychoses, there is no explanation in labeling theory for the insidious onset.

After some controversy (Gove 1970b, 1975; Gove and Fain 1973; Gove and Howell 1974; Scheff 1975), a modification to labeling theory has evolved (Link et al. 1989, Link and Cullen 1990). The *modified labeling approach* stresses the importance of more subtle consequences of receiving a diagnosis more than its power to suggest behaviors in keeping with the role of the mentally ill. For example, both patients and community residents believe "most people" will reject a mental patient and endorse strategies to avoid rejection, such as keeping the diagnosis secret, withdrawing from others, or possibly educating them slowly about mental illness. These strategies can lead to lower self-esteem, lower earning power, and reduction of social networks; and these consequences may eventually contribute to increased vulnerability to new disorder or to repeat episodes of existing disorder. The effects of labeling on income were studied in a community sample of individuals whose psychiatric impairment was measured independently of whether they had been treated for psychiatric disorder and received an official diagnosis (i.e., been "labeled"). In an analysis that included both impairment and diagnosis, adjusted for education, the effects of the diagnosis were about as strong as the effects of the impairment (Link 1982). Later studies in community and treated populations showed that the effect of labeling was at least partly explained by the effects of the stigma of being a mental patient, which changed the expectations people had of themselves and their perceptions of other persons' reactions to them (Link 1987; Link and Cullen 1990; Link et al. 1991). In a study of severely mentally ill patients at a day treatment center, the effects of treatment were contrasted with the effects of stigma on the quality of life of the patients (Rosenfield 1997). Stigma had negative effects, as a labeling theorist would predict; and treatment had positive effects, as a psychiatrist would observe. Both these effects were mediated by self-esteem and mastery, consistent with the notion of the social identity discussed earlier.

The modified approach to labeling theory has taken it away from the notion of suggestibility, and toward its effects on quality of life and performance in the system of socioeconomic stratification—hence, it reappears later in Chapter 5. But the idea that conditions of suggestibility are involved in the etiology of mental disorders should not be abandoned. The labeling theory's invocation of suggestibility was in the context of ceremonies of status degradation that, at that time in the early 1960s, took place in mental hospitals and involved individuals with severe illnesses such as schizophrenia (Scheff 1964). Schizophrenia is one of the more highly inherited disorders, as Table 1.1 shows, so that it has a credible source of primary deviation. Also, although the chaotic, complex, unpredictable, and intense behavior of the schizophrenic can be learned over many years of intimate contact (folie à deux, discussed in Chapter 4), it is, in general, very hard to imitate, even for a skilled actor. The labeling and modified labeling approaches have been evaluated more thoroughly on persons with severe mental disorders, such as schizophrenia, than on persons with less severe disorders, like depression, anxiety, and alcohol problems. Other disorders are more amenable to suggestibility, such as suicide and somatoform disorders, as shown in Chapter 6.

Labeling theory generated controversy because the policy implications of labeling were so different from those of the psychiatric and medical ideology. The labeling theorist would argue that those in society who perform the functions of psychiatrist (i.e., dealing with, processing, and, to some extent, controlling bizarre behaviors) should not be a prestigious, powerful, and organized group as psychiatrists are, so that if stereotypes of bizarre behaviors are formed, the individual is able to resist them and is more able and willing to take responsibility for the process of forming and reforming his or her social identity. If stereotypes of bizarre behavior do form, as they seem to in virtually every culture, then the labelers would argue that they should not be promulgated. The psychiatric model, on the other hand, argues for widespread public education efforts to wipe out the stigma of mental disorder and for early screening and prevention of mental disorders, which involves promulgation and early labeling, to some extent. In terms of the social construction of reality (Chapter 1), the tendency for temporary typifications to become objective and historically solidified over many generations, eventually turning into institutions, should be resisted.

STRESS AND MENTAL DISORDERS

Laboratory Models of Stress

The study of stress began in earnest with the publication of Hans Selye's *The Stress of Life* in 1956. Selye defined stress as a disruption of the natural homeostatic processes of the organism, which threatened its viability. From laboratory experiments with small animals he developed the concept of the *general adaptation syndrome* (GAS). When the animal was threatened with a noxious stimulus, such as an electric shock, or with being forced to keep its head above water, or with being poisoned, there was a reaction that was specific to the nature of the stressor. But Selye also observed a certain sequence of reactions to all the stressors, involving the sympathetic nervous system: an increase of adrenalin and certain other chemicals in the blood, an increase in the heart and respiration rates, and an expansion of the capillaries. This GAS reaction had three stages: a general and widespread alarm stage; a more specific response stage involving defense of tissues; and, eventually, if the stressor was not removed, a stage of exhaustion. Three important aspects of the GAS are (1) many different kinds of stressors all led to the same GAS; (2) the GAS affected the entire organism; and (3) the GAS sometimes *derailed*, by which Selye meant that it kept going, eventually leading to the exhaustion stage, even though the stressor had been removed.

Selye's work was not altogether different from much earlier work on dogs by Pavlov and his followers (Fox 1968; Seligman 1975). Among their many experiments was one involving the ability of the dog to discriminate between two different stimuli—for instance, that a triangle was associated with presentation of food and a circle was followed by a painful electric shock. After a while, the dog learned that the stimuli and their presentation alone would bring the appropriate response: salivation in the case of the triangle and nervous barking in the case of the circle. Then the corners of the triangle were rounded gradually, while the circle took on a more triangular shape, until the two stimuli were not distinguishable. At this point the dog began barking excitedly, straining at the traces, and could not be calmed down even when the stimuli were removed, so that eventually he became exhausted. The dog had thus acquired a "neurosis," that is, a pattern of maladaptive responses that was independent of the environmental situation. Another situation involved a dog's being administered a shock that he could escape by various responses. If the means of escape were eliminated, so that the dog was administered the shock regardless of his responses, eventually, he would stop trying to respond, even if the means of escape were then reintroduced. This particular failure to respond has been termed "learned helplessness" (Callahan et al. 1988; Seligman 1975).

The experiments of Pavlov and Selye seem to be connected to the phenomenon of *anxiety*, in a very loose sense. The psychiatric symptoms associated with anxiety involve complex symbols and behaviors, as well as the physiological behaviors studied by Selye and Pavlov, and there is as yet no agreement on exactly what the physiological concomitants of anxiety are. Learned helplessness is more relevant to depression, and, in fact, animal models for the study of depression are slightly more specific. It has been shown on the physiological and behavioral levels that monkeys and humans become depressed in a similar fashion and for similar reasons. Symptoms of depression in monkeys are a sad expression, tearing, apathy, and psychomotor retardation, as in humans. Furthermore, separation from a "loved" object (the mother or a peer) produces depression in monkeys, much as it sometimes does in humans. Treatment with antidepressant medication can forestall or prevent the depressed reaction to separation in chimpanzees (McKinney 1992).

An important generalization of Selye's GAS was that signs and symbols can be stressors, with physiological reactions equivalent to the reaction resulting from stressors such as poison and electric shock. This generalization is crucial to the study of stress in humans, and there are many good examples of the point. For instance, the adaptive reaction to inhaling noxious fumes is tearing, where saline fluid is secreted to flush out the noxious agent. But tearing is also brought about by emotional reaction to a variety of social events, such as separation and the consequent grief reaction.

Experiments by David Graham provide an elegant illustration of this idea that symbols can be stressors (cited in Mechanic 1978). He monitored the capillaries in human subjects' arms for their ability to hold blood. When the arm was struck with a hammerlike device, a red area appeared in response to the blow and showed up in his measuring instruments. Then he would repeat the blow, except that the device halted just before touching the arm. The mock blow generated the same physiological response in the arm; that is, *anticipated threat*, a symbol, generated the stress reaction. In humans symbolic processes are complex, and this has made stress research difficult. For example, in Graham's experiments, if the subject is informed first that the blow will be a mock blow, there is little or no reaction. Other vivid experiments by Lazarus (1966) reveal the same mediation of the stress response by symbolic processes: films of primitive circumcision rituals in which adolescent boys had deep cuts made in their penises and scrotums with sharpened stones produced measurable physiological responses in the audience. A more interesting result was that varied sound tracks produced either more or less response to the film:one sound track emphasized the trauma and pain; a second track was highly intellectual and detached; while in a third sound track the pain was denied. The latter two sound tracks produced lower levels of stress response, demonstrating the possibility that responses could be affected by cognitive processing.

Many important symbolic threats are social psychological situations of various kinds and have been demonstrated in laboratory situations (Crider 1970). In situations where an individual finds that his or her perception as to the length of a line on the blackboard deviates from that of a group (as in the famous Asch (1955) conformity experiments), there is a physiological stress response. If the group involved are his or her friends, there is even greater response. In the laboratory it is possible to create groups of individuals who like each other and groups of those who do not, and the level of stress response is greater in the latter. In the laboratory one can discover the prejudices of individuals and then place them with the objects of their prejudice (e.g., placing a white subject known to be prejudiced with a black experimenter or fellow subject), and there will be a noticeable stress response. A final example is the creation of a group leader in the laboratory by positively reinforcing one person's decisions; the experimenter can then create a situation where the group revolts and "deposes" the leader; this situation evokes a stress response in the leader.

Normal and Extreme Stress in Humans

Extreme stress in humans has been observed in two very different types of situations: (1) battle stress, natural disasters, and prisoner-of-war and Holocaust experiences and (2) so-called life-event stresses. Observation of the effects of battle stresses in World War II was a major impetus for research on stress in general—perhaps second in effect only to Selye's work. It was found that life-threatening episodes of battle could produce the entire range of psychiatric

Box 3.1
Story of Deborah, a Survivor of the Buffalo Creek Flood

I'm neglecting my children. I've just completely quit cooking. I don't do no house-work. I just won't do nothing. Can't sleep. Can't eat. I just want to take me a lot of pills and just go to bed and go to sleep and not wake up. I enjoyed my home and my family, but outside of them, to me, everything else in life that I had any interest in is destroyed. I loved to cook. I loved to sew. I loved to keep house. I was all the time working and making improvements on my home. But now I've just got to the point where it don't mean a thing in the world to me. I haven't cooked a hot meal and put it on the table for my children in almost three weeks.

I got to the point where I just didn't think I had anything to live for. I just didn't want to live. I thought my family would be better off without me. I just cried all the time. I'd come home from work in the evening, and I'd just sit there and cry. I couldn't do nothing. I didn't want to see people. I got to the point where I hated them. I didn't want nobody around me.

I haven't told anyone this before, but at one point, on a Saturday morning, I was so depressed that I just didn't want to live. I just took a notion that I'd end it. I got the car keys and stepped out the trailer door, but my husband and my oldest daughter at home, they had been watching me, I reckon. When I got in the car and started it, my husband grabbed the door on the driver's side and my daughter ran to the door on the opposite side. I had intended to put that car over Kelly Mountain with me in it. So they drug me back out of the car and took me back in the house and gave me some nerve medicine. I didn't feel as though I was any benefit to my family.

Source: From Kai Erikson, *Everything in Its Path: Destruction of Community in the Buffalo Creek Flood* (New York: Simon and Schuster, 1976). Reprinted by permission of Simon and Schuster.

symptomatology, including severe symptoms of psychosis, in previously normal individuals. Following the Vietnam War the diagnosis of posttraumatic stress disorder was introduced into the diagnostic manual, after petitioning from vet-erans groups (American Psychiatric Association 1980). Natural disasters are classified as stress and produced similar types of effects (Heurtin-Roberts 1993). Box 3.1 is the story of an individual who suffered the loss of her house through a surprise flood, and the picture of symptoms she presents is consistent with the criteria for major depressive disorder (Box 1.4). Consequences of battle stresses and natural disasters are often temporary, but certain types of experiences of prisoners of war (Beebe 1975) and in concentration camps (Eaton et al. 1982) have enduring psychological effects. These observations established that envi-ronmental stresses were a sufficient condition for even the most severe mental disorder.

In everyday life, battle stresses, natural disasters, and traumas are infrequent, and most episodes of intense stress are associated with sudden transformation of the social identity. In examining medical records, Hinkle and Wolf noticed that events in people's lives seemed to cluster around times of illness and disease

(Hinkle 1987), and this seemed to be in agreement with Selye's notion of disruption of homeostasis. Holmes and Rahe (1967) applied this notion by constructing a list of events requiring adaptation and change in one's life, such as divorce, marriage, taking a vacation, changing residence, becoming ill, getting a new job, and so on. They asked a sample of respondents to rate the events according to the amount of change and adaptation required, using as a reference the event of marriage, which was arbitrarily assigned a weight of 50. The resulting list of 43 events and weights is called the Social Readjustment Rating Scale (also called the Schedule of Recent Events) (Table 3.1). The weights assigned in different populations and cultures are similar enough to make the method feasible to use in a variety of Western cultures. Almost all of these events refer to status passage of one sort or another, and in role-theoretic terms, the Holmes-Rahe weights may be thought of as a quantification of status passage.

Research using the Holmes-Rahe scale and the derivative literature has shown that newly ill persons of various types have much higher scores for their recent past than well persons. The finding includes such diseases as tuberculosis, injuries on a football team, many other physical illnesses, and the range of mental disorders (Avison and Gotlib 1994; Brown and Harris 1989; Cohen et al. 1995; Dohrenwend 1998; Kaplan 1996a; Kasl 1984). The social nature of the life events in the scale was quickly understood, and the relationship between events and illness was so strong and consistent that for years this was considered the most important etiologic lead in the field of social psychiatry and social medicine generally.

For about a decade, the life events approach, essentially a methodology, was nearly synonymous with research on social stress (Wheaton 1996). The diversity of types of events included in the SRE score hindered the formulation of an etiologic theory for the disease or psychopathology that might result. Definitions of stress generally designate it as some sort of imbalance between the person and the environment but otherwise embody no specific theory of causation. Mechanic (1978) defines stress as "a discrepancy between the demands impinging on an individual, and his/her potential responses to those demands." Wheaton (1996) defines stress as "conditions of threat, demands, or structural constraints that, by the very fact of their occurrence or existence, call into question the operating integrity of the organism." Both these definitions are consistent with the nature of questions on distress in the General Health Questionnaire (as discussed in Chapter 2), that is, the feeling of being overwhelmed by circumstance. Research on stress has focused on the selection, categorization, and weighting of different types of life events in order to understand how they influence the risk for mental disorder.

The same events are perceived differently by different individuals. The process of appraisal of the stress was emphasized by Lazarus and his colleagues in their definition of stress: "a particular relationship between the person and the environment that is appraised by the person as taxing or exceeding his or her

Table 3.1
Social Readjustment Rating Scale

Life Event	Rating
Death of Spouse	100
Divorce	73
Marital Separation	65
Jail term	63
Death of close family member	63
Personal injury or illness	53
Marriage	50
Fired at work	47
Marital reconciliation	45
Retirement	45
Change in health of family member	44
Pregnancy	40
Sex difficulties	39
Gain of new family member	39
Business readjustment	39
Change in financial state	38
Death of close friend	37
Change to different line of work	36
Change in number of arguments with spouse	35
Mortgage over $10,000	31
Foreclosure of mortgage or loan	30
Change in responsibilities at work	29
Son or daughter leaving home	29
Trouble with in-laws	29
Outstanding personal achievement	28
Wife begins or stops work	26
Begin or end school	26
Change in living conditions	25
Revision of personal habits	24
Trouble with boss	23
Change in work hours or conditions	20
Change in residence	20
Change in schools	20
Change in recreation	19
Change in church activities	19
Change in social activities	18
Mortgage or loan less than $10,000	17
Change in sleeping habits	16
Change in number of family get-togethers	15
Change in eating habits	15
Vacation	13
Christmas	12
Minor violations of the law	11

Source: Holmes and Rahe (1967).

resources and endangering his or her well-being" (Lazarus and Folkman 1984: 19, in Kaplan 1996b: 176). Consistent with this line of thought, some researchers built into their measurement subjective weights by asking respondents to evaluate how much a given event they had reported upset them (Sarason et al. 1978). Subjectively weighted events were more strongly related to health and disease than the so-called objective event scores, but it seems clear that the weight of an event by an individual might be influenced by the effects it was perceived as having. Other researchers unequivocally stated the importance of objective events, as in Dohrenwend's statement: "We limit the term stressor to objective events" (cited in Wheaton 1996: 33).

The controversy over the subjective versus objective nature of life events was addressed by George Brown and colleagues in their notion of *context* (Brown and Harris 1978). They felt that life events raised risk for disorder by producing a *threat* to the individual, and that the *meaning* of the event was an important part of its power in producing threat. But they understood that if individuals in a case control study simply rated the events as to their importance, the association with health and illness would be artifactually high. The technique they developed—the Life Events and Difficulties Schedule, or LEDS—was to collect enough data on the psychological and social context of the individual experiencing the event so that its meaning could be rated by independent judges unaware of the degree of illness of the individual. A disadvantage of this approach was its cost—the interview with the respondent required many hours so that data on the context of each event could be obtained; then the data had to be put in a form that concealed the illness status of the respondent; then events were independently rated for threat by a separate panel of judges. Table 2.4 shows a result of their work on the study of depression using this method.

Elaborations of the measurement process, searching for types of events that would be most strongly associated with disorder, included many other categorizations (Thoits 1983). An early controversy was whether it was appropriate to include events that were apparently positive in their effects, such as getting married or taking a vacation (Table 3.1). The originators of the life events method included in the list any events that required adjustment of the individual, that is, any events that produced departure from homeostasis. But it became clear in reviews of research that only events regarded as negative by most people had strong effects on health and illness (Zautra and Reich 1983).

Another attempt to categorize events consisted of the contrast between events signifying entry into the social field, like marriage or the birth of a child, versus exit or loss events, such as the death of a relative or a child's leaving home. The most reliable finding relating life events to mental disorders has always been the notion, reviewed in more detail later, that the death of a spouse or close friend was related to depression; and this idea is not surprising, because of the close relationship of grief to depression. The framework put forward in this chapter suggests that we generalize the result to the basic concept of *role loss*, discussed earlier. Role loss entails a diminution in responsibilities connected to the role and a probable drop in self-esteem. Either or both of these two facets of role loss might be involved in the etiology of depression. Role gain, on the other hand, almost certainly involves additional responsibilities connected to the new role; but the effect on self-esteem depends on the antici-pated and actual outcome of the performance itself. It seems reasonable that role gain produces the anticipation of possibly poor performance and consequent feelings of anxiety that are associated with threats of all types. One research study by Finlay-Jones and Brown (1981) reports such a pattern of results: recent-onset cases of depression were more likely to have reported a loss event in the recent past; recent-onset cases of anxiety disorders were more likely to have reported a threatening event in the recent past (not too dissimilar from the con-cept of role gain); and those cases with features of anxiety and depression re-ported recent events characterized in both ways. Measurement problems are difficult in this type of research because changes in the social identity such as life events are hard to categorize in a clean fashion; for example, if a husband becomes ill and dies, the death is obviously a loss for his wife; but she may have to learn how to care for the husband during his illness before the death, and she may have to take up an occupation as a result of the death—both examples of role gain. It would seem that almost all changes in the social iden-tity bring about both loss and gain and, possibly, anxiety and depression.

Another methodologic issue in stress research was whether to include events that differed greatly in magnitude on the same lists, such as "ending school" and "death of a spouse." The Holmes-Rahe method was to calculate summed scores, using the weights in Table 3.1. There is evidence that simply counting the events is just as useful, especially if the list of events is restricted to those with the strongest weights (Thoits 1983). But the cumulation of seemingly trivial events, like the inability to find a baby-sitter or to get to the bus station on time, also might generate a potentially important stress. These types of stressors were distinguished by the name "daily hassles" or "small events" (Herbert and Cohen 1996; Kanner et al. 1981). The dividing line between hassles, major life events, and symptoms is very fine (Dohrenwend et al. 1984).

Many of the events listed in Table 3.1 are not independent of the degree of illness or health of the individual. "Personal injury or illness" is the obvious example, but other examples include "change in sleeping habits" and "change in eating habits," which are symptoms of depression. Other events could well be influenced by the disorder, even if they were not a direct symptom. For example, a depressive episode could contribute to a marital separation or trouble with the boss at work; alcoholism could lead to minor violations of the law; and physical illnesses of various types could cause a change in responsibilities at work or the wife's beginning or stopping work. To address this problem, many investigators subdivided events into those that were "independent," in that they were outside the control of the individual respondent (i.e., a layoff due to plant closing or the unexpected death of a relative); and "dependent" events, which could possibly have been influenced by the individual. Other terms used to describe this dimension are "controllable" versus "uncontrollable" and "endogenous" versus "exogenous" (Ormel and Wohlfarth 1991).

Stress and Diathesis

It is important to consider the causes of life events themselves, which may be categorized in three distinct ways: *random* causes, *social structural* causes, or *individual* causes. Each of these types of life-event cause involves a separate etiologic theory or group of theories. Randomness is involved in the clustering of independent events during a limited period of time (Smith et al. 1993). If life events occurred randomly and independently with the same probability for all persons in a population, as in a Poisson process, it is *not* true that all persons would have the same number of life events during a given period of time. The random process leads to a clustering of events in a small proportion of individuals in a given period of time, and a certain very small proportion of individuals, purely by chance, will have a very large number of life-event stresses. There is a commonsense notion to this theory—that is, sometimes people just have a "run" of bad luck. This model has important implications: if it is correct, then it may not be fruitful to search for the etiology of the stresses and, therefore, of the resulting mental disorders. It may be that the multitudinous vagaries of human life, combining and recombining by an infinite variety of routing and linking processes into these meaningful clusters, defy any sort of causal explanation.

Social structural causes of life events—called by some *systemic* (Aneshensel 1992)—are those typically studied as etiologic leads in psychiatric epidemiology. For example, it may be true that lower-class individuals have a higher rate of life events than middle-and upper-class persons. If so, this might explain why lower-class persons have higher rates of mental disorders. In this instance, life-event stresses are conceived of as mediating variables, providing a causal link between a broad structural variable and the mental disorder itself, as in Figure 1.6. These social structural causes of life-event stresses are generally fairly stable over the short term (e.g., occupation) and sometimes over the long term (e.g., race and sex are social structural positions that may affect the rate of life-event stresses).

The third type of explanation is that the life events are caused by the individual. The idea is that the individual has certain stable traits that contribute to the occurrence of life events, such as an argumentative tendency that leads to loss events like being fired or getting divorced. Since these stable traits are almost certainly linked powerfully to characteristics of mental disorder, the entire set of research findings linking life events to mental disorder can be turned on its head—mental disorders causing life events and not events causing disorders. This problem of causal interpretation is exacerbated by a related methodologic problem—that is, it may be that recently ill or mentally disordered persons are less likely to forget the occurrence of life events and more likely to distort their recall of life events, so that events occurring before the standard time period of the research are brought into the picture.

The individual causation explanation involves the corollary that different individuals may be differentially influenced by the same set of life events. The *differential vulnerability* could be explained by different appraisal of the threat of the events, as discussed earlier, or different mechanisms of coping with the events. *Coping* is the process of reacting to stress. The reaction can take various forms: Lazarus and colleagues distinguished reactions attempting to change the situation (*problem-focused coping*) from reactions designed to deal with the emotions it produced (*emotion-focused coping*); Pearlin added coping efforts designed to change the meaning of the situation. Lazarus and colleagues designed a questionnaire to measure coping that included 67 distinct coping responses; when these are factor analyzed, about 5 to 8 types of responses are found, including behavioral strategies like *confronting, seeking information,* or *leaving*; cognitive strategies like *distracting oneself* or *reinterpreting the situation*; and strategies focused on changing the emotional response, such as *exercise, medications,* or *meditation* (Thoits 1991). Individuals tend to adopt the same coping mechanisms over the course of their lives, and these individual differences have sources in both the individual's temperament and personality (Cooper and Payne 1991) (so-called *personal coping resources*), as well as in the social situations in which they are located (Eckenrode 1991) (*social coping resources*). The personal coping resources that have been studied most often involve a willingness to persist in the face of adversity, in effect, striving to master it. These include concepts like *mastery, internal locus of control, hardiness, self-efficacy,* and *sense of coherence* (Antonovsky 1991). Social differences in coping exist between gender, class, age, race, culture, and other social groups.

The temporal quality of the events is important in understanding the causal process. A random model could be specified that involved probabilistic clustering of temporally discrete events in a defined amount of time—say, one day. A heart attack or automobile accident might fit in this model, and if both happened in one day, few would disagree that the day had been stressful. But life is rarely so precise. Most events—even events with a formal date such as divorce or moving—actually take days or months to unfold. Plans for moving are made, for example, and the divorce may be anticipated for months or even years. Some stressful occurrences are more or less permanent, such as the continuing financial difficulties some families experience or the stress produced by caring for an ill and disabled relative. This logic has led researchers to distinguish between major life events and long-term difficulties (Avison and Turner 1988). The interview technique of Brown and colleagues is thus called the Life Events and Difficulties Schedule (LEDS) (Brown and Harris 1978). Long-term difficulties do not fit well into the random model of causation, but they can be produced both by systemic factors in the social structure and by factors related to the individual.

Sources of stress that may originate within the individual and vulnerabilities

Figure 3.3
Diathesis Stress Model

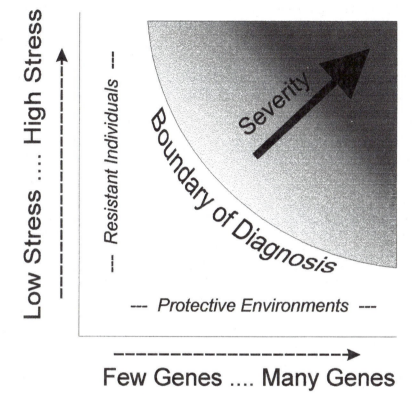

Diathesis is usually conceptualized as genetic inheritance, but could be any factor producing long-term vulnerability. Resistant individuals show little or no effects of stress, no matter how great; some environments protect even the most vulnerable of individuals from stress. An early example of the model is Zubin, Magaziner, and Steinhauer (1983).

Source: This drawing was influenced by Mirsky (1986).

to react to stress in maladaptive ways include inherited dispositions, sometimes called *diathesis*. A framework to describe the combination of the inherited disposition with stress over the course of life is the *diathesis stress model*, shown in Figure 3.3. The diathesis stress model originated in the study of schizophrenia (Mirsky 1986; Zubin et al. 1983), but is useful for any disorder that has other than a negligible degree of influence by inheritance (i.e., most of the disorders considered in this book and listed in Tables 1.1 and 2.7) (Haynes 1992). The general idea is that genes and stress add up to increased risk for disorder and increased severity of disorder if it occurs. At a high level of stress, such as in prolonged combat, almost anyone, except perhaps a few very resistant individuals who have very few of the relevant genes, will meet the criteria for disorder (upper left part of Figure 3.3). Those with many relevant genes meet the criteria for disorder even at a fairly low level of environmental stress; but some individuals with many genes never meet criteria for disorder as long as they remain within protective environments (lower right part of Figure 3.3). Those with many genes and in stressful environments have disorder of a more severe nature (upper right part of Figure 3.3).

The diathesis stress model is useful in orienting us to the combination of genes and environment but understates the complexity of the process. There are genetic models involving the addition of many independent genes acting together to produce a single dimension of vulnerability (Falconer 1965). But the notion of "stress" in the diathesis stress model has difficulty encompassing all the aspects of the environment that can combine with genes to produce disorder, that is, as shown in Figure 1.6, injuries, toxins, and infections. Even if this notion is limited to social stresses, it cannot easily encompass the entire spectrum of stresses and learning experiences that accumulate over the life span in producing risk for disorder. But the most important problem with the diathesis stress model in Figure 3.3 is the assumption that genes and environment act additively and independently of each other (Kendler 1986). Individuals tend to select their environments and shape them, depending on their genetic makeup, and this process generates new environments, which then interact with perhaps other genes, so that, at the end of the process, it may be very difficult to sort out a portion of the vulnerability that is "due" to the environment and a part that is "due" to genes (Plomin et al. 1994).

An application of the notions of diathesis and stress is shown in Figure 3.4 (Kendler et al. 1995). The data pertain to a sample of female twins in Virginia, of whom a small proportion met the criteria for major depressive disorder. The advantage of the twin sample is that genetically based risk for the disorder can be roughly quantified using the distinction between monozygotic and dizygotic twins and if the entire sample has been assessed with regard to the presence of disorder. The part of the sample at lowest genetic risk consists of those individuals whose cotwins have never met the diagnostic criteria for major depression. Monozygotic twins whose cotwins have been depressed are at highest genetic risk; dizygotic twins whose cotwins have been depressed, at an intermediate level of risk. In both the left- and right-hand side of the figure, these levels of genetic risk are operating, producing a higher rate of depression in those at higher risk. The dramatic aspect of the figure is the enormous difference in risk for those with severe life events present in the month of onset. Monozygotic cotwins of depressed individuals are about 15 times as likely to be depressed as their (genetically identical) twin if they have had a severe life event, and the prevalence rate is more than 8 percent higher than for those with low genetic loading for the disorder. For those without a severe life event, the high genetic risk group has only slightly increased prevalence compared with the low

Figure 3.4
Interaction of Life Events and Heredity: Onset of Major Depression in 2,164 Female Twins

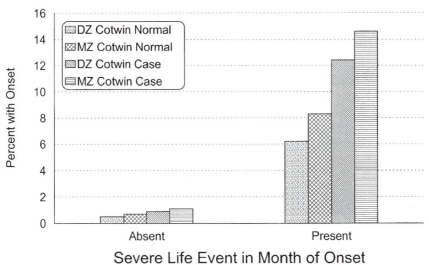

Severe Life Event in Month of Onset

Genetic vulnerability and life event stressors combine to raise risk for major depression.

Source: Adapted from Kenneth S. Kendler et al., "Stressful Life Events, Genetic Liability, and Onset of an Episode of Major Depression in Women," *American Journal of Psychiatry* 152; 833–42, 1995. Copyright 1995, the American Psychiatric Association. Reprinted by permission.

genetic risk group (statistically speaking, there is additive interaction). Thus, the severe life event acted as a potentiator of the disorder.

The concept of diathesis is appropriately extended to nongenetic factors that produce stable vulnerabilities to generate disorder under conditions of stress. These nongenetic factors may be caused by anything after conception, that is, the prenatal and perinatal period and the period of childhood and adolescence. Personality traits, for example, can form the diathesis. These factors are considered in more detail in the next chapter.

Longitudinal data are relevant to these methodologic problems and to the diathesis stress framework because they help sort out cause and effect and because they provide insight into the distinction between relatively stable vulnerabilities versus transient events and situations. Many longitudinal studies of life events and stress have taken the form of path analysis or structural equation models, such as in Figure 3.5. The numbers associated with a given path are usually standardized partial regression coefficients, or *betas*, which indicate the degree of change in a later variable, measured in standard deviation units, produced by one standard deviation unit of change in a prior variable. Path coefficients can be multiplied along paths to determine the effect of variables at the

Figure 3.5
Effects of Life Difficulties and Life Changes on Distress: Dutch Longitudinal Study of 296 Adults

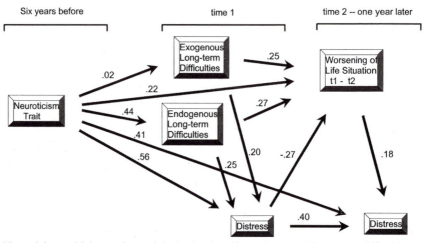

Neuroticism, which may be an inherited trait, effects short- and long-term difficulties as well as stressful events and levels of distress. Even after adjusting for neuroticism and prior distress, stressful events have significant effects on distress.

Source: Johan Ormel and Tamar Wohlfarth. "How Neuroticism, Long-Term Difficulties, and Life Situation Change Influence Psychological Distress: A Longitudinal Model," *Journal of Personality and Social Psychology* 60: 744–55. Copyright © 1991 by the American Psychological Association. Adapted with permission.

far left to variaoles at the far right. The beta may be interpreted in a fashion roughly similar to a correlation coefficient. Thus, a beta of 0.10 is small or even trivial; 0.25 is small; and a beta of 0.50 is of moderate strength. In studies of life events and psychological disorder with several waves of data collection, the life-event scores tend to be weakly correlated over time, with a beta coefficient of about 0.15. The overtime correlation of life event scores, even though small, suggests stable individual or systemic factors and is not consistent with the notion of randomness (Aneshensel and Frerichs 1982; Eaton 1978; Turner and Noh 1988). Typically, in these studies the level of distress is highly correlated from one time to the next. This stability could be explained by a stable inherited personality disposition, such as neuroticism, or a stable position in the social structure that was stressful. Psychological disorder at one time tends to predict stresses occurring later, with a beta at a level of about 0.10–0.15, giving evidence that individuals may be contributing to their own stress. Finally, the prediction of psychological disorder from life event stresses is attenuated when the earlier level of distress is controlled, but not eliminated—it is often about 0.20–0.40.

Stresses accumulate over time. Even small events can be cumulatively very distressing if there are enough of them and if they persist. Events such as the trauma of assault, war, or disaster leave a lasting impression and add to, or set the context for, current stresses (Wheaton 1996). Furthermore, the sequence in which stresses occur may be important in the cumulative nature of their effects. While it seems natural that stresses would cumulate, there may be positive effects of stress (Thoits 1995). For example, there is some evidence from longitudinal data that early stresses may inoculate individuals, in effect, teaching them to adapt and master stress, so that early stresses have a protective effect when later stresses are included in the model (Eaton 1978; Husaini and Von Frank 1985; Turner and Noh 1988). The extent to which stresses are not resolved predicts future levels of distress, and the process of resolution may be generating feelings of mastery that have the inoculation effect for future stress (Turner and Avison 1992). Different sequences of role acquisitions and losses over the life course occur at different frequencies in different cultures (Elder et al. 1996), and departures from normative sequences, including sudden changes that are stressful, have varying consequences.

The study in Holland by Ormel and Wohlfarth (1991) exemplifies many of these issues (Figure 3.5). They sampled several thousand persons from the entire nation of the Netherlands, administering a brief questionnaire that included a measure of neuroticism. As discussed earlier, neuroticism is perhaps the most important dimension of personality that has been repeatedly found in factor analytic studies of personality traits (Costa and McCrae 1992). Most definitions of neuroticism exactly fit the notion of diathesis that is important here, that is, reactivity to stress (Tyrer 1985). Six years later they interviewed a random subsample of the respondents, obtaining measures of distress, life situation, and long-term difficulties, which they divided into those influenced by factors outside the individual's control ("exogenous") and those influenced by the individual ("endogenous"). One year later they interviewed the same individuals, making a judgment about changes in the life situation of the individual. The ratings of the long-term difficulties and of the life situation change were made in the manner of the Life Events and Difficulties Schedule, that is, contextual ratings via judges who did not know the reported levels of distress. The source of data for ratings of change in life situation is obtained simultaneously to the measures of distress, as in other longitudinal studies of life events and psychological disorder. As in the other studies of this type, this measure is not strictly antecedent in time, and the causal priority is not completely undebatable. But it has the advantage of making a judgment about the entire life situation—that is, balancing improvements with deteriorations—that event scores at two points in time cannot do.

The diathesis of neuroticism has a powerful influence in the model in Figure 3.5. It has no effect on exogenous, long-term difficulties, as might be expected (standardized beta coefficient of 0.02) but a substantial effect on endogenous, long-term difficulties (0.44). Both types of long-term difficulties have a moderate effect on distress at time 1 of about 0.20–0.25, consistent with the literature.

Both types of long-term difficulties have an effect on the worsening of the life situation, indicating the relatively stable risk for crisis of persons with these difficulties. Distress at time 1 is correlated with distress at time 2, as in most studies of this type (beta of 0.40). A slight anomaly in this study is the negative effect of distress on worsening of life situation—presumably, this occurs because persons in distress at time 1 have improved their situation by recovering or "bouncing back." The influence of change in life situation on distress at time 2 is similar in magnitude to what is in the literature, although slightly smaller (beta of 0.18). It may be smaller because of the control for the diathesis, represented by the sizable effect of neuroticism on distress at time 2 (beta of 0.41).

Some analysts have charged that the development of measures in this field has become increasingly constricted due to the methodologic problems discussed earlier and that measures of life events do not tap the entire domain of stress, thus diminishing the true effects of stress (Wheaton 1996). The tendency is to use one or the other types of stress measurement, that is, either a measure of life events, a measure of chronic strains, a measure of life traumas, or a measure of daily hassles. Turner et al. (1995) have shown that when all these measures are included, the effects of stress are larger than has been the case generally in the literature. Their analysis is strictly cross-sectional, not solving the problem of mixing cause and effect and not controlling for the diathesis as has been done by Ormel and Wohlfarth. On the other hand, the work in the Dutch sample fails to capture the details of the ongoing process of dealing with stress—the *stress process* (Pearlin et al. 1981). For example, Pearlin and others estimated the effects of a single stressor (job disruption) on depression, with a coefficient of 0.34, as in many longitudinal studies of stress. More interesting were the mechanisms by which it had this effect. The occurrence of the typical life event, job disruption, influenced income, which influenced economic strain—more like a chronic difficulty. This, in turn, influenced the coping resources of social support, mastery, and self-esteem, and through these variables the effect on depression was exercised. If there are no measures of coping, and there are strong measures of diathesis, the effects of coping may end up falling into the measure of diathesis, thus overestimating its effect. This type of complexity of the stress process is an example of nonadditivity in the diathesis stress model, in that initial tendencies and vulnerabilities in the individual operate on, select into, and are molded by, different social environments.

Stress and Depressive Disorder

The difficulties of cross-sectional data are apparent in the study of stress and depressive disorder. Of all the psychiatric disorders, depression is the one most studied in the life events paradigm and the one where the data are most convincing. The range of affective disorders, from mild distress, as might be measured by the GHQ, to full-fledged disorder, as represented by the Buffalo Creek survivor reported in Box 3.1, to bipolar disorder, as represented by the woman

Box 3.2
Narrative Account of Psychosis

I was a senior in high school when I had my first attack of manic-depressive illness; once the siege began, I lost my mind rather rapidly. At first, everything seemed so easy. I raced about like a crazed weasel, bubbling with plans and enthusiasms, immersed in sports, and staying up all night, night after night, out with friends, reading everything that wasn't nailed down, filling manuscript books with poems and fragments of plays, and making expansive, completely unrealistic, plans for my future. The world was filled with pleasure and promise; I felt great. Not just great, but I felt really great. I felt I could do anything, that no task was too difficult. My mind seemed clear, fabulously focused, and able to make intuitive mathematical leaps that had up to that point entirely eluded me. Indeed, they elude me still. At the time however, not only did everything make perfect sense, but it all began to fit into a marvelous kind of cosmic relatedness. My sense of enchantment with the laws of the natural world caused me to fizz over, and I found myself button holing my friends to tell them how beautiful it all was. They were less than transfixed by my insights in to the webbings and beauties of the universe, although considerably impressed by how exhausting it was to be around my enthusiastic ramblings: You're talking too fast, Kay. Slow down, Kay. . . .

I did, finally slow down. In fact, I came to a grinding halt. . . . Then the bottom began to fall out of my life and mind. My thinking, far from being clearer than a crystal, was tortuous. I would read the same passage over and over again only to realize that I had no memory at all for what I just had read. Each book or poem I picked up was the same way. Incomprehensible. Nothing made sense. [I] was incapable of concentrated thought and turned time and again to the subject of death: I was going to die, what difference did anything make? Life's run was only a short and meaningless one, why live? I was totally exhausted and could scarcely pull myself out of bed in the mornings. It took me twice as long to walk anywhere as it ordinarily did, and I wore the same clothes over and over again, as it was otherwise too much of an effort to make a decision about what to put on. I dreaded having to talk with people, avoided my friends whenever possible, and sat in the school library in the early mornings and late afternoons, virtually inert, with a dead heart and a brain as cold as clay. . . . I aged rapidly during those months, as one must with such loss of one's self, with such proximity to death, and such distance from shelter.

Source: From K. R. Jamison, *An Unquiet Mind: A Memoir of Moods and Madness* (New York: Alfred A. Knopf, 1995). Reprinted courtesy of Random House, Inc.

reported in Box 3.2, all have been linked to stressful life events. But the causal status of the life event stresses in depressive disorder might not satisfy a skeptical epidemiologist (Kessler 1997). Paykel (1994) reviews 29 studies of life event stresses and depression, and all 29 show that life events "predict" onset of depression. The advantage of this particular review, in the view of its author, is that the depression is diagnosed by a psychiatrist "making it clear that events are implicated in such disorder, rather than only in the milder disorder and distress identified in community epidemiological samples" (52). A disadvantage is that all 29 studies are retrospective, precluding definitive statement about cause and effect. Furthermore, it could be that life events are not what makes a person depressed, but rather what makes a depressed person *get into treatment*. Since there is a large proportion of persons meeting the criteria for diagnosis that do not get into treatment (Shapiro et al. 1984), it could be that the relationship of life events to depressive disorder is very small or nonexistent in the total population of depressives. Many fewer studies, including that of Brown and Harris (1978) shown in Table 2.4, also involve community samples.

For the skeptical epidemiologist, longitudinal research on general population samples with a criterion-based diagnosis of depression is what is needed. These are difficult requirements because the incidence of depressive disorder is so low (Eaton et al. 1997). There appear to be only three studies of this type. A population-based study in Zurich, from 1978 through 1988, found that life events in 1981 predicted onset of depressive disorder as much as seven years later (Ernst et al. 1992). A problem is that the theory related to life events would not predict a latency of seven years in having the effect. Also, most of the onsets were actually recurrent episodes of depression. Finally, it is important to note that, although the initial sample was drawn from the general population, later waves of follow-up concentrated on a subsample that was drawn for reason of high scores on a measure of psychiatric symptoms, and this measure was, in fact, the strongest predictor of onset of depression (similar to the neuroticism measure in the Netherlands study earlier). A second study in Edinburgh also sampled from the general population but subsampled those at high risk for follow-up, with high risk defined by 1 or more of 11 vulnerability factors, including whether the individual had sought treatment for her or his nerves (Surtees et al. 1986). Those with onset of depression in the three weeks preceding onset were 6.5 times more likely to have had one or more severe events that were judged to be "independent," or outside their control, according to the LEDS method, and 15.5 times as likely to have one or more severe "dependent" events. As in the Zurich study, most of the onsets were recurrences.

A third population-based longitudinal study of depressive disorder advertised for respondents from the general population in Eugene, Oregon (Lewinsohn et al. 1988). As with the Edinburgh and Zurich researchers, the sample for follow-up was defined by a measure of high risk (scores on a scale of depression, which approximate the measures of psychological distress used in Netherlands research, with a slightly greater focus on depressive symptomatology). There were 85 onsets during the follow-up, of which only 9 were the first episode in the individual's life. The analysis distinguished predictors of depressive disorder from predictors of distress. Increases in distress *and* the onset of disorder were predicted by life event stresses, marital discord, and initial high levels of distress. Onset of disorder *but not* the onset of higher distress was predicted by young age, female gender, and a prior episode of depression. Higher distress levels *but not* the onset of disorder was predicted by so-called depressogenic cognitions, such as fatalism and measures of external control. This third research study elegantly integrates a rather diverse literature. The predictors of disorder only (young females with prior episodes) are consistent with the epidemiologic literature on depressive disorder (Eaton et al. 1997). The results show that stress predicts both milder forms of distress as well as the onset of disorder. There is also a tendency for milder distress to be better predicted by maladaptive patterns of thinking. Finally, both disorder and distress are predicted by earlier high levels of distress, as might be expected from the diathesis stress framework.

These three studies constitute the most powerful evidence that stress causes depression. In all three the onset of disorder is made in a strictly prospective sense, but the assessment of the timing of life events is not strictly prospective. In fact, the partly random nature of the occurrence of life events precludes strictly prospective ascertainment without impossibly high costs. In all three studies the onsets of disorder consist mostly of recurrent episodes, and in all three the best predictor of onset is some prior measure of distress or depression. Even with these weaknesses in method, the causal status of stresses in depression is quite strong. The causal status of tobacco in lung cancer is still debated, in part due to similar problems of method, and in part because, as with stress and depression, the precise causal mechanisms have not been established. In both literatures there are strong biological and animal studies supporting the general conclusion. A slight difference between the two literatures is that for the smoking–cancer relationship, there is evidence from various naturally occurring and quasi-experimental situations that a reduction in smoking is related to a reduction in the rate of lung cancer. There is no similar evidence for a reduction in stresses being related to a reduction in rate of depressive disorder.

Social Identity and the Stress Paradigm

After 50 years of research the stress paradigm has failed to elaborate a useful theory of the etiology of mental disorder. The concept of stress had the advantage of breadth, so that it helped to integrate diverse areas of interest. But the breadth developed into a handicap as it became ever clearer that there could not be a useful single concept of stressor or a single stress response. Also, the stress paradigm has not led to successful efforts at prevention of mental disorder. Here again, the breadth of the concept became its Achilles' heel. Stress and adversity exist everywhere, and it is impossible to know where to begin the efforts at prevention if the concept is so global. Only severely delimiting the concept of life events into specific situations such as divorce, natural disaster, sexual assault, widowhood, and so forth gives the possibility of intervening, either before the event occurs or immediately after (Eaton and Dohrenwend 1998). Some researchers have suggested that the concept of stress might not be useful any longer. For example, in summarizing a recent edited text on the subject, Kaplan (1996b) suggests, "Rather than expend energy on trying to clarify and defend the utility of 'stress' and related constructs, perhaps we should redirect our attention to creating theoretical structures that take into account individual, environmental, and situational factors that . . . interact with each other to . . . affect outcomes of interest." In an article entitled "Stress Is a Noun! No, a verb! No, an Adjective!" Engel (1985) argues to abandon the concept but anticipates that few researchers will actually do so: "For them stress is neither a noun, nor a verb, nor an adjective. It is an escape from reality." Another recent review concludes: "It might be argued that researchers have extended the concept of stress to the point where it is too broad to be meaningful or useful" (Avison and Gotlib 1994: 327).

For the sociologist the stress process is subsumed into the study of the formation and maintenance of the social identity. Many definitions of social stress focus on the self or the social identity. For Kaplan (1996a) stress "is defined in terms of negative self-feelings" (176). "Stressors are equivalent to threats to self. . . . For the most part, experiences of failure and rejection" (189). For Burke (1996), "Social stress results from the interruption of the continuously adjusting identity process" (148; see also Burke 1991). With a somewhat broader definition of the identity process given earlier, stress could be conceptualized as a relatively sudden shift in the shape of the social identity. Changes in shape take the form of role losses and role gains, with the roles assessed on dimensions of choice/assignment, valuation, and involvement, as in the three-dimensional model of social identity discussed earlier. The degree of suddenness could be quantified in a dynamic, time-oriented manner, if there were temporal data with sufficiently small time intervals between measurements. For the immediate situation, that is, predicting behavior from moment to moment, the crucial problem is understanding the attentional mechanisms that lead the individual to pay attention to one role versus another, that is, the salience of the roles. For the long term, where the effects of adversity and change are likely to show up in mental health outcomes, the crucial problem is the assessment of the *centrality* of a role for the social identity. The results in this area also suggest the value of more detailed study of that aspect of the social identity where most central roles reside and where the life span concept is inherent, that is, the family, which is the subject of the following chapter.

In Chapter 1 the medical model of mental disorders was contrasted with the sociological (deviance/labeling) framework. A difficulty with the sociological approach is that, consistent with the early beliefs that many or most mental disorders were actually created by the medical system, it offers little in the way of treatment recommendations, except to minimize the role of medicine. Mechanic and others have suggested that an educational model might be substituted for the medical model of mental disorders (Erickson 1957; Mechanic 1969). The educational model is well known and prescribes action and a well-developed ideology and institutional system for dealing with individuals. The educational model fits well with a scientific corpus of knowledge, that is, learning theory. A further alternative to the educational and medical model is suggested by the previous discussion of social identity. The goal of the therapist, in this model, would be to transform the social identity. For a demoralized person, selected roles that generate high valuations should be added to their social identity, and roles with low valuation should be carefully stripped away. In some sense, these types of transformations form part and parcel of various forms of interpersonal psychotherapy. As well, social workers and case managers engage in these activities on behalf of their clients. Transformations of social identity have been used in healing rituals in traditional societies for generations (Ellenberger 1970).

4

Integration: Community and Family

COMMUNITY

Integration and the Social Ecology

Integration is the process whereby individuals join, participate in, and leave groups. Two major arenas for integration to exercise its force are the community and the family. A *community* is a large group of individuals who share a common history or perceive a common future. This definition reserves the concept of community to groups larger than can meet on a face-to-face basis and includes the idea that there must be a sense of common history or future, above and beyond the simple concept of group as defined in the first chapter. Communities tend to exist around easily identifiable indicators of group status. Ethnic status is one of the most common means of identification with a large group. *Ethnic status* is an easily identifiable characteristic that implies membership in a community—the identifier of ethnic status might be race, religion, or country of origin.

An early study of the effects of integration on psychiatric disorder was Durkheim's (1966) work on rates of suicide. Durkheim analyzed national suicide rates from the nineteenth century, similar to that shown in Figure 4.1, which displays national suicide rates in 1993. Rates are presented for all countries where the reporting system was judged to be credible, and for which there were greater than 30 suicides during the reporting year. The figure shows a large range of rates and stimulates thought about causes. For example, in this particular example, the countries with the highest rates of suicide tend to have been in the old socialist block—could the high rates in these countries be the result of the fall of communism five years earlier? In Durkheim's case, the obvious national differences paralleled differences in ethnic status, as measured by re-

Figure 4.1
Suicide in 1993

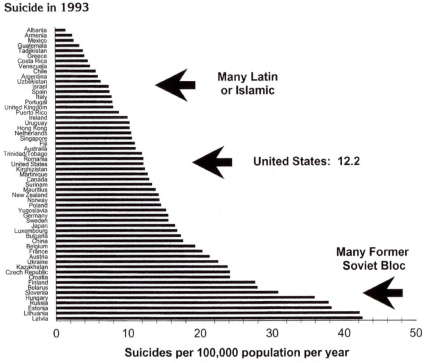

Albania
Armenia
Mexico
Guatemala
Tadjikistan
Greece
Costa Rica
Venezuela
Chile
Argentina
Uzbekistan
Israel
Spain
Italy
Portugal
United Kingdom
Puerto Rico
Ireland
Uruguay
Hong Kong
Netherlands
Singapore
Fiji
Australia
Trinidad/Tobago
Romania
United States
Kirghizistan
Martinique
Canada
Surinam
Mauritius
New Zealand
Norway
Poland
Yugoslavia
Germany
Sweden
Japan
Luxembourg
Bulgaria
China
Belgium
France
Austria
Ukraine
Kazakhstan
Czech Republic
Croatia
Finland
Belarus
Slovenia
Hungary
Russia
Estonia
Lithuania
Latvia

Many Latin
or Islamic

United States: 12.2

Many Former
Soviet Bloc

0   10   20   30   40   50

Suicides per 100,000 population per year

Variation in suicide rates across nationalities inspired one of Durkheim's most powerful works. Data on suicide look markedly different in 1993 than they did a decade earlier, before the breakup of the Soviet Union.

ligious affiliation: nations that were Catholic had a rate of suicide of 58 per million, whereas nations that were Protestant had rates of 190 per million. To control for between-country differences in culture and in the reporting of suicides, he analyzed data from countries where there was variation in religious affiliation by province, such as Prussia (Table 4.1). The provinces with many Protestants have a rate of suicide of 264.6, more than two times higher than those with few Protestants, with a rate of 95.6. Durkheim analyzed several other comparisons with regard to religious and national differences and concluded that:

the proclivity of Protestantism for suicide must relate to the spirit of free inquiry that animates this religion, . . . [and that] Protestantism concedes a greater freedom to individual thought than Catholicism, . . . because it has fewer common beliefs and practices. . . . A religious society . . . does not unite men by an exchange and reciprocity of services, a temporal bond of union which permits and even presupposes differences, but which a religious society cannot form. It socializes men only by attaching them completely to an identical body of doctrine and socializes them in proportion as this body of doctrine is

Table 4.1
Durkheim's Analysis of Egoistic Suicide (Suicide Rates in Provinces of Prussia)

Percentage of Protestants in Province	Suicides per million
More than 90% Protestant	264.6
68-89% Protestant	220.0
40-50% Protestant	163.6
28-32% Protestant	95.6

Source: Durkheim (1966: 153).

extensive and firm. . . . The greater concessions a confessional group makes to individual judgment, the less it dominates lives, the less its cohesion and vitality. We thus reach the conclusion that the superiority of Protestantism with respect to suicide results from its being a less strongly integrated church than the Catholic Church. (Durkheim 1966: 156–159) . . .

If religion protects man against the desire for self-destruction, it is not that it preaches the respect for his own person; . . . but because it is a society. What constitutes this society is the existence of a certain number of beliefs and practices common to all . . . The more numerous and strong these collective states of mind are, the stronger the integration of the religious community, and also the greater its preservative value. (170)

Following this conclusion, Durkheim analyzed data concerning two other types of society: family and political. He showed that married persons had lower rates of suicide than unmarried and that persons with children had lower rates of suicide than persons without children, regardless of whether they were married or not. Likewise, he showed that suicide was more common in cities than in rural areas, reaching the conclusion that "suicide varies inversely with the degree of integration of the social groups of which the individual forms a part" (209). He called the type of suicide in which the individual asserted himself or herself in the face of the social group *egoistic suicide*.

A second major type of suicide for Durkheim was *altruistic*. He noted that there were certain situations in which suicide was more common, such as suicides of men on the threshold of old age or stricken with illness in ancient European cultures; and the not too uncommon practice of *suttee* in early modern India, in which a woman was immolated with her husband following his death. He presented data on the higher rate of suicide in the military, shown in Table 4.2. In every country the military have higher rates of suicide, and in many countries it is markedly higher. Altruistic suicide occurs where the individual:

must be almost completely absorbed in the group and the latter, accordingly, very highly integrated. For the parts to have so little life of their own, the whole must indeed be a compact, continuous mass[where] . . . everyone leads the same life; everything is common to all. . . . The individual thus has no way to set up an environment of his own in

Table 4.2
Durkheim's Analysis of Altruistic Suicide (Suicide Rates in Soldiers and Civilians)

Country and time period:	Suicides per million: Soldiers	Civilians
Austria (1876-1890)	1,253	122
United States (1870-1884)	680	80
Italy (1876-1890)	407	77
England (1876-1890)	209	79
Wurttemburg (1846-1858)	320	170
Saxony (1847-1858)	640	369
Prussia (1876-1890)	607	394
France (1876-1890)	333	265

Source: Durkheim (1966: 228, Table 23).

the shelter of which he may develop his own nature. . . . He is only an inseparable part of the whole without personal value. Whereas [egoistic suicide] is caused by excessive individuation, [altruistic suicide] is caused by too rudimentary individuation. (Durkheim 1966: 220–21)

This discussion gives a flavor for the breadth of insight of Durkheim's thinking and the large amount of data he analyzed. The discussion of Durkheim's third major type of suicide, *anomic*, is less relevant to the notion of integration since anomic suicide had to do with fluctuations in group life, such as economic crises. Durkheim's influence persists to the present, mostly because of the conceptualizations of integration as a social fact. Similar to the concept of inequality, the concept of integration exists only on the level of the group, not the individual. It forms one of three major dimensions of social life, as discussed in Chapter 1. Integration is a dimension of social life that can be harmful in extreme excess or extreme absence, as shown in the two polar types of suicide.

Durkheim's analysis commits the *ecological fallacy*, that is, interpreting data on groups to reflect risks for individuals. For example, concluding that Protestants have higher rates of suicide from the data in Table 4.1 may be erroneous, because there may be an extremely high rate among those Catholics who live in Protestant areas. This high rate might occur because Catholics in an extreme minority status are marginalized. However, note that the notion on which the criticism is based is exactly that of integration, that is, the difficulty of forming "numerous and strong . . . collective beliefs" where those holding the beliefs are not sufficiently dense in the population. The concept of the *marginal man* was introduced by Stonequist (1937) to describe "the individual who through migration, education, marriage, or some other influence leaves one social group or culture without making a satisfactory adjustment to another and finds himself on the margin of each but a member of neither." The marginal man is thought of as a personality type that results from the introjection of two distinct cultures and thus is relevant to all situations of racial and cultural contact. Stonequist applied the concept to the situation of the individual in a disadvantaged minority group who desires complete assimilation into the majority culture but to whom majority group status is denied. The dual membership leads to divided loyalties, fluctuating opinions and attitudes, excessive self-consciousness, and, in its extreme form, "a breakdown in life organization . . . eventuating in mental disorganization and suicide." The criticism of Durkheim and the concept of the marginal man imply that rates of suicide should be higher in ethnic groups that are in the extreme minority in a given community and lower where they form a larger proportion of the population. This is the so-called *ethnic density* effect (Halpern 1993). The proportions of ethnic density that are beneficial or harmful ought to be the subject of empirical inquiry, but the idea has been put to the test only rarely. The nature of the integration that takes place as a result of increased density would depend on the complex types of integration such density promotes or reinforces. For example, it may be that cultural institutions such as churches require a certain critical threshold of population before establishing themselves in a given locale, and these critical thresholds may vary according to the particular type of religious practice, which is enhanced by the presence of an established church facility. Other religions may have practices that can be adapted to institutions with lower numbers (e.g., worship in homes). Since ethnic density may well be related to ethnic disadvantage, as discussed in this chapter, a study of the ethnic density effect must control in some manner for levels of social deprivation in the communities under study. A study in South London showed that rates of suicide in small areas (averaging about 8,000 population) were correlated inversely with ethnic densities for each of three ethnic groups, even after controlling for levels of social deprivation (Neeleman 1997). Religion and religiosity continue to be prominent subjects in the study of suicide and its relation to integration (Maris 1997; Pescosolido and Georgianna 1989).

There have not been many empirical studies of social integration at the level of the community, in spite of its theoretical importance. One of the classic psychiatric epidemiologic studies of the so-called second generation was conducted in the rural area of Stirling County, Nova Scotia. Its parallel, the *Midtown Study*, focused on the effects of social class in the city, as discussed in Chapter 5. In the *Stirling County Study* the focus was on integration and its polar opposite of disintegration. Small rural communities in the country were categorized as to whether they were disintegrated or not. Indicators of a high degree of disintegration were the presence of many broken homes; few and weak community associations; few and weak leaders; few patterns of recreation; high frequency of hostility; high frequency of crime and delinquency; and a weak and fragmented network of communications. Even after controlling for age, sex, and education, integrated areas had lower risk for mental disorder than disintegrated areas (Leighton et al. 1963).

Social Networks and Social Supports

In the epidemiologic literature the concept of integration has been explored via the idea of social networks and social supports. An influential address by Cobb (1976) proposed that individual differences in response to disease processes could be explained by the social supports of the individual. This concept fed into the models of stress and coping that were being developed at that time (Aneshensel and Frerichs 1982; Cohen and Wills 1985; Lin and Ensel 1984). Early research focused on the individual, not the community, and was almost totally directed to determine whether social supports counteracted the effects of stress. Gradually, a broader point of view has arisen that fits well into the concept of integration (House et al. 1988; Stryker and Gottlieb 1981; Veiel and Baumann 1992; Wellmann and Wortley 1990).

Social networks are relational ties between individuals that indicate a history of interaction and the potential for future interaction. Thus, in a broad sense, social networks define groups. The *personal network* is all the social networks that link to a particular individual. Personal networks form the bulk of the social identity, as defined earlier. (The remainder of the social identity is formed by diffuse roles that may involve role expectations related to abstract concepts and relationships, that is, not living human beings but constructs interpretable as aspects of the generalized other.) The personal network is often thought of as consisting of relationships defined as present or absent, but it is also possible to conceive it as relationships varying in intensity. The primary distinction is between so-called primary and secondary networks. *Primary networks* consists of persons who are seen face-to-face in a wide range of social settings, such as a spouse of other kin or close neighbors. *Secondary networks* consist of individuals with whom the interaction is limited to one particular setting, such as a coworker or a member of a specific type of club or association.

Networks can be characterized in a variety of ways. The *range* of the network is the extent of its connections to other persons. The *density* of the network is the degree of overlap in the relational ties of the network, for example, the degree to which an individual's friends know each other. The *diversity* of the network is the extent to which it extends to persons with different social characteristics. These network characteristics can be differentially related to health (Haines and Hurlbert 1992).

The existence of a personal network makes possible *social support*, which is defined as information from others that one is loved and cared for (Cobb 1976). The idea of network embodies a more strictly interactional or behavioral concept of social integration: social support is closer to Durkheim's mental definition than is social networks. Social support is often considered to be of two major types: *instrumental support*, such as services or money, and *emotional support*, such as statements of affection and understanding. An important type of social support is emotional support from a particular person in the primary network, that is, the *confidant*: someone with whom the individual is psychologically

Table 4.3
Onset of Affective Disorder, Life Stress, and Social Support

	Onset of Depressive Disorder			
	Confidant		No Confidant	
No Recent Life Stress	1%	(1/82)	3%	(1/34)
Recent Life Stress	4%	(2/45)	38%	(17/45)

Source: Brown et al. (1975).

intimate. In survey research, the confidant is sometimes identified by a question such as the following: "If you had a very serious and personal problem, is there anyone you could talk to about it?" In various surveys, more than half, and usually more than three-quarters, of the general population report the existence of such an individual in their network.

In the literature on social stress, the research often shows that the presence of a confidant is especially helpful in times of stress. The effect is analyzed as a statistical interaction, which means that it differs at different levels of stress: for those with low levels of stress, social support bears no relationship to health, but for those with moderate or large amounts of stress, there is a strong relationship between the level of social support and any disorder. Table 4.3 displays results from a widely cited work by Brown and colleagues (1975). For those with recent severe stresses and no confidant, 38 percent had a recent onset of affective disorder, compared to 4 percent of those with recent severe stresses and a confidant. For those with no recent severe stress, the percentage with a recent onset of affective disorder is quite low, regardless of whether there is a confidant. Perhaps these results ought not be so striking, in that they embody ancient wisdom such as found in Ecclesiastes IV: "Two are better than one; . . . for if they fall, the one will lift up his fellow: But woe unto him that is alone when he falleth; for he has not another to help him up."

The literature on social supports has gradually expanded beyond the focus on buffering of stress. Several studies have shown that social supports have beneficial effects on health and mental health, regardless of whether stress is present or absent (Berkman 1985). As in the case of the dimension of social power, there are general physiological consequences to social support, not necessarily mediated by conscious reflection or higher cortical processes (Uchino et al. 1996). Although primary networks and emotional support are important, secondary networks and instrumental support are also helpful in certain situations (Granovetter 1983). More detailed, longitudinal analyses have revealed that stress also can affect social support (Aneshensel and Frerichs 1982). Stress motivates individuals in the network to generate social support, but the social support and the size of the network can be diminished eventually if the crisis does not resolve (Aneshensel 1996). Research is currently directed at understanding the distribution of social supports in the community (Turner and Marino 1994) and the processes by which networks are converted to supports (Wellman and Wortley 1990).

FAMILY

Marriage and Mental Disorder

A second major arena for integration to exercise its force is in the family. Part of the social network of an individual is his or her family, and it has the potential for strong forces of social integration since the relationships are extended in time, both on a day-to-day basis and over the life course, as well as being more intense than many social relationships. Membership in a family unit is presumed to provide emotional support based not on performance of the individual but on the fact of his or her membership in the family unit. The magnitude of the association between being in a family and mental health problems is suggested by the data shown in Table 4.4 on living arrangements, from the National Institute of Mental Health (NIMH) Epidemiologic Catchment Area Program. Living arrangements include family and nonfamily groups living in the same household and those living alone. A *family* is two or more individuals related by blood, marriage, or adoption living in the same household. Here the size of the group is small enough that it is defined by interaction (e.g., around the kitchen table), not awareness as in the definition of community. In 1960 three-quarters of the households in the United States were formed around a married couple, but that figure dropped to a little more than half by 1990 (Table 4.4). There were large increases in the proportions of female-headed families, nonfamily groups, and households consisting of individuals living alone during that third of a century. The data suggest that a decline in social integrations is taking place in the United States in the second half of the century.

Data from the ECA Program show that individuals living in households formed around a married couple tend to use health services for mental health problems less frequently than others (2.43 percent in Table 4.4). Individuals living in nonfamily groups and female-headed families, and those living alone use services nearly twice as much. Many of these differences persist after controlling for individual-level characteristics like age, sex, and socioeconomic status: but, since it is not absolutely clear where the cause lies—that is, in the individual or the group—it is not clear that such a control is required (Badawi 1992).

The living arrangement is differentially associated with major depression and alcoholism. Respondents living in male-headed households and in nonfamily groups are much more likely to meet criteria for alcohol disorder than those in other living arrangements. Those living in female-headed households are much more likely to be depressed (Table 4.4).

For adults, living in a family means being married, for the most part, and there are many epidemiologic studies of the association of marital status with

Table 4.4
Living Arrangements in the United States, 1960 and 1990: Mental Disorders in Three Epidemiologic Catchment Area Program Sites

Living Arrangement	Households in the United States (000's)		Respondents in the ECA Program (three sites)		
	1960 % of total	1990 % of total	% Using Services	Prevalence (%) of:	
				Major Depression	Alcohol Disorder
Married Couple Family	74.4	56.0	2.43	1.83	2.79
Male Headed Family	2.3	3.1	2.67	2.83	9.63
Female Headed Family	8.4	11.7	4.63	5.32	4.12
Non-Family Group	1.9	4.6	5.98	3.75	10.89
Living Alone	13.1	24.6	4.84	3.69	4.64
Total percent	100.1	100.0	---	---	---
Total Frequency	52,799	93,347	12,417	9,516	9,474

Source: Badawi (1992: Tables 1, 8.1, 9.1).

Table 4.5
Marital Status and Psychoses: First Admissions to Mental Hospitals in Canada, 1950–1952

		First Admissions per 1,000 Population			
Schizophrenia	Single/Married Ratio	Never Married	Married	Widowed	Divorced
Male	9.3	0.95	0.10	0.16	0.75
Female	3.2	0.68	0.21	0.18	0.92
Bipolar Disorder					
Male	2.1	0.19	0.09	0.21	0.24
Female	1.1	0.20	0.13	0.21	0.23

Source: Gregory (1959).

risk for various types of mental disorder. Following are selected data for schizophrenia, bipolar disorder, major depressive disorder, and alcohol disorder.

For the psychotic disorders data on hospitalization in Canada are presented (Table 4.5). The data suggest that marriage is protective, both for schizophrenia and bipolar disorder, because married persons have the lowest rates for both disorders and for both males and females. For example, married males have an annual rate of first admission for schizophrenia of 0.10 per 1,000, compared to never married males who have a rate of 0.95/1,000. The differences are smaller for bipolar disorder, but in the same direction. This idea that marriage protects against mental disorder is an example of the *social causation interpretation*— that is, interpreting an association of a social variable with a mental disorder as the result of a causal process whereby the social variable causes, or protects from, the onset of disorder. The *social selection interpretation* is an interpretation of a cross-section association in the other direction—that is, the onset of mental disorder causing the individual to select himself or herself into a social category. In the case of marriage and mental disorder, the selection interpretation is as follows: if mental disorder is inherited and insidious in onset, a young person who will become mentally disordered in the future is already handicapped in the marriage market. The incipient mental patient may be less desirable as a marriage partner, because he or she is less stable emotionally, disagreeable, unpredictable, and generally difficult to get along with. During the intimacy of courtship even very subtle differences between potential mates can be recognized, and persons with psychiatric deficiencies can be rejected. This theory predicts that the unmarried population will contain a residue of persons who are prone to mental illness, while the married persons have been tested by the marriage market and are much less likely to become disordered. The social causation and social selection interpretations can be made for any cross-sectional data in which the social variable is changeable, such as marital status, or socioeconomic status (discussed further in Chapter 5).

Another argument related to marital status concerns the differential utilization of facilities by persons in different marital statuses. The presence of a spouse or other concerned family member mediates the relationship of a mentally disordered person to the community at large and may help to prevent or forestall hospitalization or other forms of treatment. Thus, when the epidemiologist considers data based on treatment facilities, as in Table 4.5, the prediction is for higher rates of disorder for single persons, regardless of the true relationship of marital status to mental disorder.

Considering the effect of gender may help in distinguishing the selection and causation explanations. The ratio of single to married is greater for males than for females, for both disorders (Table 4.5), as is true for the literature in general. Both the selection and causation theories are consistent with this sex difference. Following the line of reasoning of the causation theory, one might argue that males need the emotional security of marriage more than females do because of constant threats to their security in the occupational roles, where, traditionally, more is expected of them. However, one might just as well argue that more is expected of the single woman than the single man, because of the difficulties of sex discrimination in the marketplace. The selection theory might predict that selection by personality characteristics is more intense for men than for women: men are expected to be more active in the courtship role than women, and a withdrawn, shy, or unstable man is less likely to find a marriage partner than is a withdrawn, shy, or unstable woman. Also, it might be argued, women are more likely to be selected for their physical beauty, whereas men are more likely to be selected for their performance as breadwinner. Physical good looks are less likely to be related to the presence of incipient mental disorder than ability to perform in the economic arena. The differential utilization argument is that women who behave bizarrely are less likely to be perceived as violent and threatening and, thus, less likely to be hospitalized. In this case, the sex difference is just an artifact of differences between the sexes as to entry into treatment.

The differences between the relationship of marital status to the two types of psychosis in Table 4.5 help in untangling these issues. The single-to-married ratios, which use the category of never married as equivalent to single, are stronger for schizophrenia than for bipolar disorder. There is nothing in the causation argument that suggests why such a difference should exist. If anything, affective psychosis should be much more vulnerable to the harmful effects of loneliness and isolation than schizophrenia. The never married and divorced have similar rates of schizophrenia, but the widowed have rates close to those of single persons, suggesting that the fact of having gotten married indicates low risk, not the protective effect of marriage. However, schizophrenia is a more chronic disorder than affective psychosis and much more likely to have insidious onset. Therefore, the selection argument applies more strongly to schizophrenia. The concern over differential utilization is contradicted by the differences between the two psychoses. If differential utilization causes such an excess of admissions among single persons for schizophrenia, why does it not do so for bipolar disorder?

Further support for the selection alternative for the diagnosis of schizophrenia comes from examining the other individual categories of marital status. The widowed category is important because the event of widowed acts as a natural experiment. The never married and the widowed are equivalent as far as the causation and differential utilization theories are concerned, because both lack a spouse. However, the widowed have endured the selection process, while the never married have not. Therefore, if rates for never married are higher than rates for widowed, there is evidence of selection. The selection argument applies most strongly to never married persons but also to divorced and separated persons, where the mental disorder may have caused separation or divorce. However, the loss of one's spouse is probably unrelated to whether one is schizophrenic, and widowed persons have survived the selection process to the same degree as married persons. Therefore, if widowed persons have higher rates than married persons, (e.g., male bipolars: 0.20 versus 0.09), the causation argument is supported; if widowed and married persons have equal rates (e.g. female schizophrenics: 0.18 versus 0.21), there is no evidence for this hypothesis. For schizophrenia, the never married and divorced have extremely high rates when compared with the married and widowed, and there is little difference between the rates for married and widowed. For affective psychosis, on the other hand, the rates for never married, widowed, and divorced are practically equivalent, while the rates for married persons are much lower. Thus, for bipolar disorder psychosis, having a partner is protective against the disorder; for schizophrenia, it does not matter so much whether you have a partner as that you have been able to get one at one time or another.

The causation and selection arguments also apply to less severe disorders like major depression and alcohol abuse or dependence, but there are less evidence of inheritance for these disorders, as shown in Chapter 1; more convincing research on social causes, as shown in Chapter 3; and more research on the details of the interaction between sex roles, marital status, and mental disorder. The interaction shows up for the psychoses (Table 4.5) in the difference in higher single-to-marriage ratio for males than for females and in many other studies, particularly of depression (Gove 1972–1973; Gove et al. 1990; Radloff 1975; Warheit et al. 1976). Data on major depression and alcohol disorder from the ECA Program relevant to this issue are presented in Table 4.6. The results show that major depression is more prevalent among females than males (5.7 percent versus 2.5 percent) and that alcohol abuse or dependence is more prevalent among males than females (12.1 percent versus 2.5 percent). But there are intriguing departures from this simple relationship in the individual categories of marital status. For example, among married persons, the rate of depression is more than three times as high among females as among males (4.2 percent versus 1.3 percent) but less than twice as high among the never married (5.2 percent versus 3.3 percent). Married men have the lowest rate of depression among all categories, and the conclusion is that, for depression, marriage seems to be more protective for men than it is for women. For alcohol disorders, there

Table 4.6

Gender, Marital Status, Depression, and Alcohol Disorder (Proportion Meeting Diagnostic Criteria within Prior Year, Epidemiologic Catchment Area Program, Sites 2–5, Respondents Aged 18–54)

	DIS/DSM-III Depressive Disorder		DIS/DSM-III Alcohol Abuse or Dependence		Sample Size*	
	Male	Female	Male	Female	Male	Female
Married	1.3	4.2	9.8	0.8	1,751	2,159
Never Married	3.3	5.2	13.1	3.3	1,320	1,346
Separated/Divorced	3.9	9.5	16.7	5.0	518	1,111
Widowed	13.8	4.2	31.0	2.4	29	167
All Categories	2.5	5.7	12.1	2.5	3,618	4,783

*Sample sizes are for the depressive disorders and are not precise for alcohol disorders, due to slightly different numbers of missing diagnoses. The differences are not more than trivial.

Source: Estimated by the author.

are parallels and differences to the depression findings. But, for alcohol disorders, marriage seems to be protective for women, whose prevalence is very low in that category (0.8 percent).

There is a striking interaction in the widowed in Table 4.6. Among the widowed, the prevalence of depression is more than three times as high among men as among women (13.8 percent versus 4.2 percent). Widowhood appears to be disastrous for men in terms of drinking, whose prevalence in this category is more than 10 times the prevalence for women (31.0 percent versus 2.4 percent). Other more detailed research has shown that widowhood has different effects on men than women: for men, it disrupts management of the household; for women it produces financial insecurity (Umberson et al. 1992).

Longitudinal data on the relationship of entry into marriage to depression and alcohol disorders are especially relevant to the selection argument. In a seven-year follow-up of 1,220 young unmarried people, Horwitz et al. (1996) compared the 347 who married and remained married with the 482 who stayed unmarried. Women who were depressed at the beginning of the study were less likely to get married, but there were no effects of depression on marriage for men and no effects of drinking on marriage for men or women. Controlling for the amount of depression or drinking prior to marriage and for other risk factors, it was found that marriage protected women from depression but had no effect on their alcohol consumption. Marriage protected men from problems with alcohol consumption but had no effect on depression. The effects were strongest for those who reported good marital quality.

There are many possible explanations as to why the role of the married woman, in particular, should be harmful. Most of these explanations have as ultimate cause the changes that have come about in family life over the last few decades. One important change is the decline in the importance of the extended family. The increased prevalence of the nuclear family means that most married women working in the home have smaller social networks and are more likely to be socially isolated than in earlier times. A related change in family structure has been the decline in functions of the family, from the general economic production unit on the farm and in family businesses in the nineteenth century, to a narrower group of functions centered around consumption, where economic functions are performed outside the household and family unit. As these functions are reduced in number, the range of roles, activities, and rewards available to family members qua family members is more limited. Thus, the role of the homemaker is now restricted and tedious, or, as Jessie Bernard puts it, "Being a housewife makes women sick" (cited in Radloff 1975). Also, as family functions are lost, the power structure of the family is changed to give more power to the household head (usually the male) who supports the family financially. In earlier times, the argument goes, the male and female were much more equal in all these respects: in the early U.S. farm family, for instance, both male and female were isolated equally from social contacts, both contributed equally to the production functions of the family, as well as to various other functions such as socialization, consumption, and so forth, and both shared power equally as a result. Now, however, the housewife/homemaker is open to exploitation by the husband because she does not contribute equally to the maintenance of the family, and decisions affecting the financial support of the family tend to be made by the husband. As Turner said, "The authority of the husband to direct certain family decisions is . . . more than simply adherence to a traditional belief in male authority but a product of the institutionalized subordination of family to economic life" (Turner 1970: 263). Being in a subordinate position in a social structure means that decisions affecting one's life are made by others, and one has less control over one's environment, which is a possible cause of mental disorder. In general, the housewife/homemaker tends to have an impoverished social identity, putting her at risk for mental disorder.

Other explanations for the high rate of mild mental disorder among married women have to do with cultural changes. In recent years the idea that women should work outside the home has become increasingly prevalent, and it has been shown that adolescent girls hold this work norm (Turner 1970: 267). The norm of working outside the home, however, does not prepare them for the exigencies of married life, especially with the arrival of children. Socialization in this culture has not prepared women for working outside the home as well as it has prepared men (Ruble et al. 1993). Thus, the culture has prepared young women inadequately to meet the most common situation of their adult lives, and they may find themselves in one role while desiring to be in another—an example of *intrarole conflict*. This type of cultural contradiction can lead to poor performance in the role and consequent lower self-esteem, which may be a possible contributor to mental disorder. The addition of roles and resultant expansion of social identity for a working woman produce *inter-role conflict*, sometimes called *role strain* or *role overload*, leading to stress-reactive disorders such as anxiety and depression. The competing hypothesis of *role accumulation* predicts that entry into expanded roles leads to new satisfactions and better control over their own lives (Sieber 1974). Most studies show that women in the workforce have lower rates of depression than women working in the home, supporting the role accumulation hypothesis. The relationship depends, however, on the quality of the work environment (Lennon 1987, 1995; Lennon and Rosenfield 1992), whether or not there are children in the home to take care of (Kessler and McCrae 1982), and how much time the woman has to spend on the housework (Bird and Fremont 1991). But the role accumulation hypothesis has even been evaluated in a sample of mothers with the unusual burden of caring for an adult, mentally retarded child, and the results support the idea that an expanded social identity is healthful (Hongt and Seltzer 1995).

Growing up in Families

The orientation of the preceding discussion has evaluated the idea that social integration, when it takes the form of marriage, is good for adults. Marriages can be stressful if the quality of marital interaction is not good, of course, but the option of separation or divorce provides an escape. Where escape is not possible or is difficult, for whatever reason, a bad marriage can be injurious to mental health. Marriage may bring with it other problems, such as the burden of caring for aged adults. Thus, consistent with Durkheim, too much integration can be as bad as too little. For children growing up in a family, the option of leaving via divorce is much more difficult, and the processes by which children grow up in families is of considerable interest. The approach to socialization taken in this section builds on role theory and symbolic interactionism, as discussed in Chapter 3.

The most important tenet of symbolic interactionism for the sociology of mental disorders is that language, thought, and self-concept in a child all develop out of social interaction (Hewitt 1991; Stryker 1964). The analysis begins with a newborn infant's interaction with the mother. The infant begins to observe chains of events that occur repeatedly; for instance, he or she feels his or her own hunger and cries, the mother approaches, and eventually the infant is satisfied. Each event or gesture becomes a signal for the next event, and, thus, a "conversation of gestures" develops. After a period of interaction, both parties in the interaction come to have identical understandings of the same gestures, at which point, according to symbolic interactionists, the gesture may be termed a *significant symbol*. Significant symbols entail a plan of action or a prediction of future behavior and events.

Words and categories are significant symbols and are created through social interaction as well. For example, young infants come to associate the sound "ball" with a variety of objects that are round and that roll. Eventually in their random vocalizations they make a sound similar to "ball" and associate their own verbal performance with the round, rolling qualities. Gradually, their use of the word becomes more refined: their parents reward them in one way or another for sounds closest to "ball," and the infants learn that certain round objects that do roll should not be rolled (e.g., eggs). The word "ball" comes to mean for infants more or less exactly what it means to their parents and society.

The social identity and self-esteem are complex, significant symbols that also develop out of social interaction. The social identity, it will be remembered, is the totality of patterned activities (roles) that together constitute the object *me*. Thus, the *me* consists of plans for action, as does the "ball" concept. Learning of the social identity, the *me* concept, occurs in two stages, called *play* and *the game* by Mead (1934). In *play* the child learns to take the role of some other person, such as the mother, another child, or the Cookie Monster from Sesame Street. Even such simple games as peek-a-boo or hide-and-seek require that the child understand the role the other will play, as well as his or her own role, that is, in symbolic interactionist terms, that he or she take the role of the significant other. In *the game*, however, the child learns to respond to a complex set of roles, each related to his or her own role in specific ways—in this case, the child is taking the role of *the generalized other*, which is more characteristic of social life in general. In a baseball game, for instance, the fielder anticipates, interprets, and coordinates his or her actions with all the other players in fielding the ball; likewise, the role *boy* requires dovetailing the infant male's own behavior with numerous others, each with a specific relationship to him and to each other.

The social identity of the young child is, to a large extent, made up of family roles, and she or he cannot escape them. The most important roles are the age/generation role and the sex role. Some theorists have contended that learning these roles and the complexities of fitting them to ordinary, but constantly changing, situations are the first bit of abstract thought that an infant engages in. The learning of these roles may affect thinking processes as the infant matures, and failure in this learning process may impair permanently the thinking capability of the individual. As with any significant symbol, the social identity must have a stable, clear meaning in order to be useful in guiding behavior.

The self-esteem of the young child is dependent largely on his or her family's evaluation of his or her role performances. The child has no other standards by which to judge his or her behavior and so must accept, to some extent, the family's evaluations. From infancy to adulthood the social identity becomes increasingly complex and less and less dependent on the family of origin. Roles that compete with family roles develop from interaction with peers. The age/generation role demands increasing autonomy from the family and finally a breakaway from the family in adulthood. The young adult carries with him or her a residual social identity and self from the history of the family interactions into the wider society. In some cases these residuals have weaknesses that make it difficult or impossible for the individual to adapt to society's role demands, as described earlier in the discussion of the role of women. The question of autonomy of the individual from his or her family is crucial in the study of mental disorders.

Stages of life are defined by the passage through the life cycle and are connected to cognitive and physiological maturation (Erickson 1968; Levinson and Gooden 1985). Each stage brings with it life crises, such as entering school as a child, leaving home as a young adult, and losing friends and relatives through death as an older adult; and these life crises can be operationalized with life event measures, as discussed in the prior chapter. Each stage of life includes a social field that forms the social identity of the individual, and these various types of social fields ebb and flow in number and importance to the individual, (Kellman 1970). Each social field provides the opportunity for evaluation of the individual's performance, and thus influences the self-esteem.

Symptoms of mental disorder do not cluster in children in the same way as they do in adults, and, thus, the diagnoses that we apply to adults are not good for children. The review of epidemiology in Chapter 2 included the diagnostic categories of autism as an example of a pervasive and severe disorder and attention deficit disorder with hyperactivity as an example of a learning disorder. In adolescence, adult disorders such as panic (Hayward et al. 1989) and depression arise (Lewinsohn et al. 1994), in much the same form as exist for adults. Prior to adolescence, the symptoms may occur, even in a form permitting of diagnosis (Kovacs et al. 1984), but they do not always cluster in the same manner as in adults; they do not have the same standard epidemiologic correlates, such as gender; and the standard treatments for them are not effective or much less so (Ryan 1992). While there are continuities between childhood and adulthood in broad behavioral and emotional tendencies, specific syndromes resembling adult disorders that occur in childhood do not predict strongly their occurrence in adulthood, except for pervasive disorders like autism and a small percentage of children engaged in wide-ranging antisocial behaviors, discussed later (Cowen et al. 1973; Robins 1966; Robins et al. 1971).

Studies of Family Interaction

During the decades of the 1950s and 1960s there was a series of research studies focused on detailed observations of families with a child identified as mentally disordered. Intensive clinical studies in New Haven, Connecticut (Lidz 1973; Lidz et al. 1965), Stanford, California (Bateson et al. 1956), and Rochester, New York (Wynne et al. 1958) were led by researchers in the psychoanalytic tradition and were theoretically interesting but suffered from methodologic weakness. The goal of the studies was to discover how family processes led to mental disorder. These studies initially focused on schizophrenia but have broadened to include a wider variety of disorders and problems that occur in families (Cox and Paley 1997).

One finding is that families with a schizophrenic child have different types of power relationships. Lidz (Lidz et al. 1965) identified two major types of families that he calls skewed and schismatic. In the *skewed family* the power is distributed very unequally between the parents of the identified patient. This type of family is more likely to have a male schizophrenic child, and the power is centered in the mother. The mother is powerful and domineering, while the father is passive, withdrawn, and compliant. The *schismatic family* is one in which there is no consensus about the distribution of power in the family, with continuing conflict and considerable difficulty in making decisions. This type of family is more characteristic of female schizophrenics. A related type of deviance in families with a schizophrenic patient is the *blurring of sex and generation roles* (Wynne and Singer 1963). Sometimes a parent pushes a child into the spouse role in order to make up for qualities he or she feels the real spouse lacks. Concomitantly, the spouse may be treated as child. The wife may take on masculine characteristics and roles, and the husband feminine characteristics, or the child's sex-typed behavior may be inappropriate to what the family feels is normal. The passage of the child through stages that mark the generational process and the gradually developing independence of the child may be cut off or blocked or superstimulated, or there may be disagreement about these stages between parents.

The Palo Alto group contends that families with schizophrenic offspring were characterized by *double binds* (Bateson et al. 1956). A double bind is a very specific type of communication with several conditions. The person receiving the communication must be in a situation such that the communication is important to interpret, and she or he must not be able to leave the social situation of the communication. The message itself has two contradictory parts to it. Sometimes the contradiction is completely on the verbal level, such as, "You may go out for the movie but be back at nine o'clock" (when it is known the movie lasts beyond nine). Often the contradiction is split between the verbal and nonverbal level, as when a mother physically stiffens so as to reject the approach of her son and then, when he declines to hug her in response to the nonverbal message, asks, "Don't you love me anymore?" These researchers felt that one potential response to this situation is the pattern of withdrawal and fantasy behavior of the schizophrenic.

A cluster of behaviors in families with an identified mental patient, observed by many researchers, has to do with the *scapegoating* of the child by the parents—that is, the child can come to be victimized in order to solve a problem that the family has (Vogel and Bell 1960). Often the child symbolically represents a problem the parents have, and the problem is projected onto, and internalized by, the child. An example is a couple with severe sexual problems who focus undue attention on the masculinity of their slender, graceful son. Sometimes attention directed toward a "problem" child can draw attention away from the intense conflicts that exist between the parents. Excessive concern about a child's performance at school may symbolize and at the same time draw attention away from the doubtful performance of the father in the occupational arena. The most common function of this exploitation and scapegoating is to generate solidarity within the family. These families are conflicted and fragile, yet the members are very dependent on one another. Projection of problems onto a child creates problems for the child, to be sure, but it may preserve the existence of the family. The child is sacrificed for the good of the larger social system, the family. During this process the members act as if the family does not have severe internal problems, a type of behavior called *pseudomutuality*—the false perception of social integration within the family.

An intriguing body of research focused on the thought patterns of parents of schizophrenics (Wynne and Singer 1963). Thought patterns can be studied by asking subjects to give answers to unstructured stimuli, such as a Rorschach or Thematic Apperception Test card, and to record, transcribe, and rate certain qualities of the answers, which reveal underlying styles of thought (Johnston and Holzman 1979). Bleuler (1924) thought that the primary symptom of schizophrenia was a loosening of associations. Others have felt that the process of forming categories was deficient: categories have no rigid boundaries but slip and slide into one another. This failure in category formation has been called *overinclusiveness*—the inability to exclude unnecessary and unrelated information in the processing of stimuli, leading to information overload and withdrawal to a more controllable internal world of fantasy. Another quality characteristic of schizophrenic thought is the tendency to be egocentric—that is, for thought to be dominated by concern over existence, the body, and the boundaries of the self. Thus, a central symptom of schizophrenia is *egocentric overinclusiveness*. For example, everyone is sometimes stimulated sexually in unpredictable ways, but the schizophrenic blames it on "sexual vibrations coming through the crack underneath the door." Everyone can converse with himself or herself without speaking, but the schizophrenic may understand these conversations as messages from another planet. Everyone has some trouble becoming independent from his or her mother, but in the schizophrenic this can lead to terrifying fears of death or engulfment. All of these symptoms are examples of the failure of the schizophrenic to sort out information related to the self into appropriate, singular, nonfluid categories that allow logical processing of the information, efficient storage in memory, and easy and dependable recall. A category such as "ball" does not pose too many difficulties; it is all the categories related to the self—in effect, all the social categories—that make trouble. The complement of egocentric overinclusiveness in the child is egocentricity in the parent, and parental patterns of thought should show this quality. For instance, in a test sorting varieties of objects, parents of schizophrenics should be less likely to form categories of objects according to objective criteria such as color, shape, and utility and more likely to form categories based on their own relationship to each of the objects in question. Fruit will be sorted by its appeal to the subject, for instance, not by its color or size. For objects that are difficult to form categories around, stories will be created involving the subject and each object—for example, grouping glass, dustpan, and tray by reasoning as follows: "I drop the *glass*, it breaks, I clean it up with the *dustpan*, and put it on the *tray*." This pattern of thought is relevant to the development of schizophrenia when it concerns the social identity of the preschizophrenic. It may be that the social identity is unable to take a logical, consistent form because the boundaries of its categories are shifting constantly at the whim of the parents. For example, we have seen that the formation of sex and generational identities of the child is one of the first logical operations he or she performs. But in the family of the schizophrenic, the sex and generation lines are often blurred and/or shifting, with the male child being absorbed into the parental generation as a substitute for father, for example, and then reverting on demand into the role of baby. All the clinically based observations and theories of schizophrenia in the family—the double bind, marital schism and skew, pseudomutuality, scapegoating, and the blurring of sex and generation lines—are consistent with the idea that logical thought as regards the social identity is made difficult during family life. The social identity of the child becomes an object in the service of the unstable social relationship of the parents. The idea of leaving the family sometimes provokes fears of engulfment or death in the schizophrenic or the fear that one of the parents will die; since according to this line of reasoning, the social identity of the schizophrenic is established and maintained in habitual instability by the parents, the fear of a sort of death is not so unrealistic.

An improvement over clinical observation of families is research on patterns of interaction of families with mentally disordered individuals under some sort of laboratory conditions (Hirsch and Leff 1975; Jacob 1975). Usually, the families are asked to perform a group task, during which their interactions are observed through one-way mirrors, recorded on tape or video machines, and later coded as to important dimensions of the interaction. The dimensions coded are designed so as to tap aspects of interaction that are thought to be relevant to the mental disorder under study, and it is predicted that the families with disordered children will show deviant patterns of interaction. These studies are methodologically grounded in group interaction studies in sociology (Bales 1950), but the coding of interaction is still a new development, so that a variety of coding schemes have been developed that differ considerably in their content as well as their reliability and validity.

An example is the work of Ferreira and colleagues (1965), who used the so-called *revealed difference* technique to stimulate family interaction in a standardized way. Each member of the family was given a list of social situations that involved a definite judgment (for instance, a 14-year-old girl wishes to buy a very fashionable coat, but her parents would like her to get something that will last for more seasons—should she buy the coat she wants or listen to her parents?). Later, the family met together and discussed a limited number of these situations on which they did not agree as individuals. They were asked to come up with a family decision after discussion. Several characteristics distinguished families with a schizophrenic from other families. In normal families the individual family members tended to agree without discussion more often. During the discussion normal families were more explicit about expressing opinions, and there were fewer silences than in families with schizophrenics. The decision reached by families with schizophrenic children was less likely to fulfill the choices made by members of the family and more likely to be a decision that no individual family member favored (termed a "chaotic" decision). Other similar laboratory studies report analogous results: for example, Farina and Holzerg (1968) reported abnormal levels of conflict in families with schizophrenics, and Mishler and Waxler (1968) reported blurring of generational lines, as in the clinical observations.

All of these patterns of family behavior—schism and skew, sex and generation blurring, double binding, scapegoating, and pseudomutuality—are recognized as distinct patterns of behavior only because they originated from different research teams. In any given family these behaviors may overlap considerably, and they are conceptually close. Thus, skew almost necessarily involves sex and generation blurring; the double bind almost by definition involves pseudomutuality; and exploitation of the child by the parents is involved in one way or another in all these patterns of behavior.

Family studies of adult schizophrenics have concentrated on a concept called *emotional expression*, or EE (Kavanagh 1992). Although some studies suggested that stress in the form of life events was related to onset of schizophrenia, the findings were much weaker and less consistent than for depression, and the most convincing data were limited to samples with mixtures of first and recurrent onset cases (Brown et al. 1972; Brown and Birley 1968). Research on EE began with attempts to understand the influence of family life and family stress on relapse. A family interview was developed that, when tape-recorded, could be rated as to certain qualities of interaction involving the identified patient, such as emotional overinvolvement, hostility, and critical comment. Combinations of these produced a rating of EE for the family, and schizophrenics in families with high levels of EE were more likely to suffer a relapse, often measured by readmission to hospital, than those in families with low EE. This finding has been replicated in more than two dozen studies (Kavanagh 1992), including studies in non-Western cultures (Leff et al. 1990). The finding has contributed to the development of psychoeducational strategies for families of schizophrenics that lower the rate of relapse (Hogarty et al. 1986; Leff et al. 1989). It would seem that the measure of EE bridges an intellectual gap between studies of stress discussed in Chapter 3, family interaction discussed earlier, and the broader sociological concept of integration or cohesion; but attempts to demonstrate this linkage empirically have not been conclusive (King and Dixon 1996).

As the strength of genetic influences on schizophrenia has become clearer, it has been assumed increasingly that the insidious onset of schizophrenia in the child was the dominant influence on the family process. The decline in interest in family process may have been premature, as evidence on the power of the family process is garnered from study of other disorders. Also, even in the context of a highly genetic framework such as the Genain quadruplets, each of whom eventually became schizophrenic or schizotypal, one is struck by the bizarre quality of the family interaction and the possibility of its influence (Rosenthal 1963).

Research on mental disorder occurring in more than one person in the family—folie à deux ("madness in two": DSM-IV *shared psychotic disorder*)—also supports the idea that family patterns can generate psychotic behaviors. It is rare, but there are hundreds of published case reports. The most common appearance of this disorder occurs when two or more people share an extensive delusional system. A review of case reports from 1942 to 1993 that met DSM-IV criteria for the diagnosis of *shared psychotic disorder* showed that more than 90 percent of the cases involved either a married couple, sibling, or parent–child relationship (Silveira and Seeman 1995). In Gralnick's review (cited in Gruenberg 1957), 118 interpersonal relationships of folie à deux were presented, and of these only 9 did not involve members of the same family. There were 26 husband–wife combinations, and 83 out of the 118 were first-degree biological relatives. Males and females were affected about equally, and in about two-thirds of the cases the dyad was socially isolated. Usually, one person was dominant and induced his or her own delusional structure onto a submissive partner. Often the dominant person was diagnosed as schizophrenic, and the submissive partner had schizoid traits. There were rarer cases involving more than two persons, and one reported case of folie à douze with 12 persons involved.

Folie à deux is an extraordinary subject that could as well have been included in Chapter 6 on the social transmission of psychopathology. However, the similarity to the family studies of schizophrenia is strong. There is a close and long-term personal relationship of group members in folie à deux and in families with a schizophrenic offspring. In both cases a less powerful member of the group learns disordered behavior over a protracted period of time and in relative isolation from the rest of society. The major difference is that in folie à deux the submissive person who is thought to learn the disorder is the less deviant member of the group, whereas in the studies of schizophrenia and the family, the less powerful person ends up being the identified patient. About the same range of environmental and genetic interpretations applies to studies of schizophrenia and the family and folie à deux. Since folie à deux occurs mostly among biological relatives, one interpretation is that the family members share genes that predispose them to mental disorder of this type. The husband–wife combination could also result from assortative mating for characteristics related to mental disorders, so that in virtually all instances there could be some genetic influences.

An important feature of these descriptions of disorganized families is that they tap into the three fundamental dimensions outlined in Figure 1.6: power (e.g., schism and skew; scapegoating), integration (double binds, high EE families, and enmeshment, described later), and meaning (e.g., pseudomutuality).

Box 4.1
Abbreviated Diagnostic Criteria for Conduct Disorder

A repetitive and persistent pattern of behavior in which the basic rights of others or major age-appropriate societal norms or rules are violated, as manifested by the presence of three (or more) of the following criteria in the past 12 months, with at least one criterion present in the past 6 months:

Aggression to people and animals

1. Often bullies others
2. Often starts physical fights
3. Has used a weapon
4. Has been physically cruel to people
5. Has been physically cruel to animals
6. Has stolen while confronting the victim
7. Has forced someone into sex

Destruction of property

8. Has set fires with intent to cause serious damage
9. Has destroyed others' property

Deceitfulness or theft

10. Has broken into houses
11. Often lies
12. Shoplifting or forgery

Serious violations of rules

13. Stays out at night
14. Has run away from home
15. Is often truant from school

Source: American Psychiatric Association (1994: 90–91). Reprinted with permission from the *Diagnostic and Statistical Manual of Mental Disorders*, Fourth Edition. Copyright © 1994 American Psychiatric Association.

Family and Conduct Disorder

Conduct disorder arises in adolescence but has roots in childhood and extends into adulthood as *antisocial personality disorder* (ASP). Abbreviated criteria for conduct disorder and antisocial personality disorder are given in Boxes 4.1 and 4.2, and the overlap in behaviors is easy to see. A precursor of conduct disorder, with which it overlaps highly in late childhood and early adolescence, is attention deficit disorder with hyperactivity (*ADHD*: criteria in Box 1.6) As with the

Box 4.2
Abbreviated Diagnostic Criteria for Antisocial Personality Disorder

A. Pervasive pattern of disregard for and violation of the rights of others, occurring since age 15 years, as indicated by three (or more) of the following

1. Failure to conform to norms as expressed by the law

2. Repeated lying, use of aliases, or conning of others

3. Failure to plan ahead

4. Repeated physical fights

5. Reckless disregard for the safety of self or others

6. Consistently irresponsible work or financial behavior

7. Lack of remorse

B. At least 18 years old

C. Conduct disorder with onset before 15 years

Source: American Psychiatric Association (1994: 649–50). Reprinted with permission from the *Diagnostic and Statistical Manual of Mental Disorder*, Fourth Edition. Copyright © 1994 American Psychiatric Association.

eating disorders described later, its prevalence is so much higher in adolescence than at other ages that it is likely this stage of life is crucial to its etiology. Following the discussion of cultural and universal disorders in Chapter 1, we can loosely speak of this as a *developmental stage disorder*. Moffit (1993) and others have proposed that two varieties of conduct disorder be considered (Figure 4.2). One variety begins in childhood and continues through adolescence to evolve into adult ASP—so-called *lifelong persistent disorder*. This variety explains the relative stability, over the entire life course, of antisocial behaviors found in a small percentage of individuals (median prevalence of ASP in Table 2.7 of 1.4 percent). This variety may have a heavier genetic loading than the second type, *adolescence limited disorder*, which has a high prevalence during that life stage (prevalence of conduct disorder in children 4–16 of 5.4 percent but higher than 10 percent among adolescents in the same study (Offord et al. 1987)).

The rise and fall in prevalence of antisocial behaviors during adolescence generate the problem of explaining both how the disorder becomes frequent and how it disappears or desists. Conduct disorder evolves out of processes of family interaction and socialization in Western culture and can also be thought of as a "cultural disorder," much as *latah* is a cultural disorder in Malaysia. There is huge cross-cultural variation in the disorder, with some cultures, such as enclosed religious societies, having negligible occurrence (Eaton and Weil 1955). In our culture it is frequent relative to other psychiatric disorders (Table 2.7). It is expressed on a continuum of intensity, as is clear from the diagnostic criteria for ADHD, conduct disorder, and ASP.

Figure 4.2
Prevalence of Adolescence Limited and Lifelong Persistent Antisocial Behavior

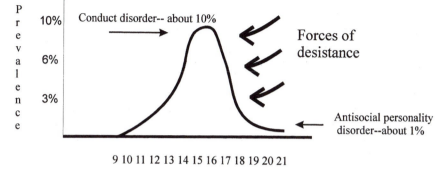

To explain the high prevalence of conduct disorder among teenage males requires the notion of the force of morbidity, as in Figure 2.1. To explain the drop in prevalence requires the notion of "forces of desistance," by which high prevalence adolescent limited conduct disorder disappears, leaving a residue of low prevalence lifelong persistent antisocial personality disorder.

Source: Adapted from the original by T. E. Moffitt, "Adolescence-Limited and Life-Course Persistent Anti-Social Behavior: A Developmental Taxonomy," *Psychological Review* 100: 674–701. Copyright © 1993 by the American Psychological Association. Adapted with permission.

Consistent with the concept of cultural disorder, the manifestations of conduct disorder express core conflicts in the culture regarding aggressive behavior, are extensions and exaggerations of normal behaviors, and are highly regarded or even held in awe. The behaviors associated with conduct disorder often lead to punitive and controlling reactions from others, as shown in studies of interactions of families with children with conduct disorder (Dishion et al. 1995; Lytton 1990; Patterson 1986). A crucial aspect of these studies is that they allow analysis of patterns and chains of interactions. An important pattern begins with a young boy behaving with "garden variety" problems such as whining, yelling, or tantrums, intended to produce immediate gratifications from parents. These attempts at coercion of the parents lead to responses that are ineffective at controlling the coercion but that may appear appropriate, such as nagging, scolding, blustering, or threatening (dubbed *nattering* by Patterson, 1986). Many children respond to the parents by adapting or stopping the coercive behavior, but some —perhaps those with a particular temperament—learn that the coercive behavior produces results that are useful or gratifying in the short term, especially in avoiding a demand for some sort of compliance by the parent. For example, the parent may ask that the meal be finished, that the child get dressed, or that the room be picked up, and the child learns to escape the task or request by whining or threatening a temper tantrum. The parent's demand also has a coercive quality to it, and the entire process of demand, coercive behavior, ineffective parental response, and escape of negative reinforcement is termed the *coercive process* (Patterson 1982). As the child becomes more coercively skillful, the chains may become longer, and after a threshold of time, measured in seconds in studies of interaction, there is a sharply rising risk of the parents' exploding, hitting the child, or both. Patterson and colleagues feel that the combination of difficult temperament and unskilled parenting puts the child at high risk for antisocial behavior and that "the primary determinant for children's antisocial behavior is to be found in family management skills" (Patterson 1986: 440.

Although it may begin in the family, the coercive process expands its influences as the child grows up. In school the coercive process may take the form of seemingly innocuous, but measurable, aggression toward schoolmates. Aggression even as early as first grade is predictive of a wide range of consequences such as early smoking, early sex, drug abuse, and eventually antisocial personality disorder (Kellam, Simon, et al. 1983; Kellam, Brown, et al. 1983; Kellam et al. 1994). The coercive habit of behavior, acquired in the family due to its short-term consequences in terms of avoiding aversive demands of the parents, also has some short-term successes in the school context. But it has long-term implications that are negative, such as failure in the academic system, where it is not effective. The problem is that the child who has acquired the habit has difficulty understanding the long-term implications and continues to be rewarded by the short-term benefits.

Another consequence of the coercive habit of behavior is its effect on peer relations. Most peers reject a coercive child, and there will be sorting process so that the child ends up associating with children with similar habits. In one longitudinal study, parenting practices, antisocial behavior at age 9–10, and earlier peer relations predicted association with deviant peers several years later (Dishion et al. 1991). Eventually, the deviant peer group comes to positively reinforce deviant behavior, and as the child grows toward autonomy, the quality of parenting that becomes most important has to do with monitoring activity of the child in relation to peer groups (Dishion et al. 1995). The effect of the peer group is so strong that therapies in which delinquent children are treated collectively can have negative, or iatrogenic, effects (Dishion and Andrews 1995).

There are aspects of this developmental process that are similar to processes of social selection, social labeling, and the self, discussed in Chapter 3. The social selection process involves the individual *shopping for environments* (Dishion et al. 1995) and the effects of mental disorders on that process. For example, the effect of a depressive or psychotic episode is to elicit social support over the short term but to diminish the size of the social network if the episode does not resolve in a short time. The social labeling framework can be applied to the perceptual habits of the parents about the child, so that a cycle is built up very gradually in which deviance is increasingly marginalized (Caprara and Zimbardo 1996). An important difference between this approach and the labeling framework is that the process is temporally more finely graded and subtle, occurring in many thousands of interactions over many years. A second important difference is that no single, stereotyped role is available to be entered; instead, thousands of subtle perceptual response biases heighten the probability of coercive, instead of cooperative, responses, on the part of both the parent and the child (Dodge 1993). The perceptual response habits are applied to the self-concept, especially as regards the potential for the future—so-called *possible selves* (Oyserman and Markus 1990)—which guide the individuals' choice of short-term and long-term behaviors.

The developmental process just described is influenced in important ways by macrosocietal factors, including processes related to stratification, integration, and culture. Parenting skills are affected by the level of economic or other stress in the family, for example (Conger et al. 1990, 1992); and the relationship of socioeconomic status to antisocial behaviors is eliminated when parenting behaviors are adjusted for—that is, as in Figure 1.6, parenting behavior mediates the relationship of socioeconomic status to disorder (Larselere and Patterson 1990). Life stresses suffered by the parents, from whatever source, also lower the effectiveness of parenting (Ge et al. 1994), as do marital stress and divorce (Allison 1989; Cherlin et al. 1991, 1998; Cowan and Hetherington 1991). At the level of the community, studies of social disorganization have used concepts similar to those used by the Leightons in the Nova Scotia study discussed earlier. For example, in a study from the British Crime Survey, social disorganization is defined as "the inability of a community structure to realize the common values of its residents and maintain effective social controls" (Sampson and Groves 1989: 777). Levels of crime were higher in communities characterized by lack of local friendship networks, little participation in formal and voluntary organizations, and inability to supervise and control teenage peer groups. These types of communities were more likely to occur where there were high residential mobility, diverse ethnic and racial groups, and high values on indices of family disruption.

The effect of culture on development of aggressive and antisocial behaviors is exercised partly through the mass media. Watching television shows that display aggressive behaviors provides a model for children that they do follow, both inside the laboratory just following the program and outside the laboratory in their everyday activities (Eron 1982). The effect is tapped by self-reported aggression as well as aggression observed by experimenters and reported by peers. The effect of television violence can be long-lasting and is reinforced by parental endorsement of sociopathic attitudes and behaviors occurring on television.

When considering application of the term *developmental stage disorder* to a pattern of behaviors, it is important to comprehend how the disorder starts and stops (Moffitt 1993). Earlier we considered how the behavior pattern is reinforced, so that its prevalence grows to nearly 10 percent in adolescent boys (Offord et al. 1987). How does one explain the small percentage—about 1 percent or less—of the population with lifelong persistent disorder? How does one explain the diminution in prevalence after adolescence? One explanation for the lifelong persistent disorder is that antisocial traits are inherited (Mednick et al. 1984). Early influences such as occurring during birth might also be important (Kandel 1991). Parenting practices may be transmitted from generation to generation, mimicking or reinforcing genetic inheritance (Patterson 1986). Inheritance, birth, and processes occurring shortly thereafter determine the temperament of the child, which forms the basis for the development of socialization, and may begin a coercive process that eventually leads to antisocial behavior (Dishion et al. 1995). The degree to which an antisocial trait—inherited or acquired early through some other mechanism—is present is indicated by how early the child begins the pattern of antisocial behavior, the breadth of antisocial behaviors engaged in, and the variety of contexts in which the behaviors are performed (Caspi and Moffitt 1995). Stabilities in behavior over time may just reflect stable causative situations, referred to as *ecological constancy* by Caspi and Moffitt (1995). For example, parenting practices in the lower social class may be less effective than in the middle class and the class status may be relatively stable over childhood and youth (Patterson 1986). Social disorganization and availability of deviant peers, as discussed earlier, may be relatively constant for a small proportion of children.

The process by which antisocial behavior develops thus begins in the highly integrated confines of the family, from which the child cannot escape. As the child grows up, patterns learned there find the social context of adolescence less integrated and organized, providing fewer social constraints on antisocial behavior. The desistance from antisocial behaviors takes place when new social constraints are introduced in the form of social bonds to a spouse, a network of friends, and a commitment to a job (Caspi and Moffitt 1995; Sampson and Laub 1990).

Family and Eating Disorders

As with conduct disorder, eating disorder emerges in the context of individuation from the family and is influenced by cultural trends in the wider society. *Anorexia* is a disorder involving refusal or resistance to eating, even to the point of starvation (diagnostic criteria in Box 4.3). *Bulimia* is a disorder involving maintenance of normal or low weight by purposefully vomiting after eating (diagnostic criteria in Box 4.3). Bulimics eat irregularly, with periods of little eating followed by binges and vomiting. Both anorexics and bulimics have obsessive features to their eating, such as hoarding, compulsions, and fantasies involving food. Anorexia and bulimia are found most frequently in adolescent girls and young women. The disorders are serious not only because they disrupt the family and social relations but also because the abnormal eating behavior can lead to death. A narrative account is given in Box 4.4.

Anorexia nervosa has been described precisely for at least some 200 years (Palazzoli 1978), but it has become important in the last few decades in North

Box 4.3
Abbreviated Diagnostic Criteria for Eating Disorders

Anorexia Nervosa

A. Refusal to maintain body weight at or above 85% of the normal weight for age and height.

B. Intense fear of gaining weight or becoming fat, even though underweight.

C. Undue influence of the effect of body weight or shape on self-evaluation.

D. In those past menarche, absence of at least three consecutive periods.

Bulimia Nervosa

A. Recurrent episodes of binge eating, that is:

   1. Eating a large amount of food in a short time;

   2. Feeling that one cannot stop eating.

B. Recurrent behaviors to avoid weight gain, such as self-induced vomiting, use of laxatives or enemas, or fasting.

C. Criteria A and B occur at least twice a week for three months.

D. Self-evaluation unduly influenced by body shape and weight.

Source: American Psychiatric Association (1994: 544–45, 549–51). Reprinted with permission from the *Diagnostic and Statistical Manual of Mental Disorders*, Fourth Edition. Copyright © 1994 American Psychiatric Association.

America (Gordon 1990). Both anorexia and bulimia are almost unheard of in non-Western cultures, even including India, where fasting is a well-known cultural ideal. Yet recently there have appeared case reports of anorexics even in India (Khandelwal et al. 1995). Figure 4.3 shows epidemiologic evidence on the upward trend reported from two of the best studies—the Mayo clinic in Rochester, Minnesota (Lucas et al. 1991) and the psychiatric case register in Aberdeen, Scotland (Eagles et al. 1995). Both studies examined a wide range of records in psychiatric and general health facilities, in inpatient and outpatient situations, and applied standardized case criteria to them to control for the possibility that clinicians might be learning about the disorder and diagnosing cases as anorexic in one time period that would not be so diagnosed in another period. Both studies show that the incidence is about 1 new case among 10,000 females each year. Both studies show a rise in incidence between 1960 and 1990: in northeast Scotland, the incidence rose from about 3 per 100,000 population to more than 15; in Rochester, Minnesota, the incidence rose from about 5 per 100,000 to more than 25. The absolute levels of incidence in the two areas are not identical, but the difference is probably due to differing diagnostic systems (DSM-IIIR in Minnesota and a standardized system based on ICD-8 in Aber-

Box 4.4
Narrative Account of Eating Disorder

Soon afterwards my essay was returned to me in a deathly hush. The paper was full of corrections in red and blue, and at the bottom was an ominous four out of ten. . . . A girl sitting in front of me raised her paper, I could see that she had nine out of ten. I gasped, and looked her over carefully. She was rather short but slim, and her hair was pulled back and fastened at the neck with a clasp. She wore a short fringe on her high forehead, and had large mischievous dark eyes. Her face was thin and pale. I was filled with profound jealousy. Her self-assurance made me feel clumsy and inadequate. I looked from her slender arms to my own which were rather plump. *For the first time in my life I felt gross, oppressed by the great weight that was pulling me down.* . . .

With evening classes started at the local church I joined with enthusiasm. The teachers were gifted, and slowly the clouds started to clear; my mind was illuminated with a new light. I started to get six out of ten at school, but I wasn't satisfied: I had to catch up with the slim girl at the top. She was forever in my thoughts, a continuous challenge. I had also begun to detest my country dresses, and kept complaining about them at home. At first my mother was disconcerted. "What ever has got into you? You never used to bother about such trifles . . ." she would say, as I kept pressing her. I felt that all my family were common people concerned only with stuffing themselves and nothing else. My father was worst of all. "You have had it too good, you have. If you had suffered hunger as I did during the war . . ." he repeated time and again. Yes, he had suffered hunger, but that was as far as his heroism had gone, I thought with contempt. . . .

. . . Sometimes I read romantic love stories, in which the hero was a kind nobleman who showed his beloved every possible consideration and was to all a perfect gentleman . . . The true lover was one who revered and respected the woman he had chosen. And my own father did anything but that . . . I would never be like mother! A woman tied to her kitchen stove, with no greater concern than to fill her husband's belly, completely uninterested in his work or aspirations, petty-minded, without a will of her own or any kind of ambition for herself. A woman who had gone to seed and had grown fat.

I was determined to be different, to make something of my life. And so I studied like one possessed, and became increasingly disgusted when I saw my father stuffing himself at table or even talking about food. . . .

I had asked a very clever schoolgirl to join us, but I felt rather ashamed of our poor house, and right from the start made a point of doing all the tidying up so that the place would not look too shabby . . . One day she suddenly asked me "What have you decided to do this autumn?" . . . "What matters is not to allow yourself to become bogged down in the petty details of a humdrum life. To work for some end," she said eventually. "That's what matters." And I suddenly felt very close to her.

At supper that night I refused to eat more than she did. My mother was surprised. "What does this mean? Only a few days ago you were eating like a horse. You have put on weight at last . . ." And she looked angrily at my friend. "You are just a copy cat," she spat at me. I was furious with her. There it was: all she cared about was fattening me up. But that was the last thing I myself wanted . . . *Suddenly it seemed to me that I had always been too fat. . . . It just couldn't go on. And next day I ate even less. They gave me castor oil. It didn't do anything. My friend went. I was left to wage my tre-mendous struggle all on my own. I knew now what I would have to do. And dieting was the first step. . . . And as I got thinner it seemed to me that my dream was coming true; I could see the slender face of the top girl of the class—I would be just like her at college. A shudder passed through me as I felt the new me stirring deep down.*

Source: From Mara Selvini Palazzoli, *Self-Starvation: From Individual to Family Therapy in the Treatment of Anorexia Nervosa* (New York: Jason Aronson, Inc., 1978). Reprinted by permission of Jason Aronson, Inc., and the author.

---

deen). The amount of the rise, however—a factor of 4–5 in 30 years—is similar. The Rochester data extend back to 1935 and show a decline until about 1950. There is some evidence that the incidence of the disorder leveled off or declined in this country in the 1990s (Heatherton et al. 1995; Willi et al. 1990).

The rise in incidence of anorexia was paralleled by an upsurge in the medical literature for anorexia and bulimia that took place starting in the late 1960s or early 1970s (Figure 4.4). There were about 25 articles in English and 25 articles in other languages (almost entirely European) each year until about 1973. Pal-azzoli's first attempt to publish a translation of her text *Self-Starvation* in English was turned down because the publisher thought the disease was such a rarity no one would purchase the book (Palazzoli 1978, noted in Gordon 1990). Hilde Bruch's classic *Eating Disorders* was published in 1973 (1973), and *Self-Starvation* in 1974 (Palazzoli 1978). These two publications, in English but by women whose professional training was in Europe, may have contributed to the mushrooming of the medical literature in the English language on this topic. It is also possible that the publication in 1972 of the Feighner criteria, which included an operational definition of anorexia, contributed (Smith and Weissman 1991). In 1982 a journal began called *The International Journal of Eating Disorders*, with a consequent burst of new articles, which peaked at more than 200 in 1985 and which has been level ever since.

Historical accounts of bulimia are rare. The word occurs in an occasional abstract once or twice in the 1960s and 1970s, but there was little medical publishing on this topic until after 1979, when an article appeared (Russell 1979) describing it as a feature of anorexia and proposing the term (Figure 4.4). From 1980 the publishing activity has been accelerating steeply, up to more than 150 articles per year.

Eating disorders fit the criteria for cultural disorder as discussed in Chapter 1. The symptoms of anorexia are direct extensions and exaggerations of normal behaviors and attitudes in the general population, often including behaviors that are widely valued; it is a pattern of misconduct that provides individuals with a means of being irrational, deviant, or crazy; and it generates highly ambivalent reactions from others, such as awe and respect, as well as punitive and con-trolling responses. The wide cross-cultural variation suggests that the disorder is culturally caused.

Figure 4.3
Incidence of Anorexia Nervosa, Minnesota and Scotland

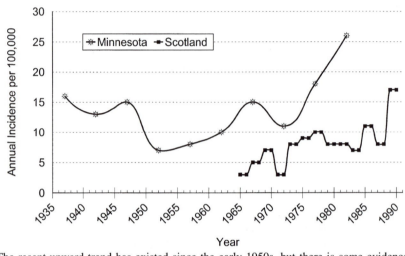

The recent upward trend has existed since the early 1950s, but there is some evidence of a downward trend from 1935 until 1955.

Sources: Minnesota data from Lucas et al. (1991); Scotland data from Eagles et al. (1995).

Regardless if anorexia and bulimia have culture as their ultimate cause, they include many accompanying physical symptoms. Anorexics have lowered estrogen levels and elevated growth hormone levels; reduced levels of neurotransmitters like norepinephrine, serotonin, and dopamine; abnormalities in temperature regulation; delayed gastric emptying; and many other physiological abnormalities. There is a sizable literature on treatment of anorexia with chemicals, especially antidepressants; and some think that it is a form of depression. Some of the physiological abnormalities are predictable results of starvation, and even some psychological symptoms, such as obsessive fantasizing about food, have been shown to result from experimentally induced starvation (Keys et al. 1950). Some of the symptoms of starvation, such as the tendency to binge, persist years after the starvation episode has been stopped and may be a form of compulsive disorder (Szmukler and Tantam 1984). After years of research on the biological aspects of anorexia, some researchers agree the cause is "psychic" (McHugh 1996) or that "the physical symptoms of anorexia are epiphenomena unrelated to the etiology of the illness" (Beumont, cited in Gordon, 1990: 20).

It may seem obvious that culture is the "cause" of anorexia and bulimia. A challenge to this interpretation is a credible genetic epidemiologic study of female twins that found a heritability estimate for bulimia of 55 percent (Kendler et al. 1991). How can 55 percent of the variance of liability to this disorder be explained by genetic factors, when there is no mention of it in the medical literature prior to 1979? This is an example of the broad range of vulnerabilities

Figure 4.4
Anorexia and Bulimia: Number of Medical Citations, 1966–1995

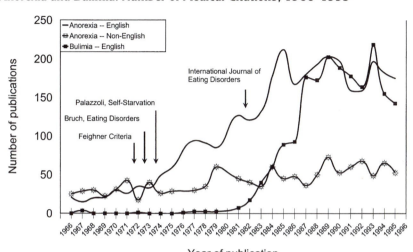

Medical literature grows as researchers become aware of the disorder, and the awareness diffuses within cultural boundaries. New avenues of publication facilitate the diffusion in the medical community. It is possible the medical literature feeds back into the mass media, actually influencing the rate of the disorder.

Source: MEDLINE.

that can be inherited and the even broader range of culturally produced expressions such vulnerabilities can take. This might be termed a *diathesis-culture* model of etiology.

How is the culture to blame for anorexia? Gordon's explanation is that the culture provides a model for behavior that addresses a new stress being experienced by young women (1990). The model for behavior is the ideal of slimness. The influence of the culture is felt in face-to-face groups, such as sororities studied by Crandall (1988), in which binge eating behaviors were observed over time and disseminated through friendship networks and were correlated with measures of popularity. The influence of the culture is also exercised without face-to-face contact through the ideal of body shape detectable in cultural artifacts. For example, contestants of the Miss America Pageant and *Playboy* centerfold models were all well under the normal weight for females of their age and height (Figure 4.5), and the percentage underweight is progressively lower from 1959 through 1978. These women are chosen after long competition, in part, because they represent the ideal form. In the most recent decade shown in the figure, 60 percent of the Miss America contestants and 69 percent of the *Playboy* centerfold models had weights 15 percent or more below normal—a major criterion for the diagnosis of anorexia nervosa in the DSM-IV (Box 4.3, pointed out by Wiseman et al. 1992). Figure 4.5 shows that the winners are

Figure 4.5
Miss America Pageant 1959–1988: Weights of Winners and Contestants

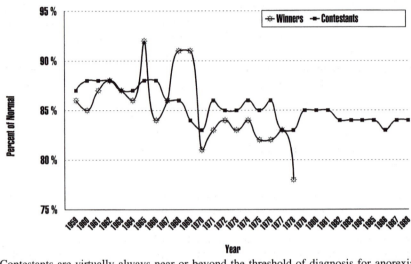

Contestants are virtually always near or beyond the threshold of diagnosis for anorexia (85% of normal); winners are usually lighter than contestants.

Sources: Garfinkel and Garner for 1959–1978 (1982); Wiseman et al. for 1979–1988 (1992).

closer to the ideal than the entire group of contestants, in that they are even more underweight. In the last decade the trend of slimness seems to have flattened out, but this may be due to a limiting factor connected to starvation and survival. Nevertheless, the prevalence of eating disorders in college populations seems to have declined during this same decade (Heatherton et al. 1995).

As with television models of violence and aggression, there are mass media influences on this ideal, with advertisements such as the famous quote by the duchess of Windsor: "You can never be too rich or too thin" or an article in *Playgirl* magazine that identified anorexics as "today's Golden Girls" (cited in Gordon 1990). A variety of dieting techniques are advertised, but some have been referred to as a "handbook for anorexia . . . the mass marketing of anorexia . . . a form of direct training in anorexic behavior" (Wooleys, as cited in Gordon 1990: 111). Case studies and observations of groups suggest that the anorexic and bulimic behaviors are highly imitative.

The new cultural ideal of slimness is coincident with new pressures on young women. As discussed earlier, they are relinquishing the traditional role of wife and mother and moving into the marketplace—yet they are still expected to live up to ideals of femininity, including doing more than half the housework and more of the nurturing of relatives and children, even if they are working as well as being married. Achieving thinness satisfies the cultural ideal of femininity while still allowing high achievement, in that the thinness is a performance of sorts. The developmental perspective, best developed in the case of conduct disorders, as discussed earlier, is important, too, as suggested by Palazolli (1978), in that women in their late teens are breaking away from the family, and anorexic behaviors can satisfy the drive toward autonomy. The teenager can rebel without appearing to be rebellious and punish without appearing to. The girl may start to diet as a result of following fashion, but the power it has over the family generates a persistence beyond normal dieting. After 40 years of study and treatment, Hilde Bruch felt that anorexia had gone from an individual disease into a social disease (cited in Gordon 1990).

In-depth clinical observations on families of adolescents with eating disorders have many similarities to the research on schizophrenia. For example, Minuchin (Minuchin et al. 1978) concludes that these families are characterized by *enmeshment*:

an extreme form of proximity and intensity in family interactions. . . . In a highly enmeshed, over-involved family, changes within one family member or in the relationship between two members reverberate throughout the system. Dialogs are rapidly diffused by the entrance of other family members. A dyadic conflict may set off a chain of shifting alliances within the whole family as other members get involved. Or one family member may relay messages from another to a third, blocking direct communication. . . . Subsystem boundaries in enmeshed families are poorly differentiated, weak, and easily crossed. This situation results in the inadequate performance of subsystem functions. For instance, the spouse relationship is subordinated to carrying out parental functions. Or, parental control of children is ineffective . . . or a child may join or enlist one parent against the other in decision making.

As with the study of EE, there are controlled trials indicating that family therapy is effective in treatment of this disorder (Dare et al. 1995).

The example of eating disorders is important for this analysis because it shows, more vividly than any other, that the epidemic transmission can occur through both face-to-face *and* mass media forms. The rise in medical interest in eating disorders is probably also not completely free from the influences and interests of the mass culture, and some of the sources of imitation may be located in the medical research interest.

5

Socioeconomic Stratification

INTRODUCTION

Definition and Measurement

Inequality is the simplest concept that applies to the group but not the individual. As such, the study of inequality has always been central to sociology. Inequality in social resources seems to be present in every current society (Flanagan 1989) and brings with it a wide range of associated differences that might be related to mental disorder. Although the study of mental disorders formed part of the earliest empirical work in sociology, as in Durkheim's *Suicide* (Durkheim 1966), the earliest work on the relationship of social inequality to mental disorder has been done by individuals in other fields (Commission on Lunacy 1971; Nolan 1917). A review of the community studies of social status and specific mental disorders in 1969 included 25 studies of social class and mental disorder, of which 20 revealed the inverse relationship between social class and prevalence of disorder, that is, the highest rate of disorder in the lowest social class (Dohrenwend and Dohrenwend 1969). A review in 1990 referred to 60 studies published between 1972 and 1989 (Ortega and Corzine 1990). Forty-six of these revealed an inverse relationship between social class and mental disorder. The strength and consistency of the relationship is impressive, as is its enduring interest for sociologists. Gradually, a picture is emerging that reflects both the complexity of mental disorders as well as the complexity of social class and socioeconomic status.

Socioeconomic stratification is the process by which individuals are accorded unequal access to rewards and resources in society. Individuals in social structures with socioeconomic stratification are hierarchically ordered as to wealth, power, and prestige, that is, economic, political, and cultural rewards and resources. Socioeconomic stratification affects the degree to which individuals can control their environment and their sense of mastery of their environment.

An important form of socioeconomic stratification is the social class structure. *Social classes* are groups of individuals who are similar in their wealth, power, and prestige and who either (1) interact with one another more frequently than randomly or (2) are aware of some common interest. This is a slightly broader definition than that in the Marxist tradition, in which social classes are groups of individuals in a society defined by their relationship to the ownership and control of the means of production or by the process of appropriation, production, and distribution of surplus value in the economy. The Marxist definition leads to at least two basic classes: those who own and control the means of production and receive the benefits of others' labor (i.e., the capitalist class) and those whose labor is exploited, in that the surplus value produced is taken from them (i.e., the working class). Although Marx emphasized the process of exploitation as the major determinant of class, later evolutions of this concept have emphasized the importance of power and the capacity of the individual to influence decisions about the structure of the economy. Individuals in similar socioeconomic strata form into social classes, in part, in order to retain control over the economic and political process (Mills 1956). Some theorists have emphasized the importance of the relational concept of exploitation based on control of productive assets, that is, beyond the material means of production to organizational power and the influence of credentials such as educational degrees, as opposed to simple measures of domination or power (Western and Wright 1994, Wright 1985). For the purposes of our discussion, the glue holding these concepts of social class together is the concept of the social group: social classes, according to this view of the Marxist tradition and its heirs, are social groups with differential control over productive assets, whereas socioeconomic stratification indicates an ordering of individuals by a slightly wider range of concepts, who may or may not be formed into groups.

The study of social class and socioeconomic stratification includes diverse traditions, and these definitions are not consistent with all of them; but they are fairly close to some well-known texts (Collins 1994; Farley 1994; Matras 1984). These various perspectives on socioeconomic stratifcation and social class have formed a central part of the discipline of sociology, and it is reasonable to consider different mental health outcomes associated with various definitions.

Education, either as years of education or as credentials such as certifications and degrees, is the most common measure of social class in psychiatric epidemiology and public health research (Liberatos et al. 1988). Its stability over adult life, reliability, efficiency of measurement, and good validity are presumably the main reasons for its popularity (Kaplan and McNeil 1993). Education represents knowledge, which might have an influence over health behaviors (Sorlie et al. 1995). But education also might increase the value of an individual's contribution to the productive process, which translates into greater social rewards. Another view is that the credential provided by educational attainment may be more a sign of lifestyle, class of origin, or "attitude" than of actual ability; but these added latent features may be what generates the higher salary.

Occupation, measured according to the Bureau of Census Classification of Occupations or as occupational prestige, is a major social class indicator in psychiatric epidemiology. Occupation strata identify technical aspects of work and also are associated with prestige, wealth, skills, and specific working conditions. Some authors in the functionalist tradition in medical sociology emphasize that occupational prestige and socioeconomic status are consequences of educational achievement (Ross and Wu 1995). Other models of occupational stratification emphasize that the rewards associated with positions that persons occupy in society derive from their location in the hierarchical structure of the workplace, not from the workers' education (Krieger et al. 1993, 1997). For example, managerial and professional occupations obtain higher wages partly as a compensation for being high enough in the hierarchy that close supervision is viewed as inappropriate—that is, they are rewarded for supervising themselves.

A third way of measuring social stratification has been the assessment of a person's *economic resources*, using measures of personal and household income (Liberatos et al. 1988), dichotomous measures of poverty (Bruce et al. 1991), and wealth (Muchtler and Burr 1991). In a money economy, income and wealth are the most straightforward measures of ability to acquire resources and influence a wide range of outcomes. But these measures present their own set of limitations. Income typically shows a higher nonresponse rate than education and occupation, supposedly due to the unwillingness of respondents to disclose their financial situation (Liberatos et al. 1988). Furthermore, although income can be conceptualized as a measure of social class, several research programs consider income as a dependent variable to be explained by social class theories (Halaby 1993; Robinson and Kelley 1990; Wright 1979). Positions in the social structure are associated with various kinds of income (e.g., rents derived from renting land versus wages derived from being an employee) and differentials in wealth (e.g., value of assets owned) (Calinicos 1989; Wright 1993). Finally, because wealth is more unequally distributed than income (Matras 1984; Wolff 1995), it is likely that reliance on income as the preferred indicator of economic resources may overlook larger differentials in mental health.

The Causes of Inequality

There are two main contending paradigms to explain the existence of social classes and socioeconomic differences (Matras 1984). One explanation arises out of the sociological theory of *functionalism*, a major paradigm in sociology in the United States (Davis and Moore 1974; Merton 1956). With respect to socioeconomic stratification, functionalists argue that in a complex, modern society there are differences in the individual qualities required for different occupations. Some occupations require extremely persistent, skillful, and intelligent individuals, while other jobs can be performed by almost anybody. In addition, some jobs are more important than others for the welfare of the society as a whole. Rewards are distributed unequally in society in order to attract individuals with specific and rare skills and abilities into important jobs. Thus, the social class system serves the function of sifting and sorting people into appropriate occupations for the greatest good of society.

The second main explanation for the existence of socioeconomic stratification and social classes comes out of the *conflict paradigm*, which finds its most developed expression in the Marxist tradition. According to this tradition, classes are thought to exist because individuals higher up in the hierarchy are more powerful, who preserve the class structure in order to hold on to privileged and advantageous positions for themselves and their heirs (Mills 1956). Such control is exercised in a variety of ways. For instance, the upper classes may attempt to manipulate the political process to favor those already in power (Ferguson 1995; Navarro 1994). High-status individuals attempt to ensure that their sons and daughters are provided with educational credentials for entering high-status positions in the occupational structure. The upper classes, consciously or unconsciously, may manipulate the mass culture so that explanations for the social-class system are expressed in terms of individual differences in ability instead of differences in power or inequalities of institutions (Chomsky 1989; Matza 1967). The functional explanation of the class system, discussed earlier, may be thought of as an ideology maintained by elites to draw attention away from their privileges and power (Laurin-Frenette 1976).

Socioeconomic stratification is a process generating a structure that tends to persist through time, even though the individuals holding positions within the structure are constantly being replaced over the generations (Erikson and Goldthorpe 1993). Each generation of individuals joins the current structure of socioeconomic stratification, in a process of *intergenerational* mobility (i.e., from one generation to the next) and *intragenerational* mobility (i.e., within one generation, over the lifetime of an individual). The process of stratification as well as the periods of highest vulnerability to mental disorder (reviewed in Chapter 2) are developmentally staged. During some stages of life, the effects of the environment, the choices made by the individual, and the successes and failures in tasks related to the social environment in particular are more important in the future evolution of the life course than at other stages. Variation in the population as to many individual characteristics tends to expand over the life course, as the combination of genetic endowment and environmental experiences produces individuals with ever more differentiated qualities (Baltes et al. 1980). A natural research focus that reflects on the functional and conflict explanations for the maintenance of social classes in the study of individual differences in ability, whether they are presumed to be inherited or the result of socialization processes. The question is, How does an individual with a given set of characteristics end up in a given social position? In the field of socioeconomic stratification, any abilities that are broadly advantageous in a range of occupational positions are important.

Many cognitive abilities are relevant to performance of occupational duties.

Some scholars feel that *intelligence*—the ability to perform in modern school systems and to survive and advance in a given culture—is a broad, stable, and general dimension along which individuals differ (Anastasi 1988). There is considerable controversy over how broad and general the trait of intelligence is (Sternberg 1995). If this concept of general intelligence is correct, then it has consequences for the functionalist theories of class, because more intelligent individuals will be suited to a wider range of jobs than less intelligent individuals. There is evidence that intelligence as measured by standard psychometric tests is correlated with socioeconomic position (Jensen 1969). The continual calibration and recalibration of intelligence tests, with validation by a range of indicators, naturally tend to produce a measure that predicts broadly for the majority of the population and is longitudinally stable. But the degree to which intelligence tests actually are predictive, whether it is fair to use them in judging an individual's abilities, and the degree of changeability over the life span are issues of intense debate (Schiff and Lewontin 1986).

Ambition is also important to consider. In a true functionalist "meritocracy," the only determinants of reward should be an individual's ambition and his or her intelligence (Young 1994). At any given level of ability, ambitious people who set high aspirations for themselves are likely to have higher educational and occupational attainments.

Other types of abilities are important to consider. Kohn (1977) feels that lower-class children are brought up in an atmosphere that encourages a *conformist orientation* without the flexibility necessary to deal with a stressful situation. Lower-class adults, perhaps because of the type of occupations in which they find themselves (Kohn and Schooler 1983), value conformity to authority more than upper-class people and socialize their children to their own value systems. Upper-class individuals and their children value self-direction more than conformity to authority. Conformity to authority contributes to inflexibility in coping with stress, and this inflexibility, interacting with genetic factors, explains some or all of the social class differences in rates of mental disorder. Abundant data from several industrialized nations show that social classes do differ in their conformity orientations in this way (Kohn 1977), but there is as yet no evidence that the differences are connected to mental disorder. The concept of conformist orientation would appear to be related to the coercive family process discussed in Chapter 4. That process involved inflexible parenting of a sort, and it is linked to socioeconomic status. But there has been no research directly linking the two concepts.

Useful empirical studies of the stratification process have taken the form of path models of intergenerational mobility, as shown in Figure 5.1 (Sewell et al. 1970). The path models in this tradition benefit from use of continuous outcome variables, such as occupational prestige or income, and therefore involve a simplification of stratification to something called the *status attainment process*. The numbers are standardized regression coefficients (betas), as described in reference to Figure 3.5 (pages 133–134).

If an individual inherits his or her class position from his or her parents,

Figure 5.1
Wisconsin Model of Status Attainment

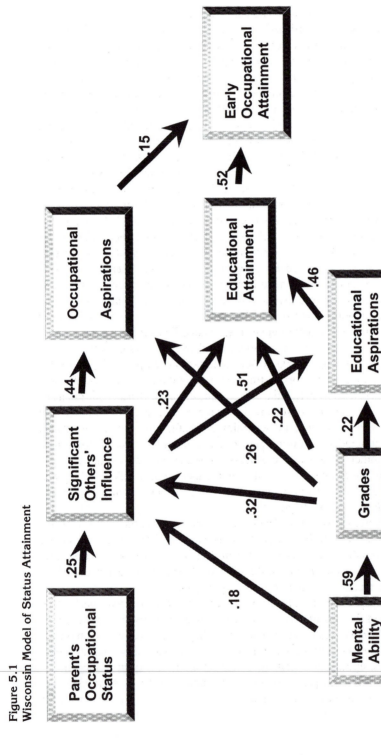

The system of social stratification maintains itself from generation to generation. The family background and the individual's ability are important, but a crucial period is during adolescence and early adulthood, when peer influences on ambition influence the eventual status attainment. In this diagram, residual and unanalyzed correlations are omitted.

Source: Sewell et al. (1970). Reprinted by permission of the American Sociological Association and the authors.

regardless of his or her personal characteristics, then the class system is said to be "rigid" or "closed," supporting the conflict interpretation for the existence of classes. If an individual can enter the upper class no matter what his or her social class background, the system is thought of as "open," and the functional theory is supported. In Western societies during the first three-quarters of the twentieth century, there was considerable intergenerational movement from the lower class into the middle and upper-middle classes. The movement is due partly to the expansion of the middle class. But along with the movement out of the lower class, there is a tendency for those born into the upper class to remain there throughout their lifetimes. In Figure 5.1, both the occupational status of the parents and the mental ability of the offspring have strong influences on ultimate attainment. In this model the sources of variation in mental ability—for example, whether it is inherited or caused by the environment—are not analyzed. Mental ability has a strong influence on grades (.59), which, in turn, affect educational ambition (.22) and educational attainment (.22). Early variables like mental ability and parental occupational status also pass effects on status attainment through social psychological variables measured in high school, such as the ambitions of the offspring and the effects of peers. But social class background also affects aspirations because the individual may become aware that upward mobility is closed to him or her or because he or she is taught that it is inappropriate to aspire to upper-class status. Thus, the Wisconsin model provides some support for both functionalist and conflict perspectives.

Adolescence and young adulthood are important developmental periods for both the process of socioeconomic stratification *and* the onset of mental disorders. As shown in Figure 5.1, high school educational and occupational aspirations (as well as other factors such as the socioeconomic position of the family of origin) are very influential in determining whether the individual attends college; college attendance is important in determining the first job (Sewell et al. 1970). Still other models of the process show that the first job has a strong influence on the entire later career (Blau and Duncan 1967). Likewise, the age of risk of first onset for many mental disorders is in adolescence and young adulthood, as described in Chapter 2.

Thus, the general focus of this developmental approach is the ongoing, reciprocal relationship between the age-graded expectations of the social system, the adequacy of the individual's performance in the context of those expectations, and the consequential mental life of the individual. The Wisconsin model (Figure 5.1) shows that performance in the school system affects future status attainment. Ratings of performance by others affect aspirations for future performance, and the school system and the occupational system regularly provide ratings of performance. These "natural" ratings affect self-esteem and feelings of mastery, which, in turn, can affect the risk for onset of mental disorders (Kellam, Brown, et al. 1983; Kellam, Simon, et al. 1983). In turn, mental disorders affect performance in school and occupation (Kessler et al. 1995).

The process of socioeconomic stratification is related to the occurrence of mental disorder in a subtle and complex manner. The effects of many variables that mediate the relationship ebb and flow over the life course, interacting back and forth in a constantly evolving codependent manner. Important aspects of this coevolution are shown in Figure 5.2. Typical sociological studies of socioeconomic status are in the top part of the figure (inter- and intragenerational mobility), and typical epidemiologic studies of psychiatric disorder are in the bottom part (familial transmission and natural history). The diagonal lines represent the confluence of the two disciplines, which is the subject of this chapter. Social class can affect the occurrence of mental disorder early in life by the way the infant and child are socialized (*early socialization* in Figure 5.2). Social class can affect the way in which adults think and cope (*later socialization*). At any given time, lower social class status may be involved with greater *stress*. Likewise, the onset of mental disorder may affect the attainment of class status early in the occupational career, even before the signs and symptoms of mental disorder are fully apparent, through the familial transmission of mental disorder. This effect shows up in less than expected occupational mobility for the individual, compared to a sample from the same cohort in history (*selection*). Onset of disorder is associated with a natural history, which may also produce downward mobility from whatever position the individual has attained up to that time (*drift*).

CAUSATION: ENVIRONMENTAL AND INDIVIDUAL FACTORS

Social Class and Mental Disorder in New Haven

The monograph *Social Class and Mental Illness* is the strongest early study of class and mental disorder, and it assumed the direction of causation from class *to* mental disorder (Hollingshead and Redlich 1958). It represents one of the strongest collaborations between sociology and psychiatry. Hollingshead, the sociologist, had created earlier the Hollingshead *Index of Social Position*, which produced five categories of social class by combining information on education, occupation, and area of residence for each respondent. This index presumes that social class can be represented and measured via a single set of ordinal categories and is consistent with the earlier definition of social classes as groups of individuals that are similar not only in terms of wealth, power, and prestige but also in structured patterns of interaction, discontinuous culture and lifestyles, and awareness of their class.

Social Class and Mental Illness had the advantage of presenting data on specific categories of disorder but the disadvantage of using data only from facilities that treat mental illness. It shares these features with other research in this "first generation" of psychiatric epidemiology. Table 5.1 presents the central findings. Psychosis is strongly associated with class, showing more than eight times the prevalence in the lower class as in the upper two classes (15.05 versus

Figure 5.2
Socioeconomic Status and Psychopathology: Inter- and Intragenerational Models

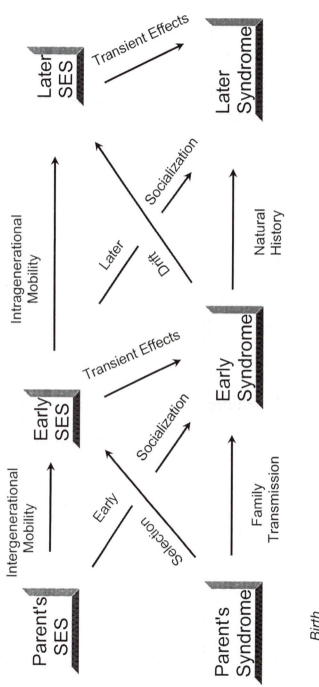

The top part of the diagram shows the process of inter- and intragenerational mobility, as is typically studied in sociology. The bottom part shows the natural history of the disorder, as is typically studied in epidemiology. The issue of causation versus selection is expressed in the diagonal linkages between the two processes.

Table 5.1
Social Class and Mental Disorder in the New Haven Study (Rates* per 1,000)

	Level of Social Class			
	I-II	III	IV	V
Neurosis				
Prevalence	3.49	2.50	1.14	0.97
Incidence	0.69	0.78	0.52	0.66
Psychosis				
Prevalence	1.88	2.91	5.18	15.05
Incidence	0.28	0.36	0.37	0.73

*Prevalence rate is point prevalence; incidence rate is annual.
Source: Hollingshead and Redlich (1958: Table 16).

1.88 per 1,000, Table 5.1). Some of this association must be due to higher chronicity among the lower classes, since the relationship of class to incidence is weaker (0.73 versus 0.28 per 1,000, Table 5.1). Chronicity of neurosis, on the other hand, is associated with higher class status, even though the relationship of neurosis to incidence is flat (Table 5.1). Treatment for psychosis was available in 1950 through publicly financial mental hospitals; but long-term treatment for neurosis had to be paid for by the patient. The higher prevalence rate of neurosis for the upper classes thus presumably is an example of the differential utilizations hypothesis (Chapter 4) resulting from a shortcoming in the methodology, which relied on data solely from treatment facilities, not the general population.

Incidence Studies

The New Haven, Connecticut, study was the first among many later examples of studies of socioeconomic stratification and mental disorder. Most of the studies are cross-sectional in nature, yielding *prevalence* rates, which means that the observed association between class position and mental disorder could have resulted either because lower class position causes mental disorder (social causation interpretation) or because those with mental disorder end up in lower class positions (social selection interpretation). Prospective studies of *incidence* of mental disorder show that the class position actually precedes the disorder and thereby establish class as a more credible potential cause. The incidence results from the New Haven study as to schizophrenia (Table 5.1) have been replicated in dozens of studies, with all but a handful showing the inverse relationship of incidence with social class (Eaton 1974, 1985), thus providing consistent support for the causation explanation. Data on schizophrenia incidence are uniformly from treatment agencies, since it is so rare. But since schizophrenia is a severely impairing disorder, most schizophrenics get treated by psychiatrists, and data from the treatment sector are more credible than for other disorders (Eaton 1985).

Data for nonpsychotic disorders are credible only if they originate from community studies, since the proportion treated for these disorders is low. But there are more limited incidence data. Indicators of poverty (Bruce et al. 1991) and occupational status and education (Anthony and Petronis 1991) are risk factors for depression in data from the ECA Program, supporting the causation model for that disorder. ECA analyses on panic disorder (Keyl and Eaton 1990), agoraphobia (Eaton and Keyl 1990), and social phobia (Wells et al. 1994) all show statistically significant relationships of indicators of low social class to incidence, supporting the causation explanation for the anxiety disorders generally.

Social Class and Stress

Some explanations for the effects of lower class status on mental disorder concentrate on the social environment of the individual, especially its stressful qualities. Other studies focus on individual differences in coping with the social environment; still other possibilities exist in the way in which socioeconomic position brings individuals into contact with the physical environment, as in the biosocial model in Figure 1.6. Increased stress is the most widely accepted causal explanation for the increase in rate of mental disorder among the lowest class. Definitions of stress given in Chapter 3—for example, the "discrepancy between the demands of the environment and the potential responses of the individual"—link into notions of power differences and differential ability to control the environment. Conflict theorists would contend that lower-class life is, at the least, less pleasant than life in the upper class, in part because of additional stresses. Many of these stresses are described in vivid detail in Marx's descriptions of life in the lower classes in nineteenth-century England (Marx 1967: Chapter 10; Engels 1958).

Life event stresses are more frequent in the developmental periods of adolescence and young adulthood (Goldberg and Comstock 1980; Turner et al. 1995). Many of these relatively normal stresses involve the economic system, where the lower-class person is at a distinct disadvantage compared with the upperclass person. The individual in the lower class is probably more likely to have financial difficulties, for instance (Wright 1979), or to lose his or her job (Granovetter 1995). Stresses resulting from illness to oneself or one's friends and deaths to friends and relatives are important causes of mental disturbance, and these illness-related stresses have repeatedly been shown to be more common in lower classes than in the upper classes (Krieger et al. 1993, Marmot and Koveginas 1987; Susser et al. 1985). Indices of stress, which collect together these types of stressful life events into a score, are related to lower social class position (Goldberg and Comstock 1980; Turner et al. 1995).

The methodology in the "second" generation of psychiatric epidemiologic

Figure 5.3
Social Class and Stress in Manhattan

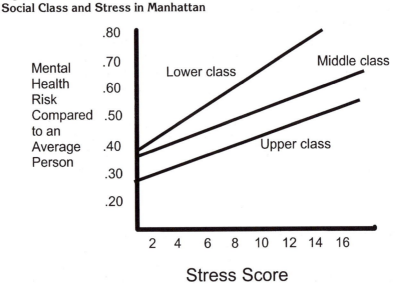

Lower-class life is connected to higher mental health impairment. In all three classes, more stress is connected to higher rate of impairment. The slope for the lower class is steeper, suggesting a greater vulnerability to the same degree of stress.

Source: Redrawn from Langner and Michael (1963: Figure 14.2).

research on class shifted considerably from the New Haven Study. An example is the *Midtown Manhattan Study* (Langner and Michael 1963). The data collection was through a household survey; and the emphasis was on a global concept of mental illness, instead of specific diagnostic categories. The substantive focus shifted from social class to social stress; but the issue of social class remained important. The concept of social stress provided an etiological explanation for the association of social class and mental disorder, as shown in Figure 5.3. The figure shows that higher levels of stress are related to higher risk for mental illness, all along the continuum of stress from very low to very high. It also shows that individuals in the lower class have a higher risk for mental illness at any given level of stress. Finally, the figure suggests that stress is a more potent activator of mental illness in the lower class than in the middle and upper class, in that the slope of the line for the lower class is steeper (Kessler 1979).

In *The Social Origins of Depression* (Brown and Harris 1978), there was evidence of a relationship of life event stressors to depression: for example, 86 percent of the recent cases from the community and 75 percent of patients had a severe event or major difficulty, but only 31 percent of the women without depression had such events or difficulties (Table 2.4). The researchers were also interested in the relationship of social class to depression (Brown et al. 1975). There was evidence of a relationship of social class to depression; for example,

25 percent of the lower class in the community residents versus 5 percent of the middle-class community residents were recent or chronic cases (Brown et al. 1975: Table 2). There was evidence that stresses were related to social class; for example, 54 percent of the lower class versus 30 percent of the middle class had a severe event or major life difficulty (Brown et al. 1975: Table 3). There was evidence that the presence of a confidant helped buffer the effects of stress, as shown in Table 4.3. What is of interest here is the elaboration of this relationship made by analyzing the data in terms of life stage, because the availability of a confidant differed by life stage (Figure 5.4). The bottom two lines in Figure 5.4 show that social class interacts with life stage in affecting depression: there are no statistically significant differences between the classes, *except* for women who have one or more children less than six years old living with them. For women at this life stage, more than 40 percent are recent or chronic cases of depression in the lower class, and only 5 percent are in the middle class. There is evidence of a separate interaction of class with the availability of a confidant in the top two lines in Figure 5.4. Here again, the classes differ most in the life stage of women who have children less than six years old living with them. Less than 40 percent of these women report having someone they can talk to about personal problems, whereas more than 75 percent of middle-class women have this kind of relationship available to them. Since most of these women are married, the suggestion appears to be that the lower-class marital life does not support or include a psychologically intimate component during this life stage.

The absence of a confidant or fewer social supports in general for lower-class persons might explain the differential vulnerability to stress by social class, which is reflected in the data from the Midtown Manhattan Study (Figure 5.3). This lack could be interpreted as a lack of environmental coping resources, in the language of Chapter 3. The differential vulnerability could also be interpreted as lack of individual coping resources, as has been done in a study by Wheaton, in what he calls an *attributional* theory (Wheaton 1980). As a result of reinforcement contingencies associated with social class position, individuals develop biases in their attributions of the causes of changes in their situations. The general notion from attribution theory is that success is more likely to be attributed to the individual's efforts, while failure is more likely to be attributed to the external environment. Lower-class individuals are less successful in the everyday challenges of life, because of their disadvantaged position in the social structure, and acquire the habit of attributing causes to the external environment. Upper-class individuals are more successful, in general, and attribute causes to their own efforts. The external attribution, termed *fatalism*, increases the vulnerability to psychological disorder because active attempts at coping are viewed by the individual as unlikely to be successful. Upper-class individuals are more optimistic because their background has led them to think of themselves as successful, and this optimism leads to greater persistence in the face of stress, which is ultimately more successful—a self-fulfilling prophecy. In this case,

Figure 5.4
Social Class and Depression in London (Life Stage and Intimacy as Mediators)

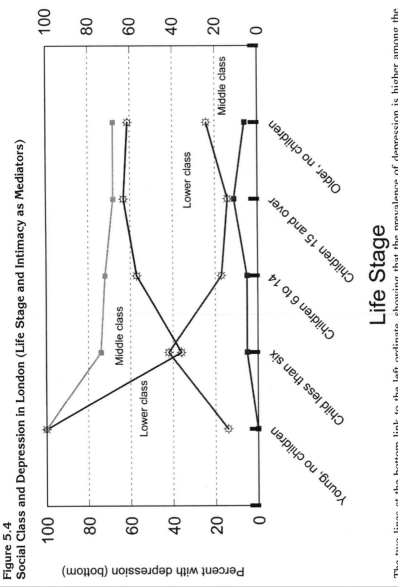

Life Stage

The two lines at the bottom link to the left ordinate, showing that the prevalence of depression is higher among the lower class, and especially so during the stage of life when children less than six are in the home. The two lines at the top link to the right ordinate, showing that women are most likely to be without emotional supports during this same period of life, especially for the lower class.

Source: Drawn from two separate tables in Brown et al. (1975).

Figure 5.5
Attributional Model of Socioeconomic Status and Psychological Disorder

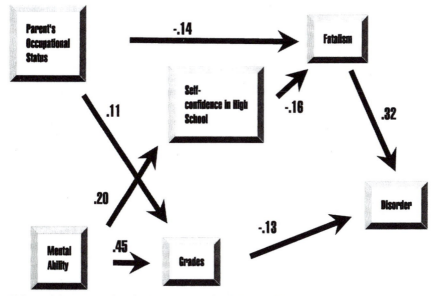

This model suggests that fatalism, an acquired, "internal" coping mechanism, is a strong mediator of the relationship of social class to mental disorder. Residual and unanalyzed correlations are omitted.

Source: Wheaton (1980: Table 5 and Figure 5). Reprinted by permission of the American Sociological Association and the author.

individual characteristics interact with the stressful environment to precipitate disorder. The individual may not emerge successfully from the stressful situation, because he or she does not attempt to deal with it actively but, rather, lets events overtake and control the situation (Seligman 1975).

Wheaton provides analyses from three separate longitudinal data sets that are consistent with the fatalism theory (Wheaton 1980). Figure 5.5 shows a simplified model from one of them. The data derive from a study of all 17-year-old male high school students in a county in Michigan in 1957. In 1972, 291 of these were reinterviewed. The father's occupational status is weakly related to the school ability of the respondent (coefficient of 0.16, not shown). School ability affects self-confidence in high school, and school ability and father's occupational status are both related to the grades received in school. The fatalistic orientation is affected both by the father's status (-0.14) and by the level of self-confidence (-0.16). Poor grades affect vulnerability to disorder (-0.13). There is a relatively strong effect of fatalism on disorder (coefficient of 0.32). The advantage of this path model is that it provides an empirical test of an explicit model of the effects of low social class on mental disorder, with mediating variables that have a foundation in social psychological theory. It is linked to studies of attribution for success and failure that have been done in laboratory settings and builds elegantly on advances in stratification theory and research.

There are important weaknesses in the test of the attributional model. First, the concept of disorder is vague. The operational definition and measurement using the 22-item index of Langner (Langner and Michael 1963) are more consistent with the notion of distress or demoralization (Link and Dohrenwend 1980) than with disorder. However, even if the model is limited to the concept of distress, it illuminates social and psychological processes that are important in the study of mental disorder, as argued earlier and elsewhere (Aneshensel 1996; Aneshensel et al. 1991). A second important weakness of the attributional model is that, in spite of its longitudinal nature, it is not possible to disentangle the fatalism variable from the disorder variable, since they were both measured at the second wave of interviews in 1972. Mental disorder and fatalism might be related to each other in a reciprocal way, as suggested by data from the labeling research of Link and colleagues, reviewed earlier. Finally, stress is omitted from the model because it was not statistically necessary (Wheaton 1980); but the linear and additive nature of the model may have missed the possibility that the interaction of stress and fatalism is more important for lower- than upper-class individuals, since they are likely to have greater stress as well as greater fatalism.

Class and the Physical Environment

The physical and biological environment can affect the individual's risk for mental disorder at any time from the moment of conception to death. Since there are differences in lifestyles between the various social classes, and since the causes of mental disorders are not well understood as yet, there are numerous other specific possibilities to explain why lower-class life may cause an increased risk for mental disorder, as shown in the biosocial model in Figure 1.6. Mediators of the relationship of social class to mental disorder may not be strictly sociological variables, but, nevertheless, are relevant to sociological research on class and mental disorder if they explain the relationship. Examples of possibly important mediating variables that link to social class are illnesses and fetal damage due to more limited access to the health care system in the lower class and increased exposure to infectious, toxic, and injurious environments through work and residence (Figure 1.6).

A variety of disturbances during pregnancy and birth can cause injury and risk for disease and death of the newborn (Bracken 1984). These pregnancy and obstetric complications can also lead to relatively subtle disturbances in mental functioning in later life (Pasamanick and Knobloch 1961). The link to social class exists because many aspects of fetal damage are more common among the lower classes, for example, mortality (Bakketeig et al. 1984); low birth weight

(Strobino et al. 1995); and prematurity (Alberman 1984). This suggests the possibility that lower-class infants are more likely to be born with some slight fetal damage, which may contribute later to a mental disorder. The pregnancy and obstetric complications also may interact with social class, in that the long-term deleterious consequences of fetal damage may be potentiated only among lower classes (Drillien 1964).

Mental disorders can be produced by injuries, infections, toxins, and physical deprivations. Many aspects of residential environments are potentially toxic and connected to lower-class life. Lead and other heavy metals, which can cause mental deficiencies (Needleman and Bellinger 1991), are likely to be more common in lower-class urban neighborhoods. Toxic waste sites are more likely to be situated in lower-class than upper-class residential neighborhoods (Bullard 1993). Dangerous occupational environments contribute to risk for mental disorder and are found more frequently in jobs held by individuals in the lower class. The dangers include toxins such as heavy metals found in battery plants and organophosphate herbicides and pesticides used by migrant workers (Needleman 1995). The dangers include the psychological characteristics of the occupational environment. For example, Link and others have suggested that jobs with certain noisome characteristics (steam, heat or cold, odors, confined spaces) contribute to risk for schizophrenia (Link et al. 1986; Muntaner et al. 1991) and that jobs where individuals have little influence over the pace of work may contribute to risk for depression (Link et al. 1993).

SELECTION AND DRIFT: INDIVIDUAL AND ENVIRONMENTAL FACTORS

Mental disorder could be inversely related to socioeconomic stratification because mental disorder or the predisposition to mental disorder affects the educational and occupational career. The notion that mental disorder leads to a lowering of socioeconomic status is here termed *drift*, and it refers to *intra*generational mobility. The notion that the predisposition to mental disorder could affect attainment of socioeconomic position, over the entire life course, is here termed *selection*. Selection can be observed in longitudinal research on *inter*generational mobility.

Mental disorders with significant chronic impairment are likely to affect attainment of achieved roles like occupation. Consider the contrast in the manner of hiring that might occur in lower- versus upper-class occupations. Application for a job as construction worker or fruit picker is sometimes as simple as showing up at the construction trailer or street corner when workers are needed. Verbal or social skills, judgment, independence, persistence, and other traits may not be assessed prior to being hired. Application for an executive or professional position is more likely to require the possession of professional certifications, assessment by professional placement firms, and interviews with prospective supervisors and coworkers, sometimes over several days. Paper-and-pencil tests, including intelligence tests, may be included in the requirements for obtaining positions or for the educational background of degrees and certifications required even to apply. Social impairment is one of the defining criteria for mental disorders, and the more severe disorders like schizophrenia involve lower cognitive ability in some persons (Bilder et al. 1992). Individuals with chronic social and cognitive impairments, as is likely to be the case for schizophrenia and antisocial personality disorders, are likely to suffer in the more rigorous selection procedure, gravitating down the social scale to positions with less demanding entrance requirements.

Lunacy and Poverty in Nineteenth-Century America

A classic early study of social class and mental disorder concluded that selection and drift were the dominant explanation. In 1854 Edward Jarvis led a legislative commission of the state of Massachusetts "to ascertain the number and condition of the insane in the State, distinguishing as accurately as may be between the insane, properly so considered, and the idiotic or *non compos*; between the furious and the harmless, curable and incurable, and between the native and the foreigner, and the number of each who are State paupers" (Commission on Lunacy 1971: 9). Letters of inquiry were sent to hospitals, to physicians in each town, and to clergy and other responsible persons in towns without physicians. It was assumed that the physicians could make a reliable diagnosis, as they were presumed to "understand the nature of defective or diseased minds, and [were] competent to testify" (Commission on Lunacy 1971: 17). The study gives the appearance of extreme effort to be comprehensive and exacting efforts in the presentation of data. At the 10th meeting of the Association of Medical Superintendents of American Institutions for the Insane (the forerunner organization of the American Psychiatric Association), a motion was unanimously adopted praising the Jarvis Commission work "as the first successful attempt, in America, to secure entirely reliable statistics on this subject" (Grob 1971: 65).

A principal finding of the Jarvis report was that poverty was associated with lunacy. There were 2,622 lunatics in a population of more than 1 million, for a prevalence proportion of 2.33 per 1,000. This proportion is slightly lower, but on the same order of magnitude, as the prevalence of psychosis today, which might be estimated as about one-half of 1 percent, or 5 per 1,000. The prevalence of lunacy among paupers, who formed about 2 percent of the population, is 65 per 1,000, or over 6 percent, as shown in Table 5.2, but only 1 per 1,000 among persons of independent means. The resulting odds ratio, estimated and presented by Jarvis in the report (Commission on Lunacy 1971: 52–53), is nearly 70—a size any modern-day epidemiologist would pay attention to.

What did Jarvis conclude from these data? One conclusion was that insanity caused individuals to become paupers, that is, the *drift* interpretation. "It needs no philosophy to show that some, perhaps many, lunatics, by their disease lose

Table 5.2
Lunacy and Idiocy in Massachusetts in 1854 (Report of the Jarvis Commission)

	Lunatics	Idiots	Total
		Paupers	
Number	1,522	418	23,125
Prevalence/1000	65.82	18.08	
		Independents	
Number	1,110	671	1,102,551
Prevalence/1000	1.01	0.61	
		Total	
Number	2,622	1,089	1,124,676
Prevalence/1000	2.33	0.97	

Source: Commission on Lunacy (1855: Tables 4, 8, 19, 21 and frequencies on page 52).

their power of self-sustenance, and are thereby removed from the independent to the pauper class" (Commission on Lunacy 1971: 53). But he also concluded that "much of poverty has a common origin with insanity" (Commission on Lunacy 1971: 55)—the *selection* interpretation:

It is worth while to look somewhat at the nature of poverty, its origin, and its relation to man and to society. It is usually considered as a single outward circumstance—the absence of worldly goods; but this want is . . . only one of its manifestations. Poverty is . . . enrooted deeply within the man . . . ; it reaches his body, his health, his intellect, and his moral powers, as well as his estate. In one or other of these elements it may predominate, and in that alone he may seem to be poor; but it usually involves more than one of the elements. . . . Hence we find that, among those whom the world calls poor, there is less vital force, a lower tone of life, more ill health, more weakness, more early death . . . less self-respect, ambition and hope, more idiocy and insanity, and more crime, than among the independent. (52)

The Jarvis report raises several issues that form themes for later work. The comprehensive definition of the target population and the intensive case finding are important; and it would appear that the Jarvis commission was more inclusive in this respect than other work until the ECA study, more than 120 years later. The use of specific categories of mental disturbance (*lunatic* and *idiot*) and the presentation of data that allow distinctive relationships to social variables between the categories contrast with some later work. The categories studied, however—both the focus variables of lunacy and idiocy and the social definition of "pauperism"—are on the rare end of continua. For example, paupers formed a category with only 2 percent of the population, which contrasts to later interest in variation along a continuum of wealth or social class as well as later interest in a range of mental disturbances with less severe outcomes than the nineteenth-century concept of lunacy. The theme of variation in thresholds of definition as well as the linearity of relationships of social status to mental disturbance are of continuing interest to this day.

The idea that mental illness produces a downward shift in the individual's financial status (drift) or that some trait or group of traits of the personality structure of the individual predisposes him or her simultaneously to pauperism and insanity (selection) is not proven in the cross-sectional work of Jarvis but is consistent with the functionalist view of the formation and maintenance of the social classes. This point of view suggests that individuals in poverty acquire that status because of their own lack of ability or ambition.

Results for the fatalism model of Wheaton (1980) are consistent with Jarvis' contention that "among those whom the world calls poor, there is less vital force, a lower tone of life, more ill health, more weakness, . . . less self-respect, ambition and hope." For "less self-respect, ambition and hope," substitute *fatalism*. Data from the Jarvis commission and the Michigan County Study, one century later, provide evidence that mental disorder is related to social class position. Jarvis' notion that a wide range of personal dispositions is associated with mental disorder *and* with social class position receives empirical support from the work of Wheaton and others. The direction of causation is presumed by each author, but differently: from disorder to class for Jarvis and from class to disorder for Wheaton. The presumption of direction may have been affected by the focus on relatively severe disorders, as with Jarvis, versus relatively milder distress, as with Wheaton.

Follow-up Studies

As is the situation with the causation framework, longitudinal data are pre-ferred for assessing the selection/drift theory because they sort out the temporal order. The selection/drift interpretation requires a longitudinal follow-up of the social class attainment of a population of individuals after the occurrence of mental disorder in some proportion of them. About a dozen studies address the issue of mobility of individuals with severe mental disorders, and most indicate some support for either the selection or drift hypothesis (Eaton and Lasry 1978). A methodologically rigorous study of intragenerational mobility in England gave strong evidence of downward mobility following an episode of schizophrenia (Goldberg and Morrison 1963). A strong study comparing intergenerational mobility of schizophrenics and control individuals born in the same cohort showed that the trajectory for individuals who would later be diagnosed as schizophrenic was not as high as that in the general population (Turner and Wagenfeld 1967). These studies of mobility suggest that the incidence findings might be an artifact of insidious onset of disorder, which hinders upward mobility. There are few follow-up studies of the effects on attainment of socioeconomic position of less severe mental disorders like depression, anxiety, and alcohol dependence.

As with the causation argument, there are individual and environmental approaches to the selection/drift model. The individual approach is characterized by Jarvis and the Commission on Lunacy: impairments associated with mental disorders, even in their insidious, pre-onset form, hinder the attainment of higher social positions. But mental disorder might affect attainment of social class position indirectly, through stigmatizing social processes associated with treatment for mental disorder—this approach focuses on the social environment more than the individual. The labeling approach to mental disorder has a long history, but its specific application to research on social class and mental disorder has not received much attention. As discussed in Chapter 3, the general idea is that in our culture, the concept of mental disorder carries with it a set of expectations that guide our reactions to those we perceive to be mentally disordered (Link and Cullen 1990; Link et al. 1989). The relationship of labeling to the status attainment process has received support in work by Link and colleagues. In one cross-sectional study, the income of individuals who had been treated for mental disorder (i.e., "labeled") was lower than for those with equivalent levels of symptoms who had not been treated; and the labeled individuals were less likely to be employed (Link 1982). In another study, it was shown that expectations of rejection and discrimination were related to demoralization, unemployment, and income loss only among individuals who had actually been treated for mental disorder ("labeled"), not among those with equivalent symptom levels who had not been treated (Link 1987; Link et al. 1989).

Studies on official labeling provide evidence on an aspect of selection and drift that is based on the social context, not on the individual's level of impairment. Extensions of labeling research bring us very close to the causation side of the argument, by considering the effects of labeling by others who do not represent the psychiatric treatment establishment. Mental disturbances and the behaviors they generate are sometimes stigmatized and labeled, and these processes can produce expectations contributing to amplification, not reduction, of the mental disturbance. Others' labels are part of the information one uses to make attributions about the disturbance (whether it is *emotional deviance* [Thoits 1985]). Eventually, these more subtle forms of labeling could influence the propensity for the mental disturbance itself. However, evidence that exists now suggests that this form of labeling by others in the nonprofessional social network is more prominent in the upper than in the lower class (Horwitz 1982). Therefore, research on nonofficial labeling theory is unlikely to lead to a potent explanation for the inverse relationship of social class to mental disorder.

OTHER CONCEPTS OF SOCIOECONOMIC DISADVANTAGE

Ethnic Disadvantage and Mental Disorder

In the study of ethnic stratification two main theoretical perspective are an assimilation perspective and a domination perspective (Greeley 1974). The *assimilation perspective* studies the ways in which a minority ethnic group integrates and assimilates into the dominant society and assumes that eventually the minority group will lose most or all of those characteristics that make it distinct. The focus of measurement is the degree to which the group has been assimilated into the majority. This perspective began with the so-called race relations cycle of the Chicago school of sociology and is applied most often to white ethnic groups such as Jews, Irish, and Italians in the United States. The implications for mental health are that partially assimilated groups experience marginality and weakened integration, as discussed in Chapter 4.

The *domination perspective* studies the ways in which the majority group maintains its power in society by exploiting smaller or weaker groups, for while ethnic differences are based on identifiers arising from cultural and historical factors, they acquire a specific added meaning having to do with the placement of the particular ethnic group in the system of socioeconomic stratification. Multiethnic societies are almost always characterized by hierarchies in terms of prestige, wealth, and power. Power and prestige are conferred by others, and in a situation where persons of a given ethnic group are perceived as less prestigious or less influential, one can say that these groups are relatively disadvantaged. Thus, the process of *ethnic stratification* is the manner in which groups attain advantage or disadvantage, relative to other groups, in the socioeconomic system. *Ethnic disadvantage* is the relative lack of prestige, power, and wealth accorded to one ethnic group in a society, vis-à-vis another. The domination perspective and the concept of ethnic disadvantage are most useful in the study of black–white relations in the United States. The implications for mental health are that disadvantaged groups may have higher levels of mental disorder.

Race is a particular type of ethnic status that provides an easily identifiable characteristic implying common genetic history (as opposed to the broader concept of common cultural history implied by ethnic status). The race identifier has to do with skin color or physiognomy. Race, a concept based in genetics, is not useful for sociologists or even for population geneticists, because racial identifiers provide so little information about genetic makeup. Important other characteristics of individuals and populations, such as disease proneness or personality, generally are not grouped in informative clusters with the racial identifier; and there is usually more variance in these other characteristics *within* any identified racial group than there is *between* racial groups (Cavalli-Sforza and Menozi 1994). However, the racial identifier tends to serve as a marker of ethnic status that forms the basis for social distinctions, such as ethnic disadvantage.

In the following discussion this ambiguity is signaled by placing the word "race" in quotation marks to alert the reader to the problem. In that it provides a marker of ethnic status and the derivative concept of ethnic disadvantage, measurement of "race" is sometimes useful. More often than not, in general use, the word "race" signifies something other than genetic makeup, much closer to ethnic disadvantage.

Indicators of ethnic disadvantage are analogous in some ways to indicators of socioeconomic status. The existence of ethnic inequality on the economic level is demonstrated by data that show that disadvantaged groups receive less pay for equivalent occupation or years of education. Education by income data for blacks and whites in the United States reveals the relative disadvantage of the blacks (Siegel 1965). On the level of prestige, survey results show that disadvantaged groups are the objects of prejudice among the general population. On the level of power, disadvantaged groups are represented sparsely in the controlling bodies of institutions such as schools, businesses, hospitals, and parliaments. All of these data show the relative lack of power, prestige, and wealth that originate in one's ethnic origin.

Although class and ethnic disadvantage have different sources, it could be that they have equivalent effects on the individual, since they both reflect differences of power and prestige. If this is so, then it is reasonable to expect disadvantaged ethnic groups to have higher rates of mental disorder than advantaged groups, even at the same level of social class. The most frequently studied consequence of ethnic disadvantage is low self-esteem, which links to the prestige aspect of inequality. Paper-and-pencil tests of self-esteem often show blacks to have lower self-esteem, and many behavioral measures of interaction provide results in the same direction. A content analysis of Richard Wright's novels shows that most of his references to blacks are derogatory, even though he is black himself (Pettigrew 1964). Disadvantaged groups are thought to have less confidence in dealing with the environment's fatalism, which, though perhaps realistic, nevertheless hampers their success in mastering crisis situations. A second general type of consequence of ethnic disadvantage is an increment in life crises, especially those that originate in the economic system. Members of disadvantaged ethnic groups are the first to be fired or laid off and the last to be hired. Disadvantaged groups tend to have higher rates of mortality and nonpsychiatric morbidity, which indicate an increment in stress. A third broad consequence of being a member of an ethnically disadvantaged group is the lessened resources to deal with any crisis situations that may arise. There are less likely to be powerful friends who can help meet the crises for members of disadvantaged groups. There is less flexibility in choosing a new residence, which might ameliorate a stressful situation. Institutions controlled by the dominant group are less likely to be sensitive to the ethnically disadvantaged individual's needs. A fourth general consequence of ethnic disadvantage is hostility. In many cases hostility is directed openly at the advantaged group; in other cases there are covert means of expressing hostility. Sometimes hostility is displaced onto another minority group in the form of prejudice or aggression. All of these factors suggest that the psychological consequences of ethnic and class disadvantage are similar.

In reviewing the evidence on social class and mental disorder, Dohrenwend and Dohrenwend (1969) helped to inaugurate the so-called third generation of research, in part because they showed that results as regards social class differed for specific disorders, thus challenging the point of view that mental disorder was a unitary concept. They decided upon a strategy of research that was based on the domination perspective of ethnic stratification and that would support either the stress or selection interpretation of the social class mental disorder relationship. As discussed earlier, the finding that social class is related to mental disorder is hard to interpret because social class status is constantly changing over the lifetime of the individual. But ethnic status does not change over the lifetime, and the causation selection problem cannot apply to immutable variables. This situation is an experiment of nature, or *quasi experiment*, which provides the leverage to decide between stress and selection as explanations for the social class–mental disorder relationship, they contended (Dohrenwend and Dohrenwend 1974b).

In analyzing data on ethnic group differences and mental disorder, it is important to compare rates in ethnic groups at the same level of social class. At any given level of social class, if stress is the explanation, then the more highly stressed individuals in the disadvantaged ethnic groups will have *higher* rates of disorder. If selection is the explanation, then upwardly mobile individuals in the advantaged groups will leave behind a residue of impaired individuals in lower levels of the class structure. Furthermore, healthy individuals in disadvantaged ethnic groups who would be upwardly mobile are held to lower-class positions by the discriminatory opportunity structure—in effect, diluting the denominator of the rate of mental disorder at any given level of class. The quasi-experimental design predicts that if selection is the interpretation, the disadvantaged ethnic groups will have a *lower* rate of mental disorder at any given level of social class.

The quasi-experimental design was executed in Israel, which was in many ways an ideal setting (Dohrenwend et al. 1992). Israel possessed excellent record-keeping systems, which facilitated drawing samples, and is sufficiently small and naive to the survey process that high completion rates could be achieved. Israeli society fitted the design requirements of an open society with substantial upward mobility, but with large differences in social advantage between certain ethnic groups. Researchers focused on the comparison between Jews born in Israel from European heritage versus those born in Israel of North African (mostly Moroccan) heritage, using educational attainment as the indicator of social class. Table 5.3 shows the results for three disorders: schizophrenia, major depression, and antisocial personality disorder. For schizophrenia, the selection interpretation is supported, because the European-heritage Jews have higher rates at each level of education for both sexes (e.g., 4.18 per 1,000

Table 5.3
Education and Ethnic Status in Israel

Educational Attainment	European n = 1197		North African n = 1544	
	Male (602)	Female (595)	Male (852)	Female (692)
Schizophrenia				
Less than High School	4.18	0.84	1.91	0.00
High School Graduate	0.29	0.39	0.17	0.00
College Graduate	0.00	0.39	0.00	0.00
Major Depression				
Less than High School	3.01	4.81	3.47	6.60
High School Graduate	2.06	2.93	4.61	12.11
College Graduate	0.66	1.68	2.94	10.70
Antisocial personality				
Less than High School	0.73	0.82	6.97	0.73
High School Graduate	0.15	0.00	0.79	0.30
College Graduate	0.00	0.00	0.00	0.00

Note: One-year prevalence in percent; diagnostic categories according to Research Diagnostic Criteria.

Source: Adapted with permission from B. Dohrenwend et al., "Socioeconomic Status and Psychiatric Disorder: The Causation Selection Issue," *Science* 225. Copyright 1992 American Association for the Advancement of Science.

for European-heritage males with low education versus 1.91 for North African-heritage males; 0.84 versus 0.0 for females with low education). The results for antisocial personality disorder, on the other hand, support the stress interpretation among males, because the North African-heritage group has higher rates than the European-heritage group at all levels of educational attainment (e.g., 6.97 per 1,000 versus 0.73 at the lower level of education and 0.79 versus 0.15 at the middle level of education). For depression the results are equivocal: even though the North African group has the higher rate at all levels of education and for both sexes, the data do not display the expected inverse relationship between social class and disorder.

The quasi-experimental strategy is bold in conception, and its execution in Israel was methodologically rigorous. However, it requires assumptions that vitiate its power. It must be assumed that the stresses associated with low social class status are similar or identical to those associated with membership in a disadvantaged ethnic group. But the perceived cause of the stress may render different psychological consequences: lower-class individuals in the dominant ethnic group may be more willing to blame themselves for the stresses they suffer, in part because of the functionalist ideology (Hochschild 1995; Matza 1967), whereas individuals in disadvantaged ethnic groups may be more likely to blame the structure of society for the stresses they suffer. The quasi experiment requires the assumption that ethnic groups do not differ in their genetic propensity for mental disorders. While there is wide variation within any given ethnic group (often greater than variation across ethnic groups) it is, nevertheless, true that a large number of diseases differ greatly in their prevalence between groups (McKusick 1967); often the differences are larger than differences shown in Table 5.3. The quasi experiment requires the assumption that mental disorders are equivalent across cultures and can be measured equivalently. The quasi-experimental data cannot determine whether or not both the causation and selection processes are operating simultaneously or not—the results reflect only the relative preponderance of one or the other process. Finally, the quasi experiment fails to provide evidence as to *how* lower social class position affects risk for mental disorder.

Neo-Marxist Indicators of Socioeconomic Position

In spite of the central importance of social class to sociology and the importance of the issue of mental disorders and social class, there has been only limited comparison of the effects of different measures of social class on the rate of mental disorder (Eaton 1974; Eaton and Kessler 1981; Kessler and Cleary 1980). Therefore, the Baltimore ECA follow-up (Eaton et al. 1997) included several measures whose effects could be compared to gain insight into the nature of the relationship between social class position and mental disorder. Results are shown in Table 5.4. The DIS produces specific diagnoses according to criteria used by psychiatrists. The analysis includes the diagnosis of major depression and the group of anxiety disorders including panic disorder, phobic disorders, and obsessive-compulsive disorder. Abbreviated diagnostic criteria for panic disorder and one type of phobia (agoraphobia) are given in Box 1.5, and Box 1.6 gives a medical case history of panic disorder. The table explores differences between the two types of mental disorders as well as differences that may exist between measures of social class. The numbers shown are odds ratios from a multivariate logistic regression, with all variables included together in the same model. Each variable includes a category that is designated as the "reference," with odds ratio of 1.0. Odds ratios for other categories in that variable are estimated relative to the reference category. When odds ratios are close to 1.0, there is no association; when they are greater than 1.0, there is positive association; and when they are less than 1.0, there is inverse association. The association is statistically significant when the confidence interval for the

Table 5.4
Social Class, Depression, and Anxiety Disorders

Prevalence, Adjusted* Odds Ratios, and 95% Confidence Intervals

Measures of Social Class	Major Depression		Anxiety Disorder	
	%	OR	%	OR
Education of Respondent				
Less than high school	1.2	1.0	16.0	1.0
High school graduate	2.5	1.9	14.8	1.3
Some college	2.7	3.5	7.6	0.3
College graduate	2.7	6.5	13.3	0.8
Graduate school	0.7	1.9	13.9	0.8
Household Income				
< $17,500	1.2	**16.2**	19.1	**2.9**
$17,500 - $34,499 -	3.8	**11.5**	16.3	1.6
$35,000 +	2.0	1.0	10.8	1.0
Household Physical Assets				
Does not own car	1.8	0.6	19.3	1.6
Owns car	2.1	1.0	13.0	1.0
Does not own home	2.2	1.3	19.3	1.1
Owns home	1.8	1.0	12.1	1.0
Household Financial Assets				
No dividend income	2.0	1.0	16.3	1.0
Dividend income	2.1	2.9	11.6	1.2
No savings income	2.9	1.5	18.3	0.6
Savings income	1.5	1.0	13.3	1.0
No property income	2.0	1.0	15.7	1.0
Property income	1.9	1.8	4.7	**0.1**

Table 5.4 (*continued*)

Respondent Occupation†

Labor	2.9	‡	14.8	0.5
Craft	1.9	1.1	8.5	0.3
Service	0.9	0.6	14.1	0.6
Technical	2.7	0.6	19.0	0.8
Professional	2.6	1.0	14.7	1.0

Respondent Organizational Assets†

Non-management	1.4	0.5	15.7	2.1
Supervisor	3.6	2.9	15.7	**2.6**
Manager	1.0	1.0	8.1	1.0

*Odds ratios are adjusted for age, gender, race/ethnicity, and other variables in the table.
†The sample for measures of occupation and organizational assets is limited to 877 respondents who were in the labor force at the time of the interview.
‡There were no sample respondents with major depressive disorder in this occupation category.

Source: Eaton and Muntaner (1999). The data are from interviews of the Baltimore Epidemiologic Catchment Area Followup conducted in 1993 and 1994, with the sample size at 1,865.

odds ratio does not include the value of 1.0—in this case the odds ratio in Table 5.4 is printed in boldface type.

Education is not significantly related to major depression or to anxiety disorder, but low household income is related to both disorders. Respondents whose household income is less than $17,500 are 16 times as likely to meet the criteria for major depressive disorder as those whose household income is over $35,000; those with household incomes in the middle range are 11 times as likely to meet the criteria for major depressive disorder. For anxiety disorders the relationship is significant but smaller (nearly three times the rate of anxiety disorder in the low-income group as in the reference group).

Measures of assets, such as owning one's own home, having a car, owning stock, or having a savings account, are not related to rate of depression or anxiety disorder, with income and education controlled. But receiving income from property, royalties, estates, or trusts is strongly associated with low rate of anxiety disorder (odds ratio of 0.1). This type of income protects the individual from year-to-year fluctuations in salary and possibly inoculates him or her in some degree from day-to-day difficulties in achieving success at work.

The occupational setting is related to depression and anxiety disorder, but not in the predicted direction. After adjusting for education, income, and assets, the respondent's occupation does not have a strong effect. But the organizational assets of the individual do have effects, in that supervisors have higher rates of depressive disorder (odds ratio of 2.9, not significant) and anxiety disorder (odds ratio of 2.6, significant) than both management and workers. The notion of organizational assets derives from a reconceptualization of Marxist class theory in the modern context (Wright 1985). The supervisor is in the lower tier of management, with authority over other workers, but has little influence over the decisions made by top management and is accountable to them for the performance of workers. This class location is often filled by former workers, who may experience role conflict and divided loyalties. They have the trappings of authority but may experience little freedom in controlling their own day-to-day work. This finding is consistent with studies of the role of direction, control, and planning in the workplace as it relates to depression (Link et al. 1993; Mausner-Dorsch and Eaton 2000).

CONCLUSION

As long as inequality exists, it is likely to be associated, to some degree, with the extent of mental disorder in society. Changes in the socioeconomic structure lead to consequent changes in the mental structure of society, including rates of mental disorders. Thus, research describing the relationship will always be central to sociology's interest in the causes and consequences of inequality, and there is a continuing role for descriptive studies of social class and mental disorder, as society evolves, because the possibilities for both causation and selection to operate will continue to exist. In the half century since the New Haven Study, many descriptive studies of prevalence of mental disorders have documented the evolving relationship. There has been slow, but measurable, progress in understanding the details, that is, the mediators: *how* social class affects mental disorder and *how* mental disorder, or the predisposition for it, affects attainment of social status. Research on the "details"—that is, the mediating variables—may eventually prove more helpful in improving the lives of individual human beings. Eliminating social inequality may be impossible. But identification of causal mechanisms may lead to societal programs, less global than eliminating inequality, that prevent the onset of mental disorder. Identification of factors mediating the process of selection may lead to programs that lessen the impact of mental disorder once it has occurred.

6

The Social Transmission of Psychopathology

INTRODUCTION

The aim of this chapter is to study together the major types of mental disturbance and bizarre behavior that show the "epidemic" form of transmission, in which the agent of the transmission is human communication of some sort. Reviews of socially transmitted psychopathology trace back at least to Gruenberg (1957), who focused on severe psychopathology such as shared psychoses. Earlier work (Hecker 1859; Mackay 1852) preceded the era in which some deviant behaviors were considered to be psychopathological. Several reviews by psychiatrists (Markush 1973; Sirois 1974; Wessely 1987) and epidemiologists (Boss 1997) have assumed a medical perspective, but there are also multidisciplinary inquiries into the occupational settings where these epidemics often take place (Boxer 1985; Colligan and Murphy 1979; Colligan et al. 1982). A brief sociological analysis by Gehlen (1977) focused on the distinction between panics and crazes. An analysis from the social psychological point of view is found in Levy and Nail (1993).

Transmission is the passage of a similar or identical complaint, behavior, sign, or symptom from one person to another. In effect, we are studying *behavioral contagion*, defined in 1951 by Grosser et al. (1951) as "a social interaction in which a 'recipient's' behavior changes to become 'more like' that of another person, and where this change has occurred in a social interaction in which the 'initiator' (other person) has not communicated intent to influence the behavior of the recipient." In this instance the concept of behavioral contagion is applied to mental disturbances and bizarre behaviors. These behaviors are generally, but not always, socially disapproved, as was the situation in early studies of behavioral contagion (Wheeler 1966); and social disapproval, with its consequent focus on lowering of restraints, is not a required part of this otherwise useful definition. The term "hysterical contagion" has also been used in this context, as defined, for example, by Kerckhoff and Back (1968), wherein "a set of experiences or behaviors which are heavily laden with the emotion of fear of a mysterious force are disseminated through a collectivity. The type of behavior that forms the manifest content . . . may vary widely . . . but all are indicative of fear, and all are inexplicable in terms of the usual standards of mechanical, chemical, or physiological causality." This term is not favored because the etymology of the word "hysteria" implies a physical structure in women, which appears to be incorrect. Inevitable linkage to the emotion of fear is not appropriate, and the notion that the epidemic is "inexplicable" in mechanical, chemical, or physiological terms is not quite on target either, as discussed later. Colligan and Murphy (1979) define "contagious psychogenic illness" as "the collective occurrence of a set of physical symptoms and related beliefs among two or more individuals in the absence of an identifiable pathogen." This definition suffers by focusing on physical symptoms only; in requiring a cluster of more than one symptom; by not requiring actual transmission between persons; and by requiring the absence of an identifiable agent.

Defining terms more carefully helps understand how this area of inquiry links together sociology and psychiatric epidemiology. *Collective psychopathology* is the most general situation where groups of individuals have high rates of disorder, for whatever reason. An *epidemic* is a more narrow form of collective psychopathology with a temporal and interpersonal element, in which a disorder spreads rapidly through a community. Collective psychopathology can exist for many reasons, without having the epidemic form of transmission occur. Ill or disordered people can gather purposively in groups, for example; and groups of individuals can become ill or disordered because of risk factors that are common to them all. This distinction is sometimes referred to as the difference between "convergence" and "contagion." The *transmission completion rate* is the equivalent of the concept of the attack rate, used by infectious disease epidemiologists, that is, the proportion successfully reproducing the illness after transmission from another. The requirement that the sign or symptom be similar or identical in the transmitter and the receiver narrows the scope of the inquiry, eliminating many social situations that affect the occurrence of psychopathology, such as situations of stress produced in human interactions; situations of long-term developmental socialization, including that occurring in the context of the family; and certain unusual types of apparently florid and volatile mental disturbances such as *latah* and the startle reaction. In all these situations the actions of the individual producing the stress are not equivalent to the reaction resulting in the receiver.

The *social transmission of psychopathology* is the experience or enactment, in one or more individuals, of a mental disturbance or behavioral disorder that has been perceived, in one or more other individuals, during a group process. The transmission involves a symbol of some sort, making these epidemics uniquely human. The term "transmission" is preferred to "learning" because the process takes place more rapidly, without the repetition connoted by the term learning or the necessity of vicarious practice or anticipation; and because it is difficult to specify the reinforcer that learning theory entails (Bandura 1977). Socially transmitted disorders may legitimately be termed *psychogenic* since, distinct from infectious and toxic disease epidemics, the individual's symbolic processing is a necessary agent for transmission. The simplest form of transmission is a *sole source epidemic*, that is, from a single source to many individuals. An example from infectious disease epidemiology is the cholera epidemic studied by John Snow, in which the source was the pump at Broad Street, which carried water with cholera bacteria. This example is not perfect since the cholera bacteria can also be transmitted from person to person after infection from the Broad Street pump water: a purer example might be an environmental catastrophe, such as the Bhopal Disaster, with a single source of exposure. The prototype for this form of epidemic in the field of psychopathology is imitative suicide. A somewhat more complex form of transmission is the *person-to-person epidemic*, which involves transmission from person to person. In epidemiology many contagious diseases take this form, such as tuberculosis and hepatitis, transmitted by bacteria; schistosomiasis, transmitted by a parasite; and colds and HIV, transmitted by viruses. In a homogeneous population where everyone is equally susceptible, and interaction is random, the cumulative attack rate for this form of epidemic takes the logistic S form. In the beginning the disease spreads slowly because not very many people are transmitting it. It spreads most rapidly when there are a fairly large number of individuals carrying the disease, as well as a large number who have not yet been exposed. Toward the end of the epidemic the curve flattens out, because there are so few individuals who have not yet been exposed. The acute somatoform epidemics reviewed later take this form.

Most psychogenic epidemics involve transmission where the presence of a group is necessary for, or very important to, the transmission. In person-to-person epidemics in the field of epidemiology generally, such as sexually transmitted diseases, the epidemic transmission can be limited to dyads. In socially transmitted psychopathology, groups larger than two enhance, or are necessary for, transmission (as shown later). This is an example of the important distinction between a dyad and larger groups (Simmel 1950). As noted earlier, a *group* is defined as two or more individuals who (1) interact with one another more than would be expected by chance *or* (2) think of themselves as possessing a common history or future. This definition of group allows a structural form (interaction) or a mental form (awareness). Where the group structure enhances, or is necessary for, transmission, the epidemic may be defined as *sociogenic* (as well as psychogenic). The term "sociogenic" has been proposed earlier (Stahl 1982), but the distinction between the two forms (psychogenic and sociogenic) has not been made before. It turns out to be important in understanding the epidemics. Sociogenic epidemics are instances of the "social fact" (Durkheim 1966).

It is helpful to organize the epidemics into categories according to their content and duration. The *content* of the epidemic is what is actually transmitted and that is the focus of concern by individuals involved. Four categories are used here: *ideas*, such as the transmission of a delusion, *emotions*, such as the transmission of panic anxiety; *behaviors*, such as suicide; and *bodily signs or symptoms*, such as headaches, rashes, or convulsions. Social transmission can generate short-term, apparently self-limiting epidemics that endure only a few days. These include mass panics and delusions, suicides, and various somatoform epidemics. But social transmission is capable of generating epidemics that endure for years or even decades, with important consequences for individuals. These include chronic fatigue syndrome, chemical and allergic reactions like multiple chemical sensitivity, and Gulf War syndrome.

ACUTE EPIDEMICS

Imitative Suicide

The example of imitative suicide is considered first because it often has the simplest form of *sole source*, not necessarily involving interaction among participants. There has been speculation for a long time that suicide had an epidemic form. An early example is the publication of Goethe's *Die Leiden des Jungen Werthers* (The Sorrows of Young Werther) in the eighteenth century. This short novel focused on an attractive, lovable, and romantic young man who was hopelessly in love and who committed suicide at the end. The book was connected to an increase of suicides and was banned in several parts of Europe. In the last two decades several studies have shown that suicides occur through imitation. For example, Phillips (1974) showed that the rate of suicide in the United States rose appreciably in the month following a well-publicized suicide such as that of movie actress Marilyn Monroe. The rise in suicide rate was not due to artifactual changes in coroners' reporting, which might have also been influenced by newspaper reports, because there was no drop in adjacent categories of cause of death, such as accidental injury. The suicides did not result from bereavement, since there were no rises in suicide rates following deaths of public figures such as President John Kennedy. There was also a dosage effect to the imitation, such that a larger number of pages of newspaper coverage for a given suicide were related to a greater rise in suicides during that month. The effect was statistically reliable, and Phillips concluded that a well-publicized suicide caused an extra 50 to 60 suicides in the country. The effect, though statistically strong when the entire country is considered, may account for only a small percentage of suicides (Gould et al. 1990). The effect has been generalized from newspaper to television movies (Gould and Shaffer 1986) and has been observed in other countries (Hafner and Schmidtke 1989). It is particularly strong among teenagers (Gould et al. 1990).

The predisposition to suicide is fairly widespread in the population. For example, data from the Epidemiologic Catchment Area Program show that about 10 percent of the general population have thoughts of death in the several weeks prior to interview, and almost 5 percent of respondents think about their own death (Moscicki et al. 1988). But less than 1 percent of the population have actually attempted suicide during their lives. Thus, there exists a probabilistic process between the vague and abstract consideration of one's own death and the actual attempt. Such a process generates a distribution of vulnerabilities with considerable variation. At any given moment, a percentage of the population is close enough to the threshold of attempting suicide that a relatively small increment in propensity, which might arise from reading a news story, will produce dozens of additional suicides in a nation of more than 200 million. The nature of the probabilistic process is thus the causal nexus but is very hard to trace since it depends on temporally fluctuating propensities in the population and idiosyncratic determinations of the meaning and significance of news events by literally millions of individuals at risk.

The phenomenon of imitative suicide, as established in the research just reviewed, has the form of the sole-source epidemic, from an individual news story to an individual suicide. But imitative suicide can take place in groups, such as in Jonestown, Guyana, in which more than 800 people died in a single occurrence; the Solar Temple cult, which led to the deaths of 74 people; and the Heaven's Gate Cult, in which 39 persons committed suicide. Reports of suicides in these group situations do not suggest that the affect of dysphoria is involved. But there does appear to be an imitative quality in that the method (plastic bag over the head in the Solar Temple cult; manner of dress and situation of the body in Heaven's Gate) is repeated. Both these cults involved the belief that the suicide transports the individual instantly to a new world somewhere in outer space. In the Jonestown and Heaven's Gate cults, there was extensive advance practice of the suicide ritual. In the 50–60 additional suicides following that of a well-known public figure, no interaction took place among those committing suicide, who did so in diverse places under different circumstances. The cult suicides are groups in the strict sense, with individuals interacting among themselves and in relative isolation from persons outside the group. The media suicides are more likely to involve young persons, whereas the cult suicides involve adults across the range of ages. However, the influence of the mass media suggests that a sort of group influence is at work at the level of the individual— that is, the individual's response, in committing suicide, may be stimulated by invoking the group awareness. This sort of group awareness is not too different from Durkheim's (1966) notion of altruistic suicide.

A Delusional Epidemic: Windshield Pitting in Seattle

An example of a short-term delusional epidemic is the episode of reports of windshield pitting that took place in Seattle in 1954 (Medalia and Larsen 1958).

Figure 6.1
Seattle Windshield Pitting Epidemic: Newspaper Coverage

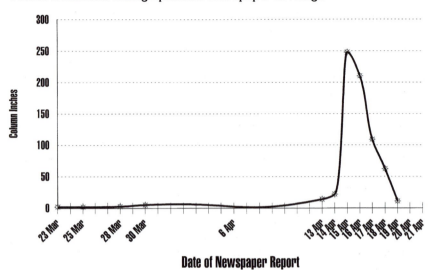

Date of Newspaper Report

Newspaper coverage is a prototype for the overtime transmission of ideas, which do not always have a material foundation.

Source: Adapted from Medalia and Larson (1958).

This occurrence is unusual because it concerns a delusional idea without much overt anxiety associated with it, but this feature makes it a good choice for analysis. In March 1954 newspapers in Seattle began carrying reports of damage to automobile windshields, about the size of a thumbnail, first in cities to the north and then gradually, by the middle of April, in Seattle itself. Newspaper coverage of the pitting peaked on April 15 (Figure 6.1), with more than 200 inches of newspaper columns on this topic in one day's edition of two newspapers. On April 14 and 15 there were 242 calls to the Police Department about pitting marks in windshields. Postulated causes for the pitting were diverse, including such possibilities as vandalism, ordinary road wear, industrial air pollution, hysterical beliefs, meteor dust, cosmic rays, sand fleas hatching in the windshield glass, and a recent atomic test conducted on a remote island in the Pacific Ocean. On April 15 the mayor of Seattle made an emergency appeal to the governor and President Eisenhower for help. In his appeal, the mayor referred to the atomic tests as a possible cause, and this eventually came to be accepted as the cause by more people than any other.

A telephone survey revealed that about one-quarter of the population of Seattle were skeptical that the pitting was anything other than ordinary road damage, and about one-quarter were undecided (Medalia and Larsen 1958). Fifty percent believed that unusual damage was caused by a physical agent, and of those, one-third attributed the cause to the atomic tests. Believers were equally distributed among males and females, but males were more likely to report actually having observed windshield pitting damage (8 percent of men versus 3 percent of women). Believers were equally distributed across the range of adult ages.

The epidemic was over by April 19 (Figure 6.1), and a puzzle for the researchers was the relatively quick extinction. They discounted the possibility that the epidemic extinguished due to the growth of a counternorm, such as a belief that it was all hysterical delusions. They postulated that the dominant belief system—the atomic test—included the notion of transitory effect and actually resolved latent anxieties about the effects of the test, suggesting that its effects were consummated and exhausted by the windshield pitting. The survey showed that even though *interest* in the windshield pitting declined, the *belief* in it remained stable. One of their conclusions is: "Acute outbursts of mass delusion are not necessarily self-limiting. Interest and belief in a phenomenon for which no scientific basis can be found may well persist for periods of time even in a culture presumably committed to science as the ultimate test of reality" (Medalia and Larsen 1958: 185). This conclusion foreshadows consideration, in the following, of chronic epidemics. It also sets the foundation for the importance of the transmission of a belief as the principal agent in the epidemics.

An Anxiety Epidemic in Harbor City

An example of an anxiety epidemic is the occurrence at Harbor City Elementary School in California in 1993 (Small et al. 1994). About 10 minutes after morning classes had begun, 10 of the 680 students in the school complained of nausea, thought to originate from odors (not too uncommon) associated with a nearby petroleum refinery. The school officials called the Fire Department, and firefighters arrived in a car and two fire trucks, parking them in front of the school. A large yellow tarp was spread out to establish a makeshift treatment area. A few minutes later the school was evacuated, by which time six to eight ambulances and emergency vehicles were parked in the parking lot, and the 10 students were being treated on the yellow tarp in front of the entire student body. School officials then approached each classroom and asked if anyone had experienced any symptoms, and children began walking over to the yellow tarp area. Sixty-six students and seven adults were ultimately taken to local hospitals, where laboratory tests of their blood found nothing abnormal. All the children and six of the seven adults were released that day, and school resumed the following day without incident. In a survey conducted shortly after the incident, 77 percent of the students reported one or more symptoms, including headache (57 percent), nausea (52 percent), dizziness (51 percent) abdominal pain (51 percent), and other symptoms (less than 30 percent).

The Harbor City occurrence is similar to many other epidemics of the anxiety form. These are often precipitated by odors (Alexander and Fedoruk 1986; Araki and Honma 1986; Bell and Jones 1958; Boxer et al. 1984; Cole et al. 1990;

Hall and Johnson 1989; Modan et al. 1983; Selden 1989). Skin or throat irri-
tation often is reported along with the typical symptoms of anxiety such as fear,
headache, nausea, and abdominal pain. The Harbor City epidemic may be the
largest one in the literature, and the transmission completion rate of 77 percent
is higher than in most other epidemics. In some of the epidemics there is a
detectable substance in the air at low levels—for example, petroleum distillate
or smog—but in some where an odor is reported there has been the failure to
find anything despite prolonged environmental tests. In many of the epidemics
there are visual cues of emergency, and in the Harbor City occurrence the number of symptoms reported by students was greater for those falling ill after the
arrival of the ambulances. A nearby school was also evacuated, because of the
fear that the odor might affect people there, but no emergency vehicles were
summoned, and no one required medical attention.

A Somatoform Epidemic: The June Bug

A more potent and dramatic form of socially transmitted psychopathology is
the somatoform epidemic, in which the symptoms take a somatic form. Somatoform illnesses are clusters of one or more *complaints* from individuals that
typically accompany bodily, or somatic, illness—that is, in the disease model,
symptoms; and one or more *behaviors* that typically accompany physical illness—that is, in the disease model, *signs*. There is evidence for social and
psychological causes in these clusters (as is true in many or even most somatic
illnesses), but they are distinct in combining the social and psychological causation with an absence of obvious physical cause.

The classic study is by Kerckhoff and Back (1968), who include the news
accounts of the epidemic given in Box 6.1. The epidemic was widely reported
in the press and attracted the attention of state and federal health officials. Local
physicians, engineers, and epidemiologists tried to locate a possible cause for
the symptoms in the air quality, in circulating toxins, and in infectious agents
but could come up with nothing, through testing either the individuals or the
factory environment. Most of the people affected were women, amounting to
about 10 percent of the white female population of the first shift at the factory.
The epidemic began mysteriously, spread quickly, and terminated in less than
two weeks.

Research on the June bug epidemic displays three characteristics of these
types of epidemics that were not known before: the source of strain connected
to the outbreak, the social character of transmission, and the distribution of belief
about the cause. Comparison of persons reporting to the factory physician (cases)
with a sample of those not reporting (controls) reveals several types of strain
more prevalent in the affected group. Cases were more likely to have been
working overtime, for one thing. Second, they were less likely than controls to
approach their supervisor when they had a complaint. Third, they were more

Box 6.1
News Reports about the June Bug Epidemic

Wednesday News Reports at 6 P.M.

Officials at Montana Mills shut down their Strongsville plant this afternoon because of a mysterious sickness. According to a report just in from Strongsville General Hospital, at least ten women and one man were admitted for treatment. Reports describe symptoms as severe nausea and a breaking out over the body. Indications are that some kind of insect was in a shipment of cloth that arrived from England at the plant today. And at the moment the bug is blamed for the outbreak of sickness.

Wednesday News Reports at 11 P.M.

During the past three weeks a number of the 200 employees have been stricken with a mysterious illness, apparently caused by an insect bite. Today about ten women and one man were stricken. Several were admitted to the hospital for treatment and observation. Company officials say they are fumigating the building. The plant is scheduled to reopen tomorrow morning at six o'clock. This station learned tonight from a company employee that the small insect attacks the skin, the bites leaving a wound similar to a gnat bite. In about twenty minutes the victim is struck with severe nausea. The company doctor informed us tonight that an entomologist is studying the problem. A report is expected later this week.

Thursday News Reports

The dressmaking division of Montana Mills opened for business this morning after a night of debugging. But the reason for a mysterious illness that has stricken 40 employees is unsolved. The outbreak of the illness had been confined to females in the sewing and stitching room at the plant, where 200 women work side by side, until yesterday when a man in the warehouse area suffered an attack. Reports that the insect might have entered the plant in an overseas shipment of cloth from England have been discounted. Last night the plant was fogged with Pyrethrum in an effort to rid the premises of a possible insect.

A plant physician treating the victims—all women except one—is quoted as saying that the diagnosis is still hanging fire, and that no one afflicted by the malady could give a specific description of the insects which many said they saw. A State College entomologist called into the case said that what caused the illness cannot be confirmed, but they are working on several theories. Hiram L. Lamont, plant personnel director, said a number of women reported for work today, when the plant resumed operations, in a highly nervous state. At least six were treated by the company physician and sent home. Dr. C.H. Foreman, Strongsville County Health Officer, reports tonight, however, that there is nothing present in the community to get excited about. The investigation continues, but Dr. Foreman said, "We haven't been able to put our fingers on a thing." And, he emphasized, although some of the women employees at the plant have been very sick, nobody is seriously ill. The predominating symptom according to physicians and company officials is anxiety. Doctors are keeping several of the stricken women at the hospital for observation in an effort to diagnose the ailment. Dr. Foreman says the doctors have ruled out a virus—since none have fever—and food poisoning. All are in good condition.

Friday News Reports

Two experts from the U.S. Public Health Service Communicable Disease Center arrived today in Strongsville to assist local health officials trying to determine the cause of the sudden outbreak of sickness which has hit employees of Montana Mills. These two physicians, along with Dr. C. H. Foreman and Dr. Daniel Gerard of the State Board of Health searched the plant today for the cause of the illnesses. Also on the premises were several plant officials, representatives of the plant's insurance company, two State College entomologists, representatives of the Strongsville Exterminating Company, and an engineer from the State Board of Health. All theories are being investigated, including the possibility that the air conditioning system in the plant could have been at fault. A thorough search was made of the vast textile plant, one of the most modern in the South, and several specimens were collected with the aid of a vacuum cleaner. The total catch consisted of one black ant, a housefly, a couple of gnats, a small variety of beetle—none with an attraction for human flesh—and one mite (a chigger) that could cause a reaction.

Nine persons remained hospitalized last night and two more have been treated in the hospital emergency room. There were unconfirmed reports this morning that at least four more persons have been hospitalized. About fifty persons have been affected.

We talked with one lady who suffered symptoms today—Mrs. Wilma Evans, a 29-year old resident of Pottsville. She said she felt a bite on her leg, then felt dizzy about thirty minutes later. She said her left arm became numb, and she felt weak all over. "I broke out in a cold sweat," Mrs. Evans said. But she could not find any evidence of a bite.

Saturday News Reports

Today Dr. C. H. Foreman and the experts from the U.S. Public Health Service conferred on the findings of the laboratory tests on several insects taken from the Montana Mills plant to be analyzed at the Communicable Disease Center. Among the specimens examined was a small chigger-like bug, known as a bird mite, which could be the insect causing the skin abrasion found on many of the afflicted employees. But, Dr. Foreman emphasizes that they are only saying the insect could be causing the extreme symptoms in evidence by most of the patients—that is, the stomach pains and dizziness. All the physicians feel that a great deal of anxiety enters the picture. They also feel that the press has played the "Mystery malady" angle too much, thus increasing the anxiety in the plants in other areas of the state.

Said Dr. Foreman: "We don't question that some of these people have been bitten . . . but certainly there is a great deal of anxiety. Fear has ballooned it out of proportion."

There was one more case of the unknown sickness at the plant today. A woman employee was sent home after she complained of being bitten by a bug, causing her to feel weak and dizzy.

Sunday News Reports

Nervous disorder, publicity and lastly a bug's bite caused the outbreak of a "very real" and mysterious sickness at Montana Mills. That's the opinion of physicians who carried out extensive investigations. The illness was characterized by nervousness, nausea, weakness, numbness and insect bites.

Monday News Reports

Business was back to normal at Strongsville's Montana Mills plant today. The elusive bug apparently is a thing of the past. And, according to all the experts the rashes and other ailments which caused the trouble can be traced to a bug all right—but a mental one rather than one which crawls or flies.

After exterminators spent all day yesterday completely spraying the building inside and out, Dr. C. H. Foreman, plant officials, and two experts from the Communicable Disease Center voiced the opinion that most, if not all, of the fifty-seven employees afflicted were victims of nothing more than extreme anxiety. They said the illness could not be blamed on any insect.

In any event, as one exterminator put it: "What has been here ain't here now."

Source: Kerckhoff and Back (1968).

---

likely to notice variation in output between members of their section. Finally, there was evidence of family responsibilities that conflicted with, or added to, the pressure of work at the factory: cases were more likely than controls to be the sole or major breadwinners in the home and more likely than controls to have a small child. The existence of prior stress or strain is not universal in the somatoform or anxiety epidemics but has been uncovered many times (7 of 28 case studies of anxiety epidemics and 23 of 24 case studies of mass motor hysteria in the 1987 review of Wessely (1987).

The June bug epidemic spread through sociometric networks, once it got started. During the start of the epidemic, six women fell ill, of whom five were considered to be isolates from the results of a sociometric questionnaire (Table 6.1: 83 percent of six cases in takeoff period). The first woman to be affected had fainted five times in the last few years. Another in this early group had

Table 6.1
June Bug Epidemic: Friendship Status by Time

Friendship Status of Cases	Period of Occurrence for Cases Percentages (n)			
	Takeoff Period	Day 1	Day 2	Resolution Period
Isolated (n = 56 cases)	83 (6)	21 (24)	23 (22)	25 (4)
Choosing Cases (n = 83 choices)	46 (11)	61 (41)	54 (28)	33 (3)
Chosen by Cases (n = 78 choices)	0 (2)	61 (41)	67 (30)	20 (5)

The n's for the second and third rows are the total choices made by the entire sample (row 2) and the choices by cases (row 3).

Source: Adapted from Kerckhoff and Back (1968: 113).

been seeing a doctor for nervousness. Yet another felt her body "swelling like a balloon," and a fourth felt a "crawling sensation" on her thigh. Thus, in this takeoff phase, the individuals were marginal to any group structure, and the symptoms did not conform to any general type. When the epidemic began to spread more rapidly (day 1 and day 2 in Table 6.1), the spread was through individuals who knew one another. Affected persons were more likely to choose as friends, and to be chosen by, other affected persons. There were 83 individuals who chose cases, but the tendency to choose day 1 cases (61 percent of 41 choices of cases in Table 6.1) was stronger than the tendency to choose takeoff period cases (46 percent of 11 choices of cases in Table 6.1). The tendency for cases to choose other cases was stronger in days 1 and 2 than during the takeoff or resolution periods (e.g., 61 percent of 41 choices made by day 1 cases were of other cases, compared to 20 percent of 5 resolution period cases chosen by cases).

There was a good deal of heterogeneity of belief as to the cause of the June bug epidemic. Those affected were more likely to believe the cause to be an insect (63 percent, even though some cases felt it was not an insect, and some controls believed that it was an insect). The degree of reaction and the group structure are related independently to belief in an insect: for instance, the stronger the reaction, the more probable that an insect was blamed (76 percent of cases who reported to the medical clinic believed in the insect, compared to 50 percent of cases who did not). But even if an individual was a control, if she was a member of a group where many were affected ("linked control" in Table 6.1), she was more likely to attribute the symptoms to an insect.

Discussion of Acute Epidemics

Several comprehensive reviews of so-called hysterical epidemics have made it possible to examine the characteristics of the acute somatoform epidemics. Sirois (1974) conducted a review in 1973 that summarized 70 published accounts from 100 years. Boss (1997) updated that work with a review of 70 further published accounts from 1973 to 1993. In terms of the categories presented earlier, the epidemics included in the reviews cover the content area of delusions, emotions, and somatoform behaviors, all with short-term duration; epidemics of suicidal behavior, even though short-lived, were not included. The somatoform complaints and behaviors in the epidemics reviewed included convulsions, fainting, coughing, numbness, headaches, nausea, vomiting, dizziness, paralysis, fatigue, and panic. The characteristics of the 140 epidemics are displayed in Table 6.2, which summarizes the two reviews.

The epidemics tend to occur in situations where group communication is facilitated, and well-defined groups exist already. Almost half of the 140 epidemics reviewed occurred in school settings, as in the Harbor City example. About half of the epidemics result in less than 30 people falling ill, and about half, more than 30. The number of persons ill is much fewer than the number

Table 6.2
Review of 140 Short-term Emotional, Delusional, or Somatoform Epidemics, 1872–1993

Location	Number of Epidemics	Percent*
School	69	49
Town or village	24	17
Factory	28	20
Hospital or Institution	10	7
Other	9	6
Number of persons ill		
Less than ten persons	29	21
10-30 persons	38	27
More than 30 persons	63	45
Unknown	7	5
Gender of persons ill		
All female	68	48
Males and females	60	43
All Males	4	3
Unknown	7	5
Age of persons ill		
All less than 20	65	46
20-40	17	12
All ages	28	20
Unknown	29	21
Duration		
Less than 3 days	30	21
3-14 days	45	32
15-30 days	16	11
More than 30 days	28	20
Unknown	21	15

*Percentages use 140 as denominator; percentages do not always add to 100 percent due to rounding.

Source: Adapted from Sirois (1974) and Boss (1997).

of persons who are involved in, or witness, the epidemic. The transmission completion rate is often about 5 or 10 percent, meaning that many hundreds of people are involved in most of the epidemics as potential cases. Cases in these epidemics are likely to be young women: in about half the epidemics the cases are exclusively women; and about half the cases consist only of persons under 20 years of age. About half the epidemics endure less than two weeks, and only 20 percent last more than a month.

The epidemics travel through social networks, not necessarily along lines through which physical contagion, by an agent such as a germ or toxin, is most plausible. For example, in occupational settings where workers of different ethnic or cultural groups are in close physical proximity, typically only one ethnic group is affected (Dawson and Sabin 1993; Kerckhoff and Back 1968, 1993; Phoon 1982), and there is evidence of transmission via friends or social networks in 19 separate case studies (Wessely 1987). The social transmission is difficult to demonstrate after the epidemic is over, and it is likely that many of these case studies do not report it because the authors do not have sufficient documentation.

Many of the epidemics summarized in Table 6.2 have been reviewed by Wessely (1987). His definition excludes the strictly delusional epidemic, and he divides the remainder into two types: "mass anxiety hysteria," where the complaints and behaviors are forms of anxiety such as fear or panic, chest pain or palpitations, shortness of breath or hyperventilation, dizziness, nausea, and headaches; and "mass motor hysteria," where the complaints and behaviors involve dissociative or conversion behaviors such as convulsions, twitching, anesthesia, paralysis, and trances. Use of the word "hysteria" is unfortunate, but the analysis is insightful in distinguishing different epidemic forms for the two types. The anxiety type spreads rapidly (often by line of sight), usually without a known index or primary case, and endures for only a few hours. It is more typical in children and adolescents, and preexisting stress is often absent. The motor type spreads more slowly, lasts longer, and is more common among adults as well as children, and preexisting stress is often present. Wessely contends, but does not show, that the group structure is necessary for the transmission of the anxiety, whereas prior stress and the secondary gain obtained from sick role behavior are involved in the motor epidemics.

CHRONIC EPIDEMICS

Chronic Fatigue

Social transmission of illness in an epidemic form can lead to chronic as well as short-term illness. The example with the longest history has to do with the symptom of fatigue and the current epidemic of chronic fatigue syndrome (Wessely et al. 1998). The feeling of fatigue is normal following physical or mental exertion or inadequate sleep. It is also a general feature of many illnesses and, aside from nonlocalized pain, is as nonspecific an indicator of illness as it is possible to experience and report. Fatigue contributes directly to failure in fulfilling role responsibilities of various types and thereby to disability by various definitions. For these reasons fatigue has always been able to generate the attention of the social network of the individual and has been noticed quickly by the medical profession.

The modern history of fatigue syndromes might begin with George Beard's description of neurasthenia in 1869, then proceed through interest in irritable heart syndrome, then chronic brucellosis, then epidemic neuromyasthenia, all involving fatigue with putative infectious models eventually discredited to evolve into psychosocial models of etiology, and then to a languishing of interest in the disease (Demitrack and Abbey 1996; Wessely 1994). This discussion picks up the story in the 1930s, when outbreaks of disabling fatigue and/or paralysis occurred in Los Angeles in 1934, Adelaide in 1949, New York state in 1950, London in 1952 and 1953, Bethesda in 1953, South Africa in 1955, and Florida in 1956. These outbreaks were sometimes temporally associated with local polio epidemics, and the initial symptoms were difficult to distinguish from polio (Dawson and Sabin 1993). The possibility that there might be a mild form of polio or other infectious paralytic disease may have contributed to naming the illness *benign myalgic encephalomyelitis*, or "ME." There were associated nonspecific symptoms, including malaise, dizziness, and nausea, but some were suggestive of infection, such as sore throat and stiff neck. The outcome of the illness was much more favorable than for polio, but some cases remained chronically ill for years or even decades. It is possible that polio provided a symbolic template for the belief structure that evolved around the complaint of mild paralysis and chronic fatigue.

These epidemics produced controversy as to their cause: a microbial agent was never identified, and the epidemics had features suggestive of social transmission. For example, some of the epidemics were concentrated in medical staff who were actively treating, or more knowledgeable about, the symptoms of polio, but not their housemates or friends. The epidemics tended to occur in populations of young women who knew each other. Several of the epidemics occurred in areas with populations of mixed cultural backgrounds, but infection was limited to one race or ethnic group. Finally, there is evidence that persons falling ill in the epidemics have personality traits historically associated with conversion and dissociative states, such as high scores on the Eysenck scales for neuroticism and extraversion (McEvedy and Beard 1973).

Epidemics of fatigue apparently did not occur during the decades of the 1960s or 1970s, perhaps connected to elimination of polio. In the early 1980s there were medical reports that persistent infection with the Epstein-Barr virus was associated with fatigue and other nonspecific symptoms (Jones et al. 1985; Tobi et al. 1982). In 1984 two general practitioners in Lake Tahoe, Nevada, noticed similarities between patients they were seeing and discussed the issue with two internists in Boston who were studying a similar condition (Buchwald et al. 1992). The illness was characterized by debilitating fatigue and associated nonspecific symptoms like headache, joint and muscle pain, swollen lymph glands, and sore throat. Many of the associated symptoms in this Lake Tahoe cluster overlapped symptoms of depression, such as sad mood, loss of appetite, and trouble sleeping. An important distinguishing feature of the Lake Tahoe illness was that it was both new to the individual and had sudden onset, often following an episode of flulike illness. The possibility that the cluster in Lake Tahoe might be the result of infection led to an investigation involving medical history and physical examination, hematologic and chemistry testing, magnetic resonance imaging, lymphocyte phenotyping studies, and assays for active infection of patients' lymphocytes with human herpesvirus type 6. The researchers cautiously

Table 6.3
**Prevalence of Selected Symptoms of Chronic Fatigue Syndrome (13,538
ECA Respondents at Four Sites; Lifetime Prevalence in Percent)**

Symptom	Prevalence (%)
Persistent fatigue	23.7
Not explained by illness or drugs	13.9
which disrupts normal activities	2.6
General muscle weakness	8.7
Muscle discomfort	18.0
Headache	20.5
Joint pain	29.2
Sleep problems	25.6

Source: Adapted from Price et al. (1992).

concluded that the patients "may have been experiencing a chronic, immuno-
logically mediated inflammatory process of the central nervous system" (Buchwald et al. 1992).

Interest in the type of illness found in the Lake Tahoe cluster was reinforced
by continuing interest in fatigue resulting from viral and bacterial infections,
both in the United States and in England and Australia, where the concept of
ME had not died out. In the 1980s there was an explosion of interest in both
the medical community and scientific community. In 1988 a case definition was
worked out and promulgated by the Centers for Disease Control (CDC) (Holmes
et al. 1988). The definition required that persistent fatigue be present for more
than six months, which led to a 50 percent or more reduction in usual activities,
with 8 signs and symptoms from a list of 14, such as mild fever, muscle discomfort, headache, sore throat, or pain in the joints. The criteria also required
that the fatigue not be due to a physical illness, substance use, or weight loss
and that no psychiatric illness be present.

Chronic fatigue is common in the general population, but the chronic fatigue
syndrome, using the CDC or other criteria, is rare (Lewis and Wessely 1992).
Table 6.3 shows the distribution in the general population of many of the symptoms used in making the diagnosis, from one study in the United States. They
are very common, which may explain some of the interest in the illness by
people in the general population. But the combination of symptoms necessary
to meet the criteria for diagnosis, incorporating the exclusion criteria, produces
a prevalence of less than 1 in 10,000 in this sample. A review of epidemiologic
estimates in 1997 summarized eight separate epidemiologic studies in which the
samples were not selected on the basis of illness (Jason et al. 1997). The esti-

mates ranged from less than 10 to 1,800 per 100,000 population—that is, a range of three orders of magnitude. The prevalence is strongly related to two factors—the choice of a threshold of fatigue (Pawlikowska et al. 1994) and the manner of excluding cases that might have psychiatric illness as a cause (Price et al. 1992).

There has been considerable interest in the chronic fatigue syndrome in the general population and the media. Strong patient support groups have been formed in both the United States and Britain. In the United States the Chronic Fatigue and Immune Dysfunction Syndrome (CFIDS) Association was established in the late 1980s. A 1994 brochure described programs and services, including toll-free and pay-per-call information lines, a journal, a referral network to more than 2,000 "support organizations, physicians, and disability attorneys," a lobbying effort in Washington, D.C., led by a professional lobbying firm, and a program of financial support for research. The lobbying effort was successful in obtaining from the National Institutes of Health specially designated funds for research and a specially designated scientific review group for chronic fatigue. Since many of the reviewers were also involved in the CFIDS Association, one of the scientific reviews took place in the same city and just prior to its annual meetings. The CFIDS Association maintains a "Physician's Honor Roll of CFIDS clinicians who understand the disorder." An educational pamphlet from the CFIDS in 1994 described in some detail the CDC criteria for diagnosis, omitting the necessity for exclusion due to psychiatric illness. In a section entitled "What Are the Symptoms?" more than 60 associated symptoms were listed, including dryness of the mouth, menstrual problems, and hair loss. The pamphlet states, "It is probable that the viruses and/or other agents that trigger CFIDS are transmissible." Rest and avoiding stress are recommended. Similar patient associations exist in the United Kingdom (Wessely 1994).

What factors predict chronicity in the chronic fatigue syndrome (CFS)? Several studies have attempted to show, via batteries of immunologic and physiologic tests, that infections or other physical agents or hormonal dysregulations were responsible for the chronicity of the disorder, without success (Clark et al. 1995; Wilson et al. 1994). Older age, chronic illness, comorbid psychiatric disorder, and beliefs about the disease turn up repeatedly as predictors of poor prognosis (Joyce et al. 1997). The belief structure involves the degree to which the individual is convinced the illness has a physical cause. About 18 percent of the sample of general practitioners' patients in England attributed general fatigue they experienced to physical causes (Pawlikowska et al. 1994). An Australian outcome study was unusual in including measures of immune function as well as psychosocial measures such as beliefs about illness (Wilson et al. 1994). Age at onset of illness, neuroticism, and measures of immune dysfunction did not predict outcome, but the strength of the belief that a physical disease process caused the symptoms strongly predicted the outcome. Other research from the psychological and anthropological perspective supports the view that the *meaning of the illness for the individual* is predictive of its course and impact

(Antoni et al. 1994; Ware and Kleinman 1992). These findings may have led CFS and ME researchers to advocate treatment from a cognitive behavioral perspective (Wessely 1996), which has been shown to be effective in controlled trials (Deale et al. 1997).

The cause of chronic fatigue syndrome has been actively sought. As discussed earlier, the notion of immune dysfunction of some sort has been popular. But no implied consequences of such dysfunction—either short-term, such as blood measures of immune dysfunction, or long-term, such as elevated rates of cancer—have yet been found (Levine et al. 1994). Studies of direct measures of immune dysfunction have been conflicting or uninformative. Komaroff (1993) reviewed laboratory abnormalities, infectious agents including human herpesvirus-6, enteroviruses, Epstein-Barr virus; retroviruses; and borrelia burgdorferi. He states that:

the data are most consistent with the hypothesis that in CFS the immune system is chronically responding to a "perceived" antigenic challenge (32), . . . [and that] CFS is primarily an immunologic disturbance that allows reactivation of latent and ineradicable infectious agents, particularly viruses. [He also states that] [a]s of this writing, no etiologic agent and no characteristic pathophysiology have been identified. (38)

Straus's (1996) opinion is slightly less positive about the role of viruses:

Numerous studies reveal that chronic fatigue syndrome patients and normal controls differ in terms of immunoglobulin responses, lymphocyte phenotype, and in vitro cytokine release. . . . Regrettably, the existing data do not show these immunologic findings to be consistent. (x–xi)

The possibility that other viruses [aside from Epstein-Barr] cause the syndrome continues to be pursued at the periphery of the main research stream. It will prove difficult to totally dispense with this model because negative studies are never viewed as conclusive, because periodically we discover new candidate microbes, and because technology affords ever more sensitive means of detecting and studying them, but the concept will languish for lack of rigorous support, as have so many other earlier models of chronic fatigue. (ix–x)

The 1996 report of the United Kingdom medical Royal Colleges was likewise dubious about the role of viruses ("Frustrating Survey" 1996). But the report produced sharp negative reaction because of its recommendation of psychosocially oriented treatment. An editorial in *Lancet* stated that the committee producing the report was "top-heavy with psychiatric experts," noting that the ME association claimed the committee was "rigged" ("Frustrating Survey" 1996). The editorial concluded on a political note: "Psychiatry has won the day for now. A decade hence, when an organic cause for at least some cases of CFS may have emerged, it would be tempting to ask the committee to reconvene."

Multiple Chemical Sensitivities

There are examples of other chronic disorders that might be somatoform epidemics. An analogue to CFS that has putative toxic, as opposed to infectious, causes, is the syndrome of *multiple chemical sensitivities* (MCS), also called multiple allergy, environmental illness, and the *sick building syndrome* (SBS). The human organism is exquisitely sensitive to foreign agents, and a variety of environmental agents and toxins, such as lead in the ambient environment, pesticide residues in food, and synthetic chemicals in fabrics, can produce symptoms. Allergic responses are sometimes dramatic and life-threatening. In the modern world, thousands of new substances are being produced each year, raising the potential for allergic reaction, leading some to dub this illness "twentieth-century disease" (Black et al. 1990). Major categories of indoor air pollutants include by-products of combustion, volatile organic compounds, various types of dusts and smoke, infectious agents, bioaerosols, and human contaminants (Chang et al. 1993; Ruhl et al. 1993). In the interest of energy efficiency, newer building designs rely more heavily on tight insulation and internal recirculation of air. About 1 million buildings in the United States have these characteristics, exposing between 30 and 70 million individuals working in them to the possibility of SBS (Kreiss 1990). Sick building syndrome is characterized by diverse, nonspecific complaints, similar to those of CFS, and is distinguished from building related illness (BRI), which has a known etiology (e.g., Legionnaire's disease), a specific symptomatologic picture, and laboratory findings (Ryan and Morrow 1992).

Studies have failed to find distinguishing allergenic markers of individuals with sensitivities to many agents (Simon et al. 1993; Terr 1986). Studies of the sick building syndrome find identifiable environmental causes, such as irritants from carpet shampoo, formaldehyde, or pesticide, only about 25 percent of the time (Hodgson 1989). Although the quality of air circulation is clearly related to symptom reports in some credible studies (Finnegan et al. 1984), some careful blind studies of air circulation find no effects on symptom reports by workers (Menzies et al. 1993). Many more people believe they are allergic to food additives (about 7 percent in a study in England) than actually test allergic under double-blind challenge (less than one-quarter of 1 percent in one study) (Young et al. 1987); 4 out of 23 were allergic to a named food in a second study (Rix et al. 1984). The technique of allergic provocation, used to determine food sensitivity in clinical practice, was found to "lack scientific validity" under double-blind conditions in one study (Jewett et al. 1990). Several studies have found psychological factors to be important in comparisons of those with SBS or MCS and controls (Black et al. 1990; Simon et al. 1990, 1993; Rix et al. 1984). One study found allergy to food additives to be linked to anorexia (Robertson et al. 1988). As with chronic fatigue, believing in a physical agent as cause of the condition is a predictor of poor prognosis (Rix et al. 1984). As with eating disorders, media characterizations seem to be important influences on the symptomatology reported in at least some cases (Stewart 1990a, 1990b). Conditioning of an initial, coincidental physical reaction to an odor or visible exposure of some sort may prolong the symptoms after the agent is no longer present (Bolla-Wilson et al. 1988). Most allergist and immunologic specialists do not accept these diagnoses as valid (American College of Physicians 1989; Howard and Wessely 1993).

Gulf War Syndrome

Another important chronic disorder that might be a socially transmitted somatoform epidemic is the *Gulf War syndrome (GWS)*. Almost 700,000 members of the U.S. armed services took part in military operations following the invasion of Kuwait by Iraq in August 1990 (Persian Gulf Veterans Coordinating Board 1995). The buildup operation was called "Desert Shield" and lasted until January 15, 1991. The war itself began with air raids on January 16, and a four-day ground war took place in February. The war stage was called "Desert Storm." There were few combat casualties, and, perhaps due to extensive medical preparations, few non-battle-related injuries and diseases. During the war in the Persian Gulf there was a fear that the enemy would use biological or chemical warfare, to the point that personnel serving in the war were inoculated. As well, the desert environment was new to many, and there were unexpected infectious and toxic exposures, such as certain types of desert bacteria and the extensive fumes resulting from burning of Iraqi oil wells.

The overall health of the veterans of the Persian Gulf War is apparently good. For example, the rates of mortality are not higher than expected, except for suicides and accidents (Kang and Bullman 1996). But several thousand veterans, at least, report signs and symptoms not explained by any illness. The symptoms include fatigue, rash, headache, and pains of various types (Table 6.4) and have been dubbed the Gulf War syndrome (GWS). There has been extensive research attempting to locate the cause. For example, there has been concern that Iraq used chemical or biological war (CBW) agents during the war. There was extensive preparation for this possibility, including inoculations of service personnel and early warning detection equipment. The detection equipment was designed to be very sensitive, so that substances other than CBW, such as dust or fumes, could trip the loud warning alarms, that is, false positive alarms. Each of thousands of alarm soundings brought about donning of protective equipment by troops. Each alarm was followed by more specific tests, and there was not a single confirmation of the use of CBW. Prophylaxis against CBW was also considered a possible cause of GWS, but the prophylactic measures used had a long history of safe use in a variety of civilian populations. Candidate infectious diseases in the Gulf region do not fit the pattern of symptoms of GWS. Exposure to petroleum fumes did not cause illness in local workers or inhabitants of nearby cities.

The government continues a determined effort to locate the cause of the illness

Table 6.4
Most Frequent Symptoms Reported by Veterans of Gulf War (Indiana Reserves and Comprehensive Clinical Evaluation Program, CCEP)

Symptom	Any occurrence*		Onset — CCEP only n varies from 469 to 3516			
	Indiana n = 79	CCEP n = 18,075	Prior to Invasion	Desert Shield	Desert Storm	Redeployment
Joint pain	54%	49%	7	15	23	50
Fatigue	47%	71%	2	16	31	47
Headache	37%	39%	6	18	25	46
Memory Loss	54%	34%	2	15	27	53
Sleep Problem	57%	32%	4	20	30	43
Rash	35%	31%	5	21	29	39
Concentration	43%	27%	2	16	30	49
Depression	42%	23%	4	18	29	46
Muscle pain	NA	21%	4	17	28	47

*By more than 20 percent of those in CCEP.

Sources: Indiana—DeFraites et al. (1992); CCEP, any symptom, CCEP (1996: Table 3); CCEP, date of onset, CCEP (1996: Table 4).

(Persian Gulf Veterans Coordinating Board 1997). The Departments of Veterans Affairs, Defense, and Health and Human Services have extensive research portfolios in the areas of epidemiology, environmental hazards, neurology, and infectious diseases, all directed at finding the cause of GWS. The Department of Defense established an office of Gulf War illnesses, and various governmental panels of experts have examined the issue since 1993. The incoming secretary of defense, William Cohen, pledged on January 22, 1997, to "get to the bottom of Gulf War illnesses" in his confirmation hearings (Gulflink 1997a). His appointee as deputy special assistant secretary of defense for Gulf War illnesses, Lieutenant General Dale Vesser, described his duties as

a unique challenge. The Gulf War illnesses are especially frustrating because we lack answers for basic questions. So many of our troops have been struck down, not by the enemy on the field of combat, but by something we don't understand. They ask: "What have I got and how did I get it?" They deserve answers. But we haven't provided them. I hope I'll be able to find some of those answers. (Gulflink 1997b)

A major program of the Defense Department in efforts to understand GWS is the Comprehensive Clinical Evaluation Program (CCEP), which conducts standardized clinical and laboratory evaluations on any veteran who has an illness that might be related to participation in the Gulf War. More than 27,000 veterans have participated. The report (Comprehensive Clinical Evaluation Program 1996) assesses the frequency of presenting complaints, self-reported exposures, and medical diagnoses. Six percent of the participants suspected they were exposed to gas or nerve agents, and 2 percent suspected they were exposed to mustard or blistering agents. The symptoms presented in the first 18,598 participants are shown in Table 6.4: joint pain, fatigue, headache, memory loss, sleep problems, rash, and depression. The report concluded that "there is no clinical evidence for a previously unknown, serious illness or 'syndrome' among Persian gulf veterans" (Comprehensive Clinical Evaluation Program 1996).

The pattern of onset of the symptoms may help in understanding the epidemic. Most participants (about 75 percent) could not recall a time of onset for the symptoms they reported. Table 6.4 is organized by recalled date of onset for the 20–25 percent who could remember the onset. Less than 5 percent recall it as occurring before the operation began, and about 15 percent as beginning during the preparatory phase (Desert Shield). Of those able to recall the onset, only about one-quarter report it to have occurred after the start of, during, or in the nine months after, the ground war (Desert Storm). For about half the participants, the symptoms are reported to have begun during the phase of redeployment. The vagueness as to onset, shown in Table 6.4, and the facts that troops from allied forces stationed close to affected U.S. service personnel were not affected and that less exposed U.S. personnel in the navy were affected in similar proportions (Comprehensive Clinical Evaluation Program 1996: Table 13) suggest social transmission, not physical. Later in the formation of the epidemic (i.e., 1996–1998) research began on Gulf War syndrome occurring in British troops. Outbreak among the British could be delayed recognition of the same toxic or infectious disease; but it could also be transmission of the disease, via the agent of communication, across the Atlantic.

An intensive study of an early outbreak in Indiana is also suggestive (De-Fraites et al. 1992). In January 1992 medical staff of the Army Reserve Command in Lafayette, Indiana, became aware of complaints of symptoms of persons who had been deployed in Desert Shield or Desert Storm. In early February 1992 a female noncommissioned officer designed and circulated a symptom questionnaire to several scores of persons. The questionnaire had the title "Medical Survey for Desert Shield/Storm Troops." After obtaining name, phone, place of duty in Southwest Asia, and unit of assignment, it began with: Do you suffer from headaches/how often/to what degree? . . . Do you have nose bleeds/How often/to what degree? . . . leaving a blank line to answer. After 36 questions on symptoms, there were four questions on exposure to anthrax inoculation, microwave towers, animals in the encampment, and whether the person had taken nerve agent prevention pills. In April the army conducted a study of the outbreak, including a medical interview, complete blood count, liver function tests, and test for antibody to Leishmania tropica and Brucella for soldiers in the unit who wished to participate. Results for symptoms closely parallel the general constellation for GWS in general, as shown in Table 6.4. The timing of the symptom onset in the Indiana outbreak is better known because the army's investigation was completed closer to the symptom report. Figure 6.2 shows that the onset of the principal symptom, fatigue, occurred throughout 1991 and 1992. However, when the onset is adjusted to the month the individual was redeployed back to the United States, as in Figure 6.3, the onset is very closely related to the process of return. This relationship to redeployment is consistent for the other symptoms reported. This delayed, but simultaneous, pattern of onset is difficult to explain with an infectious or toxic agent as cause, and the army report concluded that "there is at present no objective evidence to suggest an outbreak of any disease in 123rd ARCOM (Army Reserve Command). We feel that the documentable medical problems and illnesses found in this group are typical of what one would expect in the general population" (DeFraites et al. 1992: 27). The pattern of onset suggests that social processes, including the stress of returning, the dissembling of a group structure, and social interaction among returning troops, may have contributed to this outbreak of symptoms *and* to the general notion that a cluster of symptoms caused by the war experience actually existed.

THEORIES OF COLLECTIVE BEHAVIOR

Collective behavior in sociological terms is defined as *coordinated interaction that does not arise from preexisting norms or institutions* (Goode 1992; Smelser 1962; Turner and Killian 1987). "Coordinated interaction" fits the definition of

Figure 6.2
Onset of Fatigue in 123d Army Reserve Command, by Calendar Month

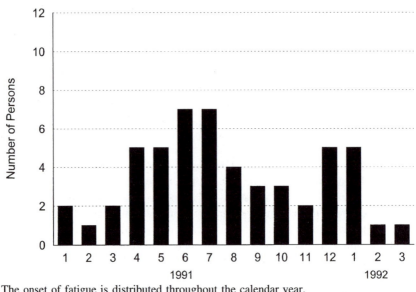

The onset of fatigue is distributed throughout the calendar year.

Source: Redrawn from DeFraites et al. (1992).

group given earlier, so another definition of collective behavior might be *the formation of one or more new groups*. In sociology it has typically included study of all types of new behaviors such as fads and fashions; crowd behaviors such as riots, panics, and lynchings; and social movements that aim to change the values or social structure of society. The area is crucial to sociology because it involves the basic processes of social change. Explanations for collective behavior have occurred in four different frameworks.

Strain

Explanations for collective behavior include theories of *strain and stress*, arising from the placement of the individual in a macrosocial situation of structural strain or a microsocial situation of social stress. Strain produced at the level of society, such as economic fluctuations, can produce frustrations in individuals that contribute to formation of collective behavior. For example, a correlation has been found between economic crises and lynchings of blacks in the South (Dollard et al. 1939). Smelser (1962) defined *strain* as ambiguity as to the adequacy of means to a given goal, conflict over the allotment of rewards, or disagreement over norms and values. Social psychological situations involving demands that the individual cannot meet or life event stressors that overwhelm the individual's ability to cope also may predispose that individual to

Figure 6.3
Onset of Fatigue in 123d Army Reserve Command, by Months Since Return

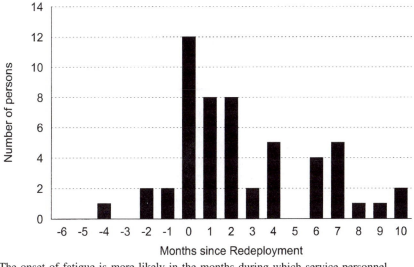

The onset of fatigue is more likely in the months during which service personnel arrive back at home.

Source: Redrawn from DeFraites et al. (1992).

engage in collective behavior. The shape that the collective behavior takes is influenced by what Smelser called the *generalized belief*. The generalized belief arises in response to a situation of strain of some sort, and it "identifies the source of the strain, attributes certain characteristics to this source, and specifies certain responses to the strain as possible or appropriate" (Smelser 1962). The generalized belief is not always accurate or realistic, and often it is semimagical in character, involving a very abstract line of reasoning or values followed by a very concrete plan of action. Five types of generalized belief were defined, each leading to a different type of social movement: the hysterical belief involves anxiety, and the resultant collective behavior is a panic or flight; the wish-fulfillment type of generalized belief leads to a craze or fad; the hostile belief, to scapegoating; the norm-oriented belief, to normative social movement; and the value-oriented belief, to value-oriented social movement.

Structure

Another type of explanation for the occurrence of collective behavior is *transmission structure*: the communication networks available in the social system that enhance or impede transmission of information related to the collective behavior. Transmission structure includes the modality, such as person-to-person communication by written word, telephone, e-mail, or face-to-face; visible transmission of information rapidly such as might occur in institutional settings where many individuals are in a large room together; and varieties of mass electronic communication such as newspaper, radio, television, and broadcast e-mail or chat room. The effects of the transmission structure on collective behavior are independent of the effects of strain and stress. Current developments in electronic networking have vastly enhanced the transmission structure of the entire world.

The strain/stress theories focus on the location of the individual in the group structure but do not require the existence of a group in producing the collective behavior. This would fit the broad definition of "collective" defined earlier, being an example of convergence. A sole-source epidemic could be based on stress or strain but appear similar to a person-to-person epidemic, unless the analysis includes the temporal and interpersonal aspect. In contrast, the transmission structure is a characteristic defined by the way individuals interact and thus, by definition, characterizes a group quality.

Contagion

A third explanation for collective behaviors—*the contagion theory*—builds upon the mental characteristics of the group, that is, group awareness, as opposed to the interactive characteristics. This theory was popularized by the work of Gustave LeBon in the nineteenth century (LeBon 1960), who emphasized the irrational nature of crowds. There was considerable interest in hypnosis in his time, and he felt that individuals in crowds could be hypnotized and manipulated by the crowd leader. Individuals in the crowd acquired a sense of invincibility due to the masses of people with whom they identified themselves. There was a sense of anonymity in the crowd situation, which lowered the feeling of individual responsibility for actions that the crowd might engage in. LeBon postulated that the crowd situation worked to release unconscious and irrational forces in the individual. All these influences worked to make the individual suggestible to manipulations by unscrupulous leaders, who used techniques of hypnosis to guide the crowd into irresponsible behavior. In the contagion theory, the crowd is perceived to be homogeneous and emotional.

Emergent Norm

A fourth explanation for the occurrence of collective behavior is the *emergent norm theory* of Turner and Killian (1987). They observe that the crowd can appear to be homogeneous due to the collective actions of a minority, even when there is considerable heterogeneity. In a problematic situation where institutionalized norms do not prescribe accepted ways of acting, the perception of homogeneity by crowd members can contribute to its development. A few members of the group may begin to respond to the problematic situation in such a way that the other members feel the response is accepted by the entire group.

Each member evaluates his or her initial reactions, in part, by deciding whether the group approves. The inference of group approval—whether correct or not—contributes to the emergence of a normative response.

The emergent norm approach does not rely on any irrational or unconscious mechanisms in explaining collective behavior, even in its most extreme forms. It does not predict that the crowd will be homogeneous, as does contagion theory. Instead, it reflects the notion of anonymity in crowds, emphasizing that the individual assesses the likely approval or disapproval of others before acting. As with the contagion theory, however, and distinct from the concepts of strain or transmission structure, the emergent norm invokes the concept of group at the mental level—that is, individuals are understanding their current situation through their awareness of the group.

RELEVANT SOCIAL PSYCHOLOGICAL PROCESSES

Social psychology is relevant to the study of collective behavior in general and to collective psychopathology in particular. Study of hypnosis, discussed in Chapter 3, is relevant. Other laboratory studies in social psychology, beginning in the 1950s, have demonstrated conclusively and repeatedly certain effects of groups larger than two that are not intuitively obvious. These include classic studies and the sizable literature that followed them of *empathy, hypnosis, norm formation, group conformity, group polarization*, and the *audience effect*. All the effects reviewed next are strong and have been replicated many times.

Dyads: Empathy and Hypnosis

Research on *empathy* has shown that humans have instinctive ability to comprehend emotions in others. This facility extends backward in the mammalian order, as studied in the nineteenth century by Darwin, among others. In primates the capacity or instinct for emotional and motor mimicry is expressed naturally throughout life. Primates understand the basic emotional content of facial expressions, for example (Brothers 1989), and responses are so quick and automatic they must be measured through film in microseconds. Imitation of physical gestures is instinctive and is probably a primitive form of empathy (Bavelas et al. 1987). Emotional contagion presumably enhances survival by communicating danger linked to emotional reactions in others and, in the infant by facilitating learning from others (Cappella 1991; Hatfield et al. 1994).

All the complaints, behaviors, signs, and symptoms discussed in this chapter have been shown to be strongly influenced by *hypnosis or suggestion*—either eliminated or strongly reduced; produced via hypnotic suggestion; or both. Two dramatic aspects of hypnosis are the notions of *dissociation* and *conversion*. The dissociation aspect is the lack of awareness of the subject. Most of the effects of hypnosis can be produced under conditions of simple rule-following or role-playing behavior (Sarbin and Coe 1972), but there remains the capacity for amnesia, which is hard to explain without a concept of unconscious or disso-ciation. Presumably, this dissociative capacity has to do with the parallel proc-essing capabilities of the brain and its capacity for multiple levels of attention. Hilgard (1977) feels that the strong attentional focus, with derailing or neglect of general attentional monitoring, is achieved through imaginative involvements and that highly hypnotizable individuals have the capacity for becoming imag-inatively involved in a wide range of books, plays, stories, and real-life events (Hilgard 1979). The other dramatic aspect of hypnosis—conversion—is its ca-pability to influence bodily functions not under voluntary control. The effects are so strong and repeated across such a range of situations as to lead one to question whether the notion of "voluntary control" is useful. Many of the be-haviors produced or influenced by hypnosis could be construed as under vol-untary control or, at least, affected by the threshold of reporting during measurement. But there are also incontrovertible examples of blind studies con-cerning so-called objective signs, such as allergic skin reaction (Black et al. 1963), hypersensitivity response (Smith and McDaniel 1983), and warts (Spanos et al. 1988, 1990).

The situation of imitation and rule following—or the more general concept of suggestion—is not limited to the original hypnotic state, with hypnotist swinging a watch in front of a subject in a quiet room. It does not require the suggestion or experience of relaxation, for example (Hilgard 1977), and is many ways indistinguishable from the role of experimental subject, as discussed in Chapter 3 (Orne 1959; Sarbin 1967). It has many similarities to various situa-tions of persuasive influence, including the relative prestige of the hypnotist and subject (Myers 1993) and the gradual shaping of requirements from general and innocuous to specific and more difficult, as discussed in Chapter 3. Discussing extremely hypnotizable subjects, Hilgard noted that many "are so talented in hypnotic performance that they gain what appears to be essentially hypnotic control through the exercise of imagination in circumstances of life in the real world where they are unconcerned about a definition of hypnosis: in riding a bicycle uphill, in distance swimming, in surgery without anesthetics. Have they then engaged in self-hypnosis? This is a question to be pondered and studied, not to be decided a priori" (Hilgard 1977: 182). Some researchers believe that the hypnotist is only an assistant in the process, that, in effect, the individual hypnotizes himself or herself (Ruch 1975). The distribution of hypnotic suscep-tibility in the population is bimodal, with about 5 percent of the population being very hypnotizable and about 1 percent being so extremely hypnotizable that they are termed *hypnotic virtuosos*, or somnambulists (Hilgard 1977).

The Effect of the Group on Norms and Arousal

Experiments by Muzafer Sherif on *creation of a norm* in a situation of un-certainty showed that a group would create an artificial belief structure (Sherif 1937). The *autokinetic phenomenon* is the perception generated when seated individuals are shown a point of light in a completely dark room. After a few moments, the light appears to move (even if it is actually stable), because there are no points of reference with which to judge its apparent movement. After seating several subjects in a darkened room and exposing them to the point of light, Sherif asked them to judge how far the light had moved. There was wide variance in judgments on how far the light had moved. But after sessions on successive days, the group tended to agree on the amount of movement, with little variation. The degree of movement, which had no basis in objective terms, acquired the status of a "fact."

Another early social psychologist, Solomon Asch, showed the effects of *group conformity* on perceptions (Asch 1955). He asked individuals to compare the lengths of three lines on successive tests. In some of the comparisons the lines were of identical length, but in some they were obviously different in length. The effect of the group was observed by placing a subject unknowingly with experimental confederates. In the first few tests, each confederate, answering in sequence before the subject, would report the line comparisons veridically— that is, either identical in length or different. On a later test, the confederates would report the lines to be of equal length, even though they were different. A large percentage of the subjects, answering at the end of the sequence of reports by confederates, falsely reported the comparison, agreeing with the group. The percentage reporting falsely depended strongly on the size of the group of confederates: there was almost no false reporting with only one confederate, but there was a sharp increase in false reporting with two or more. The tendency to falsely report in agreement with the group was sharply reduced by the disagreement of only one other confederate, even if the number in the group was very large. The Asch conformity effect has been replicated many times.

The presence of a group has an effect on decision making termed *group polarization*. In early studies of group decision making, it was found that decisions made through group discussion and consensus tended to be riskier than decisions made by the same individuals alone (Dion et al. 1970). The effect was strong and general enough to provoke a great deal of research in attempts to identify the mechanism by which the shift toward risky behavior occurred. After a decade of research it was discovered that the group's effect was not always toward risky behavior (the so-called risky shift) but could be toward a more cautious decision. It appears that the group produces enhancement of members' preexisting tendencies, that is, a strengthening of the members' average tendency. The effect occurs if the group is asked to come to a consensus on a single decision; but also, individual members of the group change their own decisions, in the direction toward the extreme, after a group process. The discussion enhances the polarization of the group, but it is not necessary for it to occur. The group polarization effect is presumed to result from several factors (Myers 1993). The group process lowers individual accountability for the decision, producing a diffusion of responsibility (Mynatt and Sherman 1975). Arguments presented in group discussion sometimes bring to light new aspects that individuals had not considered, which lead them to shift their opinions. Active participation enhances the shift, presumably because individuals creatively marshal arguments in one direction. Finally, there is the possibility that individuals incorrectly view their own initial response as very deviant; then, during the discussion or even just through a poll of the group members' opinions, they discover they are about average or even below average in the extremity of their views. The social comparison allows them to magnify their position safely. Group polarization is presumably occurring naturally all the time in such settings as fraternities, gangs, unions, and neighborhood organizations, to name a few. The groups form because of similar attitudes and interests, which are then magnified through internal discussion and evaluation, as well as relative isolation of the group from the mainstream. The process of group polarization, like the autokinetic effect, can be viewed as an example of the emergence of norms.

Studies of the *audience effect* began early in this century (Zajonc 1965). The goal of these studies was to examine the effect on performance of other people. In some cases the other people were an audience, but sometimes they were coactors, and sometimes just individuals who occasionally watched the subject at his or her task. Early experiments showed that performance of certain tasks (such as the pursuit-rotor task) was facilitated by the audience. Later results seemed to be contradictory at first, because performance of other types of tasks involving learning was poorer in the presence of others. Gradually, researchers became aware that the results were not contradictory, because acquired responses were always facilitated by the audience, and nonacquired responses (such as in a learning task) were inhibited. Zajonc (1965) generalized the effect by noting that, in the performance of an acquired response, the individual's dominant tendency is the correct one; whereas, in the performance of a learning task, the dominant tendency is usually *in*correct. Thus, he concluded that the audience enhances the emission of dominant responses.

The audience effect is believed to be one of physiological arousal related to adrenocortical activity (Zajonc 1965). It works with animals as well; for example, chickens, rats, and mice eat much more when another animal is present, and ants expend much more energy building nests when other ants are present. Learning is also inhibited in a variety of animal species when others are present. Considerable data from animal experiments show that arousal, activation, or drive levels associated with adrenocortical activity (independent of the audience effect) enhance the emission of dominant responses.

Cognitive Dissonance and Attribution Theory

The situation of individuals in their social group affects how they acquire, validate, and transmit knowledge. Many studies have been done of the drive toward consistency in the belief structure (Festinger and Carlsmith 1959); that is, given the huge number of beliefs and values that any given individual in the modern world is exposed to and comes to accept at least in part, how are they structured so that they do not conflict with one another? A related general situation is the process of inferring cause for a given event or behavior, called *attribution theory* (Jones and Davis 1965; Kelly 1973).

An early, sometimes unstated assumption of theories of consistency, dissonance, and attribution is that individuals strive to make sense of the world by having structured and consistent patterns of thought and memory that logically link together. This assumption was confirmed many times in experiments and naturalistic observations, and the drive for consistency was sometimes so strong as to be counterintuitive. For example, participants in an experiment were asked to perform an extremely dull task (turning knobs, over and over again, for an hour) (Festinger and Carlsmith 1959). Then, with a brief, bogus explanation, they asked the participants to describe the just completed hour of activity to newcomers as very interesting, not boring at all. They were paid either $1 or $20 for this "acting" part of the experiment. When asked later how much they enjoyed the experiment, those paid $20 reported little or no enjoyment, but those paid only $1 reported high levels of enjoyment—that is, it appeared that they had convinced themselves the experiment was fun. The higher level of enjoyment for less pay is sometimes called the *insufficient justification* effect and has been replicated many times (Festinger and Carlsmith 1959). The dissonance produced by the comparison of the individuals' perception of their attitude and their behavior was unpleasant: since the behavior had already been performed and could not be changed, this led to changing the attitude. The point is that engaging in the behavior can lead to a change in the attitude.

Attribution theory focused on the notion of cause. How do we infer the cause of a given social event? A classic example is an experiment in which randomly assigned students were asked to write and deliver a brief public speech either supporting or (randomly determined) attacking Fidel Castro (Jones and Harris 1967). Those watching the speeches assumed the student delivering the speech had an attitude consistent with the speech. Strangely enough, this inference existed even if those watching were told that the student had been assigned the pro or con position. Since the students at that university were generally strongly in the con position, the inference of support for Castro was mistaken most of the time. This mistake in perception is so widespread that it is called the *fundamental attribution error*: the tendency to underestimate situational influences and overestimate dispositional (trait) influences on others' behavior (Myers 1993). In effect, people end up in situations that guide their behavior, which they then attribute to personal dispositions, not situations.

In the 1970s the notions from attribution theory were applied to the self-concept by Bem (1972), and attribution theory is most useful, in the context of social transmission of psychopathology, when it is applied to the concept of the self. As discussed in Chapter 3, the self-concept is the group of cognitions and feelings an individual has about himself or herself as an object, providing the individual with the perception of constancy through time (Erikson and Gold-thorpe 1993; Rosenberg 1986; Scheibe 1995). These cognitions and feelings guide actions even when they are not prominent in consciousness. The self-concept is affected by interactions with others, and interactions with others are guided by reformulated attributions (MacKinnon 1989; Markus 1977; Swann and Read 1981). In effect, individuals seek to control their level of dissonance and resulting emotion by choosing with whom to interact and for how long. The self-concept guides the attraction into groups, which then reconstitutes the self (Turner 1987).

Both the theory of cognitive dissonance and attribution theory predict change in attitudes and inferences about the self, produced by behaviors that are discrepant with the current self-concept. The insufficient justification effect, described earlier, is an example of the fundamental attribution error, applied to the self: Why did I do that? It must be because I liked it." The reformulated self-concept is used to guide further actions and to process and encode new information, all the while changing the valences attached to various alternatives for future action. Emotional and social behaviors are likely to generate strong pressure for consistency and attribution. The tendency to infer traits and the strength of the resulting beliefs about the self are greater to the extent that the emotional or social behavior is deviant, unanticipated, or out of line with the self-concept (MacKinnon 1989). Sometimes the effect of this dissonance or attributional process can be amazingly strong. For example, a cult of individuals predicted that the world would end on a specific morning and that a spaceship would appear to pick up the few faithful members of the cult. When the spaceship did not actually appear, and the world did not end, as predicted, it might have been expected that the cult would be discredited and dissolve. Instead, they redoubled their recruitment activity and increased the strength of their faith (Festinger et al. 1956). This counterintuitive effect is predicted by both dissonance theory and self-attribution theory.

SOCIOLOGIC FRAMEWORK FOR SOMATOFORM EPIDEMICS (RESCITE)

What Is Transmitted:
Responsive Emotional Schemata (RES)

In *The Selfish Gene*, Richard Dawkins (1976) claimed that the gene was definable as a unit that replicated itself and is self-preservative. In discussing the difference between genetic and cultural transmission, he included, almost as an aside, the notion that there might exist ideas or cognitions that replicated themselves and were self-preservative—that is, the basic units of cultural transmission, much as genes are the basic units of genetic transmission. He called such ideas *memes* and stimulated an interest in what some have called the science of memetics (Fog 1996; Lynch 1996). Memetics is a young academic fashion, and it is difficult to say how important it will be in the future. But it includes several notions that are relevant to the current study. One notion is that the definition of the meme is *that which replicates itself*, from one human being to another. As with genes, memes undergo the three basic processes of creation, transmission, and persistence/reproduction (Fog 1996). New memes are created constantly, as are new genes, and they undergo processes of selection and elimination; that is, memes, like genes, are in competition, and they differ in their ability to survive and replicate in various environments.

The basic process we are evaluating is the transmission of certain symbols. By what term should we name these clusters? The term "meme" is not chosen because the basic assumption of memetics—that a unit can be replicated identically from one person to another—is not credible. The term is also not used because it seems that the founders and proponents of memetics are ignorant of much of the social psychological research reviewed earlier concerning the acquisition and transmission of knowledge. It might seem at first that what is transferred is a *delusional belief*; but this would require the difficult proof that so-called nondelusional beliefs are different in quality. Most of our beliefs originate in social groups and are validated in subjective, not objective, manner. For example, we easily conclude that the beliefs of the Heaven's Gate cult (e.g., transmission of the soul to a spaceship after death) are delusional, even though many Hindus believe in the somewhat improbable idea of reincarnation, and Christians believe in the virgin birth and Resurrection of Jesus: the point is, it is very difficult, *on the basis of the beliefs themselves*, to conclude that one is delusional and the other based in reality. The simple term *belief* might suffice, except that it connotes a verbalizable and logical structure. Smelser (1962) used the term *generalized belief* in his study of collective behavior. The generalized belief is verbalizable but, as discussed earlier, not necessarily logical. The situations of collective psychopathology would appear to involve, in Smelser's terms, either the hysterical belief or the wish fulfillment belief. But the epidemics of collective psychopathology do not always involve simple approach (as in a craze or fad) or flight (as in a panic) (Gehlen 1977), and what is transmitted does not always fit the notion of a belief that can be stated in words.

The term *schema* is used in health psychology to denote "a hypothetical entity that readies the perceiver for perceptual experience by providing a structure for assimilating new information . . . illness schema will prompt the perceiver to selectively search his/her body for illness-relevant sensations" (Pennebaker 1982:142; see also Robbins and Kirmayer 1991). This term focuses too much on the reception of the idea by the individual and not the generation and transmission of the idea; and the term has no required emotional aspects. In the study of emotions (Leventhal and Mosbach 1983), the term *schemata* has been used to denote memories or records of expressive/motor/emotional events, and this is the appropriate term here. A schemata is a cluster of one or more beliefs *and* expressive, motor, or emotional events that can be recorded in human memory and tend to be recalled as a unit. The term requires only that there be at least some cognitive, ideational, abstract, or verbalizable element; at least some emotional element involving attraction to the memory pattern or repulsion from it; and a physiological component (Leventhal and Mosbach 1983). Since emotions are basically social responses, an addition to this idea is that the schemata contains some record of the social situation. An emotional schemata is a record in memory, but it also prepares the individual to receive information in a given form, as in a health schema.

Some or all of the elements of any given emotional schemata may not be verbalizable. The notion that we can remember things that we cannot verbally express is a crucial aspect of the concept of schemata that distinguishes it from a belief. The nonverbalizable portion of memory would be called the *unconscious* in Freudian terms. Nonverbalizable memories arise in learning theory as *patterns of reinforced behavior*. The dissociation and conversion that occur in hypnosis is another example, and the fact that all of the symptoms and behaviors studied here can be brought about, or influenced by, hypnotic induction makes the relevance of this nonverbalizability clear. Experiments on the split brain show conclusively that individuals can react to complex stimuli and create complex responses without being able to state what they are doing in words (Gazzaniga 1967).

In socially transmitted psychopathology the emotional schemata in some manner or other address a puzzle or problem being experienced by one or more persons. This is the quality of the generalized belief that Smelser emphasized, saying that it "identifies the source of the strain, attributes certain characteristics to this source, and specifies certain responses to the strain as possible or appropriate" (Smelser 1962). Smelser's analysis emphasizes the logical and verbalizable quality in the belief, which is too constraining in the present context. But his insight into the responsive quality of the generalized belief to a human problem was on the mark. Here we take advantage of his wisdom to add the modifier *responsive*, leading to focus on the notion of *responsive emotional schemata* (RES).

Characteristics That Facilitate Transmission

What are the characteristics of responsive emotional schemata that make them highly transmissible, or "contagious"? Some characteristics have been studied in the field of communications theory under the rubric of *rumor transmission*. The basic two factors laid out in the 1940s that would promote the transmission of a rumor were the combination of importance of the topic and the ambiguity of the current situation, and later experiments confirmed these notions and added the dimensions of personal anxiety and general uncertainty (Rosnow 1958). That personal anxiety would promote the transmission of rumors is consistent with the notion that strain promotes collective behaviors (reviewed earlier). That general uncertainty promotes rumor transmission is consistent with the notion that the epidemics begin with an unsolved problem or puzzle.

It seems clear that other dimensions are involved in promoting the transmission of a given RES. Human beings habituate quickly and pay attention to new stimuli, so, to attract attention, transmissible RESs should be new or have a new quality to them. All of the behaviors under study here have this quality of newness about them, but the newness is sometimes engendered by the precise context or juxtaposition and confluence of circumstances. For example, women fainted in the weeks prior to the June bug epidemic, but not in the context of the possibility of insects in new shipments of cotton. Suicides occur regularly, but the suicide of a well-known public figure, written up in the newspaper and reported on television, is new. To engender transmission, the RES should be uncomplicated. The symptoms and behaviors studied here all involve a relatively simple idea that can be explained in one sentence with a straightforward declarative structure—usually, an uncomplicated disease agent like an insect, virus, or toxin (e.g., "The bug made me faint" or "Nuclear fallout pitted my windshield" or "Virus infection makes me tired"). To be reproducible, they should involve behaviors that do not have to be learned by the recipient. With the exception of suicide, all the symptoms of the acute and chronic somatoform epidemics are well known to the individual, in part because they are built into the human organism for various reasons related to survival. Obvious examples include the panic reaction, vomiting, nausea, and fatigue.

To be credible, the RES should link into a collection of ideas—a *paradigm*—already known to the recipient. The paradigm can be thought of as referring to the abstract part of the generalized belief. It is helpful to transmission if the paradigm is salient to the individual at the time that transmission is initiated and if the paradigm has considerable power to affect outcomes in the material world. Symptoms in these epidemics throughout history are drawn from a common recurring pool to become the subject of attention, according to the medical models of the time (Shorter 1992; Wessley 1994). The attraction of the paradigm of the germ theory of disease—sometimes called the "magic bullet"—is linked to its conceptual simplicity as well as its proven power to affect outcomes in a wide variety of situations. In the Heaven's Gate cult, the paradigm was an amalgam of vague allusions to Christian beliefs, and complex beliefs about astronomy and extraterrestrial life. Each epidemic fits the disease context into an existing paradigm: for example, chronic fatigue in the virus/immune dysfunction paradigm, which was strengthened by the HIV epidemic (Wessely et al. 1998); multiple chemical sensitivity in the toxin paradigm, which has become an important part of our culture since at least the publication of *Silent Spring* in 1962 (Carson 1994).

In the process of transmission, many individuals seek to validate the credibility of the schemata, and the transmission is enhanced if there is an objective substrate to which the recipient can refer for validation. The RES is more credible if it involves a *material substrate*, that is, a relatively unchanging aspect of the physical world that can serve as validation for the logic of belief involved in the RES. Material substrates are, in principle, visually perceptible. In the

Seattle epidemic there was a convenient, close, well-known place to look for the existence of the pitting (the windshield). The Hale-Bopp comet is an example of a visible material substrate that enhanced credibility of the ideology of the Heaven's Gate cult. In the somatoform epidemics there is usually a search for a physical agent like an insect, germ, or toxin. The RES can invoke a simple change in structure of threshold for identifying the material substrate, as occurred in the Seattle epidemic, in which attention directed to looking *at* the windshield, instead of *through* it, inevitably discovered evidence of pitting in some cars. In epidemics where a toxin is the purported cause, rapidly developing technologies locate lower and lower doses of chemical agents in human beings. Germs are also, in principle, visible. Fumes from burning oil wells provide another example of the material substrate, linked to the Gulf War syndrome.

The RES is more likely to persist if it involves a cognitive structure for discounting alternative beliefs. This is the analogue to inoculation. The difficulty of locating viral structures in the bloodstream provides a ready answer to negative findings pertaining to chronic fatigue syndrome, for example. Suspicions (well founded in some cases) that the government is concealing evidence contributes to discounting negative evidence about the Gulf War syndrome.

Group Influences on Transmission: The RESCITE Model

It is helpful to divide the epidemics into phases of *convergence, initiation, transmission*, and *endurance*. There are group influences at work in all phases, but the nature of the group influences and the types of susceptible individuals change with each phase. In the *convergence* phase a puzzle or problem is presented to some individuals with a group structure of some sort, in a social context where certain model individuals are present. This convergence phase is probabilistic in that the convergence of the model individuals in the given situation requires the confluence of independently acting probabilistic processes—a sampling of contexts and individuals that occasionally produces the situation of convergence. Many epidemics begin with prominent individuals who serve as *models*. Wessely (1987) tabulates 34 separate studies in which an initial case was recorded, and it must be presumed that the case was missed in yet other studies due to weakness in data collection. Model individuals with disturbances or disorders that are prominent in the convergence and initiation phases of the epidemic tend to be those who have engaged in the behavior many times earlier. For example, in somatoform epidemics the individuals in the initiation phase might be "amplifiers" (Barsky 1979) or "somaticizers" (Escobar et al. 1987; Smith 1994). In epidemics of mass anxiety the individuals in the initiation phase would score high on measures of trait anxiety. In epidemics of CFS or ME, these might be individuals who scored high on trait neuroticism, or who tended to overuse their sick leave (McEvedy and Beard 1973). The prominent individuals who end up as models are distinctive and can attract attention—sometimes these are popular individuals, but also sometimes they are social isolates (Murphy, as reported to Sirois 1982). These initial behaviors may be completely idiosyncratic and may not yet have taken an epidemic form, but they create the context for the outbreak. The epidemic process is illustrated in Figure 6.4 for a hypothetical group of 15 individuals. It is called the RESCITE model to help remember the central terms: Responsive Emotional Schemata; Convergence, Initiation, Transmission, Endurance. Each square corresponds to 1 individual with four possible tendencies to respond, labeled A,B,C, and D. The responses are enacted if the tendencies are sufficiently strong (line of three or more units of length, designated with arrow). Only one response can be made at any given time. The response structure of the five models does not change during the course of the epidemic.

The later phase of initiation, transmission, and persistence parallel the structure of biological evolution (variation, selection, reproduction) and are also used in memetics (Campbell 1975; Fog 1996). In the *initiation* phase the group becomes aware of a problem or puzzle in explaining the behaviors of the models, and news spreads of the unusual models' behaviors and their persistence: "Why did Mrs. A, and then Mrs. B, faint?"; "Why am I so tired all the time?" Some or many individuals in the group seek a solution to the puzzle. If they locate a solution without difficulty, there is no further manifestation of group activity related to the initial problem, and it may never enter the group consciousness, being forgotten by the individuals exposed to the problem. For example, a solution in the June bug epidemic might have been: "She faints all the time"; in the Gulf War it might have been: "It's hard to get used to being back in my old schedule" or "I am getting older." In most situations, then, the convergence situation, which is already not common, is resolved without group action and without taking the epidemic form. If individuals fail to solve the problem, and the situation of uncertainty persists, they seek information of other persons in their environment, much as the individuals in Sherif's experiments on the autokinetic phenomenon did, and the epidemic form of interaction begins. Other group members may be as puzzled as they are. The initial phase of the epidemic has features that suggest it is a *catastrophe or cusp*, that is, a stage of chaos where an eventually large outcome is delicately balanced on a few volatile variables (Zeeman 1976). The group structure itself may contribute to a general arousal, as in the audience effect. The arousal engendered by the audience effect pushes the group solution to include an emotional aspect, that is, a cognitive label and explanation for physiological arousal, as in the Schachterian theory of emotion (Reisenzein 1983; Schachter and Singer 1962). In the initiation stage, the models' behaviors combine with lower threshold of response due to arousal, releasing otherwise hidden response tendencies in the group as a whole. The volatile aspect is that there is no obvious dominant response, and the solution arises from the rapid and unpredictable workings of the imagination of a limited number of probabilistically assembled individuals, aiming to solve a new puzzle. Eventually, a cluster of activities, feelings, and cognitions is assembled, perhaps due to a single human performance in the public sphere or a series of them, that

Figure 6.4
RESCITE Model of Somatoform Epidemics

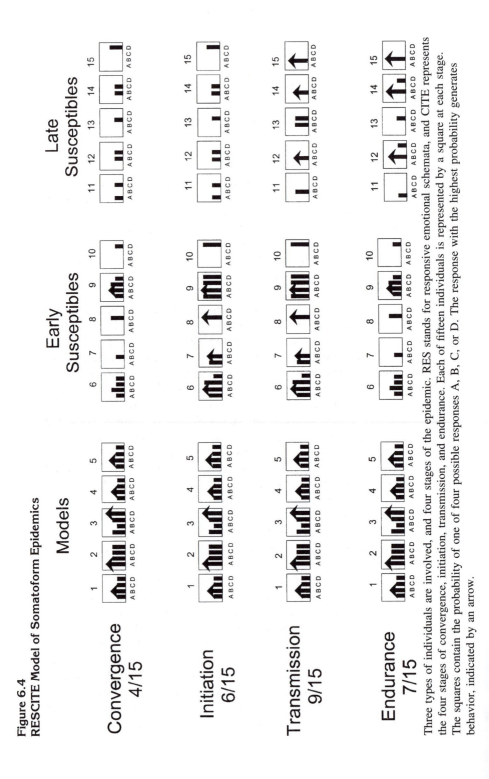

Three types of individuals are involved, and four stages of the epidemic. RES stands for responsive emotional schemata, and CITE represents the four stages of convergence, initiation, transmission, and endurance. Each of fifteen individuals is represented by a square at each stage. The squares contain the probability of one of four possible responses A, B, C, or D. The response with the highest probability generates behavior, indicated by an arrow.

is credible and transmissible—the responsive emotional schemata. This stage may involve several experiments with solutions that are evaluated and rejected by the group, as apparently occurred in the June bug epidemic.

The behavior enacted by the models is an existing and perhaps even dominant response tendency in many stress-reactive individuals, but it is inhibited by fear of disapproval or lack of salience to the current situation. Thus, in Figure 6.4, during the convergence phase, three out of the five early susceptibles have response B as one potential, and one person actually is generating the response during this phase. Experiments on group polarization show that a member's perception of the group's opinion may not be accurate and that, in fact, individuals tend to overestimate the prevalence of their own feelings and tendencies in the group. Thus, the enactors in the initiation phase are aroused because of the puzzle presented to the group, as well as by the social situation implying the need for some sort of performance. They may be inappropriately guessing the group's approval of the model's behavior and proceed to enact it themselves, producing a response that, for them, is *just barely* the dominant one, consistent with the audience effect.

The percentage of the group susceptible to initial enactments depends on the precise nature of the models' behaviors and the situation, but it may be as high as 25 percent of the general population. The susceptibles in this population may be under identifiable stress from a variety of sources. Even though it may last only a few moments, this phase may involve complex symbolic processing by the collective, engendering momentarily strong forces of conformity such as were shown to exist by Asch (1955). When the social context and the availability of individual performances in the population in that social context match, the RES emerges briefly. It must be presumed that most nascent epidemics die out because no credible RES emerges or survives the group evaluation. For example, a credible and correctable cause of an odor or fume may come to be understood by the group before any deviant or bizarre behaviors are extended beyond one or two or a small handful of individuals.

The credibility of the RES may ebb and flow with time, but at some minimal level of credibility the effects of the group on the course of the epidemic change. This is the entry into the *transmission* phase. In the transmission phase the group problem or puzzle persists, attracting focused attention, but now the RES is sufficiently credible that enacted behaviors are replicated in individuals to whom the behavior is new. There are temporarily strong pressures of conformity to the emerging RES, which is increasingly unconnected to an individual's own prior judgments of the situation, as in the Asch conformity experiments. At this point, the types of individuals who engage in the behavior change from those predisposed toward the initial symptom production as highly (convergence phase) or barely (initiation phase) dominant response, into those predisposed to suggestibility (transmission phase). In many short-term small group epidemics the transition from the initiation to the transmission phase occurs apparently as soon as the third, fourth, or fifth performance of the same behavior. In this phase of the epidemic any new information that resolves or explains the puzzle or problem may end the epidemic. In the situation of mass anxiety, the resolution occurs because the source of the fear is eliminated. In the Seattle windshield epidemic, the dominant explanation for the delusion had the notion of impermanence built in: a cloud that passed with the weather pattern.

In the transmission phase a situation similar to that of hypnotic induction (described on pages 112–115) is produced (Haberman 1986). The situation includes the following: the individual has entered a social context voluntarily; attention is highly focused on the one aspect of the social context; initially ambiguous demands have been gradually shaped into specific responses that the individual is capable of producing; and social constraints toward producing the responses have been lowered. The effect is to change the individual's typical symptom attribution style (Robbins and Kirmayer 1991), to change the threshold at which the material substrate is observed, or to change the degree of attention that is focused on a particular aspect of the body. The group problem or puzzle persists, attracting focused attention. In the transmission phase, production of a particular type of symptom or response may be quite uncharacteristic of individuals and baffling to themselves and others, much as hypnotic performances are baffling to the hypnotized individual. In fact, the performance may be out of verbalizable awareness (as in reactions like "I don't know what came over me," or "My mind went blank"). As many as 5 percent of the general population are highly suggestible, as shown by research into hypnotizability. It is important to note that the susceptible 5 percent are not necessarily highly overlapped with the approximately 25 percent stress-reactive persons who are susceptible in the initiation phase. The designation "epidemic" may occur even with a very low transmission completion rate—that is, even when only a fraction of the proportion who are susceptible actually do respond with an enactment.

A limited number of epidemics may involve a large group transmission aspect. In large epidemics this stage is reached at the point of extensive reporting by the media (David and Wessely 1995; Hefez 1985; Seydlitz et al. 1991; Small and Borus 1987). Both the Seattle windshield pitting epidemic and the study of suicide show that imitation of deviant behaviors can be induced by media in the absence of the small group, face-to-face situation. It is certainly the case that the media have played a strong role in the epidemics of chronic fatigue, Gulf War, and multiple chemical sensitivity syndromes (Wessely et al. 1998). The transmission completion rate at this second, large-group phase of transmission can be very small, since the communication process is now so widespread. Since the transmission completion rate can be much smaller, the enactments can be by individuals who are much farther away from the statistical norm in terms of their hypnotic susceptibility, as well as in other dimensions connected to the specific type of symptom or behavior. For example, although many individuals in the small Indiana outbreak of GWS reported symptoms, only 30,000 out of nearly 700,000 requested participation in the CCEP, and only a small percentage of these reported the types of symptoms linked to the GWS as of 1997. In large-group epidemics, transmission of the epidemic at this phase is not affected by face-to-face processes of emotional contagion: instead, the important influence is now the structural conduciveness of the mass media and electronic communication system.

In the *endurance* phase the effects of the group have to do with attributions and self-definition. Attribution is important because individuals seek to explain why they have engaged in behavior that is not usual for them, even bizarre for them. One attribution might be to the situation—that is, the social context produced the strange behavior. Many contexts of epidemics present a temporary or situationally oriented explanation. The explanation for behaviors connected to anxiety almost always suggests transience, both for cause, noted earlier, and for attribution to the self, suggesting why they are almost always short-lived. Deviant behavior is understandable in terms of the situation, not the self (e.g., "I was so scared I fainted"). But individuals may make the *fundamental attribution error*, as discussed earlier, in sizing up the situation; that is, they may attribute the behavior to an enduring characteristic of themselves, instead of to the situation (e.g., "I vomited because I am that way"; "I am tired because I have a chronic disease"). A counterintuitive finding from attribution theory is relevant to this phase of the epidemic; that is, the individuals for whom the deviant or bizarre behavior is most strange may end up changing their self-definition by the largest amount as a result of the attribution. This may explain why individuals who characteristically are not prone to illness behavior—deniers (Kerckhoff and Back 1968) or alexithymics (Ten Houten et al. 1986)—end up being strongly identified with the group.

The availability of labels for persistent traits or repeated patterns of behaviors enhances this endurance phase. Group behaviors may be created around the label, such as the patient groups formed around the label ME in Britain and CFS in the United States. These group activities reinforce the pertinence, strength, and salience of the attribution for the individual (Sharpe et al. 1992). Any residual uncertainty by the individual as to the cause of his or her own behavior may contribute to attempts to validate the new self-identity by group activities. Again, the individuals whose epidemic behaviors were most self-discrepant may be just those individuals who are most active in group creation and persistence, since their need for validation may be greater. In rare cases where the group becomes strong, it defines itself not just by self-awareness of a common label but also in relation to other groups, in mental terms with labels for in-group and out-group behaviors, as well as structured interactions within the group and with outsiders. Formation of other similar groups, sometimes through newly initiated "sister" epidemics, may reinforce the validity of the group definition. For example, in March 1995 army personnel working in a document-processing room with 100 percent air recirculation in Fort Leavenworth, Kansas, became sick after working with documents from Haiti, Rwanda, and the Persian Gulf. Press reports appeared in Fort Leavenworth and Kansas City newspapers as an epidemic of "sick building syndrome" (Gulflink 1996).

Trace amounts of phospine and phosgene gas were found in the air and (in roughly the same concentration) in boxes of documents from abroad. The Persian Gulf War Veterans Illnesses Investigation Team concluded that the boxes of documents were not the source of the epidemic, but after aeration of work spaces and modification of the air-conditioning system, the cause of the "History Office personnel illnesses" was alleviated. The effect of the sister epidemics and other group activities is to set up group boundaries and create techniques for differentiating itself from others. Here the group process can constrain information flow into the group in such a way as to foster the emergence of ever-more-deviant behaviors. At the extreme and very rarely, this process results in situations like folie à deux and cults.

The proportion enacting the behavior or voicing the complaint (response B in Figure 6.4) grows from the convergence through the transmission phase and then declines in the endurance phase. In the hypothetical population of 15 individuals in Figure 6.4, it grows from 4/15, to 6/15, to 9/15 and then declines to 7/15. But the four numerators are composed of different proportions of models, early (stress-reactive) susceptibles, and late (suggestible) susceptibles: 3/4 of the numerator are models in the convergence phase versus 3/6 models and 3/6 stress reactive in the initiation phase versus 3/9 models, 3/9 stress reactive, and 3/9 suggestibles in the transmission phase versus 3/7 models, 1/7 stress reactive, and 3/7 suggestibles in the endurance phase (Figure 6.4). The responses of the stress-reactive are the most volatile, appearing during the epidemic and then disappearing. The responses of the models are least volatile, being absolutely stable throughout. In the endurance phase the epidemic is dominated by individuals to whom the behavior is new. The mix of models, early and late susceptibles, is chosen to illustrate the process. The proportion of models is much lower, and the proportions of early and late susceptibles varies considerably from epidemic to epidemic.

Discussion

Recommendations in the literature conflict as to appropriate treatment for somatoform and other epidemics. One school of thought is to dismiss the putative physical cause, stating authoritatively that the epidemic has an emotional basis and dismembering the group (Cole et al. 1990; Colligan and Murphy 1979; Gehlen 1977; Selden 1989; Sirois 1974). Others imply that efforts to discount the putative material cause may backfire and that the group structure should not be openly attacked (Howard and Wessely 1993; Simon et al. 1990). These different recommendations are appropriate, but they depend on the stage of the epidemic. Epidemics in the transmission phase can be countered by a substitute form of explanation and dismemberment of the group. Epidemics in the endurance phase are strengthened by conflicting information and attempts to discourage group activity, because the group's self-definition is stronger after attack than before it.

For the short-term epidemics, there are important differences analyzed by Boss (1997) between the epidemics in the period 1872–1973 and 1973–1993 (i.e., her own review and that of Sirois (1974)). In the last two decades, epidemics have been more likely to occur in factories and less likely to occur in villages or towns. The percentage of epidemics with more than 30 cases was 28 percent in the first period but 63 percent in the last two decades. The percentage of epidemics reported where the cases were solely less than 20 years of age fell from 59 percent to 34 percent. The percentage of epidemics where the cases included both males and females grew from 11 percent in the early period to 74 percent in the last two decades. Thus, the short-term epidemics have become larger and more inclusive of a range of age and sex groups in the last 20 years, as compared with the century prior.

The change in the nature of the short-term epidemics is paralleled by the apparent rise in the number of chronic epidemics. These epidemics involve a large number of individuals, as well as a wider range of ages and more involvement by males. The long-term epidemics do not require face-to-face transmission, and, thus, the increase in the facility of rapid communications, both through the mass media and through electronic form, increases the structural conduciveness of the social system to this sort of occurrence. As a result, an epidemic of great social importance can arise in which the transmission completion rate is much lower than has been typical in the past.

In the past the tendency has been to assume that females are somehow more vulnerable due to their constitutional makeup, hence use of the term "hysteria." This biological explanation is not consistent with the shift in male–female form of participation in the chronic as opposed to the acute epidemics. Evidence shows that females are better than males at decoding nonverbal cues (Hall 1978) and more attuned to emotional responsiveness in a group setting. They are better at reading emotions in faces than are men, and they are more aware of distressing social events in their environments than are men (Kessler and McLeod 1984). Persons in positions of less social power are more attuned to the emotions in their environment (Snodgrass 1985). Since women are generally in positions of less power, it could be that the social situation, not the physiology, of women makes them prone to the epidemics. The social explanation is consistent with the change in form of the epidemics noted by Boss: that is, there may be more men involved in the epidemics nowadays because women have more equal status as compared to men than earlier.

The medical system is implicated in the initiation, transmission, and endurance phases of the chronic epidemics. Medical diagnoses provide potent and salient RESs that benefit from powerful paradigms. They provide a readily available and inexhaustible material substrate that can be searched for agents. The public health paradigm in the past has been to increase the structural conduciveness in the system in order to prevent outbreaks of certain transmissible diseases. For example, laws require notification of partners in sexually transmitted diseases, and there has been strong effort by the Defense Department to communicate openly about Gulf War syndrome. But these efforts to communicate may not be helpful in the situation of socially transmitted psychopathology, because they reinforce the RES and validate the emerging self of participants in the epidemic.

Some researchers feel that both neurasthenia and CFS are forms of culturally sanctioned illness behavior and that CFS will decline at the end of the twentieth century, just as neurasthenia did at the end of the nineteenth century (Abbey and Garfinkel 1991). Illness behavior is the reaction of the individual to his or her bodily deviations and includes help-seeking behavior, malingering, and secondary gain. Malingering is the conscious imitation of symptoms of an illness, and secondary gain is the advantages that accrue to an ill individual because of the characteristics of the sick role. There are documented instances of malingering in some of these epidemics, such as the individual who, in a follow-up study years later, reported:

I feel I must be honest. Though the illness apparently lasted for over three months in my case, I had actually recovered quickly but prolonged my stay in hospital by "cooking" a pyrexia [high fever] with cigarettes and hot water bottles. I can only explain it as a love of the attention I was receiving and a slight apprehension at going back into the outside world after such a long period of security. I have always been very sorry about doing this but have never told anyone before. (McEvedy and Beard 1973: 147)

This is an isolated example but suggests that the epidemics sometimes include frank malingerers. However, the presence of malingering and secondary gain is characteristic of all diseases whose symptoms can be credibly imitated. The notions proposed earlier to describe and explain the epidemics do not use the notion of secondary gain or malingering. Earlier it was proposed that the bodily symptoms themselves are produced as part of the social process; this process may begin prior to the illness behavior, which is a reaction to the symptoms. In most individuals and in most epidemics, the possibility of secondary gain certainly exists but is contradicted by the available evidence, which shows considerable loss in prestige, happiness, and social support in those who are ill.

There is an amazing breadth to the symptomatologic picture of disturbances, illnesses, and disorders reviewed in this chapter but also many similarities in the underlying social processes. The symptomatology seems at first to be abnormal or bizarre, but the underlying social processes are quite general. What is distinctive is the unusual social context that occasionally comes into being through the confluence of diverse circumstances, including cultural and institutional histories, lifetime experiences of individuals, and the probabilistic formation of individuals into social gatherings, which then, rarely, acquire a history and importance belied by their almost accidental origins. The nature of the social process is more important than any other contributing cause to these phenomena. But it is also the most problematic to study, since the nature of the casual phenomena are temporary and evanescent, especially as compared to causal phenomena from other disciplines, which tend to have more permanence.

7

Social Aspects of Treatment

BIZARRE BEHAVIORS AND USE OF SERVICES

There is not a direct relationship between the experience of psychiatric symptoms and the use of psychiatric services. This weak linkage between bizarre emotions and behaviors and use of services is consistent with the basic idea behind sociologic theories of deviance discussed in the first chapter, that is, that unrecognized deviance is widespread. The important part of the process of deviance is the recognition and reaction to it by the individual and by others, which has led sociologists to study the processes by which individuals are selected into psychiatric treatment facilities (Horwitz 1982).

Perception of Symptoms by Self and Others

When something goes wrong, the individual is likely to be the first to notice the problem. *Illness behavior* is "the manner in which persons monitor their bodies, define and interpret their symptoms, take remedial actions, and utilize the health-care system" (Mechanic 1983). The study of illness behavior concerns the range of bizarre emotions and behaviors, not just those that have come to be associated with mental illness. Symptoms of ill health are recognized in varying degrees, depending on the recognizability of the symptom itself, the pain associated with the symptom, the degree to which it disrupts the normal activities of the individual, and various characteristics of the individual and the situation. The study of illness behavior is important because it influences the use of treatment services and because it can affect the individual's health. Here the term *recognition* refers to the attribution of illness as the cause of feelings of demoralization. For most disorders the experience of bizarre behavior is distressing to the individual or, if not to him or her, then to those in the immediate social field. For example, the individuals in the first-person accounts of bizarre behaviors presented in Boxes 1.1, 1.2, 3.1, 3.2, and 4.4 and the medical case history in Box 1.6 all displayed considerable distress or pain during their experiences, mostly in the form either of anxiety over loss of control or of inexplicable sadness. Even the milder disorders entail a good deal of distress or demoralization. There are occasions when the symptoms of mental disorder do not involve demoralization, but in these cases there is often a failure to function, especially in the area of social relationships, that is noticed by the individual or those around him or her. Vonnegut (Box 1.2) gives a poignant example of this failure in discussing the cutting of wood, and Kay Jamison's behavior (Box 3.2) was noticed by her classmates. The experience of either distress or a failure to function leads the individual at some point to search for a cause of the distress or disability so that it might be controlled, eliminated, or at least predicted.

Symptoms of mental disorder may not be as noticeable as those of many physical illnesses. For one thing, these experiences are less recognizable because they involve a type of deviance that is inherently difficult to categorize—residual deviance. Second, the symptoms themselves—for example, the lack of insight associated with schizophrenia—may interfere with the process of recognition. For these reasons we might expect that symptoms of mental disorder may not be quickly recognizable by individuals experiencing them or by their friends and acquaintances.

Research in the general population shows that many symptoms go unrecognized. For example, Star (1952) presented 3,500 respondents with brief vignettes describing individuals with symptoms of several mental disorders, including a paranoid schizophrenic, a simple schizophrenic, a depressed neurotic, and a phobic individual. About one-sixth of the sample denied that mental illness was involved in *any* of the behaviors, and nearly half saw mental illness either not at all or only in the description of paranoid schizophrenia. Other studies have supported this general finding, but some replication studies—that is, surveys of the general population in different areas using the same vignettes—have shown much greater attribution of mental illness as the cause of the symptoms and behaviors presented. The degree to which lay individuals recognize symptoms of mental disorder has not been agreed upon among researchers, in part, because there may have been strong temporal effects that hinder the comparison of results, and, in part, because the degree of recognition seems to be affected by the exact way in which the question is asked. But clearly, a large segment of the population tends to resist attributing the cause of bizarre behaviors to the concept of mental illness.

Stigmatization is the resistance to associating with those thought to be mentally ill. Stigmatization is a form of extreme social distance, and standard instrumentation for measuring desired social distance has been used to study the stigma associated with mental illness. The Bogardus Social Distance Scales ask respondents a series of questions involving hypothetical interactions with an

Table 7.1
Desired Social Distance from the Mentally Ill in Four Studies

Percentage willing to have	Location of Study and Date			
former mental patient as:	Saskatchewan		Baltimore	North Carolina
	1954	1976	1962	1969
Spouse for child	27	45	46	52
Lover	32	40	51	44
Roommate	44	52	50	57
Rentee for apartment	60	69	–	67
Workmate	71	72	81	88
Neighbor	71	72	–	70
Member of club	78	77	–	85

Source: Brockman et al. (1979).

individual with a given personal characteristic such as race or, in this case, the fact that the individual has been mentally ill. Results from four such studies are presented in Table 7.1. Respondents are much more willing to have a mentally ill individual as a workmate or as a member in their club (roughly 80 percent responding positively) than as a lover or as a spouse for their child (roughly 40 to 50 percent responding positively).

The degree of stigmatization that occurs in actual social situations is difficult to estimate from these survey results, but it seems clear that there is considerable rejection of people who are thought of as mentally ill. Nunnally's (1961) view was that the perceived unpredictability of mentally ill individuals was the principal cause of their rejection by others. A single, severe episode of bizarre behaviors may trigger a stereotype about unpredictability that is very difficult to erase. Another possibility is the dangerousness associated with the mentally ill in the mind of the public. Both these aspects of the public perception of the mentally ill are constantly reaffirmed in the public media (Wahl 1995); the idea of unpredictability is frequently used as a vehicle for humor, for example, and mental illness appears often as an imputed cause of almost any violent behavior performed by anyone who has even the faintest history of a personal problem, let alone psychiatric outpatient or inpatient treatment. Another reason for the social rejection of the mentally ill may be that they have violated a cultural norm involving independence and the ability to manage one's own affairs.

Attitudes toward those with mental illness may reflect the public's view of its cause. Twenty-two separate studies of recognition and rejection of the mentally ill, all of which used very similar instruments to measure attitudes, were divisible into two distinct groups of researchers and research teams (Brockman et al. 1979). One group of medically oriented researchers tended to draw conclusions showing a decline in the stigma of mental illness and increased recognition of symptoms of mental illness by the public; a second group of researchers from social science disciplines were more likely to conclude that stigma was still present and recognition of symptoms low. It was concluded by the authors of the review teams (Brockman et al. 1979) that the totality of evidence was not conclusive but that the evidence from the social science orientation had fewer methodologic weaknesses and was slightly more credible. The point here is to note that the medical model of mental disorder brings with it the implication that medical treatment is beneficial and that early detection of disease is good. These implications of the medical model have led public health practitioners in psychiatry to advocate educating the public to wipe out the stigma of mental illness and to encourage early recognition of symptoms. Other models of mental illness do not entail these ideas, and some models contradict them. For example, a moral model of mental illness, in which the central cause of personal problems is thought to be a failure in individual will, implies distinctly different actions. In the moral model, stigma amounts to a type of deterrence or negative reinforcement for behaviors and problems that can be eliminated through positive thinking and willpower. It may be that a good portion of the public subscribes to this moral model, and distinguishing between the public health benefits of the two models is not an easy task.

Denial and *normalization* are interactional processes that result from the failure to recognize symptoms of mental disorder. Several studies have revealed a surprisingly strong tendency for family members and friends to deny the existence or occurrence of bizarre behaviors. If it is admitted that the behaviors actually occur, they are generally normalized by attributing them to temporary situations or normal irritations. The tendencies to deny and normalize were so strong in the early studies—mostly of individuals eventually diagnosed as psychotic—that the results were nothing less than dramatic. Recent studies of other types of disorder such as depression reveal the same tendencies. The denial occurs both in the individual exhibiting the behavior and in his or her family. Clausen et al. (1982) observe that less than one-sixth of their subjects (eventually hospitalized and diagnosed psychotic) reported on the events preceding hospitalization in a realistic or insightful way. For example, a professional in their study who had been totally out of contact and incoherent reported, "I wasn't communicating well." The depressive subjects in the study by Ginsberg and Brown (1982), on the other hand, were aware of their own symptoms and distressed by them. Both for schizophrenics and for depressives, in studies from the early 1950s to the present, however, there is pervasive denial of the symptoms by the spouse. In the study by Clausen and colleagues, more than one-fourth of the subjects were reported as having serious hallucinations or delusions, but these were frequently dismissed as "merely a reflection of being upset." In the Ginsberg-Brown study, "the majority of husbands responded to their wives' complaints of symptoms such as suicidal ideas, feelings of helplessness, and lethargy, with such comments as 'You're imagining it all', 'Stop being silly,' or 'You mustn't talk like that, there's the baby.' "

Both the family and the individual try to adapt to the bizarre behaviors in various ways to avoid recognition of the behaviors as being mentally disordered. About half of the subjects in the studies by Clausen and coworkers (1982) reported some form of adaptation such as taking a vacation, working harder, becoming more involved with religion, or, especially for employed wives, giving up work. The depressive women in the Ginsberg-Brown study most often tried to talk with their husbands about the problem, with little success in many cases: "I tried to tell him, I felt I had to let someone know, but he didn't really understand how destructive I was being to the children. I suppose he couldn't really believe I could do that (i.e., bruise the children)." This woman had already left bruises on her three-year-old child and thirteen-month old baby, but her husband dismissed her requests to talk about it. In some cases the family situation gradually becomes very distorted in order to maintain the denial and normalization. The dominant tendency is apparently to evolve into a situation of mutual noninvolvement. In the families studied by Sampson et al. (1962), the husbands almost invariably became more and more intensively involved in their work or in other interests outside the marriage, while the wife occupied herself with the children and her own affairs; eventually, the couple became so distant that there was little interaction. This pattern of accommodation would develop over many years without divorce or psychiatric treatment, even though the wife might be actively hallucinating or having acute anxiety attacks.

There are individual differences in perception of symptoms of mental disorder, in attitudes toward mental illness, and in willingness to use professional help for mental health problems. Table 7.2 presents results from a national survey (Veroff et al. 1981), showing the degree to which individuals are willing to consider referring themselves for psychiatric treatment. This table reflects recognition of symptoms, attitudes toward mental illness, and use of services as a bridge to the next section. Respondents were asked whether they had ever used any source of help for personal problems; if the answer was no, they were then asked whether they ever had gone through a situation in which they could have used help; if again the answer was no, they were asked whether they could imagine a situation in which they might need help. In response to these questions, some respondents mentioned that individuals ought to be responsible for themselves or something similar, in which case the answer was categorized as "self-help."

Women are slightly more likely to have used some sort of treatment services during their lives, and they are slightly less likely than men to mention the norm of self-help (Table 7.2). There are strong age differences, however. Young people are much more likely to have used professional help—there is a two-to-one difference in percentage (28 percent versus 13 percent) between the oldest and the youngest group. Also, older people are much more likely to espouse the norm of self-help. Finally, there are also strong effects of educational level on these variables: college graduates are twice as likely to report using services as those with only grade school education and half as likely to mention the norm

258 The Sociology of Mental Disorders

Table 7.2
Sex, Age, and Education Related to Readiness for Self-Referral

	Readiness for Self-Referral Percentages				Total Number
	Has used help	Could have used help	Self-help	Un-known	
Gender					
Male	22	32	41	5	960
Female	29	33	33	6	1,304
Age					
21-29 years	28	35	32	5	553
30-39 years	32	38	27	3	463
40-49 years	32	38	27	3	341
50-59 years	26	28	39	7	342
60-64 years	19	31	46	4	166
65 + years	13	29	50	10	397
Education					
Grade School	16	25	50	9	380
Some High School	27	32	34	7	347
High School Graduate	26	32	37	5	766
Some College	29	36	31	4	411
College Graduate	32	38	25	5	360

The second column includes their column entitled "Could have used help" and the column entitled "Might have used help"; in the third column, their "Self-Help" and "Strong Self-Help" columns are collapsed into one.

Source: Veroff et al. (1981).

of self-help. This pattern of strong relationships to age and educational level was reported in the 1957 study, which used the same measures, and also for other measures of attitudes concerning mental illness. The findings for age are not a result of a gradually increasing conservatism with increasing age. This might be a tenable explanation except for the pattern of figures in the first column, which ought by all logic to show the opposite trend with age, since older persons are reporting for the entire period of their lives, including their youth. The best explanation for both the age and education effects is that there has been a generational change in attitudes toward the mentally ill, so that younger people are actually sharing a different culture about this topic than the older generation. This generational change has accompanied the so-called psychologizing of culture in the United States since the 1950s, the publicity surrounding the community mental health care movement, and health education efforts. It is also true that a much greater percentage of the population obtains higher education than 25 years ago, so that the difference in attitudes between the age cohorts may be, in part, a simple reflection of the increasing educational level of the general population. The notion of a trend in attitudes is also supported by the data in Table 7.1 for two surveys in Blackfoot, Saskatchewan, in 1954 and 1976, conducted with very similar methods—for example, nearly twice as many were willing to consider having a mentally ill person as a spouse for their child in 1976 as in 1957 (45 percent versus 27 percent).

Seeking Help from Professionals

Most people with mental disorders do not seek or receive treatment from professional health agencies. A review identified 14 community epidemiologic studies that identified cases of disorder independently from treatment status and *also* determined whether the individual had ever used psychiatric treatment during his or her lifetime (Link and Dohrenwend 1980). These studies ranged from Jarvis' study in the nineteenth century (Commission on Lunacy 1971), to a study in New Haven, Connecticut, in 1978 (Weissman and Myers 1978). In two studies in this group, less than 10 percent of those meeting criteria for caseness had ever been in psychiatric treatment: on the high end were two studies in which just over 50 percent of those meeting criteria for caseness had ever used psychiatric treatment services. The median figure was 27 percent. The relationship depends on the type of disorder considered. For example, seven studies made the diagnosis of psychosis, independently of treatment status, and also recorded lifetime usage of psychiatric services: the range in the percentage using services in this group ran from a low of 50 percent to a high of 85 percent, with a median figure of 60 percent. For the six studies making the diagnosis of schizophrenia, the range was between 50 and 100 percent, with a median figure of 83 percent. It appears that the more severe disorders are more likely to end up in treatment. For the less severe disorders, the tendency is for many fewer than half meeting criteria for disorder to receive treatment.

In the past few decades it has become more acceptable to seek treatment from mental health professionals. Table 7.3 presents results from national surveys conducted in 1957 and 1976. The two columns on the left present findings on the hypothetical use of professional help by specific source of help in 1957 and in 1976. (The 1976 data are drawn from the same survey as in Table 7.2.) These columns allow one to examine the overall trend among the general population over the 20-year period, which shows an increased willingness, from about 33 percent to 46 percent to consider professional help from any source, and this trend exists for every professional source except for the clergy. The two right columns concern actual use of the same sources of professional help by those who had ever felt an impending nervous breakdown—about 20 percent of the sample both in 1957 and in 1976—and about half of these actually used services.

Table 7.3
Use of Professional Sources of Help in Two National Surveys (Percentage Ever Seeking Help by Source of Help)

Source of Help	All Respondents--Hypothetical use for emotional problems		Actual use by those who have ever felt an impending nervous breakdown	
	1957	1976	1957	1976
None	67	54	0	0
Clergy	18	13	3	3
Doctor	11	13	77	52
Psychiatrist or Psychologist	6	10	4	18
Other Mental Health Professional	2	8	3	10
Other Human Service Professional	6	14	13	17
Total Percentage	110*	112*	100	100
Numbers of Respondents	2,460	2,264	231	227

Percentages add to more than 100 because multiple sources could be mentioned.

Source: Veroff et al. (1981). The left two columns are taken from their Table 4.1; the right two from their Table 5.15.

Far and away the first choice of professional help in this situation is the family doctor—77 percent in 1957 and 52 percent in 1976. The decline in use of the family doctor over this period is balanced by the increased use of specialty mental health resources such as the psychiatrist/psychologist or other mental health resource (such as a community mental health center): four times as many people consider going straight to the psychiatrist or psychologist (18 percent in 1976 versus only 4 percent in 1957), and three times as many to another mental health resource (10 percent in 1976 versus 3 percent in 1957).

Many individuals meeting criteria for specific psychiatric diagnoses, even within the past six months or year, do not receive any sort of treatment. This is shown graphically for the ECA Program in Figure 2.2: nearly half of those meeting criteria for panic disorder or schizophrenia have seen a doctor in the past six months, with a much lower figure for the other disorders: for example, only about one-tenth of those meeting criteria for phobic disorder and less than a third of those meeting criteria for depressive disorder have seen a doctor for the disorder in the past six months. More recent figures from the National Comorbidity Survey are shown in Table 7.4. These figures focus on the outpatient sector but would not be greatly changed if inpatient treatment were included. Only about a fifth (21.2 percent) of those with major depressive disorder see a mental health specialist, and a total of about one-quarter (27.7 percent) see any health professional. Only about a third (36.4 percent) seek any sort of treatment at all. There are understandable differences between the specific disorders: for

Table 7.4

Percent Using Outpatient Services by Type of Psychiatric Disorder: U.S. National Comorbidity Survey, 1990–1992 (Disorders and Services Use in the 12 Months Prior to Interview)

Type of Disorder	Prevalence of Disorder	Health Care Sector			Other Sectors		Any Services
		Medical	Psychiatric	Either	Human Services	Self Help	
Major Depression	10.3	12.1	21.2	27.7	13.3	8.2	36.4
Panic Disorder	2.3	21.5	24.3	35.2	37.9	14.0	46.4
Agoraphobia	3.8	13.6	15.7	24.9	12.5	9.2	33.2
Social Phobia	7.9	5.9	11.3	15.3	8.0	7.0	23.0
Alcohol Abuse	2.5	3.3	6.5	9.4	3.6	2.4	11.6
Alcohol Dependence	7.2	4.0	11.8	13.5	10.3	13.3	24.4
Psychosis*	0.3	21.5	47.5	53.1	16.3	22.0	57.9
Any Disorder	30.8	7.9	12.4	17.3	8.9	7.4	24.7
Total Sample		3.9	5.8	8.5	5.1	3.2	13.3

*Psychosis includes schizophrenia and other non-affective psychoses.

Source: Kessler et al. (1999: Table 1).

example, nearly twice as many with panic disorder—sometimes confused with heart trouble due to the cardiovascular symptoms—seek help from the general medical sector, as is the case for depression (21.5 percent versus 12.1 percent). Those with alcohol dependence are much more likely to receive psychiatric treatment or attend a self-help group than those with alcohol abuse (e.g., 13.3 percent with dependence in self-help versus 2.4 percent with abuse in self-help). The striking figures on psychosis corroborate the earlier ECA data, showing that only about half obtain treatment in the psychiatric sector (53.1 percent), and less than three-fifths (57.9 percent) obtain any treatment whatsoever during the year. For the total sample, regardless of disorder, about 6 percent are using the psychiatric sector over the course of a year, 4 percent the medical sector, 5 percent other human services, and less than 15 percent of the population seeking help for a psychiatric problem over the course of one year.

Despite a relative decline in use over the past 20 years, Table 7.3 shows that the major source of care for those with personal problems is the family physician, a point that has not escaped the notice of public health practitioners. Primary care physicians—that is, the four major front-line groups of general and family practitioners, internists, pediatricians, and obstetrician/gynecologists—have been called the de facto mental health system. An estimated 10 percent to 20 percent of all primary care visits concern emotional problems, and often no referral is made so that the primary care physician is prescribing and administering treatment (Regier et al. 1993; Shepherd et al. 1966). The public health questions raised concern, on one hand, about the ability of the primary care practitioner to recognize and treat mental disorders; and, on the other hand, about the strategic placement of this practitioner in the system of care, where problems can be identified early and continuity of treatment is likely to be better than is generally true for the diverse psychiatric sector. Primary care practitioners are less likely to diagnose depression than psychiatrists, possibly because of the stigmatization involved or possibly because they feel less able to treat it well (Coyne et al. 1995). Unless attitudes change markedly, a good portion of the public will probably continue to prefer using family practitioners for a variety of reasons, including the increased stigmatization associated with use of psychiatrists.

Different sources of professional help have different implications for the individual in terms of the reaction of others. Phillips (1963) presented the Star symptom vignettes, discussed earlier, to respondents, along with the information that the individual in the vignette had sought one of the following types of professional help: no help sought; a member of the clergy; a physician; a psychiatrist; or admitted to a mental hospital. Then he asked respondents questions on social distance similar to those presented in Table 7.1. The average social distance score, across all vignette types, for the individuals seeking no professional help was 1.35; for those seeking aid from the clergy, the average score was 1.57; for those seeking help from a physician, the average score was 1.87; for those seeking the help of a psychiatrist, the average score was 2.56; and for those admitted to a mental hospital, the average score was 3.04. The increase in scores is interpreted as greater desired social distance or, conversely, increased unwillingness to associate with the individual.

Attitudes and subcultural differences are important influences on the specific locus of treatment chosen for help with personal problems. Several studies (Bart 1968; Greenley and Mechanic 1976; Kadushin 1969) have demonstrated that persons seeking help from psychiatrists are more likely to have developed vocabularies of distress in a culture that encourages and supports the identification of personal problems in psychiatric terms. Such cultures are more likely to exist in urban than in rural areas, to involve Jewish persons or persons not highly religious, to have high educational levels, and to have a generally cosmopolitan outlook on the world, in short, as Kadushin (1969) expressed it, to be "friends and supporters of psychotherapy." Thus, cultural and attitudinal factors are important as explanations of both the general tendency to seek help and the specific source of help sought.

THE ORGANIZATION OF TREATMENT

The Sociology of Complex Organizations

The organization of psychiatric treatment fits into the field of complex organizations in sociology. The field, a major one in sociology, crosses into the disciplines of administration and management. The organizations studied are usually corporations and factories, but human service organizations, such as welfare agencies and mental hospitals, also come under scrutiny. A *complex organization* may be defined as a patterned set of role relationships in a physical setting that produce a product. Thus, a complex organization is one type of institution (as defined in Chapter 1). In the case of human service organizations such as in psychiatry, the product is a changed, "cured," or rehabilitated individual human being.

Any complex organization can be described sociologically by its ideology, technology, and structure (Schurmann 1970). The term *ideology* has been used in many ways in sociology, but the best-known use of the term, as noted in Chapter 1, is from Mannheim's *Ideology and Utopia* (1936). Ideology serves organizational functions because it can be defined, somewhat more precisely than Mannheim did, as a systematic set of ideas with action consequences. Another way of thinking of ideology is as a goal hierarchy. The hierarchy includes abstract goals such as professionalism, or a belief in producing high-quality merchandise, and more concrete goals involving a precise conception of what a "good" product is. For a shoe company, for example, the abstract goals might be "to make a profit," "to produce quality shoes," or "to provide agreeable employment for a given number of individuals." The more precise goals involve ideas about exactly what a "good quality" shoe is—the leather used, the standards of workmanship, the durability, and so forth. Other abstract goals might entail different specific goals, and the goals are always linked in a hierarchy so that specific goals are justified by relationship to more abstract ones. Thus, the "profit" goals may entail a belief in mass production of relatively poor-quality shoes.

The *technology* of an organization includes all the methods for achieving the product-oriented goals. The ideology describes the ends desired, while the technology is the means. The technology includes the tools used in the achievement of the ends as well as certain systems of thought. The tools used are often physically visible: for a shoe factory, the workbench, the tanning fluid, the metal forms, sewing machines, and the hammer and nail. The technology also involves two basic and complementary systems of thought: a diagnostic system and an evaluation system. Both of these sets of ideas serve the ideology directly. The diagnostic systems categorize the input for the organization to indicate reliably its proper place in the process of construction. Certain types of leather are appropriate for certain types of shoes; this thread belongs on that machine; this tanning chemical is used in this line of shoes; this machine needs this type of maintenance; and so forth. The evaluation systems categorize the output of the organization to see whether the goals are being met. For the profit goal, the evaluation system involves the profession of accounting; for the "quality shoes" goal, the evaluation system involves the process of quality control, which may involve sampling the shoes produced in a systematic way to see whether the standards are being met. Although these examples are brief, it should be clear that the diagnostic and evaluation systems are not simplistic and casual; in most cases they involve fairly complex and formal systems of thought that might be taught in a course in a trade school or technical college.

When ideology and technology are brought together in a physical setting, a complex organization is created; an organized set of roles, each role having obligations and rewards attached to it. Thus, the president of the shoe company is responsible for managing the company and receives a high salary for doing so. The sewer is responsible for attaching leather together to form shoes and receives a somewhat lower salary. There are many specific roles in almost any complex organization in modern societies. The roles come directly out of the ideology and technology. They originate in ideology because they involve values, except that for roles the values are attached to the performance of a specific task by the occupant of a specific social position. They are related to technology because the performance of the task requires the exercise of the technology. The roles are the combination of ideology and technology in a given social setting.

Treatment in Traditional Nigeria

Ideology, technology, and structure combine to form an institutional structure for treatment of bizarre emotions and behaviors. In the following and in the next section, brief descriptions of this structure are given for a region in Nigeria and for the United States. The Yoruba tribe constitutes about 6 million persons concentrated in one region in Nigeria (Prince 1964). The region and tribe have their own distinctive language and culture, which includes a well-developed system of psychiatric treatment. This system is presently undergoing a good deal of change due to Western influence and modernization, but the attempt here is to describe the original indigenous treatment system. The native treatment system has a secular and religious component. The secular side centers on the *onishegun*, who is a professional healer specializing in mental disorders. These healers run small treatment centers on a profit basis (Prince 1964). A typical treatment center in Abeokuta, Nigeria, had about 20 patients. There was a main house of about 10 rooms for the healer and his family and patients who were not violent. In back of the main house was another hut for about 10 patients who were less recovered. The second hut was divided into male and female rooms, and there were separate rooms for secluding violent patients, with shackles to prevent escape. Each patient was received into the facility only if he or she paid a fee and only if a relative accompanied them to feed and clothe them. Another hut at the back of the main house was for preparing medicines, and there was a garden of herbs and medicinal plants nearby.

Psychotic patients constitute the majority of the clientele of the *onishegun*. The rate of point prevalence of psychosis has been estimated by an epidemiologic field study to be about 10 per 1,000 population (Leighton et al. 1963)— not too different from the prevalence elsewhere (Table 2.7). Often, the patient is shackled in the beginning and given rauwolfia root, a powerful antipsychotic (reserpine) "discovered" by Western medicine in the 1950s but apparently in use before that in Nigeria. Medicine is given daily until the psychotic behavior has subsided, at which time the shackles are removed, and the patient may work in the healer's garden or house. Most patients are released after several months.

Each healer has a standard approach to treatment. Healers try to decide the cause of the illness, whether natural, preternatural, or supernatural. Natural causes include heredity, nutrition, bad blood, and so forth. Preternatural causes are brought about by other human beings through witchcraft or sorcery. Supernatural causes include failure to please one's ancestors or offending deities of one form or another. Rituals and ceremonies are designed appropriate to the suspected cause. For example, in a ceremony used for sorcery, a plaster is applied to the patient's shaved scalp, then washed off with shampoo; small cuts then are made in the scalp, into which certain medicines are placed (filings of human tooth and fluid collected from a decayed human corpse). Many of the ceremonies involve animal sacrifices. If the ritual is not effective, the therapist decides that the diagnosis was incorrect and tries another approach.

Some of the ceremonies are designed only to control the patient. *Akaraba* is used to calm excited patients. This ritual uses a human skull partially covered by a cloth. A long cord is wound around the skull as the therapist chants the name of the person to whom the skull belonged and shouts, "Catch him! Catch him!" so that the spirit that once resided in the skull will bind up the patient. Discharge of the patient is usually accompanied by an elaborate ceremony to prevent possible relapse. Shaving of the head, blood sacrifices, and a sort of baptism ceremony also were involved in rituals observed by Prince (1964).

The other major professional involved in the Yoruba treatment system is the diviner-priest called *babalawo*. These men are highly trained and have great prestige. The Yoruba myth and literature are not written but rather are remembered by the *babalawos* and used by them to divine the source of a given problem, give advice on a wide range of subjects, prescribe sacrifices, recommend secular healers, and direct initiation into fraternal societies called *Orisa cults*. The Yoruba mythology is immense, and the techniques of divination require long training to acquire. Mental disorders are only one of many problems brought to the *babalawo* for solution.

Initiation into an Orisa cult may be recommended by the diviner if a secular treatment center is unsuccessful in preventing relapses or if the *babalawo* feels it would be helpful. These cults are religious groups centered around certain minor deities that may be linked to the lineage of an individual. They are centers of religious power in the community and also serve broad social functions. There is an intense and secret initiation period of several weeks during which the new member lives in the cult compound. There are annual festivals in which the members of the cult dress differently and engage in dances, masquerades, and other group behaviors that distinguish them from the community and are outside their normal activities. All of these ceremonies, rituals, and social practices fit into the broad rubric of psychotherapy. The healing process—especially that involving divination—is integrated into the entire mythology of the Yoruba people and may have considerable persuasive power. The healing process also directly involves major parts of the Yoruba social structure such as the Orisa cults. According to Prince, a Western psychiatrist, the efficacy of this healing system is at least equivalent to that of the Western system (Prince 1964).

Treatment in the United States

The system of psychiatric treatment in the United States has been subject to more complex study and analysis than the Yoruba system. Table 7.5 presents an overview of psychiatric treatment in 1992, which takes advantage of the statistical reporting system of the National Institute of Mental Health. This table covers all major types of treatment with the exception of the psychiatrists in private practice. Private practice probably represents about one-fifth of the total patient load (Bahn et al. 1996).

The system is complex, involving more than 5,000 separate organizations, including more than 500 psychiatric and 1,600 general hospitals. There are about 200,000 residents of mental hospitals or psychiatric units of general hospitals on any given day and more than 2 million admissions for overnight stay in a given year. Nearly 1 in 1,000 individuals in the United States (85.2/100,000) is residing in a psychiatric treatment facility. In 1992 about 40 percent of the additions to the rolls of these facilities involved hospitalization. There are nearly

Table 7.5
Psychiatric Treatment System in the United States in 1992

	Number of Units	Inpatient			Outpatient		Day only
		Number of Additions	Number of Residents	Residents per 100,000	Number of Additions	Additions per 100,000	Number of Additions
State and County Mental Hospitals	273	275,382	83,180	33.0	45,527	18.6	4,082
Private Psychiatric Hospitals	475	469,827	24,053	9.5	140,824	57.7	65,345
General Hospitals Psychiatric Units	1616	951,121	35,611	14.1	429,160	175.8	50,436
Veterans Hospitals	162	180,529	18,531	7.4	144,591	59.2	14,391
Residential Centers for Children	497	36,388	27,751	11.0	112,667	46.2	8,464
Freestanding Outpatient Clinics	862	--	--	--	464,499	190.3	--
Other Mental Health Centers	1613	178,815	25,588	10.2	1,544,776	632.8	139,675
All Organizations	5498	2,092,062	214,714	85.2	2,882,044	1,180.6	282,393

Source: Redick et al. (1996: Tables 7.1, 7.3, 7.4, 7.5, 7.6).

Figure 7.1
Episodes of Mental Hospitalization in the United States, 1955 and 1992

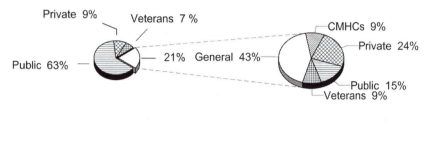

---1955---   ---1992---
1.3 million episodes   2.3 million episodes

Public mental hospitals in the 1950s have been largely replaced with psychiatric units in general hospitals, and private mental hospitals.

Source: Redick et al. (1996: Figure 7.7).

3 million additions to outpatient facilities, which may involve several visits, mostly taken up by independent outpatient clinics and multiservice mental health centers. Day hospitals represent a small percentage of the total volume in the system.

There were large changes in this treatment system during the preceding four decades. The public ("state and county") mental hospitals had the bulk of the residents in 1955, but other hospitals, especially general hospitals, absorb the majority of admissions today (Figure 7.1). In 1955, 77 percent of patient care episodes (additions to treatment roles plus persons under treatment during the year) involve hospitalization as compared with 33 percent in 1992 (Figure 7.2). There were actually no day care centers or community mental health centers as late as the 1960s, and there were only a few hundred psychiatric units in general hospitals. As these treatment centers proliferated, the mental hospital population declined—between 1955 and 1992 the resident population of public ("state and country" in Table 7.5) mental hospitals decreased from over 500,000 to just over 80,000. Episodes of mental health care are increasingly dominated by out-patient visits—from 24 percent of all episodes in 1955 to 67 percent in 1992 (Figure 7.2).

The diagnostic composition of the major treatment facilities is not very distinct. All major types of disorders are seen at all types of facilities. There is a slight tendency for schizophrenics, organic disorders (organic brain syndromes and mental retardation), and addictions (drug and alcohol) to end up at the public and veterans hospitals. Private, general, and especially outpatient clinics tend to treat the milder disorders, including depressive disorders, neuroses, and personality disorders.

Figure 7.2
Episodes of Mental Health Treatment in the United States, 1955 and 1992

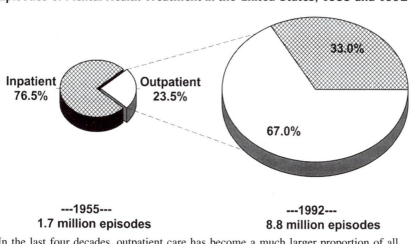

| ---1955--- | ---1992--- |
| 1.7 million episodes | 8.8 million episodes |

In the last four decades, outpatient care has become a much larger proportion of all episodes of mental health services.

Source: Redick et al. (1996: Figure 7.6).

The staffing patterns of the various facilities differ considerably (Redick et al. 1996). The major treatment facilities have professionals of many types (Table 7.6), with the greatest range of therapist types probably at the community mental health center. In all the inpatient facilities the most numerous staff is the psychiatric aide, forming about a third of the total staff (not shown in Table 7.6: about half of these have college degrees). Psychiatrists and psychologists are generally less than 10 percent of the total staff in inpatient institutions. Social workers are more numerous at outpatient clinics and multiservice centers, forming as much as 20 percent of the total patient care staff.

Unlike in Nigeria, psychotherapy in the United States does not link up with a homogeneous mythology or culture. The concepts closest to a homogeneous culture connected to psychiatry are the ideals and goals of positivistic science and medicine. But the diversification of the psychiatric professions entails a segmentation of any ideology connected to psychiatry, and this segmentation probably reduces the suggestive power of the therapies.

In both traditional Nigeria and in the United States, custom permits the psychiatrist to incarcerate the patient. In the United States this involuntary confinement is regulated strictly by law. In the land of the Yoruba, the psychiatrist may respond to the appeal of a relative simply by capturing the patient and putting him forcibly in shackles and under medication. It occurs sometimes that the patient's family fails to pay for treatment, in which case the psychiatrist will refuse to release the patient. In the traditional system there are no systematic regulations to prevent abuses of this sort.

Table 7.6
Clinically Trained Mental Health Personnel in the United States, 1996

Profession	Males	Females	Total Personnel
Psychiatry	75%	25%	28,970
Psychology	56%	44%	69,817
Social Work	23%	77%	92,841
Psychiatric Nurse	5%	95%	6,000
Counselor	22%	78%	61,600
Marriage and Family Therapy	45%	55%	46,227
Psychosocial Rehabilitation	34%	66%	9437
School Psychology	28%	72%	21,693

Source: Peterson et al. (1996: Table 10.2).

DIFFUSION OF THERAPEUTIC INNOVATIONS IN PSYCHIATRY

How has the system of care in the United States become so complex? The same social processes underlying the spread of bizarre behavior in a group, as discussed in Chapter 6, also apply to the study of therapeutic fashion in psychiatry. The major differences are the transience of collective psychopathology and its failure to produce lasting effects, in contrast to the enduring institutions produced by therapeutic fashion in psychiatry. In effect, each wave of fashion leaves an institutional residue that adds to the complexity of the system. The nearly two-century history of these movements in the United States affords an opportunity to view the subtle, long-term interplay of social change and organization. To understand fully the organization of psychiatry, one has to have a feeling for the historical background.

Uncertainty as to the efficacy of psychiatric treatment has existed from the earliest beginnings of modern psychiatry. This uncertainty is what Smelser (1962) calls structural strain, which he says can occur when there is "ambiguity as to the adequacy of means for a given goal." Efforts to correct this technologic uncertainty take the form of therapeutic fashions. In the following pages seven therapeutic movements are reviewed: the moral treatment and institutional era, the biological era, the psychotherapeutic movement, the chemotherapies, the learning therapies, the community care movement, and the human potential movement.

Moral Treatment and Institutional Era

Psychiatry was just beginning in the United States when the moral treatment movement began (Bockoven 1956; Deutsch 1949). The first hospital was constructed in Williamsburg, Virginia, in 1773, and the moral treatment movement traditionally is thought of as beginning in 1792 with the dramatic liberation of patients in Paris by Philippe Pinel and the founding of the "Retreat" in York, England, by Daniel Tuke. The gist of moral treatment was that mentally disordered persons were no longer to be treated like animals. Pinel was operating under the liberalizing influence of the French Revolution, and Tuke, within the philosophy of his Quaker religion. Both recommended maximum freedom for the mentally ill, normal human dignity, and the stabilizing effects of work and religion. Both were optimistic about the possibility of cure. With the spread of this optimism went the notion that mental disorder was caused by rapid social change, urbanization, and dislocations in society. Thus, Tuke named his asylum the "Retreat" and secluded it from the city.

At the time of the moral treatment in Europe, there were very few asylums in the United States. In the decades that followed there was intense activity in their construction. This period from 1828 to about 1875 might be called the era of institutional care and was superimposed onto the moral treatment movement. It began in 1828, when Horace Mann enunciated the principle that the insane were wards of the states. Dorothea Dix began her crusade for the construction of mental hospitals during this time. She would first canvass an entire state, investigating the treatment of the insane in great detail. Then she would make a voluminous and emotional report appealing to the state legislature for funds to construct adequate facilities for the insane. She proceeded, state by state, so that many mental hospitals are due directly to her efforts.

In the United States the ideology of moral treatment blended together with the idea of state care for the insane and with the idea that institutions were beneficial. In a peculiar twist of zeitgeist and development of medical ideas, architecture became therapeutic. There was intense interest in the proper design and administration of the mental hospital. Thomas S. Kirkbride, a leading psychiatrist, published a book in 1854 on the proper construction of asylums, with an elegant winged design (Kirkbride 1880). Many articles in psychiatric journals at about this time described various aspects of hospitals in great detail, such as the layout of the shrubbery, the type of pipes used in the plumbing, the size of the beds, and the materials used for mattresses, to a degree that seems curious to a reader of today. Included in the famous Kirkbride plan was the stipulation that the maximum population for a mental hospital should be 250.

During this era of state care, the forerunner of the American Psychiatric Association was formed: the Association of Medical Superintendents of American Institutions for the Insane. The group held its first meeting in 1844 and began to publish the *American Journal of Insanity* (the parent publication of the *Amer-*

ican Journal of Psychiatry) at about the same time. The profound therapeutic optimism that formed the raison d'être both of the moral treatment movement and of the institutional era began to decline about halfway through the nineteenth century. The zenith of this era came in 1854 with the Kirkbride plan, but in that same year the problem of large numbers of poor immigrant patients was first mentioned in the annual report of the Worcester State Hospital. In 1866 the Association of Medical Superintendents amended the approved maximum number of patients per hospital from 250 to 600. The hospital populations grew explosively, and the published cure rates, which had reached 92 percent in the 1840s, declined. During the 1870s and 1880s Pliny Earle, a renowned psychiatrist, had been examining systematically extensive available data on the rate of cure, and in 1887 he published his evaluation in *The Curability of Insanity*. He concluded that high cure rates were artifactual and, for the most part, due to methodologic errors. Reaction against institutional treatment for the insane began to grow. W. A. Hammond wrote *The Non-Asylum Treatment of the Insane* in 1879, and there were several exposés of asylum abuses published by ex-patients.

The Early Biological Era

Reaction against asylums was the seed of the biological era, but several developments external to psychiatry contributed to the rise of medical influence. One was Darwin's theory of evolution, published in 1859. Some people inferred from this theory that the insane were not among the fittest who should survive and that biologically based degenerative sickness could be considered part of the overall plan of evolution. Another development was the dramatic increase in the power of microscopes, which contributed greatly to the expansion of medicine and pathology. The environmental causes of insanity, which had been espoused since the beginning of the moral treatment movement nearly a century before, were rejected. In a publication in 1872, Dr. J. B. Gray stated, "The causes of insanity, as far as we are able to determine, are physical; that is, no moral or intellectual operations of the mind induce insanity apart from a physical lesion."

The founding of the American Neurology Association in 1875 marks the beginning of the biological era. It soon began publishing the *Journal of Nervous and Mental Disease*. This movement culminated in 1913, when syphilis bacterium was discovered in the brains of deceased paretics, establishing general paresis as the archetypal disease form of mental disorder.

The Psychotherapeutic Approach

Early in the twentieth century there were several new approaches to treatment, grouped under the term *psychotherapies*. All of them involve a more humanistic approach to the mentally ill, a willingness to talk with them and to try to understand them. Foremost among these was psychoanalysis, a European import. The earliest U.S. psychoanalytic journal (*Psychoanalytic Review*) began publication in 1913. With motivations resembling that of the era of moral treatment, the nature of psychoanalysis was to bring the insane person back to reason by helping in self-understanding. There were no administrative manipulations as in the institutional era, nor were there physical manipulations of the patient as in the early biological era. This attitude was supported by the publication in 1908 of Clifford Beers' *A Mind That Found Itself*—a subjective case history of insanity, which the average person could understand (Beers 1953). As a result, mental illness became less fearsome in the public eye.

In the next few decades many new therapies were added. Social workers and occupational therapists formed national organizations and began aiding in the treatment of mental patients. *The Journal of Consulting and Clinical Psychology* commenced in 1932, marking the entry of clinical psychologists into the mental health field. During this era the treatment of mental patients in outpatient clinics and offices became increasingly prevalent, dating from the opening of the Phipps Clinic at Johns Hopkins University Hospital in 1913 by Adolph Meyer.

After World War II there was enormous growth in psychiatry and related fields. In part, the growth was a natural tendency, the result of a long prewar takeoff period, which was accentuated by the pause of the wartime years. But several events contributed to the growth just after the war. For one thing, the war had provided irrefutable proof that various kinds of social stress could cause severe mental disorder in most, if not all, human beings. Evidence came from concentration camp survivors, prisoners of war, and battle-fatigued soldiers. These demonstrations reinforced the collaboration between psychiatry and the social sciences that had been growing ever since Freud had begun studying society as a whole in the 1920s. This tendency was accelerated still further by Hans Selye's *The Stress of Life* in 1956, which provided a physiological basis for reactions to stress that eventually was generalized to all sorts of social stresses (as described in Chapter 3). All of these tendencies were to meld around 1960, when society as a whole was identified as a stressful agent, and the movement of community psychiatry began. The federal government entered the field in 1946 with the National Mental Health Act, which set up the National Institute of Mental Health and provided resources for study and treatment. In short, the scope of psychiatry was broadened considerably, its importance for the average citizen was magnified, and resources were made available.

Many new fashions in the treatment of mental disorder reflected this growth. Here only four are discussed: the advent of psychotropic drugs, the various learning therapies, the community care movement, and the human growth movement.

The Later Biological Era

The later biological era, which continues in the present, is marked by the systematic design of chemicals to have specific psychotropic effects, the research efforts necessary for the design, including the Human Genome Project (Watson 1990), the testing of the products for safety in humans, and the marketing efforts to sell them. The diffusion of psychotropic drugs is similar to that of other successful medical and technologic innovations. Chlorpromazine provides an early and illustrative example. The family of drugs from which chlorpromazine derives is called the phenothiazines, and they were first synthesized in Heidelberg in 1883 for use in the dye industry. It is ironic that the diagnosis of schizophrenia was first made in 1896 in the same country, yet phenothiazines were not applied to the treatment of schizophrenia until more than half a century later.

Chlorpromazine was first marketed in the United States in 1954, and its use diffused with incredible rapidity throughout the psychiatric community (Swazey 1974). Eight months after its introduction, over 2 million patients had been treated. Many psychiatrists accepted the medical-biological model of mental disorders, and use of this therapy did not require any fundamental change in attitude. However, the major explanation for the rapid spread was the intensive marketing of Smith, Kline, and French, the company introducing the drug. They were confident that the drug was a powerful treatment tool and that mental hospitals would profit by using it. They were also confident that it would be profitable for them. In the first year of production it boosted their sales by one-third. Between 1953 and 1970, when their patent expired, their overall sales had expanded from $53 million to $347 million, and in 1970 they sold $26 million worth of chlorpromazine for psychiatric use. They realized that the mental hospitals were the biggest potential market and that most mental hospitals did not have a large budget for drug therapy—just money for drugs used in general medicine, like aspirin. Special requests to the state legislatures, which controlled mental hospital budgets, were needed, and Smith, Kline, and French increased their regular sales force of 300 by setting up a special task force of 50 salesmen to help lobbying efforts in state legislatures, as well as to market the drug. They soon realized that many patients would be released from hospitals shortly after treatment began, and they designed aftercare programs to help promote sales. Their efforts were rewarded, and chlorpromazine was soon in general use.

Today, hundreds of new psychotherapeutic medications are evaluated each year. Many are proven effective in clinical trials and brought to market. Between 1988 and 1998, for example, an entirely new compound was marketed each year just for the treatment of depression. Research on the genome and molecular genetics is bound to stimulate further expansion of the number of medications available that have an effect on various forms of residual deviance.

The Learning Therapies

Another therapy that was spreading just before and after the war is behavior therapy. Behavior therapy has been applied most successfully to psychiatric conditions by Wolpe and his followers (Wolpe 1969). Wolpe began treating phobic patients with a particular, circumscribed method he called systematic desensitization. Later developments involved learning through role modeling and behavior shaping through operant conditioning. Token economies based on learning theories have been used in many mental hospitals (Paul 1969), and a technology has developed to bring out specific social skills such as assertiveness, general social competence, and coping with interpersonal stress. Treatments based on learning theory are considered the most successful in the treatment of anxiety disorders (Marks 1987).

Interest in therapies based on principles of learning, as well as in the introduction of psychotropic drugs and the community care movement discussed later, was stimulated by the controversy over the success or failure of psychotherapy. A detailed review of the efficacy of psychotherapy was published by Hans Eysenck in 1952. He compared the effects of psychotherapy to results when there was no treatment at all and all concluded that psychotherapy was not demonstrably superior: in both cases about two-thirds of the patients showed improvement. Later controlled trials were to show that behavior therapy had demonstrable effectiveness for phobia, and various cognitive, behavioral, and interpersonal therapies have been proven effective in recent years, as reviewed in Table 1.1. But effectiveness of psychotherapy in general has been debated heatedly at least since Eysenck's review. The focus for a sociologist is not so much whether psychotherapy works; rather, the point is that there are considerable doubt and controversy over the effects of psychotherapy, regardless of what the "truth" is. This doubt in the psychotherapeutic professions may or may not be realistic and could conceivably have more to do with the cultural evaluation of psychotherapy by the general public than with the actual effects of psychotherapy.

The learning therapies movement also was stimulated by the attack on the medical model of psychiatry, which began to occur in this period. Learning theory and therapies always had belonged to the field of psychology, and the number of psychologists in the mental health field was growing enormously anyway. Reformists who searched for an alternative model of care recommended an educational or learning approach instead of a medical model (Erickson 1957; Mechanic 1989). These recommendations fitted well with the growth in the profession of clinical psychology.

The Community Care Movement

The community care movement began in the early 1960s with several publications by Gerald Caplan (1961, 1964) and received impetus by the inspiring message of President John F. Kennedy to Congress in 1963 in which he espoused the community approach. An aspect of the community care movement that replicated the zeitgeist of 100 years earlier was its focus on the environment as cause and social change (such as eliminating poverty or racism) as treatment. A related ideologic stimulant to the community care movement was the growing literature on institutionalism in large mental hospitals. *The Mental Hospital* (Stanton and Schwartz 1954), *Institutional Neurosis* (Barton 1959), and *Asylums* (Goffman 1961) were all published in the late 1950s and early 1960s. These works and many others concluded that mental hospitals had severe secondary effects producing withdrawal, apathy, and chronicity in patients.

The goals of the community care movement were to reformulate psychiatry in a public health framework. Much of the language of public health was incorporated into the movement: prevention of mental disorders at primary, secondary, and tertiary levels was advocated, and the sectoral concept of responsibility was adopted.

Primary prevention was designed to keep mental disorders from ever developing (Commission on Chronic Illness 1957). Mass screening was prescribed to diagnose potentially disordered children as early as possible so corrective treatment could be started. Education for positive or good mental health was advocated. Societal ills like racism, sexism, alienation, and poverty were to be treated by psychiatrists working with others through social action, demonstrations, advocacy, and eventually legislation. *Secondary prevention* involved the traditional therapies as well as newer therapies, such as crisis therapy and family therapy. In addition, part of secondary prevention was systematic evaluation whereby good therapies were to be identified and improved on. *Tertiary prevention* sought to reduce the disabilities associated with mental disorder. Public education about mental illness was to be emphasized so that the stigma of insanity was reduced. Transitional institutions such as halfway houses, day treatment centers, and foster homes were to be used to reduce the harmful effects of institutionalism and the social breakdown syndrome. In all three types of prevention, consultation was recommended with the public, religious leaders, public administrators, politicians, and so forth.

The concept of sectoral responsibility was part of the community care movement. Integrated community mental health centers were to be responsible for geographically delineated areas having between 50,000 and 200,000 residents. These community mental health centers were to have a psychiatric team headed by a psychiatrist, with a psychologist, psychiatric social workers, and a professional mental health consultant. An inpatient unit, outpatient treatment, a day treatment center, a primary prevention program, and rehabilitation services (such as occupational therapy) were important parts of the centers.

This movement was successful in reorganizing the treatment system in U.S. psychiatry. Many of the over 1,600 mental health centers in 1992 (Table 7.5) were opened during this period with funding from the federal government. Many people entered the mental health field as professionals during this period, as positions opened up in several fields—although the most dramatic increase was in the field of clinical psychology. Several related journals appeared, including *Community Mental Health Journal* and *Hospital and Community Psychiatry* (now *Psychiatric Services*).

Segmentation and structural conflict in psychiatry contributed to the growth of the community care movement. Psychiatrists favoring psychotherapy as treatment were probably somewhat threatened by Eysenck's article in 1952. The introduction of chemotherapy in the late 1950s and its enthusiastic support by biologically oriented psychiatrists contributed to psychotherapists' doubts about their own technology. In *Action for Mental Health* (1961), the report of the National Mental Health Study Group, the need to focus more resources on severe disorders and hospitalized mental patients was emphasized. Thus, again, for psychiatrists employing psychotherapy there was an increase in "ambiguity as to the means for achieving an agreed-upon goal" and a "change in the balance of power between two groups," both factors that can precipitate social movements, according to Smelser (1962). Therefore, this group was most willing to accept a therapeutic innovation that retained the humanistic ideals implicit in psychotherapeutic treatment, as the community care movement did.

Changing the principal locus of care from the mental hospital to the community has resulted in a different set of problems for the mental patient. In the era of custodial care, the central problem was the *dependency* produced by the institution; now, the problem is *continuity of care*, which involves linkages between the diversity of community institutions serving the needs of the mental patient. Ensuring that a patient would actually attend a therapeutic session was not so much of a problem in the mental hospital; in the community, referral across different mental health settings is unsuccessful in many cases, because the patient does not show up. Similarly, records are more difficult to transfer in the era of community care, and the patient has to get used to meeting a variety of caregivers.

The Human Potential Movement

The *human potential movement* refers to various groups interested in increased awareness and sensitivity to one's self, to others, and to the universe in general. Briefly considered are transcendental meditation, dianetics, and Erhard Seminars Training (EST), but scores of groups are relevant, including the encounter group movement, Arica training, Rolfing, Silva mind control, Krishna chanters, followers of the Guru Maharaj ji, and many others.

Transcendental meditation (TM) is a systematic program of meditation founded by the Maharishi Mahesh Yogi in 1958 (Orme-Johnson et al. 1974). It can be taught easily and requires only a brief period of quiet each day, during which the meditator repeats a word given him or her by the TM instructor. Credible research has shown that TM and a variety of other programmed relaxation techniques produce physiological changes associated with relaxation, such as reduced heart rate and respiration, increased skin resistance, fewer spontaneous galvanic skin responses, and changes in the brain wave pattern (Benson 1975; Smith 1975). The meditator is supposed to be happier, more creative, more alert and efficient, and more socially competent than before meditation.

The followers of the Maharishi organized an international university and a "World Plan," which calls for the training of one TM instructor for every 1,000 human beings in all parts of the globe. By 1974 over 750,000 people had received training in TM, according to the World Plan Executive Council. According to a survey in San Francisco, 5.3 percent of the adult population had taken part in TM training (Wuthnow 1976).

Scientology is a "religious philosophy containing pastoral counseling procedures intended to assist an individual attain spiritual freedom. The Mission of the Church of Scientology is . . . to help the individual attain full awareness of himself as an Immortal Being, and of his relationship to the Supreme Being." The Church of Scientology was founded by L. Ron Hubbard in 1950 with the publication of his *Dianetics*. Before 1950 Hubbard had published several science fiction novels and had traveled widely.

Dianetics itself is based on the idea that emotional experiences leave residues (called engrams) in one's mind that block creativity, spontaneous enjoyment, and objective perception. A major purpose of dianetics is to clear these engrams from the mind to allow fuller freedom. In later work (Hubbard 1974) Hubbard espouses Buddhism and even leads the reader to believe that he, Hubbard, may be Metteya, a golden-haired person prophesied to follow Buddha after 2,500 years (i.e., about 1950; Hubbard has red hair). In the San Francisco survey 1.1 percent of the population stated that they had participated in scientology (Wuthnow 1976).

Erhard Seminars Training (EST) is a program of weekend group training sessions devised by Werner Erhard. The purpose of the training is "to transform your ability to experience, so that situations you have been trying to change, or have been putting up with, clear up just in the process of life itself. It produces results that traditionally have taken years in only days." The major goal of EST is to "get it"—that is, "to be aware that you are, to experience the present fully and to take responsibility for one's own situation." There are marathon sessions in straight-backed chairs in which the trainees are repeatedly referred to as "assholes" and in which there are sharing of trainees' experiences with the group, hypnotic sessions, poetry reading, and other group experiences in a carefully programmed format. The concept of the engram is implicit in some of the training, apparently borrowed from Erhard's experience with scientology. The concept of "getting it" seems to be similar to Zen enlightenment. All this comes in a well-packaged, two-weekend course, which, in 1975, cost $250 (Brewer 1975; Rinehart 1975). EST is a multimillion-dollar business. In 1976 there was a staff of 100, some 3,500 postgraduate volunteers, and about 100,000 total graduates.

In the San Francisco survey, 1.5 percent of the respondents had participated in EST training (Wuthnow 1976).

These groups serve many of the same purposes as psychotherapy. Research studies have shown that people entering them tend to be dissatisfied with their present lives and want a change, much as do individuals entering psychotherapy—that is, in both cases they are demoralized. In many cases the group experience appears to be helpful or at least pleasant. In some cases the experience itself is so dramatic and involves such a new view of the world that comparison with religious conversion experiences is not an exaggeration.

This brief discussion has barely touched the surface of the human potential movement. For instance, an estimated 6 million have participated in encounter groups, and 350,000 in Silva mind control. Overall, more than one-fifth of the adult population of San Francisco participated in one of these human potential groups, and about three-quarters knew something about one or more of the movement's groups (Wuthnow 1976).

Recapitulation of Therapeutic Reforms

There appears to be an unsolved need for a credible technology to treat mental disorders to which these movements attempt to respond. The evidence that the need is unsolved is the repetitive and cyclical nature of the movements. This point has been made most elegantly by Andrew Scull (1975), who compared Daniel Tukes' nineteenth-century *Description of the Retreat* with Bruno Bettelheim's twentieth-century *A Home for the Heart*. Both works are humanistically oriented descriptions of treatment institutions. Even detailed, line-by-line comparisons reveal consistent, widespread similarities in style, content, and therapeutic recommendations. The major difference Scull observed is that Tuke justified his therapeutic recommendations on the grounds of common sense, whereas Bettelheim used psychoanalytic theory; for example, both recommended warm baths for the patient, but Tuke did so because the patients seemed to enjoy it, while, according to Bettelheim, it produced oceanic feelings that satisfy oral needs. Scull also compared the movement to deinstitutionalize mental patients in the 1960s with the antiasylum movement of the 1870s and found them extremely similar.

The cyclical nature of the movements involves long swings back and forth from biological to humanistic psychiatry. Thus, the moral treatment movement, the psychotherapeutic movement, and the community care movement all involve humanistic approaches interrupted by movements such as the biological era in the late 1800s and the defusion of chemotherapies in the 1950s and 1960s. Each oscillation toward one polar extreme is attached to a loss of credibility and reaction to the opposite pole with unrealistic optimism about what appears to be a "new" therapeutic method. The credibility and optimism depend, to some extent, on the evaluation of the "new" method by the mass public, and, thus, the fortunes of sectors of psychiatry are tied to changes in the general culture.

IDEOLOGY, TECHNOLOGY, AND STRUCTURE IN THE TREATMENT OF MENTAL DISORDERS

Ideologic Dilemma: Cure and Control

At the most abstract level, the ideology of treatment systems for mental disorders is the fundamental change in the individual that physicians call *cure*. The cure goal involves a notion of what illness or deviance is as well as what cure is. The dedication of Western medical doctors to curing patients of their sickness is embodied in the Hippocratic oath. Implicit in this goal is the idea that the medical doctor is the one person most capable of doing the curing.

A second abstract goal of therapists in psychiatric treatment systems is to *control* the patient for the protection of society. This leads, sometimes, to segregation on a relatively permanent basis. Society supports the profession of psychiatry partly because psychiatrists are responsible for this function, and our legal structure provides for incarceration of individuals by psychiatrists acting with the courts. The segregation of mental patients is not tied directly to the belief that they are dangerous (even though in some countries involuntary commitment is permitted only when the individual is considered dangerous to himself or herself or others). Rather, the segregation of the mentally ill occurs because of the difficulties of living with an individual who is severely disordered, because of the stigma attached to mental illness, or because his or her behavior disturbs the orderliness of society. Prior to the era of deinstitutionalization, research showed that the average released mental patient was no more dangerous to society than the so-called normal individual. Research conducted after the era of deinstitutionalization shows that some types of released patients—those with certain types of hallucinations and delusions and those with a history of drug abuse—are more likely to commit crimes than those in the general population. Other studies have shown that most families do not wish to live with severely disordered relatives, even in cultures where family links are extremely strong (Alivisatos and Lyketsos 1968).

The control function of psychiatrists is shifting away from segregation toward other forms. As the overall costs of health care are shared by the entire society, psychiatrists are likely to function as agents of the health care system, in efforts to limit treatment by malingerers but also, possibly, by persons requesting treatment who do not meet some predetermined threshold of need. In the evolving context of managed care, the task of benevolent patient care will clash with the task of making a profit or minimizing costs, and the motives of all doctors are likely to be at least somewhat tainted in the process. Psychiatrists and mental health workers may suffer more of the taint because their clientele is presumed to be unreasonable. They differ from other medical specialties in that they are performing a function not just for the patient but for the social network of the patient and the society at large. There is no reason to expect that this function will disappear in the future.

Psychiatric technology consists of certain tools and systems of thought. The most obvious part of the technology is the diagnostic system. The diagnostic system is supposed to be a practical device: once the psychiatrist has decided what type of patient the individual is, she or he should know what treatment the patient should receive and be able to predict the course of the illness. The Western diagnostic system is what was developed and formalized as part of the International Classification of Diseases as discussed in Chapter 1. The diagnostic system in this formalized version serves mainly the goal of cure. It defines the sickness, specifies the treatment, and predicts the course.

The technology resulting from the goal of control also has a diagnostic system, although it is less well known among the general public. The legal definition of insanity, which is not identical to psychiatric diagnosis, is part of this other diagnostic system; more subtle aspects have no official manual or publication. The part of the diagnostic system solely serving the interests of the cure and segregation goals links characteristics of a given patient not to aspects of treatment and cure but rather in relation to the administration of the psychiatric facility. Examples are whether the patient's condition is "acute" or "chronic." Other distinctions include "wet" or "dry," "tidy" or "untidy," "idle" or "working," "difficult" or "good," and so forth (Strauss et al. 1964). All of these essentially diagnostic categories are useful in the efficient operation of any good-sized mental health facility.

Both the cure and the control goals have special tools to achieve their respective ends. The cure goal includes tools of the various well-known therapies, such as psychotherapy, behavior therapy, milieu therapy, and so forth. As well, all the drugs used in the treatment of psychiatric patients may be thought of as tools in the process of cure. Tools in the service of the control and segregation goal are less obvious but nevertheless clear to anyone who has spent time in a mental hospital—especially a patient. The tools are privileges, rewards, and punishments, which generate the right and accepted kind of comportment necessary to the smooth operation of the facility. Moving to an open ward, transfer to the ward with the billiards table, use of the swimming pool, a larger tobacco allotment, and a decrease in the quantity of drugs prescribed are positive reinforcements for good behavior. Transfer to a locked ward, an increase in drugs, and removal of television privileges are examples of punishments for bad behavior. In Nigeria the cure goal is served by chemotherapy and psychotherapy, much as in Western psychiatry. The *akaraba* ceremony described earlier is part of the technology designed simply to control the patient.

There is a complex structure of roles in most settings where psychiatric treatment is conducted. Many facilities have psychiatrists, general physicians, general and psychiatric nurses, clinical psychologist, social workers, and psychiatric aides, all engaged in the cure and maintenance of psychiatric patients (Table

7.6). To some degree, the roles all involve specific behaviors. In the traditional mental hospital, the psychiatrist diagnoses the mental disorder and prescribes treatment (and in some cases, administers treatment); the nurse carries out the psychiatrist's instructions for treatment; the clinical psychologist conducts psychological tests and may lead group discussions; and the social worker visits the family. The aide is the only one engaged solely in the maintenance function—making sure the patient is clean and adequately fed and stays out of trouble. Many community mental health centers are directed by a psychologist or social worker, with psychiatrists available on a limited basis to prescribe drugs. Psychiatric and medical treatment facilities are different from other organizations in that patients carry a role into the structure with them: the *sick role*. In our culture the sick role has a set of expectations attached to it, but the most important prescriptions are that the sick person should agree that she or he is sick and not resist the treatment process or try to pretend she or he is well. Other important and connected parts of this role are that the patient should wait passively and obediently for the doctor to cure her or him and that the cure comes from outside the patient's efforts.

In most complex organizations the ideology is not completely coherent and consistent. The goals of the organization may be contradictory. For instance, in the case of a shoe factory the goal of large profit may conflict with the goal of producing quality shoes. In some cases the contradictory ideology is caused by the external requirements of the organization. In this case, the external requirements are that the shoe factory make a profit—otherwise it does not survive. In a market economy welfare state, industries have the profit goal imposed upon them, and human service organizations have goals that are set up or endorsed by the state. In Nigeria and many other traditional cultures, indigenous healers operate in society at large without any collaboration from the state, because people seek out their services. When the principles of the profession of psychiatry were first being formed during the moral treatment movement, the two goals of cure and control were not thought of as contradictory. During this period society was thought to cause mental illness, and the prescribed cure was to remove the individual from society. The removal also served the goal of control. At that time the state had not assumed responsibility for the mentally ill. Later, in the era of state care, mental hospitals were being publicly funded in individual states as a result of the efforts of reformers like Dorothea Dix. During this time there was great emphasis on the correct administration of the hospital in order to effect a cure—again, the goal of cure was not contradicted by the goal of control and segregation.

The idea that one cannot cure a mentally ill person at the same time that one segregates him or her from society is a product of the literature on institutionalism and one of the driving forces behind the community care movement. The most convincing evidence for the effect of institutions on individuals is the work of Erving Goffman in his *Asylum* (1961). The book is concerned with what he calls *total institutions*: residential places where the institution controls and forms the whole of inmates' lives. Examples are monasteries, prisons, boarding schools, and mental hospitals. Goffman and others have shown how the self-concept of the individual is changed gradually, so that it is less and less tied to persons and ideas outside the institution. For example, entrance into a mental hospital usually involves an extreme emotional break from key persons in the patient's environment. In the case of commitment, usually a member of the family is involved actively in procuring the patient's admission to the hospital—the end of a long process Goffman calls the *betrayal funnel*. During the stay in the institution, relationships with people on the outside atrophy because of the prolonged separation and because of the stigmatization involved in entry into the hospital. Since the institution supports the individual totally, there is no need to work, and skills involved with one's occupation may get rusty. There is work in the institutional environment, but since it is not necessary for the individual's or the institution's survival, it is often trivial. The individual's life is totally supervised in an authoritarian manner. After many years of such life, it is not surprising that the individual becomes dependent on the institution and loses his or her ability to live outside. This quality of dependency on the institution and inability to live outside it has been called *institutional neurosis* (Barton 1959) and *the social breakdown syndrome* (Gruenberg et; al. 1966; Zusman 1966).

Many well-known characterizations of total institutions portray these effects as being caused by "evil" personalities on the staff of the institution—such as Ken Kesey's portrayal of Nurse Ratched in his *One Flew over the Cuckoo's Nest* (Kesey 1964). These conceptions are in error, for it seems to be in the nature of total institutions to produce institutionalism. Even where staff are of very high quality and are dedicated to eradicating the effects of institutions, it is difficult or impossible to do so.

Another effect of total institutions is to produce *secondary deviation*. Secondary deviation is deviant behavior that is a learned reaction, defense, attack, or adaptation to situations created by the societal reaction to primary deviance (as discussed in Chapters 1 and 3). In the case of mental hospitals, secondary deviation involves bizarre behaviors that a naive observer might label as mental illness. For instance, as Goffman has pointed out, mental hospitals are boring. For an individual who has been involved in an exciting and intense outside world or for one who is used to lots of physical exercise, the hospital environment may be stifling. Reaction to this boredom can have odd consequences— fights, worm-swallowing contests, or breaking up the furniture, for example. The authoritarian nature of mental hospitals also produces secondary deviation of this sort. Having to ask the staff for trivial items like cigarettes or permission to go to the bathroom may anger the patient. When the staff is overworked, they may find it difficult to respond cordially, which may produce even more anger. Such anger can show itself in bizarre behaviors, such as urinating on the floor— in this case, the urinating could be interpreted as a political act rather than a psychiatric symptom.

The tendencies of mental hospitals to produce dependency and secondary deviation are exacerbated by the sick role that the patients occupy. The idea that the patient is supposed to wait passively for cure from outside naturally increases his or her dependency on the hospital and the doctor. Psychiatrists and psychiatric therapists are aware of this conflict and resist it by encouraging the patient to work on curing himself or herself. The idea that the patient is supposed to agree that he or she is sick is also detrimental in some ways. The patient knows that if he or she is really mentally ill, he or she is supposed to be unpredictable and do crazy things occasionally. Inhibitions are lowered by this belief, and urges that might be resisted or ignored otherwise will be followed up—for example, urinating on the floor when angry at the staff.

In epidemiologic terms, the effect of the two conflicting goals of cure and control in psychiatry may be to produce unnecessary chronicity of mental disorder. There is some evidence that treatment for mental disorders in non-Western cultures has less debilitating effects than in our own culture and that mental disorders in developing countries are less likely to be chronic. For example, in a follow-up study of the International Pilot Study of Schizophrenia, it was found that schizophrenics from Third World countries had better outcomes than those from developed countries (Jablensky et al. 1992). Earlier, Murphy and Raman (1971) had shown that the rates of first admission for schizophrenia in Mauritius and Great Britain are about equal but that the chronicity of schizophrenia in Great Britain is much greater, and this general result has been replicated elsewhere as well (Waxler 1979). It may be that other cultures, such as Mauritius, do not stigmatize mentally disordered persons as much as our culture does, and there is less need or desire to segregate them. The sick role may be less well known in these cultures than in our own. Work skills may be less complex and specific in non-Western cultures, so that the danger of their atrophy is less. The family structure in Third World cultures may be larger, with a larger number of family members living in close proximity, so that the burden of care for a schizophrenic individual can be more easily spread out, lightening the burden on close relatives such as parents, spouses, or siblings. The Yoruba treatment system has the advantage that the patient can be reintegrated directly into a major role in the social structure: the Orisa cult. Occupational therapy and employment counseling in the United States is supposed to help, but even slightly disabled persons have a difficult time finding employment in an economic structure with 5 to 10 percent of the workforce unemployed. All these factors would contribute to lower levels of chronicity in non-Western countries.

Technologic Uncertainty

The efficacy of the technology for treatment of mental disorders is called into question continually by the lay public as well as by members of the psychiatric profession. One reason for the uncertainty is the nature of the ideology itself—the goal of cure is applied almost to the entire range of human unhappiness, and elimination of these problems is unrealistic. Furthermore, if psychiatry succeeds in curing or preventing a disorder (e.g., as it has general paresis), the "cure" is forgotten, and new problems are substituted. If schizophrenia were wiped out, psychiatry would still be held accountable for its failure to eliminate depression. As noted in the first chapter, it is in the nature of psychiatry to be identified with residual deviance. To be sure, many complex organizations run well for many years on a less-than-perfectly developed technology. For example, the diagnostic system in the shoe factory may not be perfect, and sometimes work shoes may be made out of leather that would be better for ladies' fashion shoes. The machinery may break down or stitch incorrectly, and the accounting procedures may not keep up with expenses and outlays, so that the factory sometimes shows a loss. The technology of medicine itself is far from perfect— many diagnoses are little more than guesses, treatment is often ineffective, and evaluation impossible. But for the shoe factory and for medicine as a whole, the technology works, and people recognize that fact. The majority of cases that come to doctors can be dealt with effectively, like an ear infection or a broken leg, for instance. Psychiatry is distinct in that for much of its caseload, diagnosis is imperfect, treatment questionable, and evaluation of unproved quality.

Psychiatric treatments, both chemical and psychosocial, are being improved continually, and they do alleviate symptoms in some percentage of individuals. But they do not cure in the way that antibiotics cure an earache. Their effect is comparable to that of aspirin and codeine, which relieve some of the pain of the earache. The effect is a statistical one in that it works only on some patients, and one needs a good-sized group of diagnosed subjects to demonstrate statistically credible effect. Also, in some cases the side effects are so strong and noxious as to vitiate severely the value of the drug.

Structural Conflict

The ideologic dilemma and technologic uncertainty in the treatment of mental disorders contribute to chronic structural conflict. *Structural conflict* means that there is disagreement as to the content of certain roles (e.g. the role of psychiatrist) or that statuses overlap in the same role (in this case, the role of therapist), so that there is confusion as to who should be performing a role or what she or he should be doing in the role. Structural conflict is inherent in all organizations, to be sure, but in the case of psychiatry, it is not possible to reduce the conflicts conflict without changing ideology and technology, which makes things very difficult. The ideology does not seem likely to change, and the technology may be impossible to improve, especially given the residual nature of the problems that psychiatrists end up dealing with.

These problems tend to stratify the mental health professions, in terms both of therapists and of their patients. Therapists in mental hospitals are the lower class in the profession, receiving lower pay and lower prestige than others, in general. In the United States many psychiatrists in mental hospitals are foreign-trained. Psychiatrists in general hospitals are similar in lifestyle and professional prestige to other doctors in hospitals—the middle class in psychiatry. Psychiatrists in private practice have higher incomes, nicer offices, and higher professional standing. Within these divisions by location there are divisions by profession: individuals with medical training are dominant, clashing with other professionals such as psychologists, nurses, and social workers over such things as who can make diagnoses, who can receive third-party reimbursements, and who can give what sorts of treatment.

Patients are stratified, too, in terms of the treatment they receive. Lower-class patients tend to end up in large mental hospitals, middle-class patients in general hospitals, and upper-class patients in private practices or perhaps private hospitals. The tendency for this stratification seems to have existed from the beginnings of modern psychiatry in the eighteenth century: while lower-class patients ended up in large mental hospitals such as the Hospital General in Paris, upper-class patients were treated by mesmerists. There are several reasons for the stratification process. One is that the most severe and prevalent form of mental disorder (schizophrenia) is associated with lower-class status, as discussed in Chapter 5. Schizophrenia is the diagnosis most likely to require strong efforts at control, such as confinement in a mental hospital. Outpatient psychotherapy is more likely to be viewed as successful with people who are verbal and willing to be assertive and talkative with an upper-middle-class doctor. Upper-and middle-class individuals are better suited to psychotherapy for this reason (Lorion 1974). There have been some attempts to devise psychotherapies better suited to the poor, but overall, the tendency is to assign the lower-class patients to treatments that do not require personal interaction with the therapist. It also could be that the upper-middle-class therapist simply prefers upper- and middle-class patients, much as he or she would be likely to prefer them as a social acquaintance. The tendency for patients from the different social classes to be stratified along professional cleavages contributes to the prestige associated with the different types of psychiatrists. Thus, the fact that a private practicing psychiatrist has only upper- and upper-middle-class patients contributes to his or her professional prestige in comparison with the mental hospital psychiatrist who treats mainly lower-class patients.

Technologic uncertainty in the treatment of mental disorders also produces structural conflict. The failure of the therapies of psychiatrists and other healers to achieve the stated or understood goals leads to a continual search for new theories, as discussed earlier. But it is difficult to show that one therapy is better than another. The new therapies acquire legitimacy after being introduced and attracting a certain following. Eventually, there is competition among those espousing the various therapies. Thus, the technologic uncertainty explains the multitude of therapies available: thermotherapy, shock therapy, psychosurgery, psychotherapy, milieu therapy, the "total push" method, behavior therapy, occupational therapy, family therapy, reality therapy, existential therapy, cognitive behavioral therapy, interpersonal therapy, gestalt therapy, to name just a small portion of those available. In many cases the separate therapies have professional associations, journals, training institutions, and mechanisms for accrediting the institutions of training.

There is an attempt in the mental health field to generate role specificity with respect to these various therapies. One professional is assigned to a given therapy—for instance, occupational therapy—and the others are supposed to stay away from administering that treatment. However, the poor diagnostic system makes it difficult to choose which patient should get which therapy in an objective way, thus opening the door to competition among the therapies for patients. Nor are the diagnoses strongly related to the type of facility, since any type of diagnosis can be treated in just about any type of facility. Psychotherapy is one of the most widely used therapies for the treatment of mental disorder, but it is not the specific occupational realm of any particular profession in mental health. Rather, almost all the professions connected to mental disorders can practice psychotherapy if they so choose. In sociologic terms, there is overlap as to the statuses that are assigned the role of psychotherapy.

CONCLUSION: SERVING THE PUBLIC

The organization of health care and mental health care has entered the national public arena increasingly in the past few decades (Mechanic, 4th ed., 1999; Goldman et al. 1999). Health care is costly, and mental health care is an important component of the cost (about 8%, according to McKusick et al. 1998). In 1985 the costs for direct treatment of alcohol or mental health problems (excluding drug abuse), was about $50 million; the indirect costs of reduced productivity and lost days of work amounted to another $100 million (Rice et al. 1991). Programs such as the national health care system in Britain and Medicare and Medicaid in the United States have expanded the accessibility of mental health treatments to a wider range of individuals than ever before. For example, individuals in the workforce with good health care benefits can receive treatment in a good-quality private or general hospital. As a result, the existing stratification in the organization of psychiatry is evolving into new forms. In the United States the belief is widely held that unfettered access to mental health treatment by all individuals would overwhelm the system (even though it has not done so in other nations). New developments in management, therefore, attempt to use the diagnostic system as one strategy to limit costs, by setting limits on treatment dependent on the diagnosis. These strategies enlist the mental health professional in the service of the public's interest. When the public's interest includes containment of costs, these can be contradictory to interests of the individual patient.

The problem of delivering services to those who need them most has existed since the beginnings of psychiatry. In the past, the severely mentally ill were treated, in part, because society demanded their removal; and those with less important problems were treated only if they had the money to pay for it. In the current environment it is difficult to summarize where the inequity of services is greatest or how to address it. This difficulty is exacerbated by the fundamental problems inherent in the organization of services for treatment of mental disorders: ideologic dilemma, technologic uncertainty, and structural conflict.

8

Mental Disorder in the Modern World

INTRODUCTION

One of the dominant ideas in our culture today is that society is somehow sick or disordered. The idea is so diffuse, appearing in such different forms and in so many different places, that it is difficult to synthesize a sensible whole. Many commentators have contended that society has been disrupted in some way over the last few decades. The idea that the individual's relationship to the society at large is damaged, with a concomitant rise in individual disorganization and mental illness, is studied in the first section of this chapter. The focus is on risk for the individual, and standard epidemiological methods can be brought to bear. In the second section, the focus shifts to the idea that the society itself is disordered, regardless of the level of health or personal disorganization of the individuals within it. In this section the concept of variation—inherently, a group-level characteristic—is crucial. The shift in level of analysis from the individual level to the societal levels is an important conceptual change, although it has been ignored by many authors. Studying society at the macrolevel means that normal epidemiologic tools are less useful, and it makes the question more difficult to approach.

THE INDIVIDUAL IN MODERN SOCIETY

Alienation and the Self as Reflexive Project

The idea that the individual's relationship to society is disrupted is not new. For example, it was one of the driving forces behind the moral treatment movement in the early eighteenth century, as discussed in Chapter 7. Eugen Bleuler, who devised the term schizophrenia, stated that "*civilization*, so called, is one of the most important breeding places of mental diseases" (1924; 208). But society seems to have changed so much more in the last century than in earlier times that the idea is more tenable, among a larger proportion of the population, than earlier. One can get a feeling for these critiques of society in the work of Frank in 1936 (cited in Dohrenwend and Dohrenwend in 1974):

Our so-called social problems . . . are to be viewed as arising from the frantic efforts of individuals, taking any sure direction and sanctions or guiding conception of life, to find some way of protecting themselves or of merely existing in a society being remade by technology. Having no strong loyalties and no consistent values or realizable ideas to cherish, the individual's conduct is naturally conflicting, confused, neurotic, and antisocial.

A major figure in this area before World War II was Sigmund Freud, with his *Civilization and Its Discontents* (1961). The postwar era saw an avalanche of works on this topic such as Ellul's *The Technological Society* (1964), Mumford's *The Myth of the Machine* (1967), Riesman's *The Lonely Crowd* (1950), one of the top sellers ever among books written by sociologists, Dubos' *So Human an Animal* (1968), which won the Pulitzer Prize, and Toffler's *Future Shock* (1970). These are reviewed in Florman (1975) from which quotations below are drawn. The so-called postmodern movement saw important publications by Giddens (*Modernity and Self-Identity*, 1991) and Beck (*The Risk Society: Towards a New Modernity*, 1992). Work by Herbert Marcuse is considered in the second section.

The major theme running through all this literature is the concept of *alienation*. In our own time the word "alienation" has been used in works by existentialist philosophers as well as by sociologists. In earlier times the word was used in a religious sense, signifying separation from God (Ephesians 4:18: 'Having the understanding darkened, being alienated from the life of God through the ignorance that is in them, because of the blindness of their heart"). In the psychiatric sense the word indicated departure from reason (hence the term "alienist" for the forerunners of psychiatry in the nineteenth century). As Schacht (1970) has pointed out in his review, many of these writers posit an ideal self from which they contend humans are alienated—the nature of the ideal self differs from commentators to commentator. Seeman (1959) identified five separate meanings of alienation in the literature: (1) powerlessness is the expectancy held by the individual that his or her own behavior cannot determine outcomes; (2) meaninglessness is a state in which there is low expectancy that predictions about future outcomes can be made; (3) normlessness is the expectancy that socially unapproved behaviors are required to achieve important goals; (4) social isolation is a low value assigned to goals typically regarded as highly valued in the society; (5) self-estrangement is a loss of intrinsic meaning in work, so that current behavior is unconnected to future rewards. A more concise breakdown of the concept of alienation is made by combining the second and fifth of Seeman's types under the rubric of meaninglessness, since both definitions pertain to disconnection of the present from the future. Likewise, it is parsimonious to combine the third and fourth of Seeman's types under the rubric of social isolation, since both have to do with discrepancy between the individual and societal goals. The resulting framework of alienation then is consistent with the three fundamental dimensions of social life laid out in the biosocial framework of Chapter 1 (Figure 1.6) and with the structure of this book. The first concept of alienation is *powerlessness*, which is the individual's sense that the system of social environment is not in his or her control. Social aspects of powerlessness derive from the system of social stratification. The second concept is *social isolation*, referring to the individual's lack of sense of integration within the group. The third concept for alienation is *meaninglessness*, which is the individual's sense that his or her place in the world is not coherent and predictable.

These meanings of alienation are all emotion-laden, abstract cognitions experienced by an individual, that is, psychological phenomena, not strictly social. The high level of abstractness means they can come into play in a wide variety of situations. They are similar in structure to, but not identical to, concepts of individual coping considered in Chapter 3. For example, the concept of mastery is closely linked to powerlessness; the concept of meaninglessness is closely linked to fatalism; and the concept of isolation ties into the notion of social supports. Meaninglessness is the concept closest to Durkheim's notion of anomie (1966).

Some theorists contend that the importance of social class for the society and of powerlessness for the individual has declined in recent decades (Beck 1992). But modern life has expanded the importance of meaninglessness and social isolation. Meaninglessness has become more important because of the difficulty of knowing anything at all with surety. The Heisenberg principle of uncertainty—that the attempt to measure the location of an electron eliminates the possibility of actually knowing its location—is generalized to scientific knowledge in particular and practical knowledge in general. An example is the movie *Closeup*. In the movie a photographer accidentally takes pictures of what he thinks might be a murder. The plotline revolves around his attempts to improve the resolution of the photo and to determine by investigation whether the murder actually took place. In the end he is unable to know what actually happened. The final scene involves his walking in the park where the murder might have occurred and watching mimes act out a game of tennis, without using a ball. The mime tennis players hit the "ball" over the fence and gesture to him to pick it up. After some hesitation, he picks up the "ball" and throws it back, and they continue playing. He and the viewer are unsure what is real and what is not real.

Three postmodern concepts convey the idea of loss of confidence in knowledge in more depth: simulacrum, pastiche, and hyperspace (Jameson, in Ritzer 1996: 614–15). A *simulacrum* is a copy of something so true to the original that it cannot be determined which is the copy and which the original ("a copy for which no original ever existed"). An example is the painting by Andy Warhol of cans of Campbell's soup that are indistinguishable from photographs of the cans. Another example is the pseudodocumentary style of television, in which it is difficult to tell where actors are entering the plot, replacing "real" people being filmed. A *pastiche* is a collage of historical events and ideas, sometimes contradictory, woven together in an attempt to represent the past. The pastiche represents an acknowledgement that it is impossible for historians to accurately represent the past or to distinguish the past from the present. *Hyperspace* is an area where traditional concepts of space do not help to orient us. An example is the lobby of the Bonaventure Hotel in Los Angeles, designed by the post-modern architect John Portman. The lobby is surrounded by four absolutely symmetrical towers containing the rooms. The lobby as designed was so confusing that the hotel had to add color coding and directional signals to help otherwise frustrated customers find their way to their rooms.

Social isolation has become more important in modern life because the self is defined increasingly by individual choices and less by traditional group affiliations. In terms of the three-dimensional concept of social identity presented in Chapter 3, the shape of the social identity is larger on the right side, representing the "choice-achieved" end of the dimension, and relatively smaller on the "received-ascribed" end. Baumeister (1986) notes that of 10 aspects of self-definition in medieval times, 3 have been destabilized (geographical home, marriage, occupation), 5 have been trivialized (ancestral family, social rank, gender, moral virtue, and religion), and the other 2 are inherently unstable (age and bodily characteristics). He concludes:

Modern self-definition requires choice, achievement, and frequent redefinition of self; medieval self-definition generally did not (151); [and] The modern individual approaches adulthood with a chaos of options. . . . Society—both the general society at large and the specific family and social world of the individual—thus forms a rather incomplete context for identity for today. . . . Identity is a theory of self associated with an inadequate contextual framework and with a concept that injudiciously blends reality and unreality. (264–65)

Ulrich Beck (1992) makes a similar point, stating:

Individualization . . . means that each person's biography is removed from given determinations and placed in his or her own hands, open and dependent on decisions. The proportion of life opportunities which are fundamentally closed to decision-making is *decreasing* and the proportion of the biography which is open and must be constructed personally is *increasing*. . . . Decisions on education, profession, job, place of residence, spouse, number of children and so forth, . . . no longer *can* be, they *must* be made. (151; emphasis added)

The result of this modern development, according to many theorists, is to emphasize the inherently reflective quality of the self (the "looking-glass self" described long ago by Cooley and Mead, as described in Chapter 3). The self is a "reflexive project" (Giddens 1991: 32); biographies are "self-reflexive" (Beck 1992: 135). "In the individualized society the individual must therefore learn, on pain of permanent disadvantage, to conceive of himself or herself as the center of action, as the planning office with respect to his/her own biography, abilities, orientations, relationships, and so on" (Beck 1992: 135).

Social Structural Lag: Society

Major sources of alienation are disjunctures produced by changes in society. Social evolution slowly achieves a stable equilibrium, but rapid social change can be introduced by some external force (such as urbanization, technology, or migration). *Social structural lag* is the term for the disjuncture between the current social structure of society and the structure that would evolve over time in response to its current needs. The social structure includes all three dimensions introduced in Chapter 1, that is, stratification, integration, and culture. The lag can be introduced by changes in one dimension forcing a lack of balance with the other two. The change could be caused by a deprivation introduced by the environment (e.g., bad weather reducing agricultural production, leading to migration); or by technologic changes that provide the possibility of satisfying needs more efficiently, such as a new form of seed; or by cultural change involving newly recognized desires, such as the introduction of tea or refined sugar. A good example of social structural lag in the current time is the need for services and social structures for the elderly, produced by the revolution in mortality occurring during the early part of the twentieth century (Riley 1994). The social structural lag occurs because the changes in one narrow aspect of society disregard mechanisms that have evolved gradually in response to the entire range of humans' physical and spiritual needs.

Urbanization is an important type of social structural lag. In the last century the Western world has changed from a predominantly rural society to one that is overwhelmingly urban. It is only since the Industrial Revolution in the seventeenth century that a sizable proportion of the population lived in cities, and the absolute size of the cities in Europe that did exist during the Middle Ages was mostly smaller than what we could today call "towns." Today, the overwhelming majority of the population lives in large urban complexes. Urbanization has been linked to mental disorder, because increased population density is forced onto individuals and because it alienates them from nature.

Evidence that *population density* might be related to mental pathology comes from studies of rats in crowded environments (Calhoun 1962). Calhoun observed certain regularities in abnormal behavior when many rats were forced to live together: among females there was inadequate nest building; some of the males became completely passive, ignoring and being ignored by every other rat; other males became oversexed and raped other rats of both sexes; yet others became cannibalistic. Calhoun concluded that any process that collects animals together in great numbers could be termed a *behavioral sink* and had the potential to generate abnormal behavior. Studies of humans in crowded environments generally conclude that social pathologies of various types do not result directly from crowding but rather from other aggregate-level variables that may be associated with crowded areas, such as low level of income, inadequate health and community facilities per capita, low levels of literacy, and so forth (Carnahan et al. 1975; Galle et al. 1972). One study of psychiatric symptoms was conducted in Hong Kong, by far the most crowded place on earth (Mitchell, cited in Dohrenwend and Dohrenwend 1974a). It concluded that crowding did not seem to affect level of symptomatology by itself. Evidence suggests little or no effect of crowding per se on human mental disorders, but the issue is still open.

Rapid cultural change is another source of social structural lag. Anthropologists have pointed out that some societies socialize their members during their youth in ways that are maladaptive as adults. According to Alvin Toffler (1970), the increasing rate of social change makes this process endemic to modern societies—children are brought up to hold values that do not conform to the world they come to know as adults; and even if they learn new values as adults, change in their social environment always will be several steps ahead of them. Therefore, they continually feel inexperienced and inadequate in meeting new situations, and they are unable to produce a coherent, predictable view of the world. The situation that inspired Toffler's work is the experience of depression reported among returning Peace Corps volunteers. They had adapted over a two-year period to the values of the developing societies where they had been placed; when they returned to the United States, they had to "unlearn" the new values rapidly and replace them with the traditional U.S. norms they had grown up with. Both in leaving the United States and in returning, they experienced so-called *culture shock*, but it seems to have been worse on their return, perhaps because it was unexpected. In Toffler's view we are all undergoing rapidly accelerating cultural shock, which he calls *future shock*. The situation of valuelessness and cultural alienation is exacerbated by the developments in the mass media, because television and radio make us acutely aware of the heterogeneity of cultures in the world and the difficulty in discovering absolute values.

Industrialization is another source of social structural lag. The change in the nature of the work due to industrialization and technology has been the focus of important early sociologists such as Marx and Durkheim. Marx felt that "labor is alienated when it ceases to reflect one's own personality and interests, and instead comes under the direction of an alien will"; such a situation is the inevitable result of a capitalistic social structure, according to Marx (Schacht 1970: 88–89). Durkheim studied the increasing division of labor, in which tasks performed by any given person become increasingly narrow. Since individuals are performing different sorts of tasks, more effort is required to understand and interact with others on a more general level (shifting from what Durkheim called *mechanical solidarity* to what he called *organic solidarity*). The contemporary critics concur. For instance, Ellul (1964) observes that the average citizen's work is "an aimless, useless, callous business, tied to a clock; an absurdity profoundly felt and resented by the worker." Not only is contemporary work not meaningful, but it cuts the individual off from fellow human beings (House 1983; Johnson and Johansson 1991). *Taylorism* (named after the industrial planner F. W. Taylor) is the tendency to let the drive for efficiency structure the work environment, ignoring the effects of the work environment on the social structure of the workers and their psychological needs (Johnson 1991). There is epidemiologic evidence that certain occupations have higher prevalence of mental disorders (Eaton et al. 1990; Mandell et al. 1992) and speculation that social and psychological characteristics of the work environment explain the higher prevalence. For example, the ability to control the schedule of work—consistent with Marx's interest in alienated work—may be related to the prevalence of major depression (Link et al. 1993; Mausner-Dorsch and Eaton 2000). The movement away from assembly line production toward quality circles or teams of individuals who together produce the entire product, instead of assembling one single aspect of it, reflects both Marx's interest in alienation and Durkheim's focus on the effect of the division of labor on the group structure.

Technologic change produces another type of social structural lag. An example is the atom bomb, because the new technology allows for decisions made by a few persons to have a drastic effect on individuals who are only distantly connected to those few persons. The social critics also speak of the inability of the average citizen to affect the technology. Dubos (1968) speaks of an "undisciplined technology," while Ellul (1964) notes that "technique has become autonomous. . . . It has fashioned an omnivorous world which obeys its own laws." Thus, powerlessness might also be considered a result of the development of technology.

Social Structural Lag: Family

The family is a universal element in human culture because it performs the basic societal functions of *procreation*, which through childbearing generates new members for the society; and *socialization*, which trains individuals to fit properly into society according to its customs (Winch 1971). In addition to the basic functions of procreation and socialization, the family historically has attached to it other functions. The family sometimes performs a production function, by producing food, shelter, and other goods and services for its members and for others—an example is the farm family in the nineteenth-century United States. The family is also a consumption unit in many societies—that is, it serves distribution and consumption functions. Today in most Western countries the family is the most common social unit for which food, clothing, and leisure products are bought and distributed. In some societies the family serves religious functions as well; for instance, in traditional China, the peasant family was a religious unit because of the worship of ancestors in that society.

Virtually all family theorists who have made an attempt to study the family cross-culturally or historically have noticed that the traditional functions of the family have been emasculated in modern Western society (e.g., Cherlin, 1999). A good example is the comparison given by Winch (1971) between the traditional peasant family in China and the family on a kibbutz in modern Israel. In traditional China the family was a sexual, economic, political, and religious unit performing numerous functions, including procreation, socialization, production, consumption, and so forth. The family of the kibbutz performs almost none of these functions. The economic unit was the kibbutz as a whole, in terms of both production and consumption, so that adults contributed their labor to the group as a whole, and clothing and food were bought and distributed by the kibbutz group as a whole. The culture of the kibbutz discouraged traditional religions. Each individual contributed his or her vote to the political decisions to be made, so that the individual, not the family, was the political unit. Even the socialization function was performed by the kibbutz group as a whole in that babies were taken from their mothers shortly after birth and placed in a nursery. In the kibbutz studies by Winch, the family functions were whittled down to the procreative one. The family of the kibbutz is not to be regarded as the prototypical modern family, but it provides a dramatic example of a process that it believed to be very general—the loss in functions of the family. Today's modern Western family performs parts of the replacement and economic functions. The replacement function is limited to procreation and early socialization, with schools taking up much of the socialization function. The economic function is limited to consumption, with the production function being performed outside the home, for the most part.

The loss in functions of the family is accompanied by changes in the structure of the family and the nature of its life cycle. The modern family is smaller than its predecessor and has a shorter life span. With less and less of the population living on the land and being engaged in agriculture, the family is no longer geographically stable. The typical pattern now is for the younger generation to leave the family of their parents and pursue a specialized occupation, typically different from that of the parents. In many cases the career pattern of a specialized occupation demands geographic and social mobility. Thus, today the nuclear family, consisting of husband, wife, and children, is the predominant type of family structure, because it can meet demands of the economy more efficiently.

The change in the structure of the family has had positive and negative effects on its stability and importance as a social institution. The more functions an institution such as the family performs, the more powerful and stable it is (Winch 1971). The traditional family performed many functions and was strong and stable, but the stability of the family of today rests more heavily on the personal compatibility of the marital partners. Thus, we should not be surprised at the rise in the divorce rate and remarriage over the last few decades, nor should we view it as a temporary phenomenon. Rather, it reflects the change in the nature of the functions of the family.

Ironically, although the stability of the family is declining, a function of the family related to mental disorders is becoming more important—the *function of emotional security*. The present-day emphasis on achievement in our competitive society leads to *status insecurity*, that is, worry about one's status. As noted earlier in discussing the reflexive self, less and less attention is paid to ascribed statuses such as race, sex, ethnic background, or neighborhood, with the result that the individual is no longer granted automatic membership into various social groups that might provide friendship, emotional support, and self-esteem. Today the individual is more likely to have to earn membership into social groups through achievement; and even then, the group often is based on a narrow concept (bowlers, politically active women, engineers, and so on). The family is one of the last remaining social institutions that treat the individual as a whole person and automatically grant him or her membership. Status in the family is ascribed, and there is less status insecurity because a minimal level of self-esteem is guaranteed in most families. Even this quality of family life is eroding, especially for couples in a so-called *pure relationship*, "where a social relation is entered into for its own sake, for what can be derived by each person from a sustained association with another; and which is continued only in so far as it is thought by both parties to deliver enough satisfactions for each individual to stay within it" (Giddens 1992: 58). Since the importance of emotional security found within the family is greater now than before, and the family is less stable than earlier, the effects of the presence or absence of a family may be greater now than in earlier generations. The disjuncture between the increasing importance of the function of emotional security and the declining stability of the family may explain the upsurge in media portrayals of family disruptions such as child kidnapping.

The change in the structure of the family has led to an increase in potency of the *developmental crisis of autonomy* (Erickson 1968). In trying to understand what type of stress might be related to schizophrenia, Brian Murphy, a psychiatrist and anthropologist, noted it must be "a form of stress which demands responses that have no clear precedent. . . . It is only when the individual is isolated from, and has not learned the traditional answers, or when events conspire to make him seriously doubt them, that the simplicity of such stress situations is changed [and] one can expect the risk of schizophrenia to increase" (Murphy 1972: 416). He noted that three additional features of the stress are required: (1) that it is perceived as important; (2) that there is no simple solution or escape; and (3) that it is chronic. He applied this notion to a variety of epidemiologic data, including the change in rate of schizophrenia among the Tallensi in Ghana associated with rapid modernization, and the large increase in rate of schizophrenia among World War II refugees to Britain, after they had left refugee camps and "when the difficult tasks of . . . deciding one's future had to be faced," among other situations.

As the course of life evolves, opportunities are presented requiring decisions by the individual which anticipate the future, merging his or her own abilities and desires with social structural possibilities that can only be guessed at. Two important realms of decisions occurring in young adulthood affect the two basic dimensions of social life: that is, socioeconomic status—the occupational career—and social integration—marriage. The two types of planning are interwoven, as the type of mate affects the type of career, and vice versa. This activity, termed here *formulating a life plan*, is one of the most complex cognitive tasks an individual will engage in throughout his or her life (Eaton and Harrison, in press). The problem of formulating a life plan is closely connected to the formation of the social identity and the self. As noted in Chapter 3, self and social identity both have historical and futuristic aspects, in connecting individuals to their past, and in anticipating their future, producing the sense of biography which gives individuals their sense of coherence and meaning.

The formulation of the life plan involves prioritizing, selecting, integrating, and balancing among complex and subtly different future actions—what cognitive psychologists call *executive function*. This type of cognitive activity takes place in the frontal lobe, the area of the brain most different from our primate ancestors. Weak executive function is believed to be connected to schizophrenia (Goldberg and Weinberg, 1986), and its polar opposite, cognitive rigidity, has been proposed by Kohn (1977) as a risk factor for schizophrenia which arises due to socialization practices in the lower social class: "The orientational system that lower-class parents transmit to their children is not likely to provide a sufficient sense of the complexity of life or the analytic tools needed to cope with the dilemmas and problems men encounter. These deficiencies could be overcome by later educational and occupational experience; but often they are not, in part because people who have learned this orientational system are unlikely to want to overcome them, in larger part because circumstances probably would not be propitious even if they were" (199). In the context of this chapter on modernization, social structural lag induces a situation in which the individual is not prepared for the level of executive function required by the new society, producing a stress which may precipitate mental disorder. As Murphy (1968) noted, this stress coincides with the age of greatest risk for major mental disorders such as depression, schizophrenia, anxiety, and alcohol disorders: "roughly with the peak period of major decision-taking in life, since before the twenties long-range decisions can often be postponed or left to one's elders and after the twenties they have usually been taken" (89).

Our modern society involves an intergenerational mobility structure which is relatively open—an aspect we value highly. This mobility structure is one in which the life chances of an individual are poorly predicted from his or her situation at birth (or, more precisely, at conception). In medieval times, formulating a life plan was something that individuals did not have to do. The overwhelming majority were peasants, and there were few alternative life scenarios. In the nineteenth century, the majority of the populations of Europe and America converted from agricultural livelihood, with strong generation-to-generation occupational and residential stability, to non-farm occupations, in which the next generation had to formulate and choose a career different from that of their parents. Thus, the developmental crisis of autonomy is exacerbated by the change in the nature of the self from historical times to the present. For an individual, this change in the self is at its maximum acceleration when the individual is leaving the structure of the parental family and entering the "chaos of options": that is, precisely during the age of onset of the major mental disorders.

EPIDEMIOLOGIC EVIDENCE

Temporal Trend: Psychosis

Most of the words we commonly use for severe mental disorder have origins prior to the modern era and etymologies *not* connected with health and illness (examples later from the *Oxford English Dictionary*). Many expressions have to do with loss or destruction: the word "crazy," for example, has the same root as the word "crash" and was used as early as the eleventh century; other similar terms of this nature include "flipped his lid," "lost his marbles," "nervous breakdown," and so forth. Some words are connected to animality (e.g., "berserk," which has the word for "bear" in it, "looney," "batty," and so on). Other important words are connected to time and change: the word "lunatic" comes from the Latin word for moon; "mad" comes ultimately from the Latin word meaning "to change" (*mutare*) and was used as early as A.D. 1000. Only "insane" has the health–illness connotations attached to it—from the Latin *sanus* for health. Its first use in English was the "insane root" in Shakespeare's *Macbeth*.

At least some bizarre behaviors of the type we now call psychosis were described in the classical period (Roccatagliata 1991). For example, Hippocrates, in the fifth century B.C., described an illness where "the ill person often weeps without reason; unimportant things make him afraid and sometimes also sad, [he is] frightened though without reason. . . . He talks about things which bear no reference to this life . . . sometimes he sees images as if in dreams" (Roccatagliata 1991: 9) Celsus, in the first century A.D., described a chronic illness with hallucinations and delirious ravings (Roccatagliata 1991: 15). Galen described the symptom of flat affect ("a deadening of the life of the emotions" (Roccatagliata 1991: 18). Early Byzantine scholars mentioned the adolescent onset of these types of conditions (Roccatagliata 1991: 22). The clinical descriptions do not meet current criteria for diagnosis by any stretch of the imagination, but it seems probable that schizophrenia and bipolar disorder existed, if only extremely rarely, at least 2,000 years ago. Descriptions of these conditions outside the classical tradition are much harder to locate (Jeste et al. 1985).

There are no data of an epidemiologic quality that might let us estimate the frequency of the psychoses in premodern times, but we can take note of one societal response: the building of asylums. An *asylum* is a residential institution designed to segregate the mentally ill from society. The response of the modern era to the occurrence of psychoses in sufficient numbers has been to build asylums, but it is unlikely asylums were built prior to the early medieval period (Mora 1975). According to Foucault (1979), the birth of asylums occurred during the Age of Reason as a concomitant of cultural and economic developments. He also observes that during this period leprosariums existing throughout Europe were closing down because the end of the Crusades had shut off sources of contagion from the East. In some instances leprosariums were converted to asylums, and the implication is that asylums served the same cultural function. The culminating event, according to Foucault, was the *Great Confinement* of 1656 (discussed in Chapter 1). Foucault's argument would be challenged by a demographer, who might argue that mental disorders are relatively infrequent and require a certain minimum-sized population living in a small area for an asylum to be practical. A city of 500,000 would yield 500 psychotics if the rate were one per 1,000, for example. Therefore, according to this argument, the asylum would have been born when cities began to collect the required critical mass of population during this period in the seventeenth century. The critical mass of population might also serve to direct attention to psychotic behavior, regardless of whether asylums were established. This critical mass might explain the observations of psychosis in Roman literature noted earlier, since Rome had this size during the classical era.

Evidence suggests that the asylum is an invention of the Arab cultures of the eighth and ninth centuries, which spread through Muslim Spain into Europe and outward from there during the colonial conquest (Dols 1987; Mora 1975). There was an asylum in Baghdad in the eighth century, in Damascus in the ninth century, and in Cairo and Fez in the thirteenth century. In the Arab part of Spain (Granada) an asylum was established in 1365. Traditionally, the "first" asylum in Europe is thought of as Valencia, established in 1409 (Rumbant 1972), but it seems not unlikely that the inspiration may have come from Granada. Shortly thereafter, asylums were established in Seville and Lisbon, and in 1632 Vincent de Paul opened the doors to an asylum in Paris, 24 years before the Great Confinement studied by Foucault. There are vague references to other asylums in Europe at about the same time as the Valencia institution, but they were not directed solely at the mentally disordered—rather, at the poor, ill, crippled, and demented as well as the insane. There are no references to asylums in non-Western cultures that did not result clearly from colonial expansion (but see Koran 1972). Thus, the idea that there is a cultural, economic, or demographic imperative for the birth of the asylum is not demonstrated; it seems more correct to view the asylum as an invention that, like other inventions, is passed along, evaluated, and adopted if it seems to be useful.

Most of the present population of the world lives in urban areas, and, thus, the process of modernization is naturally confounded with the process of urbanization. However, it is best to attempt to separate the two processes if possible, and, fortunately, the available data allow us to keep them separate. In the following the historical trends in rates of mental disorder are considered, and in the next section the differences in rates of mental disorder between urban and rural areas are discussed.

There is no sound epidemiological data on mental disorder before the nineteenth century. During this century the distinction between the insane and the mentally deficient became widely accepted, and only at the end of the century did the present-day diagnostic system begin to take shape, including the diagnostic distinction between the category of dementia praecox (the precursor of schizophrenia) and manic-depressive insanity. The most that one can hope for is a rough estimate of the rate of psychosis in the nineteenth century. Furthermore, since diagnostic fashion varies so much from one region to another, there must be longitudinal data from just one locale. The study that meets these conditions is *Psychosis and Civilization*, a classic epidemiologic study (Goldhammer and Marshall 1953).

The purpose of *Psychosis and Civilization* was to test the hypothesis that modern civilization brings with it an increase in the incidence of psychosis. The authors present data on rates of hospitalized insanity for the state of Massachusetts from 1840 to 1930, and they choose various other sources of contemporary data from the United States as well. Generally speaking, they concluded that the rate of first admission in the age range of 20 to 50 years is about the same in the twentieth century as in the nineteenth, contradicting the critics of modern society. A secondary finding is that the contemporary rate of first admissions is much higher for those over the age of 50. They conclude that "there has been no long-term increase during the last century of the incidence of the psychoses of early and middle life" (Goldhammer and Marshall 1953: 92). The data on which they base their conclusion are reproduced in Table 8.1. This table contains data from several different places in the Goldhammer–Marshall study, as well as 1972 data from the National Reporting Program of the National Institute of Mental Health. Goldhammer and Marshall note several factors that may influence the rates of first admission without being connected to the true rate of incidence: the availability and accessibility of facilities; the motivation to use the facilities; the diagnostic range of patients admitted; and factors in the populations that may affect the incidence, such as nativity, age, culture, and so forth. They restrict their argument to specific comparisons that minimize the influence of these factors; for instance, they contend that the comparison of the rates in 1885 with the rates in 1930 (in Table 8.1) is the fairest comparison of this type because the extraneous factors are most stable between these two periods. In this specific comparison, for age groups less than 60, one can see that the later period has an equal or even slightly lower rate of first admissions.

Goldhammer and Marshall exercised considerable latitude in choosing the contemporary data to which they compare their nineteenth-century data. They repeatedly contended that they chose comparison data that were biased against

Table 8.1
First Admissions to Mental Hospitals in the Nineteenth and Twentieth Centuries (Rates per 1,000 Population)

Age	1840-1844	1885	1930
		Massachusetts	
10-19	0.12	0.22	0.26
20-29	0.50	0.96	0.91
30-39	0.72	1.11	1.12
40-49	0.80	1.10	1.25
50-59	0.78	1.03	1.28
60+	0.50	0.70	2.54

Age	1972	
	U.S.--Public	U.S.--All Inpatient
15-24	0.95	2.20
25-34	1.04	2.40
35-44	1.07	2.48
45-54	0.83	1.92
55-64	0.63	1.46
65+	0.69	1.60

Notes:
1840–1844: From Goldhammer and Marshall (1953: Table 3); includes males and females.
1885: From Goldhammer and Marshall (1953: Table 7); males only—rates for females were slightly lower than for males. Rates for both sexes together were not presented.
1930: From Goldhammer and Marshall (1953: Table 7); excludes temporary admissions. Males only—rates for females were slightly lower than for males. Rates for both sexes together were not presented.
1972–Public: From Kramer (1977: Table 8); includes both sexes at state and county mental hospitals.
1972–All Inpatient: From Kramer (1977: Table 8); includes both sexes at all inpatient facilities with a dedicated psychiatric unit, that is, state and county mental hospitals, private hospitals, Veterans Administration hospitals, inpatient psychiatric units of general hospitals, and inpatient services of community mental health centers. The rate is estimated by inflating by a factor of 2.3 to approximate the ratio of state and county episodes to total inpatient episodes in 1971 in Kramer (1977: Table 4).

their hypothesis of equality of rates. On the other hand, it is also clear that they wish to support the hypothesis that the rates have *not* changed. For instance, they note that the year 1885 is not a peak year and that they "could, perhaps, have provided more unambiguous results by continuing our series to 1890. We were, however, content to end our series when it became apparent that we had arrived at rates for the central age groups that were equal to those of today" (53). In spite of their disclaimers about conservative bias, it seems that the comparison data were chosen haphazardly at best. For the 1885–1930 comparison (Table 8.1), they focused on rates of first admission in Massachusetts, *excluding* temporary admissions from the 1930 data; for the 1855–1940 comparison (not shown) they used as modern data first admissions for psychosis to U.S. mental hospitals; for the 1840–1940 comparison (not shown) they chose, for the modern data, states with the *lowest* rates of first admission (Maine, North Dakota, and Florida). For each comparison they gave reasons that the test is conservative; for instance, they claimed the 1855–1940 comparison was fair because in the nineteenth century mental hospital admissions had a higher proportion of psychotics than admissions today. However, they consistently ignored factors that might have inflated the nineteenth-century rates, such as inability to distinguish insane individuals from other types of deviants (e.g., criminals, epileptics, and those mentally deficient); and they ignored factors that might have deflated the present-day rates, such as a decline in the rate of general paresis or the increase in the availability of private mental hospitals, general hospitals, and outpatient clinics, all of which would not have entered their "modern" statistics.

The nature of psychiatric institutions has changed so much since 1930 that it is not easy to find data comparable to those used by Goldhammer and Marshall. Therefore, two estimates for 1972 are given in Table 8.1: one estimate is based on first admissions to public mental hospitals, and the second on the more inclusive category of all inpatient psychiatric facilities. The state and county hospitals are, for the most part, the same institutions reflected in the 1930 data, but their resident population and first-admission rates peaked in 1955 and declined thereafter. The total inpatient rates include general hospital psychiatric units and inpatient units of community mental health centers, both of which had explosive growth beginning about 1960. About 50 to 60 percent of the admissions of these inpatient facilities were diagnosed as psychotic, contrasting with an estimated 80 percent in the nineteenth-century data. Strictly speaking, only the total rate of first inpatient admissions is comparable to the earlier data, but the rate of first admissions to public mental hospitals is included to let the reader get a feel for the impact of the expansion of new psychiatric facilities after World War II. Data on first admissions by age are no longer published by the National Institute of Mental Health, but, as best as can be estimated, the rate of admissions to all inpatient facilities has not declined since 1972 (Redick et al. 1996; Figure 7.3).

Extending the historical trend from 1930 to 1972 changes the pattern somewhat, because the rates climb again. A 130-year trend from 1844 to 1972 is exposed that was not so clearly evident when Goldhammer and Marshall were conducting their research. Over these 130 years the rates in the middle-aged groups have increased from about 50 to about 200 per 100,000 populations—a factor of about four.

The rise in rates has a different shape for the young and middle-aged groups than for the aged. For disorders of young and middle age, the rates rise from 1844 to 1885, then are flat from 1885 to 1930 (leading Goldhammer and Marshall to conclude there is no upward trend), and then they rise again from 1930 to 1972. For the aged, the rates rise somewhat from 1844 to 1885, then rise sharply from 1885 to 1930 (reinforcing, by comparison, their conclusion of no change for the young and middle-aged groups in this period), and then they drop. The point of noting these different trends is that the general pattern observed by Goldhammer and Marshall and interpreted by them as the absence of a historical rise in rates of mental disorder does not extend to the 1972 data. Thus, their conclusion may have been incorrect because they were unable to study a long-enough period.

A rise in rate of admissions between 1930 and 1972 could be explained by the enormous growth of mental health facilities after World War II. If this were the explanation, there would be no rise in true incidence, as Goldhammer and Marshall concluded. It is difficult to estimate the effect of new facilities on the occurrence of mental disorder. Figure 7.1 presents inpatient episode rates for the United States from 1955 to 1992 for different types of facilities. Overall episodes rose dramatically, from 1.7 million in 1955 to 8.8 million in 1992. But inpatient episodes rose less strongly, from 1.3 million in 1955 to 2.3 million in 1992. The public mental hospitals, which form the basis of the data in Goldhammer and Marshall, peaked in 1955 and declined thereafter, but the general hospital psychiatric units expanded enough to compensate for that decline. Most of the growth since 1955 has been in the outpatient clinic and the community health centers. Hundreds of community mental health centers were actually built during this period, but the increase in episode rates of outpatient clinics is due partly to hundreds of new clinics being started and partly to increased reporting of data by already existing clinics. The upshot of all this is that inpatient psychiatric facilities have not expanded dramatically since World War II, even though there has been a strong growth in facilities oriented toward less severe and nonpsychotic disorders. Thus, the rise in rate of first admissions for inpatient treatment from 1930 to 1972 (Table 8.1) is probably not the result of a simple increase in availability of treatment facilities.

Some of the rise in first hospital admission from 1930 to 1972 may be due to the increased treatment of mild psychiatric disorders in mental hospitals. However, since the psychoses make up about 50 percent of the admissions to inpatient facilities today, this factor could not increase the rate by more than a factor of 2, even if all of the nineteenth-century admissions consisted of psychotics (Taube 1975). The tentative conclusion is that there has been a slow, long-term increase in the rate of psychosis, yielding a multiple of about 3 or 4 after almost 130 years. This conclusion about the United States is consistent with similar studies in the United Kingdom (Hare 1983, 1988) but not entirely consistent with research from Denmark (Stromgren 1987).

Temporal Trend: Depression

For the nonpsychotic disorders, the data in Figure 7.2 suggests a massive increase in use of outpatient facilities over the years between 1955 and 1992, from less than one-quarter of all episodes to nearly two-thirds and with the volume of episodes rising from 1.7 to 8.8 million episodes of care. This increase is consistent with epidemiologic field studies conducted before and after 1950, which consistently showed that studies after 1950 reported higher rates of overall disorder than studies before 1950 (Dohrenwend and Dohrenwend 1974a). The studies after 1950 reported that as much as 63 percent of the population was mentally disordered, while the maximum percentage disordered reported before 1950 was 12 percent.

These data on mild psychiatric disorders are difficult to interpret. Dohrenwend and Dohrenwend concluded that research investigators after 1950 were more inclined than those before 1950 to diagnose an individual as mentally disordered. This difference probably applied more to the nonpsychotic disorders than to the psychoses. This tendency is also reflected in the growth in interest in psychiatry in general, the growth in the number of mental health professionals and mental health facilities, and the growth in awareness of psychiatric problems among the general population. But it is difficult to tell which is the cart and which is the horse—these factors could be caused by an increase in the true rate of mild psychiatric disorders, or they could contribute to an apparent increase in the rate of mild disorders. Instead of being a response to the stresses of urbanization and social change, the rise in mild psychiatric disorders might be interpreted as a shift in the cultural system, with new values oriented toward freer and more voluble expression of personal problems. Thus, for the mild psychiatric disorders, an ideological change associated with increased availability of treatment in more recent years provides an alternative interpretation for the rise in rates of mental disorders. Next is considered the most important of the nonpsychotic disorders, depression.

There are cultural records of depression in ancient times, for example, the depression of Saul (I Samuel) in the Old Testament (Mara 1975), and the depressive episodes of Rama in the Ramayana, the oldest literature in the world (Rosen 1968). Depression has been studied more or less scientifically at least from the time of Hippocrates in fifth-century B.C. Greece. He felt that depression was caused by an excess of black fluid in the body—a biochemical type of theory that has persisted for two millennia. Cicero, 300 years later, felt that depression was caused not by black bile but by violent rage, fear, or grief. Aretaus, in the first century A.D. in Asia Minor, conducted careful follow-up studies and knew, among other things, that manic and depressive episodes occur

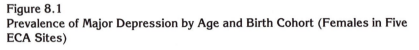

Figure 8.1
Prevalence of Major Depression by Age and Birth Cohort (Females in Five
ECA Sites)

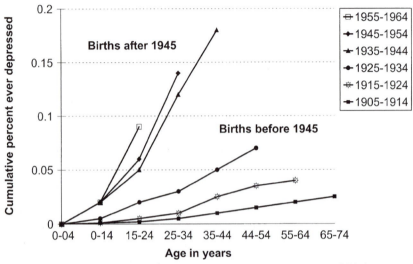

At any given age, cohorts born after World War II have higher rates of lifetime
prevalence of depressive disorders than cohorts born before World War II.

Source: Redrawn from Wickramaratne et al. (1989).

in the same person with lucid intervals in between. In the eleventh century,
Constantinus Africanus of Salerno published *De melancholia*, in which he argued that the seat of depression was in the stomach or in the brain; in the
seventeenth century, Richard Burton wrote a scholarly treatise on depression.
Finally, one of Freud's most influential pieces is his *Mourning and Melancholia*.
Thus, somewhat in contrast to schizophrenia, depression has existed and has
been studied as far back into our history as records go.

   Recent evidence suggests that the prevalence and incidence of depression have
been increasing. One source of evidence is studies such as the ECA surveys in
which individuals were questioned about the first occurrence of depression in
their lives (Klerman and Weissman 1989; Wickramaratne et al. 1989). Persons
born prior to World War II apparently have lower risk for onset of depressive
disorder at any given age (Figure 8.1). For example, consider the cumulative
probability of onset before the age of 35, by which time a sizable proportion of
the incidence of depressive disorder has occurred. Only 2 percent of the cohort
born from 1915 to 1924 had experienced a depressive episode by this age, and
only about 3 percent of those born in the following decade had experienced an
episode. Contrast these proportions to the cohorts born in 1935–1944 (about 12
percent had experienced a depressive episode by age 25) or in 1945–1954 (about
14 percent had experienced an episode by this age). Methodologic problems in

Figure 8.2
Trends in Suicide among Youth (Rates per 100,000 Population)

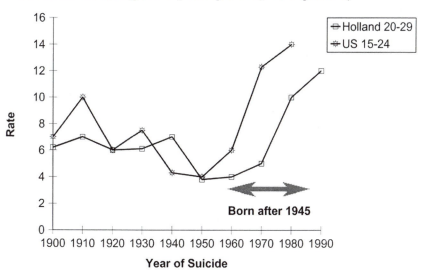

Since 1960 there has been a rise in the rate of suicide among young persons in both Holland and the United States.

Source: Diekstra (1993).

interpreting such data make definitive conclusions difficult (Simon and Von-Korff 1995). For example, it may be that persons with depressive episodes are less likely to reach the age at which an interviewer could ask the appropriate questions, than those who had not had a depressive episode. This could occur if depressives had higher rates of mortality due to suicide or physical illnesses that might be sequelae of depression. Yet the differences are so great that the difference in mortality would have to be larger than is credible to produce an effect as strong as that shown in Figure 8.1. It could also be that older individuals deny or fail to remember episodes of depression, because they are less willing to discuss them or because the strength of the memory of the episode has faded with time.

The findings on birth cohorts are consistent with other data. The only strictly prospective study is from Lundby, Sweden (Hagnell et al. 1982, 1990), and these data confirm the trend of a rise in incidence of depression, albeit not as strong as suggested by the retrospective data: from 1946 to 1957, the rate of incidence of depression among adults was 1.83 per 1,000 per person-year; from 1957 to 1972 the rate of incidence was 4.35 (Hagnell et al. 1990: Tables 48c and 48d). Another temporal trend consistent with the birth cohort findings is the rise in rate of suicide among young adults born after World War II (Figure 8.2, from Diekstra 1993). In both Holland and the United States, the rate of suicide among young adults has more than doubled in the same birth cohorts where the rise in incidence of depression is observed. In conclusion, it seems likely that there has been a historical effect to lower the age of onset of depressive disorder and raise its lifetime prevalence at any given age over the last half century.

Mental Disorder in Rural and Urban Areas

There is a small body of literature on the epidemiology of mental disorders in rural and urban areas. Table 8.2 presents a selection of results from studies in which the same investigative team identified psychiatric cases with the same methodology in both rural and urban areas. For schizophrenia and affective psychosis, studies based on treated cases are included if the case finding was comprehensive, and studies are included only if the diagnosis was made by a psychiatrist. Results for other disorders are from surveys such as the ECA, with diagnosis via survey algorithm. Studies where the population size was less than 1,000 have been eliminated. The use of the rate ratio facilitates comparisons between different types of rates, but the reader should keep in mind the differences in types of rates, especially rates that differ as much as the lifetime prevalence and the first hospitalization.

An early classic study of mental disorders in urban areas was conducted by Robert Faris and Warren Dunham in Chicago (1939) on first admissions to hospitals in 1922–1934. The boundaries of the study did not extend into rural areas, but the pattern for schizophrenia revealed a much higher rate in the center of the city—1.02 per 1,000 population per year—than at the edges of the city, five miles out—about 0.15 or 0.20 per 1,000 per year. (The "suburban" rate is not too different from the incidence rates reported in the WHO study of schizophrenia, described in Chapters 1 and 3.) For manic-depressive illness (the equivalent of today's bipolar disorder), the pattern was described as "random," since the center city rate of 0.13 per 1,000 per year was not very different from the "suburban" rate of 0.05–0.09 per 1,000.

For schizophrenia, results from studies in the 1950s and 1960s (Table 8.2) could depend on the greater utilization of facilities in urban than in rural areas. Both Jaco (1960) and Eaton (1974) report urban rates that are two or three times as high as the rural rates, using treated case data. For the two studies of prevalence in the community, the evidence is equivocal: Lin's (1953) study reports roughly similar rates, while the study by Helgason (1964) shows the rural rates to be higher. Studies of first hospitalization in Ireland and in Italy both show higher rates in rural areas. The strongest methods are in the three cohort studies from Sweden, Holland, and Denmark, which all report higher rates in urban areas. The study of Lewis et al. (1992) followed cohorts identified at the beginning of military service who had answered a questionnaire that included questions on the type of locale in which they were brought up. The study of Marcellis and van Os (1998) and of Eaton et al. (2000) followed a cohort in which the locale of the birth was recorded. The overall pattern is for higher rates of schizo-

Table 8.2
Mental Disorders in Rural and Urban Areas

Author	Location	Date	Type of Rate	Ratio of Rates Urban/Rural
Schizophrenia				
Lin	Taiwan	1953	LTP	1.17
Jaco	Texas	1960	FT?	2.44
Helgason	Iceland	1964	LTP?	0.27
Eaton	Maryland	1965	FH	2.61
Keatinge	Ireland	1988	FH	0.91
Lewis et al	Sweden	1992	C/FH	1.65
Thornicroft et al	Italy	1993	FH	0.38
Marcelis and Van Os	Holland	1998	C/FH	1.65
Eaton et al	Denmark	1998	C/FH	4.20
Affective Psychosis				
Lin	Taiwan	1953	LTP	0.71
Helgason	Iceland	1964	LTP	0.93
Marcelis and Van Os	Holland	1998	C/FH	1.16
Eaton et al	Denmark	1998	C/FH	1.08
Major Depression				
Blazer et al	N. Carolina	1985	PP	1.98
Hwu et al	Taiwan	1989	LTP	0.91
Canino et al	Puerto Rico	1987	LTP	1.26
Lee	Korea	1992	LTP	0.97
Larson	Nebraska	1996	LTP	1.39
Vega et al	California	1998	LTP	1.62
Alcohol Disorder				
Blazer	N. Carolina	1985	PP	0.82
Hwu et al	Taiwan	1989	LTP	1.25
Canino et al	Puerto Rico	1987	LTP	1.28
Lee	Korea	1992	LTP	0.97
Anthony et al	USA	1994	LTP	1.00
Larson	Nebraska	1996	LTP	1.29
Vega et al	California	1998	LTP	1.37
Personality Disorder				
Lin	Taiwan	1953	PP	2.0
Helgason	Iceland	1964	LTP	2.95
Piotrowski	Poland	1966	PP	1.92
Blazer et al	North Carolina	1985	PP	1.89
Hwu et al	Taiwan	1989	LTP	4.67

Notes:

For schizophrenia and affective psychosis, only studies that included diagnosis by a psychiatrist are included. These studies found cases through treatment facilities, except for the Taiwan study, which was a population survey including diagnosis by a psychiatrist.

For major depression only studies that did *not* rely solely on treatment facilities were included.

Alcohol disorder includes alcohol abuse and/or dependence. Only studies that did *not* rely solely on treatment facilities for case finding are included.

The personality disorder in Blazer et al. consists only of antisocial personality disorder.

Data from Larson originate in NIMH grant to David Johnson and Suzanne Ortega; comparison is with urban, defined as towns larger than 50,000, with all other residents defined as rural.

In the study by Hwu et al, the comparison is of the urban region of Taipei to rural villages, excluding small towns. The figures for alcohol disorder are for alcohol dependence.

Date is the date of the publication.

Types of rates are as follows: PP is point prevalence; LTP is lifetime prevalence; FT is first treatment in lifetime; FH is first hospitalization in lifetime; C/FH is first hospitalization for a cohort defined prior to the diagnosis.

phrenia in urban areas, and it seems unlikely that the pattern is due to migration of schizophrenics or preschizophrenics into urban areas.

For affective psychosis, the two community prevalence studies suggest slightly higher rates for rural areas. Both cohort studies show no association between place of birth and risk for bipolar disorder. Together, these studies provide a confirmation, after 60 years, of the pattern reported by Faris and Dunham, (1939)—that is, the risk for schizophrenia is associated with being born or brought up in urban areas, while the risk for bipolar disorder is not associated with locale of residence.

Depression is higher in urban areas in North Carolina and for the United States as a whole; but this pattern is not found in Taiwan and Korea. The prevalence of depressive disorder is so much lower in those cultures, however, that the type of depressive disorder uncovered in these surveys may represent a severe form. Thus, the lack of difference between rural and urban areas in Taiwan and Korea may be reflecting the same "random" pattern as exists for affective psychosis, described earlier. For alcohol disorder, there is a repeated finding of no difference between rural and urban areas. Personality disorder is more frequent in urban areas, by a factor of about 2.

MODERN SOCIETY AS INSANE

Individual and Societal Forms of Insanity

The idea that society itself is insane, even though the individuals in it may be mentally healthy, has become part of our culture in recent decades. Critics ask how a "sane" society could turn out the atom bomb and conduct the war in Vietnam, for instance. Indeed, some critics claim that the closer the individual is to the "average" member of society and the better adjusted to the society, the more sane the person is: but to be in an insane society is a form of insanity itself—a paradox. In approaching these ideas, the conceptional distinction between the individual and society must be kept constantly in view; the paradox is not unsolvable, but it requires that one take on and drop consciously frameworks for understanding the subject of study. Methodologists in sociology have dealt with this problem at considerable length. From their work one can distinguish between individual, aggregate, collective, and societal forms of insanity (Dogan and Rokkan 1969).

The *individual* form of insanity is where the clinician views the phenomenon—at the level of a single person. This form of insanity is not of interest to the sociologist qua sociology, but rather only as social facts may be involved in the etiology of the syndrome or its social consequences. In this book the most relevant chapter to the clinical approach is the one on social psychology, although social etiologies are touched on in every chapter.

The *aggregate* form of insanity is at the level of the population, where the magnitude of disorder is estimated or operationalized by aggregating information on single individuals. Thus, for example, one aggregates data on individuals diagnosed as schizophrenic at the individual level to form a rate of schizophrenia at the level of the population. This is the realm of the epidemiologist, and much of the data presented in this and other chapters is of this form.

The *collective* form of insanity is also at the level of the population, but the quality cannot be operationalized from a simple aggregation of individual-level attributes. In this form it is the quality of the interaction between the individuals that is important to observe—a quality not measured by rates of disorder, as at the individual level. This form of insanity was considered in the chapter on collective behavior, even though that chapter also dealt with individual and aggregate levels as well.

The *societal* level of insanity is yet another form and requires still different operationalizations and concepts; here it is a quality of the society itself that is evaluated. The clinical, aggregate, and collective forms all involve judgments about individuals, and the concepts of insanity used are at least analogous to each other at the three levels. But at the level of the society the concepts of insanity used do not have easy and direct analogous forms with the three other levels, and a society may be very crazy while the individuals in it are very healthy. It is a global property of the society that is evaluated, and has no relationship to individual mental health.

Most theories about the "insane society" are a muddle of concepts and ideas applying to one or more of these levels of analyses at the same time. For instance, as mentioned earlier, anthropologists have sometimes made societal-level judgments about the quality of a culture—a global attribute of a society not related to individual qualities. In some societies the culture is found to lack internal consistency; for example, young persons may be socialized to adopt certain norms or patterns of behavior that are dysfunctional for adults, leading to disorders of some sort (Benedict 1938), or the culture may include contradictory elements, generating role strain of some kind. But in both these cases, the outcome of the process is conceptualized and measured at the aggregate level in that the rate of various types of mental disorders is predicted to be higher in the society with the contradictory or dysfunctional culture.

An error in conceptualizing the insane society, which had existed at least since medieval times at the societal and individual levels of analysis, is the confusion of morality with insanity. If a society does something that a critic feels is bad, that person condemns the society as insane as a prop for his or her ethical argument. The society that produces the means of its own destruction—the atom bomb, for example—must be insane, the argument goes. Sometimes this sort of argument is extended to the leadership and general population of the society, which are held to be insane. Thus, for example, many critics have contended that Hitler displayed various forms of insanity; that the German people had authoritarian qualities, thus approaching a form of mental disorder; and that, therefore, German society as a whole was insane (Adorno et al. 1950; Fromm 1973; Lasswell 1930). These arguments are not scientific, and they mix the ethical with the objective much as medieval inquisitors mixed deviance and sin.

This section considers insanity at the collective and societal levels, as defined earlier. One criterion of poor mental health at the level of the individual is the inability to adapt to a changing environment (Jahoda 1958). If a lack of viability in a static environment is shown, or a failure to adapt to a changing environment is found, and if this failure is associated with behaviors that are distressing, dysfunctional, or "bizarre," the label of *disorder* is likely to be applied. At the collective and societal levels, the idea of adaptability suggests the theory of evolution, with its concepts of selection and the adaptation of entire species— not individuals—to ever changing environments. Population geneticists have distinguished between the adaptability and survival of individuals and those of populations. In the remainder of this chapter we consider, first, the direct application of the framework of population genetics to mental disorders at the level of the population; and we find that the concept of *genetic variation* is crucial to the argument. Second, we apply the concepts of population genetics to the idea of societal adaptation, and we find that the concept of *cultural variation* is crucial. Then we review the work of Herbert Marcuse, who has made the most potent statements about the decline in cultural variation in our modern society. Finally, we speculate about the interplay of genetic and cultural variation.

The concept of variation is central to population genetics. Variation is a population-level concept, with no analogy at the individual level. Genetic variation in a population with regard to a phenotype, such as mental health, can be good because it provides the variety of characteristics upon which the forces of selection operate. The variation can help the population adapt to the present environment, in the form of a *balanced polymorphism*. The textbook example of this phenomenon is *sickle-cell anemia* in African populations (Crow 1966). The gene for sickle-cell can have two forms—the so-called normal gene and one for a quality it induces in the blood cell that gives it a shape like a sickle. Since each gene can occur on one of two chromosomes, individuals in the population can be one of three genotypes: the individual possessing two normal genes (homozygous for the normal gene), the individual possessing two sickle-cell genes (homozygous for the sickle-cell trait), and the individual possessing one normal gene and one sickle-cell gene (heterozygous). The homozygous sickle-cell individual has an anemic disease and often does not survive to adulthood. The heterozygous individual and the homozygous normal are indistinguishable, except that the heterozygous individual is highly resistant to malaria, which is common in some parts of Africa. Thus, in terms of ability to survive in the African environment, the heterozygous individual is superior to the homozygous (normal) individual, who may die of malaria. This circumstance—the balanced polymorphism—explains one of the puzzling features of the sickle-cell disease—its survival. If individuals homozygous for the sickle-cell trait are more likely to die and less likely to have children than normal, how is it that the disease itself survives, generation after generation? The answer is that it survives because of the increased viability of the heterozygous carrier, who, though healthy himself or herself, may pass on the sickle-cell gene to his or her offspring. Thus, the health of the population depends on the maintenance of some proportion of unhealthy individuals in it.

A similar circumstance may apply to mental disorders, most of which have at least some degree of genetic inheritance in their etiology (Table 1.1). Several studies show that mentally disordered populations have higher rates of mortality than the general population and lower rates of fertility (Babigian et al. 1969; Gottesman and Erlenmeyer-Kimling 1971; Harris and Barraclough 1998; Kouzis et al. 1995). How, then, does a disorder like schizophrenia keep occurring, generation after generation? One answer is that schizophrenia occurs in the form of a balanced polymorphism (Hammer and Zubin 1968; Huxley et al. 1964). It may be a simple type of polymorphism, like sickle-cell, or it may be more complicated, involving many different genes operating in numerous combinations, some leading to increased risk for schizophrenia while others lead to a superior level of viability of the individual. If schizophrenia does take the form of a polymorphism, it is of interest to speculate on the nature of the traits occurring in heterozygous, nonschizophrenic individuals that make them more viable. Some researchers have suggested specific immunologic advantages (Carter and Watts 1971); others have hypothesized that these persons might be more creative, speculating that their minds possess the fluidity and lack of structure of schizophrenia without losing the ability to organize their thoughts systematically when necessary (Karlsson 1970; Post 1994).

The purpose of this discussion is to contrast individual- and population-level health. The balanced polymorphism maintains a certain genetic variation in the population, making it healthier on the whole. But some individuals in the population are sacrificed to contribute to that variation. Variation is beneficial to a population because it makes the population more able to survive severe changes in the environment. In fact, variation is the mechanism on which the forces of selection operate so that populations and species can evolve to higher levels. In a given environment, certain qualities may be favored, and the individuals possessing those qualities will flourish, while the number of other individuals with less of those qualities will diminish. When the environment changes, qualities that were less favored may be advantageous in the new system of things. Thus, the rule is that the greater the variation, the easier it is for a species to adapt to new conditions. Population geneticists would be unlikely to recommend a policy for humans that would reduce variation; where this has been tried in plant species, the results have sometimes been disastrous. For instance, corn was bred selectively for greater yield over a number of years with great success (Crow 1966). One year, however, a new fungus invaded the region and decimated the crops, and only the corn that had not been bred selectively survived. Thus, the reduction in variation brought about by selective breeding made the corn species less viable overall, because it was unable to adapt to this change in the environment. Again, the object is to contrast individual- with population-level health. In the case of corn, some individuals were extremely healthy, but the population as a whole was not healthy, because it lacked the heterogeneity necessary to adapt to different varieties of environmental conditions.

Cultural Diversity

The same concepts of adaptability and heterogeneity in genetics have been applied to cultures and societies, and the argument has been similar: as the society's culture becomes more homogeneous, it loses the "healthy" flexibility necessary for adaptation to a changing environment. This argument about cultural heterogeneity has appeared in many forms and is part and parcel of the literature reviewed earlier concerning the sick society. The foremost spokesman for this argument is Herbert Marcuse in his *One-Dimensional Man* (1967). The premises of his book are that society is gradually homogenizing and that the homogenization is curtailing possibilities for future change. Marcuse's argument is directly analogous to the effect of decline in variation in the corn population considered earlier. Much of the drama in his presentation comes from his explicit recognition of the contradiction and paradox of health and rationality at the level of the individual and at the level of the society. His argument is that the rationality of the individual is increasing (or at least stable) but that society itself is becoming increasingly irrational.

Marcuse reviews several different spheres of our society to show that it is becoming increasingly one-dimensional. In the political sphere, he notes that the former distinctions between the laboring classes and property-owning classes are disappearing; the economy is being concentrated increasingly into large companies; academics are increasingly doing government-supported research; in short, there is a blending and homogenizing of the political universe, so that there is no permanent, structured opposition to the status quo.

The homogenization is also taking place in the cultural sphere, according to Marcuse. In former societies there was always a higher culture that constituted another dimension of reality. True art, he states, is by nature otherworldly, involving dream, desire, need, and denial. But "the achievements . . . of this society invalidate its higher culture because the reality surpasses the culture" (Marcuse 1967: 56). The higher culture is liquidated not by denying its values in any way but rather by incorporating these values wholesale "into the established order, through their reproduction and display on a massive scale (Marcuse 1967: 57). Mass communication and mass production have turned art, religion, philosophy, and literature into commodities. For instance, the works of Plato, Shelley, and Freud are available on convenient racks in the drugstore; and while one chooses, Bach is playing over the loudspeaker as background music. In Freudian terms, artistic alienation, which is necessary for art, is based on sublimation. But now immediate gratification has replaced sublimation—as an example, observes Marcuse, compare the absolute, uncompromising, sublimated version of sex in nineteenth-century *Anna Karenina* to sex in modern works such as *A Streetcar Named Desire* or *Lolita*. "Advanced industrial society is confronted with the possibility of a materialization of ideals, and higher culture becomes part of the material culture. In this transformation, it loses the greater part of its truth" (Marcuse 1967: 58). Artists nowadays strive to make their art otherworldly, but to do so they have to break off completely the universe of discourse, so that the communication takes unpredictable forms, as in dadaism or the "random" music produced by some artists today.

Marcuse does not, apparently, begrudge or belittle the working class their reading of Shelley and Freud or listening to Bach in the drugstore, and he does not seem to mind immediate sex gratification or the production of artistic movies for mass consumption. These artistic consumption all make sense to the individual—they are rational; it is just at the level of society that the irrationality becomes apparent.

Marcuse addresses the homogenization of thought and the decline of dialectic in the thinking process. This part amounts to a virulent attack on positivism, the philosophy that recognizes only positive facts and observable phenomena. The positivist and neopositivist critique of metaphysical, nonobjectively verifiable, and inexact notions has remained strong from the time of Auguste Comte, the founder of positivism in the nineteenth century, until today. For instance, G. E. Moore's *Principia Ethica* includes the statement "Everything is what it is, and not another thing"; or compare Wittgenstein's "Die Welt ist Alles, was der Fall ist" [The world is everything, and that is the case] (in Marcuse 1967: Chapter 7), both of which amounts to statements of the noninterference of thought with reality and a denial of the usefulness or realness of mentation in humans. Marcuse feels that science, art, philosophy, and religion are "predicated on the consciousness of the discrepancy between the real and the possible, between the apparent and the authentic truth, and on the effort to comprehend and master this discrepancy" (Marcuse 1967: 229). In the modern world that discrepancy is disappearing.

The medical model of mental disorders is one part of this positivist philosophy; it involves a denial of the validity of the mental experience of the schizophrenic, for instance, as R. D. Laing (1967) has pointed out. It categorizes the schizophrenia as a fact, a disease, and neglects the opportunity for the observer to enrich himself or herself by attempts at dialogue with the schizophrenic; the doctor acts on the disease itself, not the individual, by prescribing a drug.

Positivism makes sense, of course; that is part of the problem. In fact, at the level of the individual, all of these so-called homogenizing behaviors are rational, and this rationality forms one horn of the paradox that is the central point of *One-Dimensional Man*. Marcuse clearly feels that positivism, rationality, productivity, and the conquest of nature have led to a more humane existence up to the present, and it makes sense for individuals to believe that "the real is rational, and the established system, in spite of everything, delivers the goods."

The other horn of the paradox is that these processes will not continue to lead to a more humane existence in the future.

> The industrial society which makes technology its own is organized for ever-more-effective domination of man and nature, for the ever-more-effective utilization of its resources. It becomes irrational when the success of these efforts opens new dimensions of human realization. . . . Such a qualitatively new mode of existence can never be envisaged as the mere by-product of economic and political changes. (Marcuse 1967: 17–18)

Thus, the present technological rationality is nice, Marcuse seems to say, but we could do so much better, and we are cutting down our chances of finding that better life by the very processes that have produced the good life we know. "The society tends to reduce and even absorb opposition. . . . The result is the atrophy of the mental organs for grasping the contradictions and the alternatives and, in the one remaining dimension of technological rationality, the *Happy Consciousness* comes to prevail" (Marcuse 1967: 79).

Marcuse does not specify what that better life might be or how we should search for it; he only says that we are becoming less able to be aware of it as time goes on. His argument takes a form analogous to the geneticists' argument about heterogeneity in the population of corn mentioned earlier—the corn is healthier and more productive in the present environment, but the species becomes more brittle and rigid, curtailing its potentialities for change in the future. In the study of corn, one examines the genetic variation in the population, while Marcuse examines the cultural variation in the population of humans and the reflection of this variation in individual human minds.

This argument provides us with one criterion of "mental health" of a society that fits with a commonsense view: the cultural heterogeneity should be preserved if possible. In terms of this criterion, genocidal societies such as Nazi Germany come out as the least "healthy." Totalitarian and autocratic societies also fare badly. Democratic societies with assimilationist ideologies, such as the United States, are better but still not the ideal. The ideal are heterogeneous democracies where many cultures flourish and where each individual has the maximum freedom to realize his or her own idiosyncratic potential, no matter what his or her cultural background and individual character. It is not necessary that this criterion of "mental health" of a society coincide with other important criteria concerning the functioning of societies—for instance, their political "health." Heterogeneous democracies may be politically unstable, for instance, or the political process may be tortuously slow and inefficient; there is no particular logic dictating that political and psychiatric goals coincide.

Sociogenetic Lag

A recurring theme in the literature on the insane society is the disjuncture between genetic and cultural evolution. Genetic evolution occurs at a pace governed mostly by the forces of selection and mutation. The rate of mutation is on the order of 1 in 10,000 per generation. Most mutations are fatal and do not contribute to evolution. A few mutations are beneficial, but the selective forces operating to preserve the mutation are relatively weak in any given generation, giving a relative advantage of only a few percentage points, for example. Thus, the rate of evolution is relatively languid, being measurable, for the most part, over hundreds or thousands of generations (for the human species, 1,000 years is only 30 generations, a relatively short period in the scale of evolutionary time). The invention of writing, about 10,000 years ago, permitted the accumulation of large amounts of knowledge over the generations. Since that time, the rate of cultural evolution has accelerated, but the rate of genetic evolution has not changed. *Sociogenetic lag* is the disjuncture between genetic and cultural evolution and is a potential source of mental disorder at the level of risks to the individual and at the level of society. For physical diseases, an example of sociogenetic lag is the creation of thousands of new chemicals in the industrial process, some of which are harmful or fatal to humans. Presumably, the body has adapted gradually over thousands of years to naturally occurring substances and might well acquire resistance to chemicals from industrial processes, given enough time. Likewise, production of dangerous new microorganisms through genetic experimentation is an example of sociogenetic lag.

Sociogenetic lag has shown up in works on the insane society, mostly in the form of *alienation from nature*. The evidence is more theoretical than empirical. The idea is that human beings evolved over millions of years in small, uncrowded groups in the forests and plains, and the process of urbanization has happened so quickly that they have not had the time necessary to evolve in adaptation to the new environment. Mumford (Florman 1975) points out that "the poorest peasant . . . is foot-free and mobile"; Ellul (Florman 1975) states that "man was created to have room to move about in, to gaze into far distances, to live in rooms, which, even if tiny, opened out on fields. See him now . . . in a twelve-by-twelve closet opening out on an anonymous world of city streets." The attempts of city dwellers to get out into the country on visits are scorned; Ellul refers to "a crowd of brainless conformists camping out," while Dubos writes of a "pathetic weekend in the country" (both in Florman 1975). Sociogenetic lag is also present in such developments as the atomic bomb, which is a cultural development, requiring, perhaps, a more pacific nature than has been acquired in thousands of years of genetic evolution. It could be that requirements of modern society, such as the adaptation to constantly changing social networks in urban life, are stressful because they demand mechanisms that are not built into the body through evolution.

The situation of sociogenetic lag just discussed and almost all other situations of sociogenetic lag occur because the process of cultural evolution has outdistanced the process of genetic evolution or, in some way, made demands that cannot be addressed quickly enough by genetic evolution. But one aspect of genetic evolution is highly influenced by social processes and may well have changed the prevalence of mental disorders over the last several generations. This aspect is *assortative mating*—the tendency for sexual partners to be chosen on the basis of similar characteristics. There is evidence of strong patterns of assortative mating in the United States with respect to race and social class— blacks tend to marry blacks, whites tend to marry whites, rich tend to marry rich, and so forth. Ethnic selection is also a factor, in that persons marry those whose religion or country of heritage is similar to their own (Mare 1991). The personality of the prospective mate influences the choice, and persons with similar personalities are likely to be more attracted to one another than persons with different personalities (Eaves et al. 1989; Merikangas 1982; Myers 1993). In other words, the notion that persons with complementary personalities are attracted to one another is not supported by the research evidence: rather, "like attracts like" is the rule.

Assortative mating based on personality is likely to affect the extent of mental disorder in the population. As discussed in Chapter 3, *personality traits* are tendencies to behave in certain ways that endure through long periods in the lifetime of the individual and that are consistent through a variety of social situations. Personality traits are best considered as continuous, normally distributed dimensions reflecting predispositions to behave in a given manner. These dimensions bear a strong resemblance to dimensions of personality disorder, on one hand (Nestadt et al. 1994), and to the forms of mental disorder, on the other hand. The dimensions of personality are apparently as strongly inherited as are most mental disorders (Eaves et al. 1989). In the search for genes responsible for mental disorders, no single gene or group of genes has been identified. It seems likely that the vulnerability for the common mental disorders is inherited as a quantitative trait, with many genes having small influences, all adding up to a relatively continuous vulnerability to disorder. Quantitative inheritance involves scores or hundreds of genes, and it is unlikely that the genes for vulnerability for mental disorders form a distinct set from the genes that underlie the dimensions of personality. A threshold may exist for dimensions of personality in the general population, beyond which diagnosis of mental disorder is much more likely (dotted line in Figure 8.3). Assortative mating by personality characteristics affects the distribution of vulnerability for mental disorders by producing more variation (flatter and more dispersed curve in Figure 8.3). An increase in the level of assortative mating in the population according to dimensions of personality increases the variation in the population for dimensions of personality, as well as the variation vulnerability to mental disorders. The increase in variation shows up as longer tails of the distribution, as shown in Figure 8.3. On the "bad" tail of the expanded distribution (i.e., the tail associated with mental disorder as opposed to mental health), the same threshold for disorder produces many more persons with mental disorders (Figure 8.3).

Changes in the structure of mating have occurred as the structure of society and of family life has changed. As noted earlier, the nuclear family is a relatively new development in family life, reinforced by the need for geographic and social

Figure 8.3
Variation of Personality Traits and Prevalence of Mental Disorders

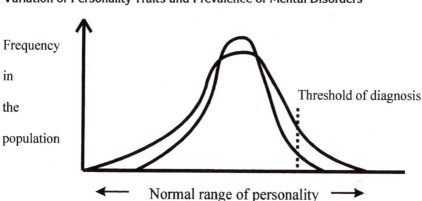

The diagnostic threshold for mental disorder produces an area under the curve and to the right of the threshold which corresponds to the prevalence of mental disorder. An increase in assortative mating according to a personality trait will produce an increase in variation of the trait, with resultant increase in the prevalence of the mental disorder associated with the trait.

mobility in the labor force. The relatively new process of leaving the family of origin behind has changed the nature of the marriage process. In the traditional family the spouse lived with or near his or her in-laws, and the relationships with them and other kin in the extended family were highly important, so that they exercised considerable influence in the choice of mates of their offspring. In premodern Western societies and in many non-Western societies today, marriage partners are chosen by parents on the basis of ascribed characteristics such as race, caste, and social class. This structure of marriage may explain why assortative mating by personality has been only weak or moderate to date (Eaves et al. 1989). Increasingly, however, mate selection is done for reasons of personal compatibility and mutually held values (Giddens 1992; Mare 1991). Ascribed characteristics are less important, and the parents and extended family have less say in the matter (Surra 1990). In contrast to thousands of years of human culture, in the past few generations, personal attraction to the prospective mate is of paramount importance. Symptoms of mental disorders are among many of the personal qualities that may have more influence on the mate selection process now than in the traditional family. Presumably, these symptoms lead to avoidance and rejection, as discussed in Chapter 7. The result is that, for the population as a whole, persons with symptoms will be more likely to marry persons with symptoms, and persons without symptoms will be more likely to marry persons without symptoms. Furthermore, in the era of deinstitutionalization and enhanced protection of civil liberties, persons with mental disorders are more likely to be fertile than in earlier times. In conclusion, then, the shifts in family structure over the past several generations, with consequent increase in assortative mating according to personality, should have produced an unusual form of sociogenetic lag, in which the increased variation in personality and mental disorder vulnerability has proceeded in advance of societal adjustments to receive the increased variation.

This discussion has focused on the interplay of two types of variation that can be useful in evaluating mental health at the level of the society: the genetic and the cultural. There are many sources of cultural and genetic variation (the determinants of sociogenetic lag) other than those previously discussed. It could be argued that the genetic variation in our world is increasing rapidly. The force of selection tends to reduce variation in the population normally, but now it is tempered by modern health programs that increase the viability of a wider range of genotypes (e.g., those predisposed to have diabetes). At the same time, the form of assortative mating is changing, so that mates are chosen for personal qualities such as character and intelligence instead of simple or physical qualities like race, religion, cultural background, and so forth. Both these tendencies increase the genetic variability of the population as to these personal qualities; these tendencies have been operating with increasing force, especially since the beginning of this century—for about two or three generations. But, according to Marcuse, the cultural variation over this same time period has been declining sharply. The situation is almost as if we had a Peg-Board, with multiformed pegs to fit into multiformed holes, except that the variety of shapes of pegs is increasing, and the variety of shapes of holes is decreasing. If this hypothesis is correct, one should expect to see a reaction in the culture to increase the variation; and the type of thing that did happen in the generation of the 1960s— the reaction that seemed to make Marcuse's work out of date shortly after it was published in 1964. During the 1960s one of the dominant trends was the establishment of alternative cultures and institutions to provide more cultural variation and more freedom for individuals who were different from the majority. Communes and free schools were established, for instance. New musical forms were discovered, and new cultural heroes set up. There was also a revival of ethnicity in the formerly assimilationist United States. Even in the field of sociology, elements of so-called *postmodernism*, such as *the linguistic turn* and the focus on *localisms*, continue to reflect this trend (Ritzer 1996). All of these trends contributed to an increase in cultural heterogeneity and, according to our definition, to an increase in health at the level of the society.

Conclusion

It is possible now to summarize and combine findings on the effects of modern urban society on the mental health of the individual. The trend in rate of first hospitalization for psychosis, dominated by schizophrenia, over more than a century shows a strong increase, but the evidence is weakened by the suspected presence of more nonpsychotic disorders in the later data and the increase in availability of facilities in more recent years. The 130-year trend is a fourfold increase, and these factors are unlikely to explain the entire trend. The trend is consistent with the best evidence concerning urban and rural differences of a higher rate in urban areas, for schizophrenia only. It seems probable that something about urbanization and/or modernization increases the vulnerability to schizophrenia, but not to bipolar disorder.

The data on milder psychiatric disorders are slightly more consistent. The trend is shorter but shows a dramatic increase in use of facilities by persons with mild psychiatric disorders since World War II. The urban–rural comparisons from community studies show urban areas to have almost twice the rate of depressive disorder and personality disorder, but there is consistently no difference in rates for alcohol disorder. These studies provide strong evidence because the methodologies are identical in both urban and rural areas and because most of the studies show the same finding. Social factors have the potential for a total explanation—that is, both diathesis and stress—for the rise in rates of disorder. For example, the change in assortative mating provides an etiologic possibility for a diathesis, and the difficulty in formulating the life plan an etiologic possibility for the stress. Thus, the urban critics may be correct after all, and we can continue to search for etiologic clues in the tangled mass of psychological conditions that we connect to urban residence and modern life.

CONCLUSION: THE SOCIOLOGY OF MENTAL DISORDERS

The sociology of mental disorders represents a collaboration between sociologists and the disciplines of psychiatry and psychology. In this collaboration sociology has the opportunity to contribute to the understanding of the etiology of the disorders, as defined in these other disciplines. For the most part, this contribution takes the nature of the social fact—that is, social circumstances that constrain the actions of individuals. Such constraints raise or lower the risk of disorder in the myriad ways discussed in the body of this book.

Social scientists have proposed that factors such as inequality be considered as *fundamental causes* of health and disease, because they continue to exert influences even after mediating causes are eliminated, or evolve into different forms (Link and Phelan 1996). Thus, social factors operate indirectly, as antecedent influences on chains of causes, in which elements of the chain more proximal to the disorder might be called "mediators" by sociologists and, perhaps, "real" causes by biologically oriented physicians. The idea of the fundamental cause thus slips easily into a disciplinary polemic. But notice that focusing on process which are strictly and solely social, or assuming that social factors have casual priority, may blind us to important social processes mediated by nonsocial variables. Thus, in consideration of the social causes of mental disorders in Chapter 1, any casual chain which had, somewhere in its length, a social factor, was included in the framework shown in Figure 1.6.

In spite of some caution about the notion of a "fundamental" cause, it is true that sociology is fundamental in many ways to the study of mental disorders. As we learn more about the brain, we learn how awkward and dysfunctional is the concept of the split between the mind and the brain (Ciompi 1991; Damasio 1994; Goodman 1991). We understand with increasing precision and detail how strongly brain process and structure are modified by experience (Kandel 1998). The experiential modifications are often exquisitely social (Eisenberg 1995). Recent research in animal models reveals that the powerful effects of social interaction and social structure can modify brain structure and function immediately, without the necessity of feelings of distress or even higher mental processing or consciousness (e.g., Jones et al. 1995; Yeh et al. 1996). As the Human Genome Project progresses (Watson 1990), a crucial aspect of the consequences of social life will be revealed when social experiences are combined with the genetic background of the individual. The polemics about gene *versus* environment are receding, and the study of gene environment interactions is in its infancy. Thus, the social environment will provide a powerful tool for helping to understand the effects of genes on behavior—perhaps, with some stretching, this important possibility could be called the *biosocial fact*, in the spirit of Durkheim.

The sociology of mental disorders also provides data and understanding for sociology itself. It enriches our understanding of the fabric of social life, providing new insights into the operation of the basic social processes of stratification, integration, and culture. In this way of thinking, the outcomes of distress and mental disorders are tools of understanding and assessment—much like a thermometer, prism, or transit rod—not ends in themselves (Aneshensel et al. 1991).

Ultimately the most important aspect of sociology for the study of mental disorders is its definitional capability. It is not trivial that the definition of mental disorder given in Chapter 1—bizarre and disabling emotions or behaviors—does not rely on the collaborating disciplines, being strictly in sociological terms. But the more important role of the sociological framework is epistemologic, in showing how we as a group come to define any given emotion or behavior as important. This orientation allows us to temporarily adopt one or another paradigm, comparing intellectual and practical results between them. In this respect—the social construction of knowledge—sociology has no peer and truly is the "Queen of the Sciences." Our definitions of insanity, at the level of society, and of mental disorder, at the level of the individual, come from within us, as well as from the natural world.

References

Abbey, S. E., and P. E. Garfinkel. 1991. "Neurasthenia and Chronic Fatigue Syndrome: The Role of Culture in the Making of a Diagnosis." *American Journal of Psychiatry* 148(12):1638–46.

Adorno, T. W., E. Frenkel-Brunswick, D. J. Levinson II, and R. N. Sanford. 1950. *The Authoritarian Personality*. New York: Harper & Row.

Alberman, Eva. 1984. "Low Birthweight." In *Perinatal Epidemiology*, ed. Michael Bracken. New York: Oxford University Press.

Alexander, Ralph W., and M. J. Fedoruk. 1986. "Epidemic Psychogenic Illness in a Telephone Operators' Building." *Journal of Occupational Medicine* 28(1):42–45.

Alivisatos, G. and G. Lyketsos. 1968. "A Preliminary Report of a Research concerning the Attitude of the Families of Hospitalized Mental Patients." In *The Mental Patient: Studies in the Sociology of Deviance*, ed. S. P. Spitzer and N. K. Denzin. Toronto: McGraw-Hill.

Allison, Paul D., and F. Furstenberg. 1989. "How Marital Dissolution Affects Children: Variations by Age and Sex." *Development Psychology* 25(4):540–49.

American College of Physicians. 1989. "Position Paper: Clinical Ecology." *Annals of Internal Medicine* 111:168–78.

American Psychiatric Association (APA). 1968. *Diagnostic and Statistical Manual* 2d ed. Washington, D.C.: American Psychiatric Association.

———.1980. *Diagnostic and Statistical Manual*. 3d ed. Washington, D.C.: American Psychiatric Association.

———. 1994. *Diagnostic and Statistical Manual of Mental Disorders*. 4th ed. Washington, D.C.: American Psychiatric Association.

Anastasi, Anne. 1988. *Psychological Testing*. 6th ed. New York: Macmillan.

Anderson, Jessie, and John S. Werry. 1994. "Emotional and Behavioral Problems." In *The Epidemiology of Childhood Disorders*, ed. Ivan B. Pless. New York: Oxford University Press, 304–38.

Aneshensel, Carol S. 1992. "Social Stress: Theory and Research." *Annual Review of Sociology* 18:15–38.

———. 1996. "Consequences of Psychosocial Stress: The Universe of Stress Outcomes." In *Psychosocial Stress: Perspectives on Structure, Theory, Life Course, and Methods*, ed. Howard B. Kaplan. New York: Academic Press, 111–36.

Aneshensel, Carol S., and Ralph R. Frerichs. 1982. "Stress, Support, and Depression: A Longitudinal Causal Model." *Journal of Community Psychology* 10:363–76.

Aneshensel, C. S., C. M. Rutter, and P. A. Lachenbruch. 1991. "Social Structure, Stress, and Mental Health: Competing Conceptual and Analytic Models." *American Sociological Review* 56:166–78.

Angst, J. 1990. "How Recurrent and Predictable Is Depressive Illness?" In *The Long-Term Treatment of Depression*, ed. S. A. Montgomery and F. Rouillon. Sussex, England: Wiley, 1–13.

Anthony, James C., William W. Eaton, and A. S. Henderson. 1995. "Looking to the Future in Psychiatric Epidemiology." *Epidemiologic Reviews* 17(1):240–42.

Anthony, James C., M. F. Folstein, A. Romanoski, M. Von Korff, G. Nestadt, R. Chahal, A. Merchant, C. H. Brown, S. Shapiro, M. Kramer, and E. M. Gruenberg. 1985. "Comparison of the Lay Diagnostic Interview Schedule and a Standardized Psychiatric Diagnosis: Experience in Eastern Baltimore." *Archives of General Psychiatry* 42667–75.

Anthony, James C. and K. R. Petronis. 1991. "Suspected Risk Factors for Depression among Adults 18–44 Years Old." *Epidemiology* 2123–32.

Anthony, James C., Lynn A. Warner, and Ronald C. Kessler. 1994. "Comparative Epidemiology of Dependence on Tobacco, Alcohol, Controlled Substances, and Inhalants: Basic Findings from the National Comorbidity Survey." *Experimental and Clinical Psychopharmacology* 2(3):244–68.

Antoni, Michael H., Andrew Brickman, Susan Lutgendorf, Nancy Klimas, Ann Imia-Fins, Gail Ironson, Ruth Quillian, Maria J. Miguez, Flavia van Riel, Robert Morgan, Roberto Patarca, and Mary A. Fletcher. 1994. "Psychosocial Correlates of Illness Burden in Chronic Fatigue Syndrome." *Clinical Infectious Diseases* 18(Suppl. 1):S73–78.

Antonovsky, A. 1979. *Health, Stress, and Coping*. San Francisco: Jossey-Bass.

———. 1991. "The Structural Sources of Salutogenic Strengths." In *Personality and Stress: Individual Differences in the Stress Process*, ed. Cary L. Cooper and Roy Payne. New York: John Wiley & Sons, 67–101.

———. 1993a. "Complexity, Conflict, Chaos, Coherence, Coercion, and Civility." *Social Science & Medicine* 37(8):969–81.

———. 1993b. "The Structure and Properties of the Sense of Coherence Scale." *Social Science & Medicine* 36(6):725–33.

Araki, Shunichi, and Tetsuo Honma. 1986. "Mass Psychogenic Systemic Illness in School Children in Relation to the Tokyo Photochemical Smog." *Archives of Environmental Medicine* 41(3):159–62.

Asch, Solomon E. 1952. *Social Psychology*. New York: Prentice-Hall.

———. 1955. "Opinions and Social Pressure." *Scientific American* (November):31–35.

Avison, William R., and Ian H. Gotlib, ed. 1994. *Stress and Mental Health: Contemporary Issues and Prospects for the future*. New York: Plenum Press.

Avison, William R., and R. J. Turner. 1988. "Stressful Life Events and Depressive Symptoms: Disaggregating the Effects of Acute Stressors and Chronic Strains." *Journal of Health and Social Behavior* 29:253–64.

Babigian, Haroutune M. 1985. "Schizophrenia: Epidemiology." In *Comprehensive Textbook of Psychiatry/IV*, 4th ed., ed. Harold I. Kaplan and Benjamin J. Sadock. Baltimore: Williams & Wilkins, 643–50.

Babigian, Haroutune, et al. 1969. "The Mortality Experience of a Population with Psychiatric Illness." *American Journal of Psychiatry* 126:470–480.

Badawi, Mohamed. 1992. "Household Living Arrangements, Attempted Suicide, Depression, and Alcoholism." Johns Hopkins University School of Hygiene and Public Health, Baltimore.

Badawi, Mohamed, Morton Kramer, and William W. Eaton. 1996. "Use of Mental Health Services by Households in the United States." *Psychiatric Services* 47(4):376–80.

Bahn, Anita K., E. A. Gardner, L. Alltop, G. L. Knatterud, and M. Solomon. 1966. "Admission and Prevalence Rates for Psychiatric Facilities in Four Register Areas." *American Journal of Public Health* 56(12):2033–51.

Bakketeig, L. S., H. J. Hoffman, and A. R. Titmuss-Oakley. 1984. "Perinatal Mortality." In *Perinatal Epidemiology*, ed. M. B. Bracken. New York: Oxford University Press, 99–151.

Baldessarini, R. J. 1970. "Frequency of Diagnosis of Schizophrenia and Affective Disorder from 1944–1968." *American Journal of Psychiatry* 127:759–63.

Baldwin, J. A., and J. H. Evans. 1971. "The Psychiatric Case Register." *International Psychiatric Clinics* 8(3):17–38.

Bales, R. F. 1950. *Interaction Process Analysis: A Method for the Study of Small Groups.* Cambridge, Mass.: Addison-Wesley.

Baltes, Paul B., Hayne W. Resse, and L. P. Lipsitt. 1980. "Life-Span Developmental Psychology." *Annual Review of Psychology* 31:65–110.

Bandura, A. 1977. *Social Learning Theory.* Englewood Cliffs, N.J.: Prentice-Hall.

Barlow, David H., and Cassandra L. Lehman. 1996. "Advances in the Psychosocial Treatment of Anxiety Disorders." *Archives of General Psychiatry* 53:727–35.

Barsky, Arthur J. 1979. "Patients Who Amplify Bodily Sensations." *Annals of Internal Medicine* 91:63–70.

Bart, Pauline B. 1968. "Social Structure and Vocabularies of Discomfort: What Happened to female Hysteria?" *Journal of Health and Social Behavior* 9:188–93.

Bartholomew, R. E. 1994. "Disease, Disorder, or Deception? Latah as Habit in a Malay Extended Family." *Journal of Nervous and Mental Disease* 182:331–38.

———. 1995. "The Idiom of Latah: Reply to Dr. Simons." *Journal of Nervous and Mental Disease* 183:184–85.

Barton, Russell. 1959. *Institutional Neurosis.* Bristol, U.K.: John Wright and Sons.

Bateson, Gregory D., D. Jackson, J. Haley, and J. H. Weakland. 1956. "Towards a Theory of Schizophrenia." *Behavioral Science* 1:251–64.

Baumeister, Roy F. 1986. *Identity: Cultural Change and the Struggle for Self.* New York: Oxford University Press.

Bavelas, J. B., A. Black, C. R. Lemery, and J. Mullett. 1987. "Motor Mimicry as Primitive Empathy." In *Empathy and Its Development*, ed. N. Eisenberg and J. Strayer. New York: Cambridge University Press, 317–38.

Bebbington, Paul E., ed. 1991. *Social Psychiatry: Theory, Methodology, and Practice.* London: Transaction.

Bebbington, P., and R. Ramana. 1995. "Epidemiology of Bipolar Disorder." *Social Psychiatry and Psychiatric Epidemiology* 30(6):279–92.

Beck, Ulrich. 1992. *The Risk Society: Towards a New Modernity*. London: Sage.

Becker, Howard S. 1967. "History, Culture, and Subjective Experience: An Exploration of the Social Bases of Drug-Induced Experiences." *Journal of Health and Social Behavior* 8:163–76.

Beebe, Gilbert W. 1975. "Follow-up Studies of World War II and Korean War Prisoners: Morbidity, Disability, and Maladjustments." *American Journal of Epidemiology* 101:400–422.

Beers, C. W. 1953. *A Mind That Found Itself*. Garden City, N.Y.: Doubleday.

Bell, A., and A. T. Jones. 1958. "Fumigation with Dichlorethyl Ether and Chordane: Hysterical Sequelae." *The Medical Journal of Australia* (August 23):258–63.

Bem, D. J. 1972. "Self-Perception Theory." In *Advances in Experimental Social Psychology*, vol. 6, ed. L. Berkowitz. New York: Academic Press.

Benedict, R. 1938. "Continuities and Discontinuities in Cultural Conditioning." *Psychiatry* 1:161–67.

Bennet, Douglas H., and Hugh L. Freeman, ed. 1991. *Community Psychiatry: The Principles*. Edinburgh: Churchill Livingstone.

Benson, H. 1975. *The Relaxation Response*. New York: Morrow.

Berger, Peter, and Thomas Luckmann. 1967. *The Social Construction of Reality*. New York: Anchor.

Berkman, L. 1985. "The Relationship of Social Networks and Social Support to Morbidity and Mortality." *Social Support and Health*, ed. Sheldon Cohen and S. Leonard Syme. Orlando: Academic Press.

Berkson, J. 1946. "Limitations of the Application of Fourfold Table Analysis to Hospital Data." *Biometrics* 2:47–53.

Bhugra, Dinesh, and Julian Leff, ed. 1993. *Principles of Social Psychiatry*. London: Blackwell Scientific.

Bilder, R. M., L. Lipschutz-Bruch, G. Reiter, S. H. Geisler, D. I. Mayerhoff, and J. A. Lieberman. 1992. "Intellectual Deficits in First-Episode Schizophrenia: Evidence for Progressive Deterioration." *Schizophrenia Bulletin* 18(3):437–48.

Bird, Chloe E, and Allen M. Fremont. 1991. "Gender, Time Use, and Health." *Journal of Health and Social Behavior* 32:114–29.

Bishop, Yvonne M. M., Stephen E. Fienberg, and Paul W. Holland. 1975. *Discrete Multivariate Analysis: Theory and Practice*. Cambridge: MIT Press.

Black, D., A. Rathe, and R. Goldstein. 1990. "Environmental Illness: A Controlled Study of 26 Subjects with '20th Century Disease.' " *JAMA* 264:3166–70.

Black, S., J. H. Humphrey, and J.S.F. Niven. 1963. "Inhibition of Mantoux Reaction by Direct Suggestion under Hypnosis." *British Medical Journal* 6:1649–52.

Blalock, H. M. 1979. *Social Statistics*. 2d ed. New York: McGraw-Hill.

Bland, R. C., H. Orn, and S. C. Newman. 1988. "Lifetime Prevalence of Psychiatric Disorders in Edmonton." *Acta Psychiatrica Scandinavica* 77(Suppl. 338):24–32.

Blashfield, Roger K., and Kenneth Fuller. 1996. "Predicting the DSM-V." *The Journal of Nervous and Mental Disease* 184(1):4–7.

Blau, P. M., and O. D. Duncan. 1967. *The American Occupational Structure*. New York: Wiley.

Blazer, D. G., L. K. George, R. Landerman, M. Pennybacker, M. L. Melville, M. Woodbury, K. G. Manton, D. Jordan, and B. Z. Locke. 1985. "Psychiatric Disorders: A Rural/Urban Comparison." *Archives of General Psychiatry* 42651–56.

Bleuler, Eugen. 1924. *Textbook of Psychiatry*, trans. by A. A. Brill. New York: Macmillan.

Blum, J. 1978. "On Changes in Psychiatric Diagnosis over Time." *American Psychologist* 1017–31.

Bockoven, J. S. 1956. "Moral Treatment in American Psychiatry." *Journal of Nervous and Mental Disease* 124:292–331.

Bolla-Wilson, K., R. Wilson, and M. Bleecker. 1988. "Conditioning of Physical Symptoms after Neurotoxic Exposure." *Journal of Occupational Medicine* 30:684–86.

Borgatta, Edgar F. 1961. "Role Playing Specification, Personality, and Performance." *Sociometry* 24:218–33.

———. 1964. "The Structure of Personality Characteristics." *Behavioral Science* 9:8–17.

Boss, Leslie. 1997. "Epidemic Hysteria: A Review of the Published Literature." *Epidemiologic Reviews* 19(2):233–43.

Boxer, Peter A. 1985. "Occupational Mass Psychogenic Illness: History, Prevention, and Management." *Journal of Occupational Medicine* 27(12):867–72.

Boxer, Peter A., Mitchell Singal, and Richard W. Hartle. 1984. "An Epidemic of Psychogenic Illness in an Electronics Plant." *Journal of Occupational Medicine* 26(5):381–85.

Bracken, M. B., ed. 1984. *Perinatal Epidemiology*. New York: Oxford University Press.

Braginsky, Benjamin, M. Grosse, and K. Ring. 1966. "Controlling Outcomes through Impression-Management." *Journal of Consulting Psychology* 30:295–300.

Brewer, M. 1975. "Erhard Seminars Training: We're Gonna Tear You Down and Put You Back Together." *Psychology Today* 9:35ff.

Brockman, J., C. D'Arcy, and L. Edmonds. 1979. "Facts or Artifacts? Changing Public Attitudes toward the Mentally Ill." *Social Science and Medicine* 13A:673–82.

Brothers, L. 1989. "A Biological Perspective on Empathy." *American Journal of Psychiatry* 146:10–19.

Brown, G., and J.L.T. Birley. 1968. "Crises and Life Changes and the Onset of Schizophrenia." *Journal of Health and Social Behavior* 9:203–14.

Brown, G. W., M. N. Bhrolchain, and T. Harris. 1975. "Social Class and Psychiatric Disturbance among Women in an Urban Population." *Sociology* 225–54.

Brown, G. W., J.L.T. Birley, and J. K. Wing. 1972. "Influence of Family Life on the Course of Schizophrenic Disorders: A Replication." *British Journal of Psychiatry* 121:241–58.

Brown, G. W., and T. Harris. 1978. *The Social Origins of Depression: A Study of Psychiatric Disorder in Women*. London: Tavistock.

———, ed. 1989. *Life Events and Illness*. New York: Guilford.

Brown, Roger. 1965. *Social Psychology*. New York: Free Press.

Bruce, Martha L., David T. Takeuchi, and Phillip J. Leaf. 1991. "Poverty and Psychiatric Status." *Archives of General Psychiatry* 48:470–74.

Bruch, Hilde. 1973. *Eating Disorders*. New York: Basic Books.

Bryson S. E., B. S. Clark and I. M. Smith. 1988. "First Report of a Canadian Epidemiological Study of Autistic Syndromes." *Journal of Child Psychology and Psychiatry* 29(4):433–45.

Buchwald, Dedra, Paul R. Cheney, Daniel L. Peterson, Berch Henry, Susan B. Wormsely, Ann Geiger, Dharam V. Ablashi, S. Z. Salahuddin, Carl Saxinger, Royce Biddle, Ron Kikinis, Ferenc A. Jolesz, Thomas Folks, N. Balachandran, James B. Peter, Robert C. Gallo, and Anthony L. Komaroff. 1992. "A Chronic Illness Characterized by Fatigue, Neurologic and Immunologic Disorders, and Active Human Herpesvirus Type 6 Infection." *Annals of Internal Medicine* 116(2):103–13.

Bullard, R, ed. 1993. "Confronting Environmental Racism: Voices from the Grassroots." Boston: South End Press.

Burke, P. J. 1991. "Identity Process and Social Stress." *American Sociological Review* 56:836–49.

———. 1996. "Social Identities and Psychosocial Stress." In *Psychosocial Stress: Perspectives on Structure, Theory, Life Course, and Methods*, ed. Howard B. Kaplan. New York: Academic Press, 141–74.

Burton, Russell P. D. 1998. "Global Integrative Meaning as a Mediating Factor in the Relationship between Social Roles and Psychological Distress." *Journal of Health and Social Behavior* 39:201–215.

Bury, M. R. 1986. "Social Constructionism and the Development of Medical Sociology." *Sociology of Health & Illness* 8(2):137–69.

Butler, Neville R., and Eva D. Alberman. 1969. "Perinatal Problems: The Second Report of the 1958 British Perinatal Survey." Edinburgh: E. & S. Livingston.

Calhoun, J. B. 1962. "Population Density and Social Pathology." *Scientific American* 206:138–48.

Calinicos, A., and Harman, C. 1989. *The Changing Working Class*. Chicago: Bookmarks.

Callahan, Leigh F., Raye H. Brooks, and Theodore Pincus. 1988. "Further Analysis of Learned Helplessness in Rheumatoid Arthritis Using a 'Rheumatology Attitudes Index'." *The Journal of Rheumatology* 15(3):418–26.

Campbell, D., and J. Stanley. 1975. "On the Conflicts between Biological and Social Evolution." *American Psychologist* 30(December).

Campbell, Donald T., and Julian C. Stanley. 1971. *Experimental and Quasi-Experimental Designs for Research*. Chicago: Rand McNally and Company.

Canino, G., H. Bird, P. Shrout, M. Rubio-Stipec, M. Bravo, R. Martinez, M. Sesman, and L. Guevara. 1987. "The Prevalence of Specific Psychiatric Disorders in Puerto Rico." *Archives of General Psychiatry* 44:727–35.

Cannon, W. B. 1942. "Voodoo Death." *American Anthropologist* 44:169–81.

Caplan, G. 1961. *An Approach to Community Mental Health*. New York: Grune & Stratton.

———. 1964. *Principles of Preventive Psychiatry*. New York: Basic Books.

Cappella, J. N. 1991. "The Biological Origins of Automated Patterns of Human Interaction." *Communication Theory* 1:4–35.

Caprara, Gian-Vittorio, and Philip G. Zimbardo. 1996. "Aggregation and Amplification of Marginal Deviations in the Social Construction of Personality and Maladjustment." *European Journal of Personality* 10(2):79–110.

Carnahan, D., W. Gove, and O. Galle. 1975. "Urbanization, Population Density, and Overcrowding." *Social Forces* 53:62–72.

Carson, Rachel (1962) 1994. *Silent Spring*. New York: Houghton Mifflin.

Carter, M., and C. Watts. 1971. "Possible Biological Advantages among Schizophrenics." *British Journal of Psychiatry* 118:453–60.

Caspi, Avshalom, and Terrie E. Moffitt. 1995. "The Continuity of Maladaptive Behavior:

From Description to Understanding in the Study of Antisocial Behavior." In *Developmental Psychopathology, Volume 2: Risk, Disorder, and Adaptation*, ed. Dante Cicchetti and Donald J. Cohen. New York: John Wiley & Sons, 472–511.

Cavalli-Sforza, L. L., and P.P.A. Menozi. 1994. *The History and Geography of Human Genes*. Princeton, N.J.: Princeton University Press.

Chambless, Dianne L., and Martha M. Gillis. 1993. "Cognitive Therapy of Anxiety Disorders." *Journal of Consulting and Clinical Psychology* 61(2):248–60.

Chang, C. C., R. R. Ruhl., J. M. Halpern, et al. 1993. "The Sick Building Syndrome. I. Definition and Epidemiological Considerations." *Journal of Asthma* 30:297–308.

Cheng, Sheung-Tak. 1996. "A Critical Review of Chinese Koro." *Culture, Medicine, & Psychiatry* 20:67–82.

Cherlin, Andrew J. 1999. *Public and Private Families: An Introduction*. 2d ed. Boston: McGraw Hill.

Cherlin, A., F. Furstenberg, L. Chase-Lansdale, K. Kiernan, P. Robbins, D. Morrison, and J. Teitler. 1991. "Longitudinal Studies of Effects of Divorce on Children in Great Britain and the United States." *Science* 253:1386–88.

Cherlin, Andrew, Lindsay Chase-Lansdale, and Christine McRae. 1998. "Effects of Parental Divorce on Mental Health throughout the Life Course." *American Sociological Review* 63(2):239–49.

Chomsky, Noam. 1989. *Necessary Illusions: Thought Control in Democratic Societies*. Boston: South End Press.

Chowdhury, Arabinda N. 1996. "The Definition and Classification of Koro." *Culture, Medicine, & Psychiatry* 20:41–65.

Ciompi, Luc. 1991. "Affects as Central Organising and Integrating Factors: A New Psychosocial/Biological Model for the Psyche." *British Journal of Psychiatry* 159: 97–105.

Clark, Michael R., Wayne Katon, Joan Russo, Phalla Kith, Mariana Sintay, and Dedra Buchwald. 1995. "Chronic Fatigue: Risk Factors for Symptom Persistence in a 2½ Year Follow-Up Study." *American Journal of Medicine* 98:187–95.

Clarkin, John F., Paul A. Pilkonis, and Kathryn M. Magruder. 1996. "Psychotherapy of Depression: Implications for Reform of the Health Care System." *Archives of General Psychiatry* 53:717–23.

Clausen, J. A., N. G. Pfeffer, and C. L. Cuffine. 1982. "Help-Seeking in Severe Mental Illness." In *Symptoms, Illness Behavior, and Help-Seeking*, ed. D. Mechanic. New Brunswick, N.J.: Rutgers University Press.

Cobb, S. 1976. "Social Support as a Moderator of Life Stress." *Psychosomatic Medicine* 38(5):300–314.

Cohen, Patricia, and Jacob Cohen. 1984. "The Clinician's Illusion." *Archives of General Psychiatry* 41:1178–82.

Cohen, Sheldon, Ronald C. Kessler, and L. Underwood Gordon, ed. 1995. *Measuring Stress: A Guide for Health and Social Scientists*. New York: Oxford University Press.

Cohen, Sheldon, and Thomas A. Wills. 1985. "Stress, Social Support and the Buffering Hypothesis." *Psychological Bulletin* 98(2):310–57.

Cole, Thomas B., Terence L. Chorba, and John M. Horan. 1990. "Patterns of Transmission of Epidemic Hysteria in a School." *Epidemiology* 1(3):212–18.

Colligan, Michael J., and Lawrence R. Murphy. 1979. "Mass Psychogenic Illness in Organizations: An Overview." *Journal of Occupational Psychology* 52:77–90.

Colligan, Michael J., James W. Pennebaker, and Lawrence R. Murphy, ed. 1982. *Mass Psychogenic Illness: A Social Psychological Analysis*. Hillsdale, N.J.: Lawrence Erlbaum Associates.

Collins, Randall. 1994. *Four Sociological Traditions*. New York: Oxford University Press.

Commission on Chronic Illness. 1957. *Chronic Illness in the United States*. Cambridge: Harvard University Press.

Commission on Lunacy (1855) 1971. *Report on Insanity and Idiocy in Massachusetts*. Boston: Harvard University Press.

Comprehensive Clinical Evaluation Program. 1996. "Comprehensive Clinical Evaluation Program for Persian Gulf War Veterans: CCEP Report on 18,598 Participants." http://www.ha.osd.mil/pgulg/18k-1.

Conger, R. D., K. J. Conger, G. H. Elder, F. O. Lorenz, R. L. Simons, and L. B. Whitbeck. 1992. "A Family Process Model of Economic Hardship and Adjustment of Early Adolescent Boys." *Child Development* 63:526–41.

Conger, R. D., G. H. Elder, F. O. Lorenz, K. J. Conger, and R. L. Simons. 1990. "Linking Economic Hardship to Marital Quality and Instability." *Journal of Marriage and the Family* 52:643–56.

Conrad, Peter, and Joseph W. Schneider. 1980. "Looking at Levels of Medicalization: A Comment on Strong's Critique of the Thesis of Medical Imperialism." *Social Science & Medicine* 14A:75–79.

———. 1992. *Deviance and Medicalization: From Badness to Sickness*. Expanded ed. Philadelphia: Temple University Press.

Cooper, B., and H. G. Morgan. 1973. *Epidemiological Psychiatry*. Springfield, Ill.: Charles C. Thomas.

Cooper, Cary L., and Roy Payne, ed. 1991. *Personality and Stress: Individual Differences in the Stress Process*. New York: John Wiley & Sons.

Cooper, John. 1995. "On the Publication of the Diagnostic and Statistical Manual of Mental Disorders: Fourth Edition (DSM-IV)." *British Journal of Psychiatry* 166: 4–8.

Costa, P. T., and R. R. McCrae. 1988. "Personality in Adulthood: A Six Year Longitudinal Study of Self-Reports and Spouse Ratings on the NEO Personality Inventory." *Journal of Personality and Social Psychology* 54:853–63.

———. 1992. "The Five-Factor Model of Personality and Its Relevance to Personality Disorders." *Journal of Personality Disorders* 6:343–59.

Cowan, P. A., and E. M. Hetherington, ed. 1991. *Family Transitions*. Hillsdale, N.J.: Lawrence Erlbaum Associates.

Cowen, E. M., A. Pederson, H. Babigian, L. Izo, and M. A. Trost. 1973. "Long-term Follow-up of Early Detected Vulnerable Children." *Journal of Consulting and Clinical Psychology* 41:438–46.

Cox, Martha J., and Blair Paley. 1997. "Families as Systems." *Annual Review of Psychology* 48:243–67.

Coyne, J. C., T. L. Schwenk, and S. Fechner-Bates. 1995. "Nondetection of Depression by Primary Care Physicians Reconsidered." *General Hospital Psychiatry* 17:3–12.

Crandall, C. S. 1988. "Social Contagion of Binge Eating." *Journal of Personality and Social Psychology* 55:588–98.

Crider, A. 1970. "Experimental Studies of Conflict-Produced Stress." In *Social Stress*, ed. S. Levine and N. Scotch. Chicago: Aldine.

Cross-National Collaborative Group. 1992. "The Changing Rate of Major Depression: Cross-National Comparisons." *Journal of the American Medical Association* 268: 3098–3105.

Crow, James. 1966. *Genetics Notes*. Minneapolis: Burgess.

Crow, T. J. 1991. "The Origins of Psychosis and 'The Descent of Man.' " *British Journal of Psychiatry* 159 (suppl. 14):76–82.

Crow, T. J., D. J. Done, and A. Sacker. 1996. "Birth Cohort Study of the Antecedents of Psychosis: Ontogeny as Witness to Phylogenetic Origins." In *Search for the Causes of Schizophrenia*, vol. 3, ed. H. Hafner and W. F. Gattaz. Heidelberg: Springer, 3–20.

Damasio, Antonio R. 1994. *Descartes' Error: Emotion, Reason, and the Human Brain.* New York: Avon.

Dare, Christopher, Ivan Eisler, Mireille Colahan, Catharine Crowther, Rob Senior, and Eia Asen. 1995. "The Listening Heart and the Chi Square: Clinical and Empirical Perceptions in the Family Therapy of Anorexia Nervosa." *Journal of Family Therapy* 17:31–57.

David, Anthony S., and Simon C. Wessely. 1995. "The Legend of Camelford: Medical Consequences of a Water Pollution Accident." *Journal of Psychosomatic Research* 39(1):1–9.

Davis, K., and W. Moore. 1974. "Some Principles of Stratification." In *Social Stratification: A Reader*, ed. J. Lopreato and L. S. Lewis. New York: Harper & Row.

Dawkins, Richard. 1976. *The Selfish Gene*. Oxford: Oxford University Press.

Dawson, David M., and Thomas D. Sabin. 1993. "History and Epidemiology." In *Chronic Fatigue Syndrome*, ed. David M. Dawson and Thomas D. Sabin. Boston: Little, Brown.

Deale, A., T. Chalder, I. Marks, and S. Wessely. 1997. "A Randomised Controlled Trial of Cognitive Behavior versus Relaxation Therapy for Chronic Fatigue Syndrome." *American Journal of Psychiatry* 154:408–14.

DeFraites, Robert F., Robert Wanat, Ann E. Norwood, Stephen Williams, David Cowan, and Timothy Callahan. 1992. "Investigation of a Suspected Outbreak of an Unknown Disease among Veterans of Operation Desert Shield/Storm, 123rd Army Reserve Command, Fort Benjamin Harrison, Indiana, April, 1992."

de Girolamo, G., and J. H. Reich. 1993. *Personality Disorders*. Geneva: World Health Organization.

Demitrack, Mark A., and Susan E. Abbey, eds. 1996. *Chronic Fatigue Syndrome: An Integrative Approach to Evaluation and Treatment*. New York: Guilford.

Deutsch, A. 1949. *The Mentally Ill in America: A History of Their Care and Treatment from Colonial Times*. New York: Columbia University Press.

Devereux, G. 1980. *Basic Problems of Ethnopsychiatry*. Chicago: University of Chicago Press.

Diekstra, R.F.W. 1993. "The Epidemiology of Suicide and Parasuicide." *Acta Psychiatrica Scandinavica* 371(suppl.):9–20.

Dion, K. L., R. S. Baron, and N. Miller. 1970. "Why Do Groups Make Riskier Decisions Than Individuals?" In *Advances in Experimental Social Psychology*, vol. 5, ed. L. Berkowitz. New York: Academic Press.

Dishion, T. J., and D. W. Andrews. 1995. "Preventing Escalation in Problem Behaviors with High-Risk Young Adolescents: Immediate and 1-Year Outcomes." *Journal of Consulting and Clinical Psychology* 63:538–48.

Dishion, T. J., G. R. Patterson, M. Stoolmiller, and M. Skineer. 1991. "Family, School, and Behavioral Antecedents to Early Adolescent Involvement with Antisocial Peers." *Developmental Psychology* 27:172–80.

Dishion, Tom, Doran C. French, and Gerald R. Patterson. 1995. "The Development and Ecology of Antisocial Behavior." In *Developmental Psychopathology, Volume 2: Risk, Disorder, and Adaptation*, ed. Dante Cicchetti and Donald J. Cohen. New York: Wiley, 421–71.

Dodge, K. A. 1993. "Social-Cognitive Mechanisms in the Development of Conduct Disorder and Depression." *Annual Review of Psychology* 44:559–84.

Dogan, M., and S. Rokkan. 1969. *Social Ecology*. Cambridge: MIT Press.

Dohrenwend, B. P., and B. S. Dohrenwend. 1969. *Social Status and Psychological Disorder: A Causal Inquiry*. New York: Wiley.

———. 1974a. "Psychiatric Disorders in Urban Settings." *Handbook of Psychiatry*, 2d ed., S. Arieti. New York: Basic Books.

———. 1974b. "Social and Cultural Influences on Psychopathology." *Annual Review of Psychology* 25:417–52.

———. 1982. Perspectives on the Past and Future of Psychiatric Epidemiology: The 1981 Rema Lapouse Lecture. *American Journal of Public Health*. 72:1271–79.

Dohrenwend, Barbara S., Bruce P. Dohrenwend, Margaret Dodson, and Patrick Shrout. 1984. "Symptoms, Hassles, Social Supports, and Life Events: Problem of Confounded Measures." *Journal of Abnormal Psychology* 93(2):222–30.

Dohrenwend, Bruce P., ed. 1998. *Adversity, Stress, and Psychopathology*. New York: Oxford University Press.

Dohrenwend, Bruce P., Itzahak Levav, Patrick E. Shrout, Sharon Schwartz, Guedlla Naveh, Bruce G. Link, Andrew E. Skodol, and Ann Stueve. 1992. "Socioeconomic Status and Psychiatric Disorders: The Causation-Selection Issue." *Science* 255: 946–52.

Dollard, J. L., N. E. Doob, N. E. Miller, O. H. Mowrer, and P. R. Sears. 1939. *Frustration and Aggression*. New Haven, Conn.: Yale University Press.

Dols, M. W. 1987. "Insanity and Its Treatment in Islamic Society." *Medical History* 31: 1–14.

Done, D. J., Eve C. Johnstone, Christopher D. Frith, et al. 1991. "Complications of Pregnancy and Delivery in Relation to Psychosis in Adult Life: Data from the British Perinatal Mortality Survey Sample." *BMJ* 302:1576–80.

Drillien, C. M. 1964. *The Growth and Development of the Prematurely Born Infant*. Baltimore: Williams and Wilkins.

Dubos, R. 1968. *So Human and Animal*. New York: Scribner.

Durkheim, E. 1966. *Suicide: A Study in Sociology*. New York: Free Press.

Eagles, J. M., M. I. Johnston, D. Hunter, M. Lobban, and H. R. Millar. 1995. "Increasing Incidence of Anorexia Nervosa in the Female Population of Northeast Scotland." *American Journal of Psychiatry* 152(9):1266–71.

Eaton, J. W., and R. J. Weil. 1955. *Culture and Mental Disorders*. Glencoe, Ill.: Free Press.

Eaton, William W. 1974. "Residence, Social Class, and Schizophrenia." *Journal of Health and Social Behavior* 15289–99.

———. 1978. "Life Events, Social Supports, and Psychiatric Symptoms: A Re-Analysis of the New Haven Data." *Journal of Health and Social Behavior* 19230–34.

———. 1980. *The Sociology of Mental Disorders.* New York: Praeger.

———. 1985. "The Epidemiology of Schizophrenia." *Epidemiologic Reviews* 7105–26.

———. 1994a. "Social Facts and the Sociological Imagination: The Contributions of Sociology to Psychiatric Epidemiology." *Acta Psychiatrica Scandinavica* 90(suppl.385):25–38.

———. 1994b. "A Ten-Year Retrospective on the NIMH Epidemiologic Catchment Area (ECA) Program (Editorial)." *International Journal of Methods in Psychiatric Research* 488.1.

———. 1995. "Progress in the Epidemiology of Anxiety Disorders." *Epidemiologic Reviews* 17(1):1–8.

Eaton, William W., James C. Anthony, Joseph Gallo, Guojun Cai, Allen Tien, Alan Romanoski, Constantine Lyketsos, and Li-Shiun Chen. 1997. "Natural History of DIS/DSM Major Depression: The Baltimore ECA Follow-up." *Archives of General Psychiatry* (54):993–99.

Eaton, William W., James C. Anthony, W. M. Mandell, and R. A. Garrison. 1990. "Occupations and the Prevalence of Major Depressive Disorder." *Journal of Occupational Medicine* 321079–87.

Eaton, William W., James C. Anthony, S. Tepper, and A. Dryman. 1992. "Psychopathology and Attrition in the Epidemiologic Catchment Area Surveys." *American Journal of Epidemiology* 1351051–59.

Eaton, William W., Mohamed Badawi, and Beth Melton. 1995. "Prodromes and Precursors: Epidemiologic Data for Primary Prevention of Disorders with Slow Onset." *American Journal of Psychiatry* 152(7):967–72.

Eaton, William W., and Bruce P. Dohrenwend. 1998. "Individual Events." In *Adversity, Stress, and Psychopathology*, ed. Bruce P. Dohrenwend. New York: Oxford University Press.

Eaton, William W., A. Dryman, and M. M. Weissman. 1991. "Panic and Phobia." In *Psychiatric Disorders in America: The Epidemiologic Catchment Area Study*, ed. L. N. Robins and D. A. Regier. New York: Free Press, 155–79.

Eaton, W. W., and G. Harrison. In press. "Social Deprivation and Schizophrenia." *Acta Psychiatrica Scandinavica*, supplement.

Eaton, William W., and L. G. Kessler. 1981. "Rates of Symptoms of Depression in a National Sample." *American Journal of Epidemiology* 114528–38.

———, eds. 1985. *Epidemiologic Field Methods in Psychiatry: The NIMH Epidemiologic Catchment Area Program.* Orlando: Academic Press.

Eaton, William W., R. C. Kessler, H-U Wittchen, and W. J. Magee. 1994. "Panic and Panic Disorder in the United States." *American Journal of Psychiatry* 151413–20.

Eaton, William W., and P. M. Keyl. 1990. "Risk Factors for the Onset of DIS/DSM-III Agoraphobia in a Prospective, Population-Based Study." *Archives of General Psychiatry* 47819–24.

Eaton, William W., Morton Kramer, James C. Anthony, Amy Dryman, S. Shapiro, and Ben Z. Locke. 1989. "The Incidence of Specific DIS/DSM-III Mental Disorders: Data from the NIMH Epidemiologic Catchment Area Program." *Acta Psychiatrica Scandinavica* 79163–78.

Eaton, William W., and Jean-Claude Lasry. 1978. "Mental Health and Occupational Mobility in a Group of Immigrants." *Social Science & Medicine* 1253–58.

Eaton, William W., and J. McLeod. 1984. "Consumption of Coffee or Tea and Symptoms of Anxiety." *American Journal of Public Health* 7466–68.

Eaton, W. W., and K. R. Merikangas. 2000. "Psychiatric Epidemiology: Progress and Prospects in the Year 2000." *Epidemiologic Reviews.*

Eaton, W. W., P. B. Mortensen and M. Frydenberg, 2000. Obstetric complications, Urbanziation, and Psychosis. *Schizophrenia Research.* 43: 117–23.

Eaton, William W., and Carles Muntaner. 1999. "Socioeconomic Stratification and Mental Disorder." In *Sociology of Mental Health and Illness,* ed. A. V. Horwitz and T. L. Scheid. New York: Cambridge University Press.

Eaton, William W., D. A. Regier, B. Z. Locke, and C. A. Taube. 1981. "The Epidemiologic Catchment Area Program of the National Institute of Mental Health." *Public Health Reports* 96319–25.

Eaton, William W., J. J. Sigal, and M. Weinfeld. 1982. "Impairment in Holocaust Survivors after 33 Years: Data from an Unbiased Community Sample." *American Journal of Psychiatry* 139773–77.

Eaton, William W., M. M. Weissman, James C. Anthony, L. N. Robins, D. G. Blazer, and M. Karno. 1985. "Problems in the Definition and Measurement of Prevalence and Incidence of Psychiatric Disorders." In *Epidemiologic Field Methods in Psychiatry: The NIMH Epidemiologic Catchment Area Program,* ed. William W. Eaton and L. G. Kessler. Orlando, Fla.: Academic Press, 311–26.

Eaves, L. J., H. J. Eysenck, and N. G. Martin. 1989. *Genes, Culture, and Personality: An Empirical Approach.* London: Academic Press.

Eckenrode, John, ed. 1991. *The Social Context of Coping.* New York: Plenum Press.

Elder, Glen H., Linda K. George, and Michael J. Shanahan. 1996. "Psychosocial Stress over the Life Course." In *Psychosocial Stress: Perspectives on Structure, Theory, Life Course, and Methods,* ed. Howard B. Kaplan. New York: Academic Press.

Ellenberger, H. F. 1970. *The Discovery of the Unconscious.* New York: Basic Books.

Ellul, Jacques. 1964. *The Technological Society.* New York: Knopf.

Engel, Bernard T. 1985. "Stress Is a Noun! No, a Verb! No, an Adjective!" In *Stress and Coping,* ed. Tiffany M. Field, Philip M. McCabe, and Neil Scheiderman. London: Lawrence Erlbaum Associates, 3–12.

Engels, F. 1958. *The Condition of the Working Class in England,* trans. O. W. Henderson and W. H. Chalones. Stanford, Calif.: Stanford University Press.

Erickson, Kai T. 1957. "Patient Role and Social Uncertainty—a Dilemma for the Mentally Ill." *Psychiatry* 20:263–74.

———. 1966. *Wayward Puritans: A Study in the Sociology of Deviance.* New York: Wiley.

Erikson, E. H. 1968. *Identity: Youth and Crisis.* New York: Norton.

Erikson, R. E., and J. H. Goldthorpe. 1993. *The Constant Flux. A Study of Class Mobility in Industrial Societies.* Oxford: Clarendon Press.

Ernst, Cecile, Gary Schmid, and Jules Angst. 1992. "The Zurich Study: XVI. Early Antecedents of Depression. A Longitudinal Prospective Study on Incidence in Young Adults." *European Archives of Psychiatry and Clinical Sciences* 242:142–51.

Eron, L. D. 1982. "Parent–Child Interaction, Television Violence, and Aggression of Children." *American Psychologist* 37:197–211.

Escobar, J. I., M. A. Burnam, M. Karno, A. Forsythe, and J. M. Golding. 1987. "Somatization in the Community." *Archives of General Psychiatry* 44713–18.

Eysenck, H. J. 1952. "The Effects of Psychotherapy: An Evaluation." *Journal of Consulting Psychology* 16:319–24.

Ezzy, Douglas. 1993. "Unemployment and Mental Health; a Critical Review." *Social Science & Medicine* 37(1):41–52.

Falconer, D. S. 1965. "The Inheritance of Liability to Certain Diseases Estimated from Incidence among Relatives." *Annals of Human Genetics* 29:51–76.

Falloon, I.R.H., J. H. Coverdale, and C. Brooker. 1996. "Psychosocial Intervention in Schizophrenia: A Review." *International Journal of Mental Health* 25(1):3–21.

Farina, A., and J. D. Holzberg. 1968. "Interaction Patterns of Parents and Hospitalized Sons Diagnosed as Schizophrenic or Non-schizophrenic." *Journal of Abnormal Psychology* 73:114–18.

Faris, R. E., and W. Dunham. 1939. *Mental Disorders in Urban Areas*. Chicago: University of Chicago Press.

Farley, John E. 1994. *Sociology*. 3rd ed. Englewood Cliffs, N.J.: Prentice-Hall.

Farquhar, J. W., S. P. Fortmann, J. A. Flora, C. B. Taylor, W. L. Haskell, P. T. Williams, N. Maccoby, and P. D. Wood. 1990. "Effects of Communitywide Education on Cardiovascular Disease Risk Factors: The Stanford Five-City Project." *American Journal of Epidemiology* 132:359–65.

Ferguson, Thomas. 1995. *Golden Rule: The Investment Theory of Party Competition and the Logic of Money-Driven Political Systems*. Chicago: University of Chicago Press.

Ferreira, A. and W. Winter. 1965. "Family Interaction and Decision Making." *Archives of General Psychiatry* 13:214–23.

Festinger, L., and J. M. Carlsmith. 1959. "Cognitive Consequences of Forced Compliance." *Journal of Abnormal and Social Psychology* 58:203–10.

Festinger, Leon, H. Riecken, and S. Schachter. 1956. *When Prophecy Fails*. Minneapolis: University of Minnesota Press.

Finlay-Jones, Robert, and George Brown. 1981. "Types of Stressful Life Event and the Onset of Anxiety and Depressive Disorders." *Psychological Medicine* 11:803–15.

Finnegan, M. J., C.A.C. Pickering, and P. S. Bunge. 1984. "The Sick Building Syndrome: Prevalence Studies." *British Medical Journal* 189:1573–75.

Fitti, Joseph E., and M. G. Kovar. 1987. *The Supplement on Aging to the 1984 National Health Interview Survey. Vital and Health Statistics*. Washington, D.C.: Government Printing Office.

Flanagan, James G. 1989. "Hierarchy in Simple Egalitarian Societies." *Annual Review of Anthropology* 18:245–66.

Fleiss, Joseph L. 1981. *Statistical Methods for Rates and Proportions*. 2d ed. New York: John Wiley & Sons.

Florman, S. C. 1975. "In Praise of Technology." *Harper's Magazine* 251:53–72.

Foege, W. H. 1996. "Alexander D. Langmuir—His Impact on Public Health." *American Journal of Epidemiology* 144(8) (suppl):S11–S15.

Fog, Agner. 1996. *Cultural Selection*. Copenhagen: Agner Fog.

Fombonne, Eric. 1995. "Eating Disorders; Time Trends and Possible Explanatory Mechanisms." In *Psychosocial Disorders in Young People: Time Trends and Their Causes*, ed. Michael Rutter and David J. Smith. New York: Wiley, 613–85.

———. 1999. "The Epidemiology of Autism: A Review." *Psychological Medicine* 29: 769–86.

Fombonne, E., and C. du Mazaubrun. 1992. "Prevalence of Infantile Autism in Four French Regions." *Social Psychiatry and Psychiatric Epidemiology* 27:203–100.

Foucault, Michel. 1979. *Discipline and Punish: The Birth of the Prison*. New York: Vintage.

Fox, M. 1968. *Abnormal Behavior in Animals*. Philadelphia: W. B. Saunders.

Frank, J. D. 1974. *Persuasion and Healing: A Comparative Study of Psychotherapy*. New York: Schocken.

Frank, L. K. 1936. "Society as the Patient." *American Journal of Sociology* 42:335–44.

Freud, S. 1961. *Civilization and Its Discontents*. New York: Norton.

Fromm, E. 1973. *The Anatomy of Human Destructiveness*. New York: Holt, Rinehart, and Winston.

"Frustrating Survey of Chronic Fatigue." 1996. *The Lancet* 348:971. Editorial.

Galle, O. R., W. R. Gove, and J. M. McPherson. 1972. "Population Density and Pathology: What Are the Relations for Man?" *Science* 176:23–30.

Gardener, H. 1983. *Frames of Mind: The Theory of Multiple Intelligences*. New York: Basic Books.

Garfinkel, H. 1956. "Conditions of Successful Degradation Ceremonies." *American Journal of Sociology* 61:420–24.

Gazzaniga, M. S. 1967. "The Split Brain in Man." *Scientific American* 217:24–29.

Ge, X., R. D. Conger, F. O. Lorenz, and R. S. Simons. 1994. "Parents' Stressful Life Events and Adolescent Depressed Mood." *Journal of Health and Social Behavior* 35:28–44.

Gehlen, F. L. 1977. "Toward a Revised Theory of Hysterical Contagion." *Journal of Health and Social Behavior* 18:27–35.

Giddens, Anthony. 1991. *Modernity and Self-Identity: Self and Society in the Late Modern Age*. Stanford, Calif.: Stanford University Press.

———. 1992. *The Transformation of Intimacy: Sexuality, Love, and Eroticism in Modern Societies*. Stanford, Calif.: Stanford University Press.

Gilbert, Paul. 1992. *Depression: The Evolution of Powerlessness*. Hove, U.K.: Lawrence Erlbaum Associates.

Gillberg, C. 1984. "Infantile Autism and Other Childhood Psychoses in a Swedish Urban Region: Epidemiological Aspects." *Journal of Child Psychology and Psychiatry*. 25:35–43.

Ginsberg, S., and G. Brown. 1982. "No Time for Depression: A Study of Help-Seeking among Mothers of Preschool Children." In *Symptoms, Illness Behavior, and Help-Seeking*, ed. David Mechanic. New Brunswick, N.J.: Rutgers University Press.

Gleitman, Henry. 1981. *Psychology*. New York: W. W. Norton.

Goffman, Erving. 1961. *Asylums: Essays on the Social Situation of Mental Patients and Other Inmates*. New York: Anchor.

———. 1962. "Cooling the Mark Out: Some Aspects of Adaptation to Failure." In *Human Behavior and Social Processes*, ed. A. M. Rose. Boston: Houghton Mifflin.

Goldberg, D. 1995. "Epidemiology of Mental Disorders in Primary Care Settings." *Epidemiologic Reviews* 17(1):182–90.

Goldberg, D., and P. Huxley. 1980. *Mental Illness in the Community; the Pathway to Psychiatric Care*. London and New York: Tavistock.

Goldberg, D. P. 1972. *The Detection of Psychiatric Illness by Questionnaire*. London: Oxford University Press.

Goldberg, David P. 1978. *Manual of the General Health Questionnaire*. Windsor, U.K.: NFER.

Goldberg, E., and G. Comstock. 1980. "Epidemiology of Life Events: Frequency in General Populations." *American Journal of Epidemiology* 111:736–52.

Goldberg, E. M., and S. L. Morrison. 1963. "Schizophrenia and Social Class." *British Journal of Psychiatry* 109:785–802.

Goldberg, T. E., and D. R. Weinberg. 1986. "Methodological Issues in the Neuropsychological Approach to Schizophrenia." In *Handbook of Schizophrenia*, vol. 1, *The Neurology of Schizophrenia*, ed. H. A. Nasrallan and D. R. Weinberger. Amsterdam: Elsevier.

Goldhammer, H., and A. W. Marshall. 1953. *Psychosis and Civilization: Two Studies in the Frequency of Mental Disease*. New York: Free Press.

Goldman, Howard H., Patricia Rye, and Paul Sirovatka, eds. 1999. *Mental Health: A Report of the Surgeon General*. Washington, D.C.: Government Printing Office.

"Goodbye, Neurosis!" *Washington Post*, September 7, 1978. Editorial.

Goode, Erich. 1992. *Collective Behavior*. Fort Worth, Tex.: Harcourt Brace Jovanovich.

Goodman, Aviel. 1991. "Organic Unity Theory: The Mind-Body Problem Revisited." *American Journal of Psychiatry* 148:553–63.

Gordon, R. 1983. "An Operational Classification of Disease Prevention." *Public Health Reports* 98:107–9.

Gordon, Richard A. 1990. *Anorexia and Bulimia: Anatomy of a Social Epidemic*. Cambridge, Mass.: Basil Blackwell.

Gottesman, I. I., and L. Erlenmeyer-Kimling. 1971. "Differential Reproduction in Individuals with Mental and Physical Disorders." *Social Biology* 18 (suppl.).

Gould, M. S., and D. Shaffer. 1986. "The Impact of Suicide in Television Movies: Evidence on Imitation." *The New England Journal of Medicine* 315:690–94.

Gould, M. S., S. Wallenstein, M.H.O.P. Kleinman, and J. Mercy. 1990. "Suicide Clusters: An Examination of Age-Specific Effects." *American Journal of Public Health* 80: 211–12.

Gove, Walter R. 1970a. "Societal Reaction as an Explanation of Mental Illness: An Evaluation." *American Sociological Review* 35:873–84.

———. 1970b. "Who Is Hospitalized: A Critical Review of Some Sociological Studies of Mental Illness." *Journal of Health and Social Behavior* 11:294–303.

———. 1972–1973. "The Relationship between Sex Roles, Marital Roles, and Mental Illness." *Social Forces* 51:34–44.

———. 1975. "The Labeling Theory of Mental Illness: A Reply to Scheff." *American Sociological Review* 40:242–48.

Gove, Walter R., and T. Fain. 1973. "The Stigma of Mental Hospitalization: An Attempt to Evaluate Its Consequences." *Archives of General Psychiatry* 28:494–500.

Gove, Walter R., and P. Howell. 1974. "Individual Resources and Mental Hospitalization: A Comparison and Evaluation of the Societal Reaction and Psychiatric Perspectives." *American Sociological Review* 39:86–100.

Gove, W. R., C. B. Style, and M. Hughes. 1990. "The Effect of Marriage on the Well-Being of Adults." *Journal of Family Issues* 11:4–35.

Granovetter, Mark. 1983. "The Strength of Weak Ties: A Network Theory Revisited." In *Sociological Theory—1983*, ed. Randall Collins. San Francisco: Jossey-Bass.

———. 1995. *Getting a Job. A Study of Contacts and Careers*. Chicago: University of Chicago Press.

Gray, J. B. 1872. "Thoughts on the Causes of Insanity." *American Journal of Insanity* 29:277–90.

Greeley, A. 1974. *Ethnicity in the United States: A Preliminary Reconnaissance*. New York: Wiley.

Greenley, J. R., and D. Mechanic. 1976. "Social Selection in Seeking Help for Psychological Problems." *Journal of Health and Social Behavior* 17:249–62.

Gregory, I. 1959. "Factors Influencing First Admission Rates to Canadian Mental Hospitals: III; an Analysis by Education, Marital Status, Country of Birth, Religion, and Rural-Urban Residence, 1950–1952." *Canadian Psychiatric Association Journal* 4:133–51.

Grob, Gerald N. 1971. "Introduction." *Report of the Commission on Lunacy, 1855.* Boston: Harvard University Press.

Gross, N., W. S. Mason, and A. W. McEachern. 1957. *Explorations in Role Analysis: Studies of the School Superintendency Role.* New York: Wiley.

Grosser, D., N. Polansky, and R. A. Lippitt. 1951. "A Laboratory Study of Behavioral Contagion." *Human Relations* 4:115–42.

Gruenberg, E. M. 1957. "Socially Shared Psychopathology." In *Explorations in Social Psychiatry*, ed. A. H. Leighton, J. A. Clausen, and R. A. Wilson. New York: Basic Books.

Gruenberg, E. M., S. Brandon, and R. V. Kasius. 1966. "Identifying Cases of the Social Breakdown Syndrome." *Milbank Memorial Fund Quarterly* 44:150–55.

Gulflink. 1996. "Non-Specific Illnesses in Personnel." http://www.dtic.mil:80/gulflink/ft-leav.htm.

———. 1997a. "Secretary Cohen Pledges to 'Get to the Bottom of Gulf War Illnesses.' " http://www.dtic.mil:80/gulflink/press.

———. 1997b. "Retired General Vesser Name Deputy Chief of Gulf War Illnesses Office." http://www.dtic.mil:80/gulflink/news.

Gurland, Barry, John Copeland, Judith Kuriansky, Michael Kelleher, Lawrence Sharpe, and Laura L. Dean. 1983. *The Mind and Mood of Aging: Mental Health Problems of the Community Elderly in New York and London.* London: Croom Helm.

Guze, Samuel B. 1995. "Book Review of Diagnostic and Statistical Manual of Mental Disorders, 4th Ed. (DSM-IV)." *American Journal of Psychiatry* 152(8):1228.

Haberman, H. A. 1986. "Spontaneous Trance as a Possible Cause for Persistent Symptoms in the Medically Ill." *American Journal of Clinical Hypnosis* 29:171–76.

Hafner, H., and A. Schmidtke. 1989. "Do Televised Fictional Suicide Models Produce Suicides?" In *Suicide among Youth: Perspectives on Risk and Prevention*, ed. D. R. Pfeffer. Washington, D.C.: American Psychiatric Press.

Hagnell, Olle, Erik Essen-Moller, Jan Lanke, Leif Ojesjo, and Birgitta Rorsman. 1990. *The Incidence of Mental Illness over a Quarter of a Century.* Stockholm: Almqvist & Wiksell.

Hagnell, Olle, Jan Lanke, Birgitta Rorsman, and Leif Ojesjo. 1982. "Are We Entering an Age of Melancholy? Depressive Illnesses in a Prospective Epidemiological Study over 25 years: The Lundby Study, Sweden." *Psychological Medicine* 12: 279–89.

Haines, Valerie, and Jeanne S. Hurlbert. 1992. "Network Range and Health." *Journal of Health and Social Behavior* 33:254–66.

Halaby, C.N.W.D.L. 1993. "Ownership and Authority in the Earnings Function: Non-nested Tests of Alternative Specifications." *American Sociological Review* 58:16–30.

Hall, Ellen M., and Jeffrey V. Johnson. 1989. "A Case Study of Stress and Mall Psychogenic Illness in Industrial Workers." *Journal of Occupational Medicine* 31(3): 243–50.

Hall, Judith. 1978. "Gender Effects in Decoding Nonverbal Cues." *Psychological Bulletin* 85:845–57.

Halpern, David. 1993. "Minorities and Mental Health." *Social Science and Medicine* 36(5):597–607.

Hammer, M. 1963. "Influences of Small Social Networks as Factors on Mental Hospital Admissions." *Human Organization* 22:243–51.

Hammer, M., and J. Zubin. 1968. "Evolution, Culture, and Psychopathology." *Journal of General Psychology* 78:151–64.

Hammond, W. A. 1879. *The Non-Asylum Treatment of the Insane.* New York: Putnam.

Hare, E. H. 1974. "The Changing Content of Psychiatric Illness." *Journal of Psychosomatic Research* 18:283–89.

———. 1983. "Epidemiological Evidence for a Viral Factor in the Aetiology of the Functional Psychoses." *Advances in Biological Psychiatry* 12:52–75.

———. 1988. "Schizophrenia as a Recent Disease." *British Journal of Psychiatry* 153: 521–31.

Harris, E. C., and B. Barraclough. 1998. "Excess Mortality of Mental Disorder." *British Journal of Psychiatry* 173:11–53.

Hatfield, Elaine, John T. Cacioppo, and Richard L. Rapson. 1994. *Emotional Contagion.* Cambridge: Cambridge University Press.

Haynes, Stephen N. 1992. *Models of Causality in Psychopathology.* New York: Macmillan.

Hayward, Chris, J. D. Killen, and C. B. Taylor. 1989. "Panic Attacks in Young Adolescents." *American Journal of Psychiatry* 146:1061–62.

Hearst, Patricia C. 1982. *Every Secret Thing.* Garden City, NY: Doubleday.

Heatherton, Todd F., Patricia Nichols, Fary Mahamedi, and Pamela Keel. 1995. "Body Weight, Dieting, and Eating Disorder Symptoms among College Students, 1982 to 1992." *American Journal of Psychiatry* 152(11):1623–29.

Hecker, J.F.C. 1859. *The Epidemics of the Middle Ages.* 3d ed. London: Trubner.

Hefez, Albert. 1985. "The Role of the Press and the Medical Community in the Epidemic of 'Mysterious Gas Poisoning' in the Jordan West Bank." *American Journal of Psychiatry* 142(7):833–37.

Helgason, T. 1964. "Epidemiology of Mental Disorders in Iceland." *Acta Psychiatrica Scandinavica* (suppl. 173).

Heller, Joseph. 1996. *Catch 22.* New York: Scribner. Reprint.

Helzer, John E., and Glorisa J. Canino, ed. 1992. *Alcoholism in North America, Europe, and Asia.* New York: Oxford University Press.

Helzer, John, P. Clayton, L. Pambakian, T. Reich, R. Woodruff, and M. Reveley. 1977. "Reliability of Psychiatric Diagnosis: II. The Test/Retest Reliability of Diagnostic Classification." *Archives of General Psychiatry* 34:136–41.

Helzer, J., L. Robins, M. Taibleson, R. Woodruff, T. Reich, and E. Wise. 1977. "Reliability of Psychiatric Diagnosis: A Methodological Review." *Archives of General Psychiatry* 34:129–33.

Henderson, A. S. 1994. *Dementia.* Geneva: World Health Organization.

Hennekens, Charles H., and Julie E. Buring. 1987. *Epidemiology in Medicine,* ed. Sherry L. Mayrent. Boston: Little, Brown.

Herbert, Tracy B., and Sheldon Cohen. 1996. "Measurement Issues in Research on Psychosocial Stress." In *Psychosocial Stress: Perspectives on Structure, Theory, Life Course, and Methods,* ed. Howard B. Kaplan. New York: Academic Press.

Herbst, Arthur L., Howard Ulfelder, and David C. Poskanzer. 1971. "Adenocarcinoma of the Vagina: Association of Maternal Stilbestrol Therapy with Tumor Appearance in Young Women." *The New England Journal of Medicine* 284(16):878–81.

Hewitt, J. P. 1991. *Self & Society: A Symbolic Interactionist Social Psychology.* 5th ed. Boston: Allyn and Bacon.

Hilgard, E. R. 1977. *Divided Consciousness: Multiple Controls in Human Thought and Action.* New York: John Wiley & Sons.

Hilgard, J. R. 1979. *Personality and Hypnosis: A Study of Imaginative Involvement.* 2d ed. Chicago: University of Chicago Press.

Hinkle, Lawrence. 1987. "Stress and Disease: The Concept after 50 Years." *Social Science and Medicine* 25:561–67.

Hirsch, S. J., and J. P. Leff. 1975. *Abnormality in Parents of Schizophrenics: A Review of the Literature and an Investigation of Communication Defects and Deviances.* London: Oxford University Press.

Hochschild, J. L. 1995. *Facing Up to the American Dream.* Princeton, N.J.:Princeton University Press.

Hodgson, M. J. 1989. "Clinical Diagnosis and Management of Building Related Illness and Sick Building Syndrome." *Occupational Medicine* 4:593–606.

Hogarty, G. E., C. M. Anderson, D. J. Reiss, S. J. Kornblith, D. P. Greenwald, C. D. Javna, M. J. Madonia, and Environmental/Personal Indicators in the Course of Schizophrenia Research Group. 1986. "Family Psychoeducational, Social Skills Training, and Maintenance Chemotherapy in the Aftercare Treatment of Schizophrenia." *Archives of General Psychiatry* 43:633–42.

Hollingshead, A. B., and F. C. Redlich. 1958. *Social Class and Mental Illness.* New York: Wiley.

Holmes, G. P., J. E. Kaplan, N. M. Gantz, A. L. Komaroff, L. B. Schonberger, S. E. Straus, et al. 1988. "Chronic Fatigue Syndrome: A Working Case of Definition." *Annals of Internal Medicine* 108:387–89.

Holmes, T. H., and R. H. Rahe. 1967. "The Social Readjustment Rating Scale." *Journal of Psychosomatic Research* 11:213–18.

Hongt, Jinkok, and Marsha M. Seltzer. 1995. "The Psychological Consequences of Multiple Roles: The Non-Normative Case." *Journal of Health and Social Behavior* 36:386–98.

Horwitz, A. V. 1982. *The Social Control of Mental Illness.* New York: Academic Press.

Horwitz, Allan V., Helene R. White, and Sandra Howell-White. 1996. "Becoming Married and Mental Health: A Longitudinal Study of a Cohort of Young Adults." *Journal of Marriage and the Family* 58:895–907.

House, James S. 1983. *Work Stress and Social Support.* Reading, Mass.: Addison-Wesley.

House, James S., Debra Umberson, and Karl Landis. 1988. "Structures and Processes of Social Support." *Annual Review of Sociology* 14:293–318.

Howard, Louise M., and Simon Wessely. 1993. "The Psychology of Multiple Allergy." *The British Medical Journal* 307(September 25):747–48.

Hsu, L.K.G. 1996. "Epidemiology of the Eating Disorders." *The Psychiatric Clinics of North America* 19(4):681–700.

Hubbard, L. R. 1974. *Hymn of Asia: An Eastern Poem.* Los Angeles: Church of Scientology.

————. 1975. *Diantics: The Modern Science of Mental Health*. Ontario, Canada: Simon & Schuster of Canada.

Husaini, Baqar A., and April Von Frank. 1985. "Life Events, Coping Resources, and Depression: A Longitudinal Study of Direct, Buffering, and Reciprocal Effects." In *Research in Community and Mental Health: A Research Annual*, vol. 5, ed. James R. Greenley. Greenwich, Conn.: JAI Press, 111–36.

Huxley, J., E. Mayr, H. Osmond, and A. Hoffner. 1964. "Schizophrenia as a Genetic Morphism." *Nature* 204:220–221.

Hwu, G., E. Yeh, and L. Chang. 1989. "Prevalence of Psychiatric Disorders in Taiwan Defined by the Chinese Diagnostic Interview Schedule." *Acta Psychiatrica Scandinavica* 79:136–47.

Jablensky, A., N. Sartorius, G. Ernberg, M. Anker, A. Korten, J. E. Cooper, R. Day, and A. Bertelsen. 1992. "Schizophrenia: Manifestations, Incidence and Course in Different Cultures: A World Health Organization Ten-Country Study." *Psychological Medicine* 20:1–97 (Supplement).

Jaco, E. G. 1960. *The Social Epidemiology of Mental Disorders*. New York: Russell Sage Foundation.

Jacob, T. 1975. "Family Interaction in Disturbed and Normal Families: A Methodological and Substantive Review." *Psychological Bulletin* 82:33–65.

Jahoda, M. 1958. *Current Concepts of Positive Mental Health*. New York: Basic Books.

Jason, Leonard A., Michael T. Ropacki, Nicole B. Santoro, Judith A. Richman, Wendy Heatherly, Renee Taylor, Joseph R. Ferrari, Trina M. Haney-Davis, Alfred Rademaker, Josee Dupuis, Jacqueline Golding, Audrius Plioplys, and Sigita Plioplys. 1997. "A Screening Instrument for Chronic Fatigue Syndrome: Reliability and Validity." *Journal of Chronic Fatigue Syndrome* 3(1):39–59.

Jensen, A. R. 1969. "How Much Can We Boost IQ and Scholastic Achievement?" *Harvard Educational Review* 39:1–123.

Jeste, Dilip V., Rebecca del Carmen, James B. Lohr, and Richard J. Wyatt. 1985. "Did Schizophrenia Exist before the Eighteenth Century?" *Comprehensive Psychiatry* 26(6):493–503.

Jewett, D. L., G. Fein, and M. H. Greenberg. 1990. "A Double-Blind Study of Symptom Provocation to Determine Food Sensitivity." *New England Journal of Medicine* 323:429–33.

Johnson, Jeffrey V. 1991. "Collective Control: Strategies for Survival in the Workplace." In *The Psychosocial Work Environment: Work Organization, Democratization, and Health*, ed. Jeffrey V. Johnson and Gunn Johansson. Amityville, N.Y.: Baywood, 121–32.

Johnson, Jeffrey V., and Gunn Johansson, ed. 1991. *The Psychosocial Work Environment: Work Organization, Democratization, and Health: Essays in Memory of Bertil Gardell*. Amityville, N.Y.: Baywood.

Johnston, M. H., and P. S. Holzman. 1979. *Assessing Schizophrenic Thinking*. San Francisco: Jossey-Bass.

Joint Commission on Mental Illness and Health. 1961. *Action for Mental Health*. New York: Science Editions.

Jones, E. E., and E. Davis. 1965. "From Acts to Dispositions: The Attribution Process in Personal Perception." In *Advances in Experimental Social Psychology*, vol. 2, ed. L. Berkowitz. New York: Academic Press.

Jones, E. E., and V. A. Harris. 1967. "The Attribution of Attitudes." *Journal of Experimental Social Psychology* 3:2–24.

Jones, I. H., D. M. Stoddart, and J. Mallick. 1995. "Towards a Sociobiological Model of Depression: A Marsupial Model (Petaurus Breviceps)." *British Journal of Psychiatry* 166:475–79.

Jones, J. F., C. G. Ray, L. L. Minnich, M. J. Hicks, R. Kibler, and D. O. Lucas. 1985. "Evidence for Active Epstein-Barr Virus Infection in Patients with Persistent, Unexplained Illnesses: Elevated Anti-Early Antigen Antibodies." *Annals of Internal Medicine* 102:1–7.

Joyce, J., M. Hotopf, and S. Wessely. 1997. "The Prognosis of Chronic Fatigue and Chronic Fatigue Syndrome: A Systematic Review." *Quarterly Journal of Medicine* 90:223–33.

Kadushin, Charles. 1969. *Why People Go to Psychiatrists*. New York: Atherton Press.

Kaelber, Charles T., Douglas E. Moul, and Mary E. Farmer. 1995. "Epidemiology of Depression." In *Handbook of Depression*, 2d ed., ed. E. E. Beckham and William R. Leber. New York: Guilford Press, 3–35.

Kandel, Elizabeth S. M. 1991. "Perinatal Complications Predict Violent Offending." *Criminology*. 29(3):519–29.

Kandel, Eric R. 1998. "A New Intellectual Framework for Psychiatry." *American Journal of Psychiatry* 155; 457–469.

Kang, H., and T. Bullman. 1996. "Mortality among U.S. Veterans of the Persian Gulf War." *New England Journal of Medicine* 335:1498–1504.

Kanner, Allen D., James C. Coyne, Catherine Schaefer, and Richard S. Lazarus. 1981. "Comparison of Two Modes of Stress Measurement: Daily Hassles and Uplifts versus Major Life Events." *Journal of Behavioral Medicine* 4(1):1–39.

Kaplan, G. A., and J. E. McNeil. 1993. "Socioeconomic Factors and Cardiovascular Disease: A Review of the Literature." *Circulation*:1973–98.

Kaplan, Howard B., ed. 1996a. *Psychosocial Stress: Perspectives on Structure, Theory, Life Course, and Methods*. New York: Academic Press.

———. 1996b. "Themes, Lacunae, and Directions in Research on Psychosocial Stress." In *Psychosocial Stress: Perspectives on Structure, Theory, Life Course, and Methods*, ed. Howard B. Kaplan. New York: Academic Press, 369–403.

Karlsson, Jon L. 1970. "Genetic Association of Giftedness and Creativity with Schizophrenia." *Hereditas* 66:177–82.

Kasl, Stanislav. 1984. "Stress and Health." *Annual Review of Public Health* 5:319–41.

Kavanagh, David J. 1992. "Recent Developments in Expressed Emotion and Schizophrenia." *British Journal of Psychiatry* 160:601–20.

Keatinge, Carolyn. 1988. "Psychiatric Admissions for Alcoholism, Neuroses, and Schizophrenia in Rural and Urban Ireland." *International Journal of Social Psychiatry* 34:58–69.

Kellam, S. G., C. H. Brown, B. R. Rubin, and M. E. Ensminger. 1983. "Paths Leading to Teenage Psychiatric Symptoms: Developmental Epidemiological Studies in Woodlawn." In *Childhood Psychopathology and Development*, ed. S. N. Guze, F. J. Earls, and J. W. Barrett. New York: Raven Press.

Kellam, S. G., M. B. Simon, and M. Ensminger. 1983. "Antecedents in First Grade of Teenage Substance Use and Psychological Well-Being: A Ten-Year Community Wide Prospective Study." In *Origins of Psychopathology*, ed. B. Dohrenwend and D. Ricks. New York: Cambridge University Press, 17–42.

Kellam, S. K. 1970. "Theory and Method in Child Psychiatric Epidemiology." In *Studies of Children*, ed. F. Earls. New York: Prodist.

Kellam, Sheppard G., George W. Rebok, Nicholas Ialongo, and Mayer Lawrence S. 1994. "The Course and Malleability of Aggressive Behavior from Early First Grade into Middle School: Results of a Developmental Epidemiologically-Based Preventive Trail." *Journal of Child Psychology and Psychiatry* 35(2):259–81.

Kelley, H. H. 1973. "The Process of Causal Attribution." *American Psychologist* 28:107–28.

Kendler, Kenneth S.L.E. 1986. "Models for the Joint Effect of Genotype and Environment on Liability to Psychiatric Illness." *American Journal of Psychiatry* 143(3): 279–89.

————.1988. "The Impact of Varying Diagnostic Thresholds on Affected Sib Pair Linkage." *Genetic Epidemiology* 5:407–19.

Kendler, Kenneth, Andrew Heath, Nicholas Martin, and Lindon Eaves. 1987. "Symptoms of Anxiety and Symptoms of Depression—Same Genes, Different Environments?" *Archives of General Psychiatry* 44:451–57.

Kendler, Kenneth S., Ronald C. Kessler, Ellen E. Walters, Charles MacLean, Michael C. Neale, Andrew C. Heath, and Lindon J. Eaves. 1995. "Stressful Life Events, Genetic Liability, and Onset of an Episode of Major Depression in Women." *American Journal of Psychiatry* 152:833–42.

Kendler, Kenneth S., Charles MacLean, Michael Neale, Ronald Kessler, Andrew Heath, and Lindon Eaves. 1991. "The Genetic Epidemiology of Bulimia Nervosa." *American Journal of Psychiatry* 148(12):1627–37.

Kenny, M. 1978. "Latah: The Symbolism of a Putative Mental Disorder." *Culture, Medicine, and Psychiatry* 2:209–31.

————. 1983. "Paradox Lost: The Latah Problem Revisited." *Journal of Nervous and Mental Disease* 171:159–67.

————. 1990. "Latah: The Logic of Fear." In *Emotions of Culture—a Malay Perspective*, ed. W. J. Karim. Singapore: Oxford University Press, 123–41.

Kerckhoff, A. C., and K. W. Back. 1968. *The June Bug: A Study of Hysterical Contagion*. New York: Appleton-Century-Crofts.

Kesey, K. 1964. *One Flew over the Cuckoo's Nest*. New York: Viking Press.

Kessler, R. C. 1979. "A Strategy for Studying Differential Vulnerability to the Psychological Consequences of Stress." *Journal of Health and Social Behavior* 20:100–108.

————. 1995. "The National Comorbidity Survey: Preliminary Results and Future Directions." *International Journal of Methods in Psychiatric Research* 5:140–51.

————. 1997. "The Effects of Stressful Life Events on Depression." *Annual Review of Psychology* 48:191–214.

Kessler, R. C., and P. D. Cleary. 1980. "Social Class and Psychological Distress." *American Sociological Review* 45:463–78.

Kessler, R. C., C. L. Foster, and W.B.S.P.E. Saunders. 1995. "Social Consequences of Psychiatric Disorders; I: Educational Attainment." *American Journal of Psychiatry* 152:1026–32.

Kessler, R. C., and James E. McCrae. 1982. "The Effects of Wives' Employment on the Mental Health of Married Men and Women." *American Sociological Review* 47: 216–27.

Kessler, R. C., K. A. McGonagle, and C. B. Nelson. 1994. "Sex and Depression in the National Comorbidity Survey; II: Cohort Effects." *Journal of Affective Disorders* 30:15–26.

Kessler, R. C., K. A. McGonagle, Z. Shanyang, C. B. Nelson, M. Hughes, S. Eshelman, H. Wittchen, and K. S. Kendler. 1994. "Lifetime and 12-Month Prevalence of DSM-III-R. Psychiatric Disorders in the United States." *Archives of General Psychiatry* 51:8–19.

Kessler, R. C., and J. D. McLeod. 1984. "Sex Differences in Vulnerability to Undesirable Life Events." *American Sociological Review* 49:620–31.

Kessler, R. C., S. Zhao, S. J. Katz, A. C. Kouzis, R. G. Frank, M. Edlund, and P. J. Leaf. 1999. "Past Year Use of Outpatient Services for Psychiatric Problems in the National Comorbidity Survey." *American Journal of Psychiatry* 156:115–123.

Kety, Seymour S., David Rosenthal, Paul H. Wender, Fini Schulsinger, and Bjorn Jacobsen. 1975. "Mental Illness in the Biological and Adoptive Families of Adopted Individuals Who Have Become Schizophrenic: A Preliminary Report Based on Psychiatric Interviews." In *Genetic Research in Psychiatry*, ed. R. R. Fieve, D. Rosenthal, and H. Brill. Baltimore: Johns Hopkins University Press, 147–65.

Kety, Seymour S., Paul H. Wender, Bjorn Jacobsen, Loring J. Ingraham, Lennart Jansson, Britta Faber, and Dennis K. Kinney. 1994. "Mental Illness in the Biological and Adoptive Relatives of Schizophrenic Adoptees: Replication of the Copenhagen Study in the Rest of Denmark." *Archives of General Psychiatry* 51:442–55.

Keyl, P., and William W. Eaton. 1990. "Risk Factors for the Onset of Panic Attacks and Panic Disorder." *American Journal of Epidemiology* 131:301–11.

Keys, A., J. Brozek, A. Henschel, O. Mickelsen, and H. L. Taylor. 1950. *The Biology of Human Starvation*. Vol. 1. Minneapolis: University of Minnesota Press.

Khandelwal, S. K., P. Sharan, and S. Saxena. 1995. "Eating Disorders: An Indian Perspective." *International Journal of Social Psychiatry* 41(2):132–46.

Kiecolt, K. J. 1994. "Stress and the Decision to Change Oneself: A Theoretical Model." *Social Psychology Quarterly* 57:49–63.

Kielholz, P. 1973. *Masked Depression*. Bern, Switzerland: Hans Huber.

Kiev, Ari. 1972. *Transcultural Psychiatry*. New York: Free Press.

King, Suzanne, and Mike J. Dixon. 1996. "The Influence of Expressed Emotion, Family Dynamics, and Symptom Type on the Social Adjustment of Schizophrenic Young Adults." *Archives of General Psychiatry* 53:1098–1104.

Kinzie, J. D., Paul K. Leung, James Boehnlein, Don Matsunaga, Robert Johnson, Spero Manson, James H. Shore, John Heinz, and Mary Williams. 1992. "Psychiatric Epidemiology of an Indian Village: A 19-Year Replication Study." *Journal of Nervous and Mental Disease* 180:33–39.

Kirk, S. A., and H. Kutchins. 1992. *The Selling of DSM*. New York: Aldine DeGruyter.

Kirkbride, Thomas S. 1880. *On the Construction, Organization, and General Arrangements of Hospitals for the Insane, with Some Remarks on Insanity and Its Treatment*. 2d ed. Philadelphia: Lippincott.

Kitsuse, J., and A. Cicourel. 1963. "A Note on the Use of Official Statistics." *Social Problems* 11:131–39.

Kleinbaum, David G., Lawrence L. Kupper, and Hal Morgenstern. 1982. *Epidemiologic Research. Principles and Quantitative Methods*. Belmont, Calif.: Lifetime Learning.

Klerman, G. L. 1978. "The Evolution of a Scientific Nosology." In *Schizophrenia: Science and Practice*, ed. J. C. Shershow. Cambridge: Harvard University Press, 99–121.

Klerman, G. L., and M. M. Weissman. 1989. "Increasing Rates of Depression." *JAMA* 261:2229–35.

Kohn, M. 1977. *Class and Conformity*. 2d ed. Chicago: University of Chicago Press.

Kohn, Melvin L., and Carmi Schooler. 1983. *Work and Personality: An Inquiry into the Impact of Social Stratification*. Norwood, N.J.: Ablex.

Komaroff, Anthony L. 1993. "Experience with Sporadic and 'Epidemic' Cases." In *Chronic Fatigue Syndrome*, ed. David M. Dawson and Thomas D. Sabin. Boston: Little, Brown.

Koran, L. M. 1972. "Psychiatry in Mainland China: History and Recent Status." *American Journal of Psychiatry* 128:970–78.

Kouzis, Anthony C., William W. Eaton, and Phil Leaf. 1995. "Psychopathology and Mortality in the General Population." *Social Psychiatry and Psychiatric Epidemiology* 30165–70.

Kovacs, M., T. L. Feinberg, M. A. Crouse-Novak, S. L. Paulauskas, and R. Finkelstein. 1984. "Depressive Disorders in Childhood." *Archives of General Psychiatry* 41: 229–37.

Kovar, M. G., J. E. Fitti, and M. Chyba. 1992. *The Longitudinal Study of Aging: 1984–90*. Hyattsville, Md.: U.S. Department of Health and Human Services.

Kramer, Morton. 1957. "A Discussion of the Concepts of Incidence and Prevalence As Related to Epidemiologic Studies of Mental Disorders." *American Journal of Public Health* 47(7):826–40.

———. 1969a. *Applications of Mental Health Statistics: Uses in Mental Health Programmes of Statistics Derived from Psychiatric Services and Selected Vital and Morbidity Records*. Geneva: World Health Organization.

———. 1969b. "Cross-National Study of Diagnosis of the Mental Disorders: Origin of the Problem." *American Journal of Psychiatry* 125 (suppl. 10).

———. 1977. *Psychiatric Services and the Changing Institutional Scene*. Rockville, Md.: National Institute of Mental Health.

Kramer, Morton, Michael VonKorff, and Larry Kessler. 1980. "The Lifetime Prevalence of Mental Disorders: Estimation, Uses and Limitations." *Psychological Medicine* 10:429–35.

Kreiss, K. 1990. "The Sick Building Syndrome: Where Is the Epidemiologic Basis?" *American Journal of Public Health* 80:1172–73.

Krieger, N. 1994. "Epidemiology and the Web of Causation: Has Anyone Seen the Spider?" *Social Science and Medicine* 39(7):887–903.

Krieger, N., D. L. Rowland, A. A. Herman, B. Avery, and M. T. Phillips. 1993. "Racism, Sexism, and Social Class: Implications for Studies of Health, Disease, and Well-Being." *American Journal of Preventive Medicine* 9(6):82–122.

Krieger, N., D. R. Williams, and N. E. Moss. 1997. "Measuring Social Class in U.S. Public Health Research—Concepts, Methodologies, and Guidelines." *Annual Review of Public Health* 18:341–78.

Lahey, Benjamin B., Brooks Applegate, Russel A. Barkley, Barry Garfinkel, Keith McBurnett, Lynn Kerdyk, Laurence Greenhill, George W. Hynd, Paul J. Firck, Jeffrey Newcorn, Joseph Biederman, Thomas Ollendick, Elizabeth Hart, Dorcas Perez, Irwin Waldman, and David Shaffer. 1994a. "DSM-IV Field Trials for Oppositional Defiant Disorder and Conduct Disorder in Children and Adolescents." *American Journal of Psychiatry* 151(8):1163–71.

————. 1994b. "DSM-IV Field Trials for Attention Deficit Hyperactivity Disorder in Children and Adolescents." *American Journal of Psychiatry* 151:1673–85.

Laing, R. D. 1967. *The Politics of Experience.* New York: Pantheon.

Lam, D. H. 1991. "Psychosocial Intervention in Schizophrenia: A Review of Empirical Studies." *Psychological Medicine* 21:423–34.

Langner, Thomas S., and Stanley T. Michael. 1963. *Life Stress and Mental Health.* New York: Free Press.

Larselere, R. E., and G. R. Patterson. 1990. "Parental Management: Mediators of the Effect of Socioeconomic Status on Early Delinquency." *Criminology* 28:301–23.

Lasswell, H. 1930. *Psychopathology and Politics.* Chicago: University of Chicago Press.

Laurin-Frenette, N. 1976. *Functionalist Theories of Social Class: Sociology and Bourgeois Ideology.* Paris: Editions Anthropos.

Lawless, Jerald F. 1982. *Statistical Models and Methods for Lifetime Data.* New York: John Wiley & Sons.

Lazarus, Richard S. 1966. *Psychological Stress and the Coping Process.* New York: McGraw-Hill.

————. 1993. "From Psychological Stress to the Emotions: A History of Changing Outlooks." *Annual Review of Psychology* 44:1–21.

LeBon, G. 1960. *The Crowd: A Study of the Popular Mind.* New York: Viking Press.

Lee, Sing. 1996. "Reconsidering the Status of Anorexia Nervosa as a Western Culture-Bound Syndrome." *Social Science & Medicine* 42(1):21–34.

Leff, J., R. Berkowitz, N. Shavit, A. Strachan, I. Glass, and C. Vaughn. 1989. "A Trial of Family Therapy: A Relatives Group for Schizophrenia." *British Journal of Psychiatry* 154:58–66.

Leff, J. P., M. Fischer, and A. Bertelsen. 1976. "A Cross-National Epidemiologic Study of Mania." *British Journal of Psychiatry* 129:428–37.

Leff, J., N. N. Wig, H. Bedi, D. K. Menon, L. Kuipers, A. Korten, G. Ernberg, R. Day, N. Sartorius, and A. Jablensky. 1990. "Relatives' Expressed Emotion and the Course of Schizophrenia in Chandigarh: A Two-Year Follow-Up of a First-Contact Sample." *British Journal of Psychiatry* 156:351–56.

Leighton, A. H., T. A. Lambo, C. C. Hughes, D. C. Leighton, J. M. Murphy, and D. B. Macklin. 1963. *Psychiatric Disorder among the Yoruba.* Ithaca, N.Y.: Cornell University Press.

Leighton, Dorothea C., John S. Harding, David B. Macklin, Allister M. Macmillan, and Alexander H. Leighton. 1963. *The Character of Danger: Psychiatric Symptoms in Selected Communities.* New York: Basic Books.

Lemert, Edwin. 1951. *Social Pathology.* New York: McGraw-Hill.

Lennon, M. C. 1987. "Sex Differences in Distress: The Impact of Gender and Work Roles." *Journal of Health and Social Behavior* 28:290–305.

————. 1995. "Work Conditions as Explanations for the Relation between Status, Gender, and Psychological Disorders." *Epidemiologic Review* 17(1):120–27.

Lennon, M. C., and S. Rosenfield. 1992. "Women and Mental Health: The Interaction of Job and Family Conditions." *Journal of Health and Social Behavior* 33:316–27.

Leventhal, Howard, and Peter A. Mosbach. 1983. "The Perceptual-Motor Theory of Emotion." In *Social Psychophysiology: A Sourcebook,* ed. John T. Cacioppo and Richard E. Petty. New York: Guilford Press, 353–88.

Levine, Paul H., Martin Atherton, Thomas Fears, and Robert Hoover. 1994. "An Approach to Studies of Cancer Subsequent to Clusters of Chronic Fatigue Syndrome: Use of Data from the Nevada State Cancer Registry." *Clinical Infectious Diseases* 18(suppl.1):S49–53.

Levinson, D. J., and W. E. Gooden. 1985. "The Life Cycle." In *Comprehensive Textbook of Psychiatry/IV*, 4th ed., ed. H. I. Kaplan and B. J. Sadock. Baltimore: Williams & Wilkins, 1–12.

Levy, David A., and Paul R. Nail. 1993. "Contagion: A Theoretical and Empirical Review and Reconceptualization." *Genetic, Social, and General Psychology Monographs* 119(3):235–83.

Lewinsohn, P. M., G. N. Clarke, J. R. Seeley, and P. Rohde. 1994. "Major Depression in Community Adolescents: Age at Onset, Episode Duration, and Time to Recurrence." *Journal of the American Academy of Child and Adolescent Psychiatry* 33(6):809–18.

Lewinsohn, P. M., H. M. Hobernam, and M. Rosenbaum. 1988. "A Prospective Study of Risk Factors for Unipolar Depression." *Journal of Abnormal Psychology* 97: 251–64.

Lewis, G., A. David, and S.A.P. Andreasson. 1992. "Schizophrenia and City life." *The Lancet* 340:137–40.

Lewis, G., and S. Wessely. 1992. "The Epidemiology of Fatigue: More Questions Than Answers." *Journal of Epidemiology and Community Health* 46:92–97.

Liberatos, Penny, Bruce G. Link, and Jennifer L. Kelsey. 1988. "The Measurement of Social Class in Epidemiology." *Epidemiologic Reviews* 10:87–122.

Lidz, T. 1973. *The Origin and Treatment of Schizophrenic Disorders*. New York: Basic Books.

Lidz, T. S., S. Fleck, and A. R. Cornelison. 1965. *Schizophrenia in the Family*. New York: International Universities Press.

Lilienfeld, David E., and Paul D. Stolley. 1994. *Foundations of Epidemiology*. New York: Oxford University Press.

Lin, Nan, and W. M. Ensel. 1984. "Depression-Liability and Its Social Etiology. The Role of Life Events and Social Support." *Journal of Health and Social Behavior* 25:176–88.

Lin, T. 1953. "A Study of the Incidence of Mental Disorder in Chinese and Other Cultures." *Psychiatry* 16:313–36.

Link, B. 1982. "Mental Patient Status, Work, and Income: An Examination of the Effects of a Psychiatric Label." *American Sociological Review* 47:202–15.

———. 1987. "Understanding Labeling Effects in the Area of Mental Disorders: An Assessment of the Effects of Expectations and Rejection." *American Sociological Review* 52:96–112.

Link, B., and F. T. Cullen. 1990. "The Labelling Theory of Mental Disorder: A Review of the Evidence." In *Research in Community and Mental Health: A Research Annual: Mental Disorder in Social Context*, vol. 6, ed. J. R. Greenley. Greenwich, Conn. JAI Press, 75–105.

Link, B., Francis T. Cullen, Elmer Struening, Patrick E. Shrout, and Bruce P. Dohrenwend. 1989. "A Modified Labeling Theory Approach to Mental Disorders: An Empirical Assessment." *American Sociological Review* 54:400–423.

Link, B., and B. P. Dohrenwend. 1980. "Formulation of Hypotheses about the True Prevalence of Demoralization in the United States." In *Mental Illness in the*

United States: Epidemiologic Estimates, ed. B. S. Dohrenwend, M. S. Gould, B. Link, R. Neugebauer, and R. Wunsch-Hitzig. New York: Praeger.

Link, B., Bruce P. Dohrenwend, and Andrew E. Skodol. 1986. "Socio-Economic Status and Schizophrenia: Noisome Occupational Characteristics as a Risk Factor." *American Sociological Review* 51:242–58.

Link, B., Mary C. Lennon, and Bruce P. Dohrenwend. 1993. "Socioeconomic Status and Depression: The Role of Occupations Involving Direction, Control and Planning." *American Journal of Sociology* 98(6):1351–87.

Link, B., Jerrold Mirotznik, and Francis T. Cullen. 1991. "The Effectiveness of Stigma Coping Orientations: Can Negative Consequences of Mental Illness Labeling Be Avoided?" *Journal of Health and Social Behavior* 32:302–20.

Link, B., and Jo C. Phelan. 1996. "Understanding Sociodemographic Differences in Health—The Role of Fundamental Social Causes." *American Journal of Public Health* 86:471–73.

Linton, R. 1956. *Culture and Mental Disorders*. Springfield, Ill.: Charles C. Thomas.

Loffler, W., H. Hafner, B. Fatkenheuer, K. Maurer, A. Riecher-Rossler, J. Lutzhoft, S. Skadhede, P. Munk-Jorgensen, and E. Stromgren. 1994. "Validation of Danish Case Register Diagnosis for Schizophrenia." *Acta Psychiatrica Scandinavica* 90: 196–203.

Lorion, R. P. 1974. "Patient and Therapist Variables in the Treatment of Low-Income Patients." *Psychological Bulletin* 81:344–54.

Los Angeles Times. "Recruiting Done over Internet?" March 28, 1997. *Eugene (Oregon) Register-Guard*, A, 4.

Lucas, Alexander R., C. M. Beard, W. M. O'Fallon, and Leonard T. Kurland. 1991. "50-Year Trends in the Incidence of Anorexia Nervosa in Rochester, Minn.: A Population-Based Study." *American Journal of Psychiatry* 148(7):917–22.

Lydiard, R. B., Olga Brawman-Mintzer, and James C. Ballenger. 1996. "Recent Developments in the Psychopharmacology of Anxiety Disorders." *Journal of Consulting and Clinical Psychology* 64(4):660–68.

Lynch, Aaron. 1996. *Thought Contagion: How Belief Spreads through Society, the New Science of Memes.* New York: Basic Books.

Lyon, G. R., and Norman A. Krasnegor, ed. 1996. *Attention, Memory, and Executive Function.* Baltimore: Paul H. Brookes.

Lytton, Hugh. 1990. "Child and Parent Effects in Boys' Conduct Disorder: A Reinterpretation." *Developmental Psychology* 26:683–97.

Mackay, C. 1852. *Extraordinary Popular Delusions*. Boston: Page.

MacKinnon, Neil J. 1989. *Symbolic Interactionism as Affect Control.* Albany: State University of New York.

MacMahon, B., T. F. Pugh, and J. Ipsen. 1960. *Epidemiologic Methods.* Boston: Little, Brown.

Magee, William J., William W. Eaton, Hans-Ulrich Wittchen, Katherine McGonagle, and Ronald Kessler. 1996. "Agoraphobia, Simple Phobia, and Social Phobia in the National Comorbidity Survey." *Archives of General Psychiatry* 53159–68.

Mandell, W., William W. Eaton, James C. Anthony, and R. Garrison. 1992. "Alcoholism and Occupations: A Review and Analysis of 104 Occupations." *Alcoholism: Clinical and Experimental Research* 16734–46.

Mannheim, Karl. 1936. *Ideology and Utopia.* New York: Harcourt, Brace, and World.

Marcelis, M., and J. van Os. 1998. "High Rates of Psychosis in Urban Areas: Effect of

Urban Birth or Residence?" *Ninth Biennial Winter Workshop on Schizophrenia,* Davos, Switzerland.

Marcuse, H. 1967. *One-Dimensional Man.* Boston: Beacon Press.

Mare, Robert D. 1991. "Five Decades of Educational Assortative Mating." *American Sociological Review* 56(1):15–32.

Maris, Ronald. 1997. "Social Forces in Suicide: Life Review, 1965–1995." In *Review of Suicidology, 1997,* ed. Ronald Maris, Morton M. Silverman, and Silvia S. Canetto. New York: Guilford Press.

Marks, Isaac M. 1987. *Fears, Phobias, and Rituals.* New York: Oxford University Press.

Markus, H. 1977. "Self-Schemata and Processing Information about the Self." *Journal of Personality and Social Psychology* 35:63–78.

Markush, R. E. 1973. "Mental Epidemics: A Review of the Old to Prepare for the New." *Public Health Reviews* 2(4):353–442.

Marmot, M. G., and Elston M. A. Koveginas. 1987. "Social/Economic Status and Disease." *Annual Review of Public Health* 8:111–35.

Marsella, Anthony J. 1993. "Sociocultural Foundations of Psychopathology: An Historical Overview of Concepts, Events and Pioneers Prior to 1970." *Transcultural Psychiatric Research Review* 30:97–142.

Marx, Karl. 1967. *Capital: A Critique of Political Economy.* New York: International.

Matras, J. 1984. *Social Inequality, Stratification, and Mobility.* 2d ed. Englewood Cliffs, N.J.: Prentice-Hall.

Matza, D. 1967. "The Disreputable Poor." In *Class, Status, and Power,* ed. R. Bendix and S. M. Lipset. London: Routledge and Kegan-Paul.

Mausner-Dorsch, H. and W. W. Eaton. 2000. "Psychosocial Work Environment and Depression: Epidemiologic Assessment of the Demand Control Model." Under revision for *American Journal of Public Health.*

Mausner, Judith S., and Shira Kramer. 1985. *Mausner & Bahn Epidemiology: An Introductory Text.* 2d ed. Philadelphia: W. B. Saunders.

McCarthy, P., M. Fitzgerald, and M. A. Smith. 1984. "Prevalence of Childhood Autism in Ireland." *Irish Medical Journal,* 77(5):179–80.

McEvedy, C. P., and A. W. Beard. 1973. "A Controlled Follow-Up of Cases Involved in an Epidemic of Benign Myalgic Encephalomyelitis." *British Journal of Psychiatry* 122:141–50.

McHugh, P. R. 1996. "Psychic Epidemic: Anorexia Nervosa," presentation in the Johns Hopkins Medical Institutions Humanities Series, November 20.

McHugh, Paul R., and Phillip R. Slavney. 1986. *The Perspectives of Psychiatry.* Rev. ed. Baltimore: Johns Hopkins University Press.

McKinney, William T. 1992. "Animal Models." In *Handbook of Affective Disorders,* 2d ed., ed. Eugene S. Paykel. Edinburgh: Churchill Livingstone, 209–17.

McKusick, D., T. L. Mark, E. King, R. Harwood, J. A. Buck, and J. Dilanardo. 1998. "Mental Health and Substance Abuse Expenditure Trends and Projections." *Health Affairs* 17(5):147–57.

McKusick, V. A. 1967. "The Ethnic Distribution of Disease in the United States." *Journal of Chronic Disease* 20:115–18.

Mead, George H. 1934. *Mind, Self and Society: From the Standpoint of a Social-Behaviorist,* ed. Charles Morris. Chicago: University of Chicago Press.

Mechanic, D. 1969. *Mental Health and Social Policy.* Englewood Cliffs, N.J.: Prentice-Hall.

————. 1978. *Medical Sociology*. 2d ed. New York: Free Press.

————. 1983. "The Experience and Expression of Distress: The Study of Illness Behavior and Medical Utilization." In *Handbook of Health, Health Care, and the Health Professions*, ed. David Mechanic. New York: Free Press, 591–607.

————. 1989. *Mental Health and Social Policy*. 3d ed. Englewood Cliffs, N.J.: Prentice-Hall.

Mechanic, D., Donna McAlpine, Sarah Rosenfield, and Diane Davis. 1994. "Effects of Illness Attribution and Depression on the Quality of Life among Persons with Serious Mental Illness." *Social Science & Medicine* 39(2):155–64.

Mechanic, D., and E. Volkart. 1961. "Stress, Illness Behavior, and the Sick Role." *American Sociological Review* 26:51–58.

Medalia, Nahum Z., and Otto N. Larsen. 1958. "Diffusion and Belief in a Collective Delusion: The Seattle Windshield Pitting Epidemic." *American Sociological Review* 23:180–86.

Mednick, Sarnoff A., W. F. Gabrielli, and B. Hutchings. 1984. "Genetic Factors in Criminal Behavior: Evidence from an Adoption Cohort." *Science* 224:891–93.

Meltzer, H., B. Gill, M. Petticrew, and K. Hinds. 1995. *Prevalence of Psychiatric Morbidity among Adults Living in Private Households*. London: Her Majesty's Stationery Office.

Mendlewicz, J., and G. N. Papadimitriou, ed. 1995. *Genetics of Mental Disorders Part I: Theoretical Aspects*. London: Bailliere Tindall.

Menzies, R., R. Tamblyn, J. P. Farant, J. Hanley, F. Nunes, and R. Tamblyn. 1993. "The Effect of Varying Levels of Outdoor Air Supply on the Symptoms of Sick Building Syndrome." *New England Journal of Medicine* 328:821–27.

Merikangas, K. R. 1982. "Assortative Mating for Psychiatric Disorders and Psychological Traits." *Archives of General Psychiatry* 39:1173–80.

Merton, R. K. 1956. *Social Theory and Social Structure*. Rev. and enlarged ed. New York: Free Press.

Milgram, D. 1965. "Some Conditions of Obedience and Disobedience to Authority." *Human Relations* 18:57–76.

Miller, G. A., E. Galanter, and K. H. Pribram. 1960. *Plans and the Structure of Behavior*. New York: Holt, Rinehart, and Winston.

Mills, C. W. 1956. *The Power Elite*. New York: Oxford University Press.

Minuchin, S., B. L. Rosman, and L. Baker. 1978. *Psychosomatic Families: Anorexia Nervosa in Context*. Cambridge: Harvard University Press.

Mirsky, Allan F.C.D. 1986. "Etiology and Expression of Schizophrenia." *Annual Review of Psychology* 37:291–319.

Mischel, W. 1968. *Personality and Assessment*. New York: Wiley.

Mishler, E., and N. Waxler. 1968. *Interaction in Families*. New York: Wiley.

Modan, Baruch, Moshe Tirosh, Emil Weissenberg, Cilla Acker, T. A. Swartz, Corina Costin, Alexander Donagi, Moshe Revach, and Gaston Vettorazzi. 1983. "The Arjenyattah Epidemic: A Mass Phenomenon: Spread and Triggering Factors." *The Lancet* (December 24/31):1472–74.

Moffitt, T. E. 1993. "Adolescence-Limited and Life-Course Persistent Antisocial Behavior: A Developmental Taxonomy." *Psychological Review* 100:674–701.

Mora, George. 1975. "Historical and Theoretical Trends in Psychiatry." In *Comprehensive Textbook of Psychiatry*. 2d ed., ed. A. M. Freedman, H. J. Kaplan, and B. J. Sadock. Baltimore: Williams and Wilkins.

Morgan, A. H. 1973. "The Heritability of Hypnotic Susceptibility in Twins." *Journal of Abnormal Psychology* 82:55–61.

Morgan, A. H., D. L. Johnson, and E. R. Hilgard. 1974. "The Stability of Hypnotic Susceptibility: A Longitudinal Study." *International Journal of Clinical and Experimental Hypnosis* 22:249–57.

Morris, J. N. 1975. *Uses of Epidemiology*. 3d ed. Edinburgh: Churchill Livingstone.

Mortensen, Preben B. 1995. "The Untapped Potential of Case Registers and Record-Linkage Studies in Psychiatric Epidemiology." *Epidemiologic Reviews* 17(1):205–9.

Moscicki, E. K., P. O'Carroll, D. S. Rae, B. Z. Locke, A. Roy, and D. A. Regier. 1988. "Suicide Attempts in the Epidemiologic Catchment Area Study." *Yale Journal of Biology and Medicine* 61259–68.

Mrazek, P. J., and R. J. Haggerty, ed. 1994. *Reducing Risks for Mental Disorders*. Washington, D.C.: National Academy Press.

Muchtler, J. E., and J. A. Burr. 1991. "Racial Differences in Health and Health Service Utilization in Later Life: The Effect of SES." *Journal of Health and Social Behavior* 32:342–56.

Mueller, Daniel. 1980. "Social Networks: A Promising Direction for Research on the Relationship of the Social Environment to Psychiatric Disorder." *Social Science and Medicine* 14A:147–61.

Mumford, L. 1967. *The Myth of the Machine*. New York: Harcourt, Brace & World.

Munk-Jorgensen, P. 1986. "Schizophrenia in Denmark: Incidence and Utilization of Psychiatric Institutions." *Acta Psychiatria Scandinavica* 73:172–80.

Munson, M. L., H. Orvaschel, E. A. Skinner, E. Goldring, M. Pennybacker, and D. M. Timbers. 1985. "Interviewers: Characteristics, Training and Field Work." In *Epidemiologic Field Methods in Psychiatry: The NIMH Epidemiologic Catchment Area Program*, ed. William W. Eaton and L. G. Kessler. Orlando, Fla.: Academic Press, 69–83.

Muntaner, Carles. 1988. Personal communication.

Muntaner, C., A. Y. Tien, William W. Eaton, and R. Garrison. 1991. "Occupational Characteristics and the Occurrence of Psychotic Disorders." *Social Psychiatry and Psychiatric Epidemiology* 26273–80.

Murphy, H.B.M. 1968. "Sociocultural Factors in Schizophrenia Compromise Theory." In *Social Psychiatry*, New York: Grune & Stratton.

———. 1972. "The Evocative Role of Complex Social Tasks." In *Genetic Factors in Schizophrenia*, ed. A. R. Kaplan. Chicago: Charles C. Thomas.

Murphy, Jane M., Donald M. Berwick, Milton C. Weinstein, Jonathan F. Borus, Simon H. Budman, and Gerald L. Klerman. 1987. "Performance of Screening and Diagnostic Tests." *Archives of General Psychiatry* 44:550–55.

Myers, David G. 1993. *Social Psychology*. 4th ed. New York: McGraw-Hill.

Myers, J. K., M. M. Weissman, G. L. Tischler, C. E. Holzer, P. J. Leaf, H. Orvaschel, James C. Anthony, et al. 1984. "Six-Month Prevalence of Psychiatric Disorders in Three Communities: 1980–1982." *Archives of General Psychiatry* 41959–67.

Mynatt, C., and S. J. Sherman. 1975. "Responsibility Attribution in Groups and Individuals: A Direct Test of the Diffusion of Responsibility Hypothesis." *Journal of Personality and Social Psychology* 32:1111–18.

Nathan, P. E., and J. Gorman. 1998. *A Guide to Treatments That Work*. New York: Oxford University Press.

Navarro, V. 1994. *The Politics of Health Policy. The U.S. Reforms, 1980–1994*. Boston: Blackwell.

Needleman, H. L. 1995. "Behavioral Toxiocology." *Environmental Health Perspectives* 103(suppl. 6):77–79.

Needleman, H. L., and D. Bellinger. 1991. "The Health Effects of Low Level Exposure to Lead." *Annual Review of Public Health* 12:111–40.

Neeleman, Jan. 1997. "The Social and Epidemiological Context of Suicidal Behavior." Dissertation. Rijksuniversiteit Groningen, Rotterdam.

Nestadt, Gerald, William W. Eaton, Alan J. Romanoski, Roberta Garrison, Marshal F. Folstein, and Paul R. McHugh. 1994. "Assessment of DSM-III Personality Structure in a General-Population Survey." *Comprehensive Psychiatry* 35(1):54–63.

Neufeld, K., K. Swartz, J. Bienvenu, W. Eaton, and G. Cai. 1999. "Incidence of DIS/ DSM-III-R Social Phobia in Adults." *Acta Psychiatrica Scandinavica* 100(3): 186–92.

Nielsen, J., and J. A. Nielsen. 1977. "Eighteen Years of Community Psychiatric Service in the Island of Samso." *British Journal of Psychiatry* 131:41–48.

NIMH Genetics Workgroup. 1997. *Report of the National Institute of Mental Health's Genetics Workgroup*. Bethesda, Md.: National Institute of Mental Health.

Nolan, W. J. 1917. "Occupations and Dementia Praecox." *State Hospital Quarterly* 3: 127–54.

Norman, W. T. 1963. "Toward an Adequate Taxonomy of Personality Attributes: Replicated Factor Structure in Peer Nomination Personality Ratings." *Journal of Abnormal and Social Psychology* 66:574–83.

Nunnaly, J. C. 1961. *Popular Conceptions about Mental Health*. New York: Holt.

Offord, D. R., M. H. Boyle, P. Szatmari, N. I. Rae-Grant, P. S. Links, D. T. Cadman, J. A. Byles, J. W. Crawford, Blum H. Munroe, C. Byrne, H. Thomas, and C. Woodward. 1987. "Ontario Child Health Study: II. Six-Month Prevalence of Disorder and Rates of Service Utilizaton." *Archives of General Psychiatry* 44:832–36.

Ojesjo, Leif, Olle Hagnell, and Jan Lanke. 1982. "Incidence of Alcoholism among Men in the Lundby Community Cohort, Sweden, 1957–1972." *Journal of Studies on Alcohol* 43(11):1190–98.

Orme-Johnson, D. W., L. Domash, and J. Furrow. 1974. *Scientific Research on Transcendental Meditation: Collected Papers*. Los Angeles: Maharishi International University.

Ormel, Johan, and Tamar Wohlfarth. 1991. "How Neuroticism, Long-Term Difficulties, and Life Situation Change Influence Psychological Distress: A Longitudinal Model." *Journal of Personality and Social Psychology* 60:744–55.

Orne, M. T. 1959. "The Nature of Hypnosis: Artifact and Essence." *Journal of Abnormal and Social Psychology* 58:277–99.

Ortega, S. T., and J. Corzine. 1990. "Socioeconomic Status and Mental Disorders." In *Research in Community and Mental Health: A Research Annual: Mental Disorder in Social Context*, vol. 6, ed. J. R. Greenley. Greenwich, Conn.: JAI Press, 149–82.

Oyserman, Daphna, and Hazel R. Markus. 1990. "Possible Selves and Delinquency." *Journal of Personality and Social Psychology* 59(1):112–25.

Palazzoli, Mara S. 1978. *Self-Starvation: From Individual to Family Therapy in the Treatment of Anorexia Nervosa*. Trans. Arnold Pomerans. New York: Jason Aronson.

Panse, F., and H. J. Schmidt. 1967. *Pieter Bruegels Dulle Griet: Bildnis Einer Psychisch Kranken*. N.p.: Bayer Lehrerkursen.

Papadimitriou, G. N., and J. Mendlewicz, eds. 1996. *Genetics of Mental Disorders Part II: Clinical Issues*. London: Bailliere Tindall.

Parker, G. 1987. "Are the Lifetime Prevalence Estimates in the ECA Study Accurate?" *Psychological Medicine* 17:275–82.

Parsons, T. 1951. "Illness and the Role of the Physician: A Sociological Perspective." *American Journal of Orthopsychiatry* 21:452–60.

Pasamanick, B., and H. Knobloch. 1961. "Epidemiologic Studies on the Complications of Pregnancy and Birth Process." In *Prevention of Mental Disorders in Children*, ed. G. Caplan. New York: Basic Books.

Patterson, Gerald R. 1982. *Coercive Family Process*. Eugene, Oreg.: Castalia.

———. 1986. "Performance Models for Antisocial Boys." *American Psychologist* 41 (4):432–44.

Paul, G. L. 1969. "Chronic Mental Patient: Current Status—Future Directions." *Psychological Bulletin* 71:81–94.

Pawlikowska, T., T. Chalder, S. R. Hirsch, P. Wallace, D.J.M. Wright, and S. C. Wessely. 1994. "Population-Based Study of Fatigue and Psychological Distress." *BMJ* 308: 763–66.

Paykel, Eugene S. 1994. "Life Events, Social Support, and Depression." *Acta Psychiatrica Scandinavica* 377 (suppl.):50–58.

Pearlin, L. I., E. G. Menaghan, M. A. Lieberman, and J. T. Mullen. 1981. "The Stress Process." *Journal of Health and Social Behavior* 22:337–56.

Pennebaker, James W. 1982. "Social and Perceptual Factors Affecting Symptom Reporting and Mass Psychogenic Illness." In *Mass Psychogenic Illness: A Social Psychological Analysis*, ed. Michael J. Colligan, James W. Pennebaker, and Lawrence R. Murphy. Hillsdale, N.J.: Lawrence Erlbaum Associates, 139–54.

Persian Gulf Veterans Coordinating Board. 1995. "Unexplained Illnesses among Desert Storm Veterans: A Search for Causes, Treatment, and Cooperation." *Archives of Internal Medicine* 155:262–68.

Persian Gulf Veterans Coordinating Board: Ronald R. Blanck, Joel Hiatt, Kenneth C. Hyams, Han Kang, Susan Mather, Frances Murphy, Robert Roswell, and Stephen B. Thacker. 1997. "Unexplained Illnesses among Desert Storm Veterans: A Search for Causes, Treatment, and Cooperation." http://www.ha.osd.mil/cs/pgulf/arch.

Pescosolido, Bernice, and Sharon Georgianna. 1989. "Durkheim, Suicide, and Religion: Toward a Network Theory of Suicide." *American Sociological Review* 54:33–48.

Peterson, Brennan D., Joyce West, Harold A. Pincus, Jessica Kohout, Georgine M. Pion, Marlene M. Wicherski, Rita Vandivort-Warren, Margaret Palmiter, Elizabeth Merwin, Jeanne C. Fox, Tom W. Clawson, Kathryn K. Rhodes, Rex Stockton, John P. Ambrose, Laura Blankertz, Kevin P. Dwyer, Victoria Stanhope, Michael S. Fleisher, Harold S. Goldsmith, Michael J. Witkin, Joanne E. Atay, and Ronald W. Manderscheid. 1996. "An Update on Human Resources in Mental Health." In *Mental Health, United States, 1996*, ed. Ronald W. Manderscheid and Mary A. Sonnenschein. Washington, D.C.: Government Printing Office.

Pettigrew, T. A. 1964. *Profile of the Negro American*. Princeton, N.J.: Van Nostrand.

Phillips, D. L. 1963. "Rejection: A Possible Consequence of Seeking Help for Mental Disorders." *American Sociological Review* 28:963–72.

Phillips, D. P. 1974. "The Influence of Suggestion on Suicide: Substantive and Theoretical Implications of the Werther Effect." *American Sociological Review* 39(June): 340–54.

Phoon, W. H. 1982. "Outbreaks of Mass Hysteria at Workplaces in Singapore: Some Patterns and Modes of Presentation." In *Mass Psychogenic Illness: A Social Psychological Analysis*, ed. Michael J. Colligan, Jamees. W. Pennebaker, and Lawrence R. Murphy. Hillsdale, N.J.: Lawrence Erlbaum Associates, 21–32.

Pincus, Harold A., Allen Frances, Wendy W. Davis, Michael B. First, and Thomas A. Widiger. 1992. "DSM-IV and the New Diagnostic Categories: Holding the Line of Proliferation." *American Journal of Psychiatry* 149(1):112–17.

Piotrowski, A. "Individual Interview and Clinical Examination to Determine Prevalence of Mental Disorders." *Proceedings of the Fourth World Congress of Psychiatry*, Madrid.

Plomin, Robert, Michael J. Owen, and P. McGuffin. 1994. "The Genetic Basis of Complex Human Behaviors." *Science* 264(June 17):1733–39.

Popay, Jennie, Mel Bartley, and Charlie Owen. 1993. "Gender Inequalities in Health: Social Position, Affective Disorders and Minor Physical Morbidity." *Social Science & Medicine* 36(1):21–32.

Post, Felix. 1994. "Creativity and Psychopathology: A Study of 291 World-Famous Men." *British Journal of Psychiatry* 165:22–34.

Price, Rumi K., Carol S. North, Simon Wessely, and Victoria J. Fraser. 1992. "Estimating the Prevalence of Chronic Fatigue Syndrome and Associated Symptoms in the Community." *Public Health Reports* 107(5):514–22.

Prince, R. H. 1964. "Indigenous Yoruba Psychiatry." In *Magic, Faith, and Healing*. New York: Free Press.

———. 1985. "The Concept of Culture-Bound Syndromes: Anorexia Nervosa and Brain-Fag." *Social Science & Medicine* 21:197.

Prior, Margot, and Ann Sanson. 1986. "Attention Deficit Disorder with Hyperactivity: A Critique." *Journal of Child Psychology and Psychiatry* 27(3):307–19.

Radloff, L. 1975. "Sex Differences in Depression: The Effects of Occupation and Marital Status." *Sex Roles* 1:249–65.

Redick, Richard W., Michael J. Witkin, Joanne E. Atay, and Ronald W. Manderscheid. 1996. "Highlights of Organized Mental Health Services in 1992 and Major National and State Trends." In *Mental Health, United States, 1996*, ed. Ronald W. Manderscheid and Mary A. Sonnenschein. Washington, D.C.: Government Printing Office.

Regier, D. A., W. E. Narrow, D. S. Rae, R. W. Manderscheid, Ben Z. Locke, and F. K. Goodwin. 1993. "The De Facto U.S. Mental and Addictive Disorders Service System: Epidemiologic Catchment Area Prospective 1-Year Prevalence Rates of Disorders and Services." *Archives of General Psychiatry* 5085–94.

Reisenzein, R. 1983. "The Schachter Theory of Emotion: Two Decades Later." *Psychological Bulletin* 94:239–64.

Rice, D. P., S. Kelman, and L. S. Miller. 1991. "Estimates of Economic Costs of Alcohol and Drug Abuse and Mental Illness, 1985 and 1988." *Public Health Reports* 106(3):280–92.

Rickwood, D. J., and V. A. Braithwaite. 1994. "Social-Psychological Factors Affecting

Help-Seeking for Emotional Problems." *Social Science & Medicine* 39(4):563–72.

Riesman, D. 1950. *The Lonely Crowd: A Study of the Changing American Character.* New Haven, Conn.: Yale University Press.

Riley, M., and J. Riley. 1994. "Age Integration and the Lives of Older People." *The Forum* 34(1):110–15.

Rinehart, L. 1975. *The Book of EST.* New York: Holt, Rinehart, and Winston.

Ritzer, George. 1996. *Sociological Theory.* 4th ed. New York: McGraw-Hill.

Rix, K., D. Pearson, and S. Bentley. 1984. "A Psychiatric Study of Patients with Supposed Food Allergy." *British Journal of Psychiatry* 145:121–26.

Robbins, James M., and Lawrence J. Kirmayer. 1991. "Attributions of Common Somatic Symptoms." *Psychological Medicine* 21:1029–45.

Robertson, D., R. Ayres, C. Smith, and R. Wright. 1988. "Adverse Consequences Arising from Misdiagnosis of Food Allergy." *BMJ* 297:719–20.

Robins, L. N. 1966. *Deviant Children Grown Up.* Baltimore: Williams & Wilkins.

Robins, L. N., J. E. Helzer, J. Croughan, and K. S. Ratcliff. 1981. "National Institute of Mental Health Diagnostic Interview Schedule: Its History, Characteristics, and Validity." *Archives of General Psychiatry* 38381–89.

Robins, L. N., J. E. Helzer, M. M. Weissman, H. Orvaschel, E. M. Gruenberg, J. D. Burke, and D. A Regier. 1984. "Lifetime Prevalence of Specific Psychiatric Disorders in Three Sites." *Archives of General Psychiatry* 41949–58.

Robins, L. N., G. E. Murphy, R. A. Woodruff, and L. J. King. 1971. "Adult Psychiatric Status of Black Schoolboys." *Archives of General Psychiatry* 24:338–45.

Robins, L. N., and Darrel A. Regier, ed. 1991. *Psychiatric Disorders in America—The Epidemiologic Catchment Area Study.* New York: Free Press.

Robinson, R. V., and J. Kelley. 1990. "Class As Conceived by Marx and Dahrendorf: Effects on Income Inequality, Class Consciousness, and Class Conflict in the U.S. and Great Britain." *American Sociological Review* 55:827–41.

Roccatagliata, Guiseppe. 1991. "Classical Concepts of Schizophrenia." In *The Concept of Schizophrenia: Historical Perspectives*, ed. John G. Howells. Washington, D.C.: American Psychiatric Press.

Rogan, Walter J., and Beth Gladen. 1978. "Estimating Prevalence from the Results of a Screening Test." *American Journal of Epidemiology* 107:71–76.

Rosen, George. 1968. *Madness in Society: Chapters in the Historical Sociology of Mental Illness.* Chicago: University of Chicago Press.

Rosenberg, M. 1986. *Conceiving the Self.* New York: Basic Books.

————. 1992. *The Unread Mind: Unraveling the Mystery of Madness.* New York: Lexington Books.

Rosenfield, Sarah. 1997. "Labeling Mental Illness: The Effects of Received Services and Perceived Stigma on Life Satisfaction." *American Sociological Review* 62:660–72.

Rosenhan, D. L. 1973. "On Being Sane in Insane Places." *Science* 179:250–58.

Rosenthal, David. 1963. *The Genain Quadruplets: A Case Study and Theoretical Analysis of Heredity and Environment in Schizophrenia.* ed. David Rosenthal et al. New York: Basic Books.

Rosnow, Ralph L. 1958. "Rumor as Communication: A Contextual Approach." *Journal of Communication* 38(Winter):12–28.

Ross, Catherine E., and Chia-ling Wu. 1995. "The Links between Education and Health." *American Sociological Review* 60:719–45.

Rothman, Kenneth J. 1986. *Modern Epidemiology*. Boston: Little, Brown.

Ruble, Diane N., Faith Greulich, Eva M. Pomerantz, and Barbara Gochberg. 1993. "The Role of Gender-Related Processes in the Development of Sex Differences in Self-Evaluation and Depression." *Journal of Affective Disorders* 29:97–128.

Ruch, J. C. 1975. "Self-Hypnosis: The Result of Heterohypnosis or Vice Versa." *International Journal of Clinical and Experimental Hypnosis* 23:282–304.

Ruhl, Ronald, A., Christopher C. Chang, Georges M. Halpern, and M. E. Gershwin. 1993. "The Sick Building Syndrome. II. Assessment and Regulation of Indoor Air Quality." *Journal of Asthma* 30(4):297–308.

Rumbant, R. D. 1972. "The First Psychiatric Hospital of the Western World." *American Journal of Psychiatry* 128:1305–9.

Russell, G.F.M. 1979. "Bulimia Nervosa: An Ominous Variant of Anorexia Nervosa." *Psychological Medicine* 9:429–48.

Ryan, Christopher M., and Lisa A. Morrow. 1992. "Dysfunctional Buildings or Dysfunctional People: An Examination of the Sick Building Syndrome and Allied Disorders." *Journal of Consulting and Clinical Psychology* 60(2):220–24.

Ryan, Neal D. 1992. "The Pharmacologic Treatment of Child and Adolescent Depression." *Psychiatric Clinics of North America* 15(1):29–40.

Sacker, Amanda, John Done, Timothy J. Crow, and Jean Golding. 1995. "Antecedents of Schizophrenia and Affective Illness Obstetric Complications." *British Journal of Psychiatry* 166:734–41.

Sampson, H., S. L. Messinger, and R. D. Towne. 1962. "Family Processes and Becoming a Mental Patient." *American Journal of Sociology* 68:88–96.

Sampson, R. J., and W. B. Groves. 1989. "Community Structure and Crime: Testing Social Disorganization Theory." *American Journal of Sociology* 94:774–802.

Sampson, R. J., and J. H. Laub. 1990. "Crime and Deviance over the Life Course: A Salience of Adult Social Bonds." *American Sociological Review* 55:609–27.

Sarason, Irwin G., James H. Johnson, and Judith M. Siegel. 1978. "Assessing the Impact of Life Changes: Development of the Life Experiences Survey." *Journal of Consulting and Clinical Psychology* 46(5):932–46.

Sarbin, T. R. 1967. "Hypnosis as Role Enactment." In *Handbook of Clinical and Experimental Hypnosis*, ed. J. E. Gordon. New York: Macmillan.

———. 1968. "Notes on the Transformation of Social Identity." In *Comprehensive Mental Health: The Challenge of Evaluation*, ed. L. M. Roberts, N. S. Greenfield, and M. H. Miller. Madison: University of Wisconsin Press.

Sarbin, T. R., and V. L. Allen. 1968. "Role Theory." In *Handbook of Social Psychology*, 2d ed., vol. 1, ed. G. Lindzey and E. Aronson. Reading, Mass.: Addison-Wesley.

Sarbin, T. R., and W. C. Coe. 1972. *Hypnosis: A Social Psychological Analysis of Influence Communication*. New York: Holt, Rinehart, and Winston.

Sartorius, N. 1988. "International Perspectives of Psychiatric Classification." *British Journal of Psychiatry* 152 (suppl. 1):9–14.

Satorius, N., A. Jablensky, A. Korten, G. Ernberg, G. Anker, J. Cooper, and R. Day. 1986. "Early Manifestations and First-Contact Incidence of Schizophrenia in Different Cultures." *Psychological Medicine* 16:909–28.

Schacht, R. 1970. *Alienation*. Garden City, N.Y.: Doubleday.

Schachter, S., and J. E. Singer. 1962. "Cognitive, Social and Physiological Determinants of Emotional State." *Psychological Review* 69:379–99.

Scheff, T. 1963. "The Role of the Mentally Ill and the Dynamics of Mental Disorder: A Research Framework." *Sociometry* 26:436–53.

———. 1964. "The Societal Reaction to Deviance: Ascriptive Aspects in the Psychiatric Screening of Mental Patients in a Midwestern State." *Social Problems* 11:401–13.

———. 1975. "Reply to Chauncey and Gove." *American Sociological Review* 40:252–57.

Scheibe, Karl E. 1995. *Self-Studies: The Psychology of Self and Identity*. Westport, Conn.: Praeger.

Schiff, Michel, and Richard Lewontin. 1986. *Education and Class: The Irrelevance of IQ Genetic Studies*. Oxford: Clarendon Press.

Schlesselman, James J. 1982. *Case-Control Studies Design, Conduct, Analysis*. New York: Oxford University Press.

Schoenberg, B. S., E. Kokmen, and H. Okazaki. 1987. "Alzheimer's Disease and Other Dementing Illnesses in a Defined United States Population: Incidence Rates and Clinical Features." *Annals of Neurology* 22:724–29.

Schurmann, F. 1970. *Ideology and Organization in Communist China*. 2d ed. Berkeley: University of California Press.

Scull, A. T. 1975. "Cyclical Trends in Psychiatric Practice: The Case of Bettleheim and Tuke." *Social Science and Medicine* 9:633–40.

Seeman, Melvin. 1959. "On the Meaning of Alienation." *American Sociological Review* 24:783–91.

Selden, Brad S. 1989. "Adolescent Epidemic Hysteria Presenting as a Mass Casualty, Toxic Exposure Incident." *Annals of Emergency Medicine* 18(8):892–95.

Seligman, M.E.P. 1975. *Helplessness: On Depression, Development, and Death*. San Francisco: W. H. Freeman.

Selye, Hans. 1956. *The Stress of Life*. New York: McGraw-Hill.

Sewell, William H., A. O. Haller, and G. W. Ohlendorf. 1970. "The Educational and Early Occupational Status Attainment Process: Replication and Revision." *American Sociological Review* 35:1014–27.

Seydlitz, Ruth, J. W. Spencer, Shirley Laska, and Elizabeth Triche. 1991. "The Effects of Newspaper Reports on the Public's Response to a Natural Hazard Event." *International Journal of Mass Emergencies and Disasters* 9(1):5–29.

Shapiro, S., E. A. Skinner, L. G. Kessler, M. Von Korff, P. S. German, G. L. Tischler, P. J. Leaf, L. Benham, L. Cottler, and D. A. Regier. 1984. "Utilization of Health and Mental Health Services, Three Epidemiologic Catchment Area Sites." *Archives of General Psychiatry* 41971–78.

Sharpe, M., K. Hawton, Seagroatt V., and G. Pasvol. 1992. "Followup of Patients with Fatigue Presenting to an Infectious Diseases Clinic." *British Medical Journal* 302:347–52.

Shepherd, Michael, Brian Cooper, Alexander C. Brown, and Graham W. Kalton. 1966. *Psychiatric Illness in General Practice*. London: Oxford University Press.

Sherif, M. 1937. "An Experimental Approach to the Study of Attitudes." *Sociometry* 1:90–98.

Shorter, E. 1992. *From Paralysis to Fatigue: A History of Psychosomatic Illness in the Modern Era*. New York: Free Press.

Sieber, S. D. 1974. "Toward a Theory of Role Accumulation." *American Sociological Review* 39:567–78.

Siegel, P. 1965. "On the Cost of Being a Negro." *Social Inquiry* 35:41–57.

Simmel, Georg. 1950. *The Sociology of Georg Simmel*, ed. trans. Kurt Wolff. New York: Free Press.

Simon, Gregory E., William Daniell, Henry Stockbridge, Keith Claypoole, and Linda Rosenstock. 1993. "Immunologic, Psychological, and Neuropsychological Factors in Multiple Chemical Sensitivity: A Controlled Study." *Annals of Internal Medicine* 119(July 15):97–103.

Simon, Gregory E., Wayne J. Katon, and Patricia J. Sparks. 1990. "Allergic to Life: Psychologic Factors in Environmental Illness." *American Journal of Psychiatry* 147:901–6.

Simon, Gregory E., and Michael Von Korff. 1995. "Recall of Psychiatric History in Cross-Sectional Surveys: Implications for Epidemiologic Research." *Epidemiologic Reviews* 17(1):221–27.

Simons, R. C. 1996. *Boo! Culture, Experience, and the Startle Reflex.* New York: Oxford University Press.

Simons, R. C., and C. C. Hughes, eds. 1985. *The Culture Bound Syndromes: Folk Illnesses of Psychiatric and Anthropological Interest.* Dordrecht: D. Riedel.

Sirois, F. 1974. "Epidemic Hysteria." *Acta Psychiatrica Scandinavica* (suppl. 252).

———.1982. "Perspectives on Epidemic Hysteria." In *Mass Psychogenic Illness: A Social Psychological Perspective,* ed. Michael J. Colligan, James W. Pennebake, and Lawrence R. Murphy. Hillsdale, N.J.: Lawrence Erlbaum Associates, 217–36.

Small, Gary W., and Jonathan F. Borus. 1987. "The Influence of Newspaper Reports on Outbreaks of Mass Hysteria." *Psychiatric Quarterly* 58(4):269–78.

Small, Gary W., David T. Feinberg, David Steinberg, and Mark T. Collins. 1994. "A Sudden Outbreak of Illness Suggestive of Mass Hysteria in Schoolchildren." *Archives of Family Medicine* 3:711–16.

Smelser, N. J. 1962. *Theory of Collective Behavior.* New York: Free Press.

Smith, A. L., and M. M. Weissman. 1991. "The Epidemiology of Depressive Disorders: National and International Perspectives." In *Diagnosis of Depression. Perspectives in Psychiatry,* vol. 2, ed. J. P. Feighner and W. F. Boyer. John Wiley & Sons, 17–30.

Smith, Carolyn A., Christopher J. Smith, Robin A. Kearns, and Max W. Abbott. 1993. "Housing Stressors, Social Support and Psychological Distress." *Social Science & Medicine* 37(5):603–12.

Smith, G. R. Jr., and S. McDaniel. 1983. "Psychologically Mediated Effect on the Delayed Hypersensitivity Response by Direct Suggestion under Hypnosis." *Psychosomatic Medicine* 45:65–69.

Smith, G. R. 1994. "The Course of Somatization and Its Effects on Utilization of Health Care Resources." *Psychosomatics* 35(3):263–67.

Smith, S. C. 1975. "Meditation as Psychotherapy: A Review of the Literature." *Psychological Bulletin* 82:558–64.

Snodgrass, S. E. 1985. "Women's Intuition: The Effect of Subordinate Role on Interpersonal Sensitivity." *Journal of Personality and Social Psychology* 49:146–55.

Sorlie, P., E. Backlund, and J. B. Keller. 1995. "U.S. Mortality by Economic, Demographic and Social Characteristics: The National Longitudinal Mortality Study." *American Journal of Public Health* 85:903–5.

Spanos, N. P., R. J. Stenstrom, and J. C. Johnston. 1988. "Hypnosis, Placebo, and Suggestion in the Treatment of Warts." *Psychosomatic Medicine* 50:245–60.

Spanos, N. P., Victoria Williams, and Maxwell I. Gwynn. 1990. "Effects of Hypnotic,

Placebo, and Salicylic Acid Treatments on Wart Regression." *Psychosomatic Medicine* 52:109–14.

Spector, Malcolm. 1977. "Legitimatintg Homosexuality." *Society* (July–August):52–56.

Spector, Malcolm, and John I. Kitsuse. 1977. *Constructing Social Problems*. Menlo Park, Calif.: Benjamin Cummings.

Spitzer, Robert L., Miriam Gibbon, Andrew E. Skodol, et al. 1989. *DSM-III-T Casebook: A Learning Companion to the Diagnostic and Statistical Manual of Mental Disorders*. 3d ed., rev. Washington, D.C.: American Psychiatric Press.

Srole, L., and A. K. Fischer. 1989. "Changing Lives and Well-Being: The Midtown Manhattan Panel Study, 1954–1976." *Acta Psychiatrica Scandinavica Supplement* 348:35–44.

Stahl, Sidney M. 1982. "Illness as an Emergent Norm, or, Doing What Comes Naturally." In *Mass Psychogenic Illness: A Social Psychological Analysis*, ed. Michael J. Colligan and James W.M.L.R. Pennebaker. Hillsdale, N.J.: Lawrence Erlbaum Associates, 183–98.

Stallones, R. A. 1980. "To Advance Epidemiology." *Annual Review of Public Health* 1: 69–82.

Stanton, A. H., and M. S. Schwartz. 1954. *The Mental Hospital*. New York: Basic Books.

Star, S. A. 1952. "The Public's Ideas about Mental Illness." *Annual Meeting of the National Association of Mental Health*.

Steffenburg, S., and C. Gillberg. 1986. "Autism and Autistic-like Conditions in Swedish Rural and Urban Areas: A Population Study." *British Journal of Psychiatry* 149: 81–87.

Steinhausen, H. C., D. Gobel, M. Breinlinger, and B. Wohlleben. 1986. "A Community Survey of Infantile Autism." *Journal of the American Academy of Child Psychiatry* 25:186–89.

Sternberg, R. J. 1995. "For Whom the Bell Curve Tolls: A Review of the Bell Curve" *Psychological Science* 6(5):257–61.

Stevens, Anthony, and John Price. 1996. *Evolutionary Psychiatry: A New Beginning*. London: Routledge.

Stewart, D. 1990a. "The Changing Faces of Somatization." *Psychosomatic Medicine* 31: 153–58.

———.1990b. "Emotional Disorders Misdiagnosed as Physical Illness: Environmental Hypersensitivity, Candidiasis Hypersensitivity and Chronic Fatigue Syndrome." *International Journal of Health* 19:56–68.

Stonequist, Everett V. 1937. *The Marginal Man: A Study in Personality and Culture Conflict*. New York: Charles Scribner's Sons.

Straus, Stephen E. 1996. "Chronic Fatigue Syndrome: "Biopsychosocial Approach May Be Difficult in Practice." *British Medical Journal* 313:831–32.

Strauss, A., et al. 1964. *Psychiatric Ideologies and Institutions*. New York: Free Press.

Strauss, J. S., K. S. Gabriel, R. F. Kokes, B. A. Ritzler, B. VanOrd, and E. Tarana. 1979. "Do Psychiatric Patients Fit Their Diagnoses?: Patterns of Symptomatology As Described with the Biplot." *Journal of Nervous and Mental Disease* 167(2):105–13.

Strobino, Donna M., Margaret E. Ensminger, J. Kim Young, and Joy Nanda. 1995. "Mechanisms for Maternal Age Differences in Birth Weight." *American Journal of Epidemiology* 142(5):504–14.

Stromgren, Erik. 1987. "Changes in the Incidence of Schizophrenia?" *British Journal of Psychiatry* 150:1–7.

Strong, P. M. 1979. "Sociological Imperialism and the Profession of Medicine: A Critical Examination of the Thesis of Medical Imperialism." *Social Science & Medicine* 13A:199–215.

Stryker, Sheldon. 1964. "The Interactional and Situational Approaches." In *Handbook of Marriage and the Family*, ed. H. T. Christensen. Chicago: Rand McNally.

———.1968. "Identity Salience and Role Performance: The Relevance of Symbolic Interaction Theory for Family Research." *Journal of Marriage and the Family* 30: 558–64.

Stryker, Sheldon, and A. Gottlieb. 1981. "Attribution Theory and Symbolic Interactionism: A Comparison." In *New Directions in Attribution Research*, ed. J. H. Harvey, W. Ickes, and R. Kidd. Hillsdale, N.J.: Lawrence Erlbaum Associates.

Stryker, Sheldon, and Richard T. Serpe. 1994. "Identity Salience and Psychological Centrality: Equivalent, Overlapping, or Complementary Concepts?" *Social Psychological Quarterly* 57:16–35.

Sudman, Seymour. 1976. *Applied Sampling*. New York: Academic Press.

Surra, C. A. 1990. "Research and Theory on Mate Selection and Premarital Relationships in the 1980s." *Journal of Marriage and the Family* 52:844–65.

Surtees, P. G., P. M. Miller, J. G. Ingham, N. B. Kreitman, D. Rennie, and S. P. Sashidharan. 1986. "Life Events and the Onset of Affective Disorder: A Longitudinal General Population Study." *Journal of Affective Disorders* 10:37–50.

Susser, Mervyn, and Ezra Susser. 1996. "Choosing a Future for Epidemiology." *American Journal of Public Health* 86:668–77.

Susser, M., W. Watson, and K. Hopper. 1985. *Sociology in Medicine*. New York: Oxford University Press.

Swann, W. B., and S. J. Read. 1981. "Self-Verification Process: How We Sustain Our Self-Conceptions." *Journal of Experimental Social Psychology* 17:351–72.

Swazey, J. P. 1974. *Chlorpromazine in Psychiatry: A Study of Therapeutic Innovation* Cambridge: Massachusetts Institute of Technology Press.

Szasz, Thomas. 1970. *The Manufacture of Madness*. New York: Dell.

Szmukler, G. 1985. "Weight and Food Preoccupation in a Population of English Schoolgirls." In *Understanding Anorexia Nevosa and Bulimia: 4th Ross Conference on Medical Research*, ed. J. G. Bergmann. Columbus, Ohio: Ross Laboratories, 21–28.

Szmukler, G. I., and D. Tantam. 1984. "Anorexia Nervosa: Starvation Dependence." *British Journal of Medical Psychology* 57:303–10.

Taube, C. 1975. *Utilization of Mental Health Facilities, 1971*. Rockville, Md.: National Institute of Mental Health.

ten Horn, C. H., R. Giel, W. H. Gulbinat, and J. H. Henderson, ed. 1986. *Psychiatric Case Registers in Public Health—A Worldwide Inventory 1960–1985*. Amsterdam: Elsevier Science.

Ten Houten, W. D., Klaus D. Hoppe, Joseph E. Bogen, and Donald O. Walter. 1986. "Alexithymia: An Experimental Study of Cerebral Commissurotomy Patients and Normal Control Subjects." *American Journal of Psychiatry* 143:312–16.

Terr, A. 1986. "Environmental Illness: A Clinical Review of 50 Cases." *Archives of Internal Medicine* 146:145–49.

Thase, Michael E., and David J. Kupfer. 1996. "Recent Developments in the Pharmacotherapy of Mood Disorders." *Journal of Consulting and Clinical Psychology* 64:646–59.

Thoits, P. A. 1983. "Dimensions of Life Events That Influence Psychological Distress: An Evaluation and Synthesis of the Literature." In *Psychological Stress: Trends in Theory and Research*, ed. H. B. Kaplan. New York: Free Press, 33–103.

———. 1985. "Self-Labeling Processes in Mental Illness: The Role of Emotional Deviance." *American Journal of Sociology* 91(2):221–49.

———. 1986. "Multiple Identities: Examining Gender and Marital Status Differences in Distress." *American Sociological Review* 51:259–72.

———. 1990. "The Sociology of Emotions." *Annual Review of Sociology* 15:317–42.

———. 1991. "Gender Differences in Coping with Emotional Distress." In *The Social Context of Coping*, ed. John Eckenrode. New York: Plenum Press, 107–63.

———. 1992. "Identity Structures and Psychological Well-Being—Gender and Marital Status Comparisons." *Social Psychology Quarterly* 55(3):236–56.

———. 1995. "Stress, Coping, and Social Support Processes: Where Are We? What Next?" *Journal of Health and Social Behavior* 36 (Extra issue):53–79.

Thornicroft, Graham, Giulia Bisoffi, Domenico De Salvia, and Michele Tansella. 1993. "Urban–Rural Differences in the Associations between Social Deprivation and Psychiatric Service Utilization in Schizophrenia and All Diagnoses: A Case-Register Study in Northern Italy." *Psychological Medicine* 23:487–96.

Tien, A. Y. 1991. "Distribution of Hallucinations in the Population." *Social Psychiatry & Psychiatric Epidemiology* 26(6):287–92.

Tobi, M., A. Morag, Z. Ravid, I. Chowers, V. Feldman-Weiss, Y. Michaeli, et al. 1982. "Prolonged Atypical Illness Associated with Serologic Evidence of Persistent Epstein-Barr Virus Infection." *Lancet*:61–64.

Toffler, A. 1970. *Future Shock*. New York: Random House.

Tsuang, Ming, Mauricio Tohen, and Gwen Zahner. 1995. *Textbook in Psychiatric Epidemiology*. New York: Wiley-Liss.

Tune, L. 1998. "Treatment for Dementia." In *A Guide to Treatments That Work*, ed. P. E. Nathan and J. Gorman, New York: Oxford University Press.

Turner, J. C. 1987. *Rediscovering the Social Group: A Self-Categorization Theory*. New York: Basil Blackwell.

Turner, R. H. 1970. *Family Interaction*. New York: Wiley.

Turner, R. J., and William R. Avison. 1992. "Innovations in the Measurement of Life Stress: Crisis Theory and the Significance of Event Resolution." *Journal of Health and Social Behavior* 33:36–50.

Turner, R. J., and Franco Marino. 1994. "Social Support and Social Structure: A Descriptive Epidemiology." *Journal of Health and Social Behavior* 35:193–212.

Turner, R. J., and Samuel Noh. 1988. "Physical Disability and Depression: A Longitudinal Analysis." *Journal of Health and Social Behavior* 29:23–37.

Turner, R. J., and M. O. Wagenfeld. 1967. "Occupational Mobility and Schizophrenia." *American Sociological Review* 32:104–13.

Turner, R. J., Blair Wheaton, and Donald A. Lloyd. 1995. "The Epidemiology of Social Stress." *American Sociological Review* 60:104–25.

Turner, Ralph H., and Lewis M. Killian. 1987. *Collective Behavior*. 3d ed. Englewood Cliffs, N.J.: Prentice-Hall.

Tyrer, P. 1985. "Neurosis Divisible?" *Lancet* 8430:685–88.

Tyrer, Peter, and Derek Steinberg. 1993. *Models for Mental Disorder: Conceptual Models in Psychiatry*. 2d. ed. New York: John Wiley & Sons.

Uchino, B. N., J. T. Cacioppo, and J. K. Kiecolt-Glaser. 1996. "The Relationship between Social Support and Physiological Processes: A Review with Emphasis on Underlying Mechanisms and Implications for Health." *Psychological Bulletin* 119: 488–531.

Umberson, Debra, Camille B. Wortman, and Ronald C. Kessler. 1992. "Widowhood and Depression: Explaining Long-Term Gender Differences in Vulnerability." *Journal of Health and Social Behavior* 33:10–24.

Vega, W. A., B. Kolody, S. Aguilar-Gaxiola, E. Alderete, R. Catalano, and J. Caraveo-Anduaga. 1998. "Lifetime Prevalence of DSM-III-R Psychiatric Disorders among Urban and Rural Mexican Americans in California." *Archives of General Psychiatry* 55(9):771–78.

Veiel, Hans O. F., and Urs Baumann, eds. 1992. *The Meaning and Measurement of Social Support.* New York: Hemisphere.

Veroff, J., E. Douvan, and R. A. Kulka. 1981. *The Inner American.* New York: Basic Books.

Vogel, E. F., and N. W. Bell. 1960. "The Emotionally Disturbed Child as the Family Scapegoat." In *A Modern Introduction to the Family*, ed. N. W. Bell and E. F. Vogel. New York: Free Press.

Von Korff, M., L. Cottler, L. K. George, William W. Eaton, P. J. Leaf, and A. Burnam. 1985. "Nonresponse and Nonresponse Bias in the ECA Surveys." In *Epidemiologic Field Methods in Psychiatry: The NIMH Epidemiologic Catchment Area Program*, ed. William W. Eaton and L. G. Kessler. Orlando: Academic Press, 85–98.

Wahl, Otto F. 1995. *Media Madness: Public Images of Mental Illness.* New Brunswick, N.J.: Rutgers University Press.

Ware, Norma C., and Arthur Kleinman. 1992. "Culture and Somatic Experience: The Social Course of Illness in Neurasthenia and Chronic Fatigue Syndrome." *Psychosomatic Medicine* 54:546–60.

Warheit, George J., Charles E. Holzer, Roger A. Bell, and Sandra A. Arey. 1976. "Sex, Marital Status, and Mental Health: A Reappraisal." *Social Forces* 55:459–70.

Watson, J. D. 1990. "The Human Genome Project: Past, Present, and Future." *Science* 248:44–49.

Waxler, Nancy E. 1979. "Is Outcome for Schizophrenia Better in Nonindustrial Societies?: The Case in Sri Lanka." *Journal of Nervous and Mental Disease* 167(3): 144–60.

Weissman, M. M., G. L. Klerman, J. S. Markowitz, and R. Ouellette. 1989. "Suicide Ideation and Suicide Attempts in Panic Disorder and Attacks." *New England Journal of Medicine* 321:1209–14.

Weissman, M. M., J. F. Leckman, K. R. Merikangas, G. D. Gammon, and B. A. Prusoff. 1984. "Depression and Anxiety Disorders in Parents and Children: Results from the Yale Family Study." *Archives of General Psychiatry* 41:845–52.

Weissman, M. M., and J. K. Myers. 1978. "Affective Disorders in a U.S. Urban Community: The Use of Research Diagnostic Criteria in an Epidemiological Survey." *Archives of General Psychiatry* 25:1304–11.

Wellman, Barry, and Scot Wortley. 1990. "Different Strokes from Different Folks: Community Ties and Social Support." *American Journal of Sociology* 96:558–88.

Wells, J. C., A. Y. Tien, R. Garrison, and William W. Eaton. 1994. "Risk Factors for the Incidence of Social Phobia As Determined by the Diagnostic Interview Schedule according to DSM-III in a Population-Based Study." *Acta Psychiatrica Scandinavica* 90:84–90.

Wender, Paul H., and Barry D. Garfinkel. 1989. "Attention-Deficit Hyperactivity Disorder: Adult Manifestations." In *Comprehensive Textbook of Psychiatry/V* 5th ed., vol. 2, ed. Harold I. Kaplan and Benjamin J. Sadock. Baltimore: Williams & Wilkins, 1837–42.

Wessely, Simon. 1987. "Mass Hysteria: Two Syndromes?" *Psychological Medicine* 17: 109–20.

———. 1994. "The History of Chronic Fatigue Syndrome." In *Chronic Fatigue Syndrome*, ed. S. Straus. New York: Marcel Dekker, 41–82.

———. 1996. "Cognitive Behavior Therapy: Why?" In *Chronic Fatigue Syndrome: An Integrative Approach to Evaluation and Treatment*, ed. Mark A. Demitrack and Susan. E. Abbey. New York: Guilford Press, 212–39.

Wessely, Simon, Matthew Hotopf, and Michael Sharpe. 1998. *Chronic Fatigue and Its Syndromes*. Oxford: Oxford University Press.

Westermeyer, J. 1973. "On the Epidemicity of Amok Violence." *Archives of General Psychiatry* 28:873–76.

Western, Mark, and Erik O. Wright. 1994. "The Permeability of Class Boundaries to Intergenerational Mobility among Men in the United States, Canada, Norway and Sweden." *American Sociological Review* 59:606–29.

Wheaton, B. 1980. "The Sociogenesis of Psychological Disorder: An Attributional Theory." *Journal of Health and Social Behavior* 21:1001–1124.

———. 1996. "The Domains and Boundaries of Stress Concepts." In *Psychosocial Stress: Perspectives on Structure, Theory, Life Course, and Methods*, ed. Howard B. Kaplan. New York: Academic Press.

Wheeler, L. 1966. "Toward a Theory of Behavioral Contagion." *Psychological Review* 73:179–92.

Wickramaratne, P. J., M. M. Weissman, P. J. Leaf, and T. R. Holford. 1989. "Age, Period and Cohort Effects on the Risk of Major Depression: Results from Five United States Communities." *Journal of Clinical Epidemiology* 42(4):333–43.

Willi, J., G. Giacometti, and B. Limacher. 1990. "Update on the Epidemiology of Anorexia Nervosa in a Defined Region of Switzerland." *American Journal of Psychiatry* 147:1514–17.

Williams, Janet B. W., Miriam Gibbon, Michael B. First, Robert L. Spitzer, Mark Davies, Jonathan Borus, Mary J. Howes, John Kane, Harrison G. Pope, Bruce Rounsaville, and Hans-Ulrich Wittchen. 1992. "The Structured Clinical Interview for DSM-III-R (SCID): II. Multisite Test-Retest Reliability." *Archives of General Psychiatry* 49:630–36.

Williams, Paul, Greg Wilkinson, and Kenneth Rawnsley, eds. 1989. *The Scope of Epidemiological Psychiatry: Essays in Honor of Michael Shepherd*. London: Routledge.

Williams, Simon J., and Michael Calnan. 1996. "The 'Limits' of Medicalization?: Modern Medicine and the Lay Populace in 'Late' Modernity." *Social Science & Medicine* 42(12):1609–20.

Wilson, Andrew, Ian Hickie, Andrew Lloyd, Dusan Kadzi-Pavlovic, Clem Boughton, John Dwyer, and Denis Wakefield. 1994. "Longitudinal Study of Outcome of Chronic Fatigue Syndrome." *The British Medical Journal* 308:756–59.

Winch, R. 1971. *The Modern Family*. New York: Holt, Rinehart, and Winston.

Wing, J. K., J.L.T. Birley, J. E. Cooper, P. Graham, and A. D. Isaacs. 1967. "Reliability
of a Procedure for Measuring and Classifying 'Present Psychiatric State.' " *British
Journal of Psychiatry* 113:499–515.

Wiseman, Claire V., James J. Gray, James E. Mosimann, and Anthony H. Ahrens. 1992.
"Cultural Expectations of Thinness in Women: An Update." *International Journal
of Eating Disorders* 11(1):85–89.

Wittchen, Hans-Ulrich, and Thomas Bronisch. 1992. "Alcohol Use, Abuse, and Depen-
dency in West Germany: Lifetime and Six-Month Prevalence in the Munich
Follow-Up Study." In *Alcoholism in North America, Europe, and Asia*, ed. John
E. Helzer and Glorisa J. Canino. New York: Oxford University Press.

Wittchen, H. U., C. A. Essau, D. von Zerssen, J. C. Krieg, and M. Zaudig. 1992. "Lifetime and Six-Month Prevalence of Mental Disorders in the Munich Follow-Up
Study." *European Archives of Psychiatry and Clinical Neuroscience* 241:247–58.

Wolff, E. N. 1995. *Top Heavy: A Study of Wealth Inequality in America.* New York:
Twentieth Century Fund.

Wolpe, J. 1969. *The Practice of Behavior Therapy.* New York: Pergamon.

Wright, Erik O. 1979. *Class Structure and Income Determination.* New York: Academic
Press.

———. 1985. *Classes.* London: Verso.

———. 1993. "Typologies, Scales, and Class Analysis: A Comment on Halaby and
Weakliem." *American Sociological Review.* 58:31–34.

Wuthnow, R. 1976. "The New Religions in Social Context." In *The New Religious
Consciousness*, ed., C. Y. Glock and R. N. Bellah. Berkeley: University of California Press.

Wynder, Ernst L. 1994. "Studies in Mechanism and Prevention: Striking a Proper Balance." *American Journal of Epidemiology* 139(6):547–49.

Wynne, L. C., I. M. Ryckoff, S. Day, and S. I. Hirsch. 1958. "Pseudomutuality in the
Family Relations of Schizophrenics." *Psychiatry* 21(2):205–20.

Wynne, L. C., and M. T. Singer. 1963. "Thought Disorder and Family Relations of Schizophrenics." *Archives of General Psychiatry* 9:191–206.

Yap, P. M. 1951. "Mental Diseases Peculiar to Certain Cultures: A Survey of Comparative Psychiatry." *Journal of Mental Science* 97:313–27.

Yeh, Shih-rung, Russell A. Fricke, and Donald H. Edwards. 1996. "The Effect of Social
Experience on Serotonergic Modulation of the Escape Circuit of Crayfish." *Science* 271(January 19):366–69.

Young, E., S. Patel, M. Stoneham, R. Rona, and J. Wilkinson. 1987. "The Prevalence
of Reaction to Food Additives in a Survey Population." *Journal of the Royal
College of Physicians* 721:241–47.

Young, Michael. 1994. *The Rise of the Meritocracy, with a New Introduction by the
Author.* New Brunswick, N.J.: Transaction.

Zajonc, R. B. 1965. "Social Facilitation." *Science* 149:269–74.

Zautra, A. J., and J. W. Reich. 1983. "Life Events and Perceptions of Life Quality: Development in a Two-Factor Approach." *Journal of Community Psychology* 1:121–
32.

Zeeman, E. C. 1976. "Catastrophe Theory." *Scientific American* 234:65–83.

Zola, Irving K. 1975. "In the Name of Health and Illness: On Some Socio-Political
Consequences of Medical Influence." *Social Science & Medicine* 9:83–87.

Zubin, J., J. Magaziner, and S. Steinhauer. 1983. "The Metamorphosis of Schizophrenia: From Chronicity to Vulnerability." *Psychological Medicine* 13:551–71.

Zusman, J. 1966. "Some Explanations of the Changing Appearance of Psychotic Patients." *Milbank Memorial Fund Quarterly* 44:363–94.

Index

Entries are in alphabetic order by subject. Within subject headings, entries begin with "definition" or "diagnostic criteria," if available, and are followed by alphabetized entries.

About the Author

WILLIAM W. EATON is Professor of Mental Hygiene in the School of Hygiene and Public Health at Johns Hopkins University. He is also Director of the NIMH Training Program in Psychiatric Epidemiology at Johns Hopkins University. In addition to the first and second edition of *The Sociology of Mental Disorders* (1980 and 1985), he has authored numerous scientific articles and coedited three books.